Contemporary British Music

The twenty-five years from
1945 to 1970

Also by Francis Routh

Contemporary Music

Francis Routh

Contemporary British Music

**The twenty-five years from
1945 to 1970**

Macdonald . London

Contents

List of Illustrations

Between pages 140 and 141

Plate 1 Extract from an article on Chabrier by Constant Lambert, which appeared in *Apollo*, October 1926.
Author's manuscript ; reproduced by permission.

Plate 2 The opening page of Alan Rawsthorne's *Third Symphony*, showing the dedication to his wife.
Composer's manuscript ; reproduced by permission
© *Copyright 1965 by Oxford University Press*

Plate 3 Extract from the first movement of Alan Rawsthorne's *Third Symphony*, showing the approach to the climax-chord at 15.
Composer's manuscript ; reproduced by permission
© *Copyright 1965 by Oxford University Press*

Plate 4 Extract from No. 6 of Denis ApIvor's *Overtones*. This piece is called after the Klee painting 'Sonnen und Mond Blumen' ('Sun and Moon flowers'). The two sections of the orchestra play, and are grouped, antiphonally; the soprano section (Orch. I) is associated with the idea 'Moon-flower', the bass section (Orch. II) with the idea 'Sun-flower'.
Composer's manuscript ; reproduced by permission

Plate 5 The opening page of Roberto Gerhard's *Violin Concerto*, showing the dedication to a Cambridge scientist and his wife, friends of the composer. The bold directions pp, and rit . . . Io, are a conductor's blue-pencil marking.
Composer's manuscript ; reproduced by permission

Plate 6 Extract from the first movement of Roberto Gerhard's *Violin Concerto*, showing some of the composer's characteristic corrections and cuts in the printed score. This forms part of the *Molto vivace con spirito* section following the cadenza and includes a reference to the violinist Yfrah Neaman, who was the soloist for the recording of this work.
© *Copyright 1960 by Mills Music Ltd. ; reproduced by permission*

Plate 7 Extract from Andrzej Panufnik's *Universal Prayer*, showing the end of the 12th verse of Alexander Pope's poem, set for bass solo, and the organ solo leading to the last verse. The key signatures for the harps indicate the pedal-settings, which remain unaltered throughout the work.
Composer's manuscript ; reproduced by permission
© *Copyright 1970 by Boosey & Hawkes Music Publishers Ltd.*

Preface

This study forms the second part of a trilogy. The first part, *Contemporary Music*, was a broadly based introduction to the varied and controversial developments in Western music since 1900. This second part is specifically concerned with British composers, whose work has multiplied so exceedingly since 1945, particularly as London is now the musical capital of Europe, if not of the Western world.

The third part (*The Aesthetics of Music – A Study of Tonality*) will form the interpretative conclusion to the series, based on the factual foundation of the first two. The entire trilogy is intended as an assessment of the contemporary environment.

The principles governing this book are the same as those underlying the first, *Contemporary Music*: it is a study in aesthetics. That is to say, it is not intended as an encyclopaedia; nor as a complete catalogue of every work of every British composer; nor does it claim to be history. Instead, I have tried to identify the individual motivation of certain composers, and to identify the direction in which their personal creativity has led. It is no function of a practising composer to attempt to put price-tags on the work of his colleagues; indeed, as they and he form parts of a living and constantly evolving organism, this would be a highly dubious undertaking. And in-so-far as criticism is taken, as it usually is, to mean the pronouncement of a value-judgment, or the expression of an opinion, this book is not intended as criticism. What the function of criticism could be, and what it is today, are two very distinct things. The critic should not attempt simply to measure the music against the rigid slide-rule of his own experience; rather he should, on each encounter with a fresh art-work, enlarge the range of his experience. Aesthetics is concerned not with the opinion of the critic, but with the nature of the art-work. But a reasoned assessment of the contemporary situation in this country is a very different matter; it will act as a life-line in a period of growth and evolution.

It is necessary to define terms. The term *contemporary* is taken, by its dictionary definition, to mean *belonging to our time*; by *our time* is meant the period since 1945, which forms a convenient starting point for historical, political and social, as well as musical, reasons.

The word *contemporary* is sometimes misused, particularly by certain of today's more articulate *avant-garde*, and made to apply qualitatively and exclusively only to those works which are consistent with their own immediate philosophy; the implication being that all others are to some extent irrelevant to today's listeners, and somehow not genuinely *contemporary*.

Such a doctored use of the word, with the lopsided view of today's musical art that it entails, is based on a false aesthetic standard. The only question to ask of an art-work is not whether it is *contemporary*, which is a purely neutral term, but whether, and if so why, it is artistically effective. If an art-work is effective, it will contribute actively to its tradition; if it is ineffective, it will not. What matters about a composer's style is not that he uses this or that particular idiom (however up-to-the-minute), but what use he makes of it. So tradition may be defined as that element in art which is relevant for those who come after. An active contemporary tradition is both a cumulative thing, and a constant growth; but an attempt to confine the use of the term *contemporary* to one specific aspect of today's many-sided musical activity is doubly unfortunate; it is out of touch with the dictionary definition, and it misunderstands the way in which musical traditions evolve.

That we are now witnessing such an evolution of an active musical tradition in this country is assumed, self-evident. Moreover, tradition may be defined also as that part of an art-work which gives it some claim to lasting, as distinct from merely ephemeral, value.

The term *British* is taken to include those composers who live and work in this country, or who consider themselves to be British citizens, wherever their work has been heard.

The term *music* is taken to include as many aspects of the composer's work as fall under the heading *art-work*. An art-work is one which makes some claim on our serious attention. This implies a creative, unique purpose on the part of the composer, and an active response on the part of the listener; it implies that the composer possesses and uses both vision and technique, and that the listener in return is expected to bring to bear his full intelligence. This excludes non-art music, such as pop music, whose purpose is chiefly, if not entirely, commercial. Pop groups are big business; they are socially significant; there is no question that they form a remarkable contemporary phenomenon—but this does not make the result into an art-work, and to consider it as if it were is an illogical affectation.

The activity of contemporary British composers presents a variegated pattern, like a mosaic, made up of innumerably variable particles, each reflecting and illustrating a different aspect of art; some more, some less, some apparently very little; but each differently expressive, each with a different contribution to make to the overall pattern of the contemporary tradition. Any attempt to identify, and confine, contemporary music within any one of these particles is neither prudent, nor, historically speaking, very sensible. It would be to confuse a part for the whole.

Inevitably, selection implies judgement; and judgement may well seem personal or arbitrary to those whose opinions are already formed. Some composers whose work may be widely played and comparatively well-known have received scant reference; others whose work is much less familiar, if known at all, have been treated more fully. The underlying factor is the uniqueness of their art—to which neither fluency nor notoriety are necessarily the passport. Starting with the music itself, I have been concerned with its underlying nature and purpose; not so much with the outward facts surrounding a composer's career, however well publicized these may have been. In the case of a few composers, their work has been so well noised abroad, and their every move so well documented, that further comment is superfluous.

It should hardly be necessary to point out that the order of the chapters in no way follows a chronological progression; nor should it be taken to imply artistic precedence or 'progress'. This would be foreign to the entire concept of this book. It is incorrect aesthetically to consider a composer who uses a particular idiom or style as more 'advanced' than one who uses another. Rather should they be seen as each developing a different aspect of a many-sided tradition.

Tradition is that factor which allows music to grow. It is not merely something derived from the past. Therefore a tradition that is healthy and vital is capable of growth in as many directions as there are composers of uniqueness. It is these composers whose work I have attempted to describe in these pages.

As the book is not an encyclopaedia, nor an up-to-the-minute work of reference, I have omitted check-lists of composers' works, except where such a list is used to illustrate a particular point, or where it is otherwise unobtainable. In the majority of cases, check-lists are issued by publishers. Works referred to in the text are check-listed in the index.

The intention of Appendices III, IV and V is—in taking a cross-section of concerts in one typical season from the twenty-five years covered by the scope of this book—to show, by means of figures and tables, the place allotted to the contemporary British composer in the output of the principal orchestras, organizations and festivals. The season chosen is 1968/9.

October, 1971   FRANCIS ROUTH

Introduction

British Music up to 1939

Contemporary music is never a complete entity, a thing in itself, which can be measured and assessed at any one moment in time. Rather is it a process of growth, many-sided, organic. Its properties are biological; it has its roots in the past, while, plant-like, some newly-formed shoot is always springing up. Hopefully and curiously, we can only wonder whether a new growth will blossom forth into a flowering plant of recognizable beauty and unique character, or wither away into nothingness. The reasonably informed musician, like the reasonably informed gardener, may make a reason-based guess. But it is only a guess.

However, what is not so much a matter of guesswork, but more susceptible of expert assessment, is the new growth that is beyond the seedling stage, the bud that has already begun to flower. To the gardener who is acquainted with grafting and splicing, with soil fertilization and the care of plants, the appearance of the new bloom will not come entirely as a surprise. And in the case of a musical growth, the same laws operate; the nature of a composer's work is decided already by the priorities he sets himself at the formative stage, by his artistic point of departure; also by his environment, which represents the soil in which his creativity develops and grows.

It is unreasonable to consider a seedling as if it were a flower. It may well develop into a flower later; or it may not. But speculation is not valid criticism. And, in the same way, it is no merit in itself that a composition should be the work of a 'young composer'; indeed, it may well be a disservice to a composer to overrate his immature student-work. Not until the bud opens out into flower is it possible to discuss its true nature. And many a composer (Britten, Rawsthorne, Tippett, for example) has withdrawn his early attempts.

Two main questions underlie any reasoned enquiry into the development of British music up to 1939. First, what was the nature and purpose of the composers' achievements? Secondly, what was the environment within which they worked?

The first question is considerably easier to answer than the second. The environment itself was constantly changing, compounded of several factors, and it varied from place to place. Historians and critics of the time give widely differing accounts, according to their prejudices and differing backgrounds; and to accept one as definitive means to ignore others. Moreover, the most active musicians, and the most articulate, are not always those whose work is most lasting. One cannot necessarily form a complete picture solely from the accounts of individual writers, composers and critics. Cecil Gray provides a particularly clear example of an important writer whose remarkably shrewd insight into the work of a small group of composers (Delius, Van Dieren, Warlock, Lambert), for whom he acted as spokesman, was matched by an almost complete antipathy towards composers of a different allegiance. The picture he presents is therefore a partial one. But his *History of Music* was remarkable for its erudition, and for its catholicity of taste: mediaeval music, plainchant, Monteverdi, lesser known eighteenth-century opera, were included in his survey—all of which have since come into their own. His concern with Russian music, and Berlioz, and his distaste for Wagner, Schoenberg, and the nineteenth-century hegemony of Teutonic music, and above all his fervour in the cause of Sibelius, all accurately reflect the mood of his day; moreover, his style of opinionated writing did much to establish the critic's function today as primarily one of passing judgment and giving an opinion.[1] He represents the composer's lot (and no doubt in this he was also giving articulate expression to a considerable body of opinion) as a never-ending, uphill struggle against a bureaucratic and philistine Establishment. That British musical society at this time did contain some members whose chief characteristics were their extreme limitations of outlook is beyond doubt. Such people can be found today, if one is sufficiently interested to enquire. But fortunately they form only a part, and a small and insignificant part at that, of the overall pattern of musical achievement.

Generally speaking, the period up to 1939 was one of activity, development and expansion. As far as the concert-going public was concerned, there were one or two chief centres of music-making. Pride of place, because of its roots in the past, must be given to the Three Choirs Festival, which provided Elgar's environment, and which reached its heyday between the wars.

The great works of Elgar, choral and symphonic, are the musical and spiritual embodiment of Worcester Cathedral or the Malvern Hills. The qualities of his music—the emotional stillness and tranquillity, the gentle, melting harmonies, with their leisurely rate of harmonic change, the

1. See the preface to his *A Survey of Contemporary Music*.

sequential themes—all arise naturally and inherently from the resonant dignity of an English cathedral.

Many a composer, including Vaughan Williams, derived great benefit from this centre of music-making. Other centres were found at Leeds and at Bournemouth. The Leeds Festival in 1931, saw the first performance of Walton's *Belshazzar's Feast*, while at Bournemouth Sir Dan Godfrey, with his municipal orchestra, promoted the work of a number of composers, many of whom were invited to conduct themselves.

As far as London was concerned, the story of music-making up to the war is mainly the story of Queen's Hall. When Queen's Hall was destroyed in an air raid on May 10th 1941, this marked not only the end of a concert-hall in London, which was the focal point for the country as a whole; it also marked the end of that formative period of the renaissance of British music, with which it was more or less coeval (1893–1941). By 1939, the regular symphonic repertoire had been established in this country; orchestras had been formed which were of a professional standing, and comparable in quality with other leading world orchestras; standards had been set which formed the norm for composers, audiences, critics, and performers. In short, the foundations of a tradition had been laid.

One musician whose work had a certain visionary quality was Henry Wood. He was not so much a great conductor as a great personality, and one whose work, through the medium of the Proms, which he founded, brought him into direct touch with the ordinary music-loving public,[1] which he himself had created. His contribution to the developing tradition of British music was to teach the public to accept the work of the British composer. In this respect he was the first[2], though other conductors of this period, notably Adrian Boult, Thomas Beecham and Dan Godfrey, followed his example in their different ways.

His words are prophetic:[3]

They said there wasn't a public for great music 47 years ago. The critics wagged their heads. But Robert Newman said we'd *make* a public, and we did. He asked me to be the permanent conductor of a new orchestra he was forming, the Queen's Hall Orchestra—and I jumped at the chance. Out of that came the Proms. It was a bold venture, in 1895.

Bach and Haydn, Mozart, Beethoven and Brahms are not dry-as-dust names to be shuddered at these days. They've become friends now, and well-loved friends, to all sorts and kinds of people, who had never heard of them till the

1. No one captures this mood more aptly than J. B. Priestley, when he describes in *Angel Pavement* a visit by the central character, Mr. Smeeth, to a Queen's Hall concert.
2. The first Promenade Concert was on 10th August 1895, at Queen's Hall.
3. Taken from a broadcast of August 1941.

B

Proms started. It meant years of hard work, and, I quite admit, a certain amount of cunning. We had to go slow at first; cornet solos and all that sort of thing. Nowadays, I can put on a work like the *London Symphony* of Vaughan Williams, one of the finest composers we have in Britain today, and then you see how the Proms have changed. I've arrived at what I set out to do.

If, after 1945, a new concert-hall was to take the place of the burnt-out Queen's Hall, it would be because the tradition of British music-making was so secure that a new concert-hall was felt to be necessary. Such a hall was, indeed, built ten years later—the Royal Festival Hall—which was part of the Festival of Britain in 1951; and it has since been extended to include two smaller auditoria. It is, therefore, true to say that, during the period up to 1939, the groundwork of the renaissance, whose fruits were to become more and more apparent after 1945, was securely and truly laid. Standards were established; and a public was seen to exist. In short, the soil was prepared.

There was, however, a very wide gap between the music being played at concerts during this period, the works being written in this country, and the developments taking place on the continent of Europe. European composers who, for better or for worse, were altering the face of music at this time, included chiefly Busoni and Hindemith, with their neo-classical inclinations; Weill and Brecht; Satie and the Ecole d'Arceuil; Stravinsky and Bartok; and the Viennese school of Schoenberg, Berg and Webern. Many developments in British music since 1945[1] have had their origin in the work of these pre-war European composers, but at the time their works were hardly known or played at all in this country.

What performances there were, stand out because they were so isolated. The Sackbut[2] concerts promoted Bartok; Erwin Stein directed Schoenberg's *Pierrot Lunaire* in April 1930, in a celebrated performance at Westminster Central Hall, with Erika Wagner and the Pierrot Ensemble; in 1933 Edward Clark and Adrian Boult presented a broadcast of *Wozzeck*, though this had to wait twenty years before being staged at Covent Garden, conducted by Erich Kleiber. Stravinsky appeared several times at Queen's Hall, where he both played and conducted.

Some of the most enterprising concerts were conducted in 1921 by Eugene Goossens with his specially formed Goossens Orchestra. This series included, in June 1921, the first performance in England of Stravinsky's notorious *Le Sacre du Printemps*, 'which created such a sensation that it was repeated by general desire at a subsequent concert in the same series'.[3] Other composers represented were Schoenberg,

1. With the notable exception of electronic music. See p. 297.
2. See p. 14.
3. Quoted from Robert Elkin, *Queen's Hall*, p. 47.

Debussy, Bliss, Bax, Ireland, Delius and Lord Berners. Goossens' compositions were in the romantic tradition, but as a conductor he was lost to England because there was no demand for his concerts. He went instead to America.

Seen against a European background, and particularly in historical perspective, it might seem that Vaughan Williams's folk-song school, or the Sibelius movement, were an irrelevance to the growth of British music.

It naturally happened that some individual musicians, whose vision was more internationally orientated, would have preferred the rate of development to be different, or quicker, or both. Such men as Edward Dent, Edward Clark, Constant Lambert, were aware of developments in other European countries, and wished to bring them to the notice of their more sluggish fellow-countrymen. But it was not to be expected that the radical innovations of Stravinsky or Schoenberg, Krenek or Hindemith, would find ready acceptance by a British public whose acquaintance with the standard nineteenth century repertoire was so comparatively recent. What they had so laboriously learnt they were not prepared to unlearn. Contemporary music was, therefore, the concern of the minority, who formed into small, private societies.

Edward Clark at the B.B.C. would arrange broadcast performances, often at a conspiratorial hour late at night; more often than not with inadequate rehearsal. One musician summed up the conditions under which such work was done: 'It was every man for himself—and the devil take the Hindemith!'

In general at this time, performances of contemporary music were very infrequent; the British composer could only take his work to the L.C.M.C., or the Macnaghten Concerts.[1] This is in marked contrast to the situation in 1970, when it is very much easier for new work to be heard; and as far as the B.B.C. is concerned, the situation has been transformed, as can be seen by comparing the pioneer work of Edward Clark with the long list of premières in 1970, to say nothing of other performances which were not premières, or were of composers other than British. In many ways the B.B.C. by 1970 swung too far the other way, and did not differentiate between a workshop rehearsal and a public recital.[2] Many of the works were of relevance only to a small minority, and made no impact on the majority of listeners.

Vaughan Williams adopted a different approach from Clark or Lambert. His concern was not so much to find out about the latest developments in music that were happening on the continent, as to set about realising and fulfilling the musicality that, so he believed, was inherent in the English

1. See p. 21.
2. See p. 18.

make-up. He therefore wished, more than most composers of his generation, first to win acceptance by the broad mass of his fellow-countrymen.
Great music, he feels, springs from a tradition; and a tradition needs
national roots. There is nothing narrowly chauvinistic, or mistakenly
patriotic, about such a view; it is purely observable common sense.

Indeed, for this reason, our contemporary tradition starts with Vaughan
Williams. He foresaw that it would take several generations before an
endemic British tradition could flourish, and he set about establishing
roots for such a national music, secure and deep. So far from being
narrow or provincial in outlook, Vaughan Williams was, on the contrary,
a composer of wide-ranging vision, revolutionary in thought. He set to
work to touch and influence the musical life of his country at as many
points as possible; at the orchestral concert level; at the university level,
which he rightly thought was very important for the propagation of a
positive musical taste; at the amateur level which, again, he was very far
from despising; at the level of church music, which was at a particularly
low ebb, and has remained so for most of the contemporary period; at the
level of chamber music and song-writing, since the love of domestic
music-making is one of the hall-marks of an active tradition.

As he essayed such a bewildering diversity of work, it was inevitable
that he would be misunderstood. But the underlying purpose of his work
may be seen partly as a spiritual thing; a search for a foundation for a
British musical tradition that would have sufficient toughness and validity
to grow over the coming decades, and that would strike a responsive note
in the musical instincts of the people which, he felt, had for too long been
repressed and frustrated. It can be seen partly also as a technical thing.
If music is to survive it requires not only a certain distinctive individuality
and grandeur; it must also have technical expertise.

As far as British music was concerned, Vaughan Williams saw a rich
heritage from the past, waiting to be claimed by composers, and other
artists, of the present. But first it was necessary to win acceptance, not
so much from the critics and other self-styled experts, whose knowledge
of other traditions, past or present, was largely second-hand, as from
the mass of the people. Folk-song, and the use of a modal idiom, which
we recognize as one of the features of nationalism, was to Vaughan
Williams the means of achieving such a general acceptance, and a link
with past periods. To later composers and to us today who, thanks largely
to him, can take for granted a certain measure of popular acceptance, the
use of folk-song material may seem unnecessary, an anachronism; and to
those of his contemporaries who were influenced by his dominating
personality into the unthinking imitation of his style, the device proved a

particularly unqualified dead end. But the same may be said for any technique or style. It is the universal characteristic of second-rate and derivative composers that they copy this or that original without the insight which is essential if they are to use their mentor's style in an effective way. Audiences prefer an original to a pale copy—and rightly so.

If Henry Wood was the earliest champion of the British composer, and his go-between and advocate before the broad concert audience, and if Cecil Gray was the spokesman of the more thinking musicians of his day, the most articulate spokesman of the advanced set was Constant Lambert. His *Music Ho!* is both knowledgeable and witty, a true barometer of the times. The period following 1918 was partly, though not entirely, a period of trivialities, of undergraduate pranks, of the antics of the Sitwells, of the jazz age; but it was also a period of reaction, after the war, against all things German; particularly Wagnerian romanticism. The smart, and therefore correct, thing to be was an admirer of things French, such as Debussy or Berlioz; of things Russian, such as the Russian ballets of Stravinsky, or the works of Borodin, Mussorgsky; or, if you wanted a model symphonist, of Sibelius. The very last resort of the destitute was to be satisfied with the homespun product of your native land; indeed, the British composer, along with the British public, needed to be jolted out of his narrow provincialism into a greater awareness of the world about him. Colour, exoticism, Life—low or high—were the essentials necessary for salvation. Thus spake Constant Lambert.

But Vaughan Williams thought differently. The acceptance of a contemporary British composer by his own countrymen would depend on many other considerations than just musical ones. A composer needs to make a correct evaluation of British society; its social barriers, its conventions, its taboos. To offend in any important particular might result in total rejection, however excellent the music.

One such force in society, and perhaps the most influential of all, is the power of the Establishment. Though a nebulous thing, it is, like the British Constitution, a force that is all the stronger for being felt rather than seen. Its rules are unwritten conventions rather than an absolute code of conduct; against its verdict there can be no appeal. And one of the strengths of Vaughan Williams was his acceptance of, and by, the Establishment.

Another force in British society, which Vaughan Williams recognized and fully allowed for, is the cult of amateurism. Whether in politics, in law, in sport, or in art, the British instinctively exalt the amateur—and correspondingly downgrade the expert. Clearly this presents the composer with a disturbing choice. Is not expertise the one decisive factor that separates the truly ambitious artist from the dilettante; the work of some permanent value from the work of ephemeral interest only ? Yet expertise by itself will in no way win acceptance by a British public taught, in truly democratic style, that a 'do-it-yourself' job has some intrinsic merit, from that very fact; and that the expert, unless controlled, may assume a superiority over his fellows, which is to be mistrusted.

This cult of the amateur can sometimes invite and breed hypocrisy of a particularly disturbing kind. It no more abolishes the need for expertise than prohibition abolishes drinking; but what it can achieve is an outward denial and devaluation of skill. If a composer is to survive, and find some acceptance, in British society, he must tend to belittle the technical and specialist excellence of his work, which are what chiefly qualify it for serious consideration, and stress instead his possession of those neutral qualities of ordinariness and sameness that make him indistinguishable from his fellows—his fondness for gardening, his concern for the local football team, his partiality for an occasional pint—all those absurd activities that appear under 'recreations' in *Who's Who*. But whatever happens, he must make no admission of artistic endeavour, or effort of any kind, as this will be of no avail.

So it comes about that the much-reputed 'reserve' of the English is as much due to self-preservation as to national modesty. Vaughan Williams met the challenge inherent in this aspect of British society by seeking, wherever he could, to establish and maintain contact with as many people as possible, and to interest them in what he was doing.

A third characteristic force inherent in British society, which Vaughan Williams took fully into account, is an insatiable curiosity about other cultures and other traditions. Partly for commercial reasons, partly as a mark of social distinction, the British have always been inveterate travellers; and a traveller is essentially an observer of a scene; he is in no way committed to, or involved in, what he observes. The Grand Tour of the eighteenth century was obligatory for the cultured English gentleman; he was expected to capture something of the habits and customs of other countries—the more exotic the better—and thus return home armed with interesting conversation. Music was included among the objects to be observed; it was something that foreigners did so much more naturally, and so much better than the English. Such an approach to contemporary music can be seen in the history of music of Dr. Charles Burney, which is more of an eighteenth-century travel-diary than a music history. But the philosophy underlying it is anything but out of date; indeed, it is still felt today; namely, that if you wished to become a musician you had to go to Vienna or Leipzig in order to do so. It has been accepted for very many years by the British that other traditions and cultures, particularly of the more respectable European countries, are vastly more interesting than anything that could be produced at home. The story of British music, at least since the seventeenth century, can be interpreted in the light of the acceptance—or the rejection—of this philosophy. It has fundamentally affected the cultural ethos, and the general musical receptivity, of the intelligentsia of this country.

And even today, when London is now the musical capital of Europe, and when music is heard in London in greater quantity, and of a higher standard, than in any other city in the world, the British people are still quite extraordinarily slow to cast aside this self-denigrating philosophy, which automatically places the work of foreign composers, however negligible, on a higher level of interest and artistic achievement than the corresponding work of their British counterparts.

This inherent desire to investigate and to extol foreign traditions was fully understood by Vaughan Williams. Indeed, he himself shared it; he was fully abreast of all the latest developments. But he exercised his composer's right of choice, and was not content to be merely the propaganda-agent of another composer's style.

And so the musical environment in England between the wars showed a differing degree of acceptance of the British composer among different sections of people. Vaughan Williams won acceptance; and through him, and Henry Wood, the gate was opened to a considerable number of British composers whose music was nostalgically romantic. There arose a considerable romantic movement, twenty years or more after this had occurred in Germany and other European countries. This mood was perfectly caught by Beecham, when he sponsored the music of Delius, who would otherwise have remained virtually unknown here, though his work was extensively played on the continent. Curiously, the work of this emigré Englishman, whose revolutionary score *Paris* (1896) antedates, in terms of sheer modernity, the early works of Stravinsky and Schoenberg, most aptly illustrates the result of an absence of the impetus of an active tradition, within which a composer can live and work. By the twenties, when Beecham promoted his work, the music of Delius was already being superseded in Europe by various other movements; but the developments in music of the twentieth century had scarcely begun to be recognized in England, except by a handful, and the romantic movement between the wars was popularly acceptable because it postponed the necessity of recognition; at least for a while. But it meant that impetus was lacking in this country.

A measure of this lack of impetus can be seen in the work and career of Constant Lambert. This remarkable musician, whose father was a painter and whose brother a sculptor, was primarily a man of the theatre, and the

first British composer to be commissioned by Diaghilev to write a ballet—
a remarkable achievement for a young man. But his ballet scores, starting
with *Romeo and Juliet*, never succeeded as much as his other better-known
work, *The Rio Grande* (1928), which has a zestful vitality lacking in some
later works, such as *Horoscope*. *Tresias* was peremptorily dismissed by the
critics, though not primarily for musical reasons. Indeed, the music is by
no means to be dismissed; Rawsthorne later wrote an orchestral piece
round a theme from this score. *Summer's Last Will and Testament* is
another remarkable choral work; not gay or witty, but containing many
references to earlier styles, such as the madrigal.

Lambert was not entirely to be identified with the prevailing mood of
romantic nostalgia. Though he was associated with the group centred
round Philip Heseltine and Cecil Gray, he later lost favour with their
tendency to an ingrown Englishry which resolutely refuses to admit outside influences. His own criticism of Stravinsky in *Music Ho!* was largely
personal, since Stravinsky's outstanding success with Diaghilev was in
such marked contrast with the failure of his *Romeo and Juliet*.

The mood of romanticism, however, is much more truly reflected in the
symphonies and choral works of Bax, Ireland, and the songs of Warlock,
Van Dieren. If Bax's symphonies and tone-poems show the characteristic
romantic predilection for a big orchestral tone, Ireland's romanticism
was, on the contrary, condensed into his piano works, which greatly
exceed his pieces for orchestra in both number and scope. Several later
composers were deeply impressed by Ireland's piano-writing, notably
Alan Rawsthorne.

Warlock's brooding melancholy, the Heseltine side of his personality,
is most fully realized in his settings of Yeats—a poet who also greatly
affected Bax. Both Delius and Van Dieren wrote major works on
Nietzsche's texts (*Also sprach Zarathustra*) and the Hans Bethge translations from the Chinese, which also inspired Mahler's *Third Symphony*
and *Das Lied von der Erde*.

Van Dieren at this period was the central figure in an important group
of composers, which included Bliss and the young Walton. Though his
music had a strongly romantic flavour, he anticipated, in a number of
ways, certain trends which were later developed by Webern—complex
contrapuntal writing, for instance, for groups of solo instruments. This
was, no doubt, a direct influence of Busoni—his wife Frida was Busoni's
pupil—but it does no service to Van Dieren to claim for him, as Cecil
Gray did, the mantle of the Messiah. His gentle romanticism was highly
aristocratic and refined, but of its period.

It is commonly said, and with some truth, that trends and movements
in European music reach England at least ten years later; that there is a

time-lag in the receptivity of English audiences. This may well explain the non-appearance of up-to-the-minute styles among British composers. The flippancy and satirical humour of so much French music, for instance, in the 20's, was hardly reflected at all on this side of the channel. Indeed, while French audiences were, we presume, responding in the appropriate manner to the facetious humour and disrespectful antics of Satie, or to the small theatre works of Stravinsky, the audiences in England were too busy catching up on their romantic past to pay much attention.

Not until forty years later, with the rise of the *avant-garde* in the 60's, and of groups such as Maxwell Davies's Pierrot Players, did flippancy and humour become acceptable; then these early works of the twentieth century produced a considerable progeny in Davies, Goehr and others. Would Lambert have approved of such a latter-day fulfilment of a fifty-year-old movement such as appeared in Dada or Surrealism? Not, we may be sure, if the joke has to be explained, like the patter of a stale comedian. The only test of a joke is whether or not it is funny. Would Lambert have been amused by Hoffnung's extravaganzas in the 50's, or were they pouring hot water on to old tea leaves? In 1930 Constant Lambert might point out the merits of zest and levity in music, whether in his own *Rio Grande*, or in his book, *Music Ho!*; but apart from Walton's *Façade*, and one or two attempts by Bliss and Berners, this was neither expected nor approved of by the English public. The Establishment was not amused.

Meanwhile, another aspect of British music was being developed, with very great promise for the future; that was the re-discovery of early music. An awareness of the great strength of past periods of English music had first been shown by Vaughan Williams in his movingly austere *Tallis Fantasia*; and the desire to recover something of the splendour of the past was felt increasingly during the inter-war period.

Peter Warlock was a pioneer in his work on the English Ayre, and brought to bear, in his re-discovering of music of the Elizabethan and Jacobean periods, a unique combination of scholarship and creative insight. His transcriptions included songs, English and French Ayres, and pieces for strings by Purcell, Dowland, Matthew Locke and many others. He and Cecil Gray also wrote the first study of the life and work of Gesualdo, who was entirely unknown, but later, thanks largely to Stravinsky's interest, became something of a cult figure.

Lambert edited and performed works by seventeenth- and eighteenth-century composers, such as John Blow and William Boyce. E. H. Fellowes began his monumental work of editing Tudor music, and Margaret Glyn pioneered the rediscovery of the Elizabethan virginalists. Charles Kennedy Scott and Boris Ord were two musicians particularly concerned with establishing a standard of choral singing which would equal that of the great orchestras; they founded the Oriana Madrigal Society and the Cambridge University Madrigal Society respectively. Thus began that revolutionary movement in British choral singing, which was to have such marked effects after 1945.[1]

The time when Alldis formed his choir (1962) was the time when the serialist movement was at its height; his chosen repertoire was, therefore, strongly inclined towards Schoenberg, Webern, Messiaen, Stockhausen, and their English derivatives Wood, Lutyens and Smalley.

The discovering and performance of contemporary music between the wars was confined to a minority—a handful of small societies, and one or two individual musicians of a somewhat idealistic turn of mind. Apart from the group who gathered round the Sitwell family, some distinctive concerts, the Sackbut concerts, were promoted by Cecil Gray and Peter Warlock (Philip Heseltine). Works by Van Dieren and Delius were juxtaposed with those of Purcell; Schoenberg and Bartok with Gesualdo. Such programmes, with which we are now more familiar, were entirely unknown fifty years ago. Warlock was a friend of Bartok, who later in the 30's came several times to this country, largely through the I.S.C.M.[2] Another composer who greatly influenced the trends in British music during this period was Busoni; not only as a pianist, and composer, but also through personal contact, through the I.S.C.M., he had a great effect on the two British musicians who were chiefly instrumental in bringing about the swing towards the contemporary composer, that began to be apparent after 1945—Edward Clark and Edward Dent.

1. One musician, who was a member of the choir at King's College, Cambridge (1949–52), under Boris Ord, subsequently formed his own professional choir, and extended these principles beyond Tudor and early English music, to the contemporary repertoire. John Alldis has described (in *Composer*, No. 33, Autumn 1969) something of his intention:

   '(At Cambridge) I had become accustomed to a standard of choral singing which, in those days, did not exist anywhere else. This was due to Boris Ord, who, in my opinion, 'invented' that intense, clear sound (as opposed to the woolly choral society sound) that we all now try to achieve in English choral singing. I also wished to expand beyond the Renaissance repertoire which the post-war flood of scholarship had led everyone to perform. I chose professionally trained singers, of high general intelligence, who were beginning to succeed as individual performers. I wished to do something of a virtuoso kind. I was not seeking to blend voices into a "choral", non-individualistic sound.

   (I favour) 20 to 24 in number, more or less equally divided, but unlike some, I occasionally increase the number of voices as they get lower. This can have a striking effect on the total sonority. I normally have a counter-tenor in the alto section—it seems to add a special quality to the sound without being in itself obtrusive.'

2. See p. 20.

Dent, Professor of Music at Cambridge, and biographer of Busoni, was a musician of international vision, through whom Britain was included in the I.S.C.M.. Edward Clark was an enlightened champion of contemporary music through the medium of radio performances. He promoted works unheard of in this country, such as Busoni's *Dr Faust* and *Arlecchino*, and Berg's *Wozzeck*; he befriended British composers, much as Adrian Boult did as a conductor. Both filled a need.

When Boult was appointed to conduct the newly formed B.B.C. Symphony Orchestra, this ensured a central and important place for the symphonic work of the romantic British school of composers of the period—Vaughan Williams, Holst, Delius, Bax and John Ireland. It was largely due to him that their work became securely established. So, in the story of the gradual evolution of contemporary British music—certainly as far as orchestral music is concerned—Adrian Boult occupies a central position. He sought to be, not so much the great virtuoso conductor, as simply the friend and colleague of the composers of his time, many of whom he knew personally, and for whom he acted as intermediary and advocate with the public. In 1919 Hugh Allen, the Director of the Royal College of Music, invited him to join the staff of the College. It was an inspired and highly propitious appointment, and the next five years proved a particularly fruitful period for British music, when such works as Holst's *Planets*, Vaughan Williams' *Pastoral Symphony*, John Ireland's *Forgotten Rite* and Delius's *Violin Concerto* were first rehearsed and played under Boult's direction. For sheer activity, and concert work, the centre of gravity of British music in 1920 lay at the Royal College of Music.

This ceased when Boult was appointed in 1924 to conduct the Birmingham orchestra; and in 1930 he moved from there to be the first conductor of the new B.B.C. Orchestra, a post which he retained for twenty years, in close association with Edward Clark. His departure brought an insecurity to composers from the 50s onwards.[1]

While Boult was forming the B.B.C. Symphony Orchestra, another orchestra was being formed by that most colourful of musical individualists, Sir Thomas Beecham. On October 7th, 1932, at Queen's Hall, the London Philharmonic made its first appearance. Beecham was a perfectionist, with an acute ear for the constituent strands of sound that make up the orchestral ensemble; and indeed Alldis was to follow the same principle when he founded his choir thirty years later.[2]

Beecham's unique achievement, in this period of musical growth in England, was to set standards. He was himself an inveterate founder of orchestras, starting with the Beecham Orchestra of 1909, to say nothing

1. After 1950 he was associated with the L.P.O.
2. See p. 14.

of the Beecham Opera Company; the Royal Philharmonic Orchestra was also to be his creation, in 1947. But it was not enough in itself simply to found orchestras. The quality of ensemble playing and orchestral sound had to stand comparison with that of the finest foreign orchestras, whose tradition went back much further. It was necessary therefore that as soon as possible the newly-founded orchestra should tour abroad; and this the London Philharmonic duly did—to Germany in 1936, to Paris in 1937.[1] Beecham set a standard of ensemble, of phrasing, of orchestral balance, that made him comparable with the European virtuoso conductors of his generation—Furtwängler, Toscanini, Walter. But the only British composer whose work he promoted to any great extent was Delius.

In addition to the founding of symphony orchestras of international standard, which could, under the right direction, serve the British composer, another development took place in the 30's, one which achieved spectacular success remarkably soon, and quickly became a focal point for the British composer; that was the Sadler's Wells Ballet, later renamed the Royal Ballet.

The achievement of Dame Ninette de Valois in founding a British ballet company is in a sense more remarkable than that of Sir Thomas Beecham in founding orchestras. She was not only starting a new group of dancers; she was initiating a tradition where hitherto, in this country, there was little or none.[2]

After dancing with the Diaghilev company, which she left in 1926, she considered the possibility of appearing with dancers in municipally-owned repertory theatres in England. She knew that there was a stock of dancing talent of a very high order in this country, only waiting to be used properly. Her first achievement was in work with W. B. Yeats at the Abbey Theatre in Dublin, in his dance-dramas, which were much influenced by Japanese Nō plays. But the decisive moment came when Lilian Baylis suggested a joint venture whereby a new dance company would present performances, partly at the Old Vic theatre, partly at Sadler's Wells theatre in Islington. This company would therefore be called the Vic-Wells Ballet. And so in 1931, with six dancers, the Sadler's Wells Ballet was born. There also started, however insecurely, a ballet school—without which no ballet company can exist.

They were referred to in one newspaper as 'the Islington dancers'; and the company stayed at Sadler's Wells until 1939, when the theatre closed. The chief conductor was Constant Lambert, and under his

1. Described in *The Baton and the Jackboot*, by Berta Geissmar.
2. Only the Ballet Rambert existed as an independent company, founded by Marie Rambert, who had also been associated with the Diaghilev company as a teacher of Dalcroze eurhythmics.

dynamic direction a wholly fresh repertoire of British ballets was built up, starting with Bliss, Walton, Lambert himself. Like Dame Ninette, Constant Lambert had been associated with Diaghilev, and it was the combined vision of these two that gave the balanced impetus to this idealistic enterprise, and brought success. But Lambert was much more than just the conductor; he controlled the dancers as well as the musicians; he directed the decor, and provided just the overall musical leadership that the newly founded company needed.

The public in the 30's was small, but during the war years the company was compelled to travel round the country, playing in different theatres and camps. From this necessity came virtue. They soon realised that they were not only filling a need by providing art and colour during a period of enforced austerity; they were also establishing their own identity among a wide public—which has grown ever since. Immediately after the war they toured abroad, first to Brussels and Paris in 1946, then to America and Russia—where with some understandable satisfaction Dame Ninette decided to perform Stravinsky's *Firebird*. Thus her British company brought the chicken home to roost, and won great international acclaim. Perhaps the greatest international triumph was the opening at the Metropolitan in New York of *The Sleeping Beauty*, conducted by Constant Lambert, with Margot Fonteyn in the role of Aurora.

So ballet developed earlier and quicker than opera in this country during the inter-war years. Indeed, opera was still an exclusive affair at this time. The Covent Garden season was for just three months during the summer, and the repertoire was confined to German, Italian or Russain opera, while the newly founded Glyndebourne was modelled on some private, princely theatre of the baroque period, and derived its artistic life-blood from the opera houses of Germany, whose work it reflected.

During the war Covent Garden opera house became a dance-hall, while Sadler's Wells was closed. When Covent Garden opened again in 1945, Dame Ninette's company, and school, played there for a year, until the opera joined them. Thus the Royal Ballet was securely established. Yet, strangely, more prestige attaches to opera than to ballet in this country. You have 'Grand Opera'; you do not have 'Grand Ballet'.

The tradition and technique of dancing that inspired Dame Ninette were in line with the classical Western style of Denmark, France and Italy—which had also been the source and origin of the Russian style. But the characteristics of the British Royal Ballet are a greater development of footwork, greater movement from the waist downwards, and character-dancing. Physical style is something inherent in the national dance of a country, and in the case of the Royal Ballet it has evolved naturally. The success, and the example, of Dame Ninette's vision acted as a spur to Britten, and others, in 1946 in forming a corresponding company for opera—the English Opera Group.

Constant Lambert died in 1951; but numerous British ballets continued to be played by the Royal Ballet. ApIvor, Arnold, Searle, Rawsthorne, Britten and several other composers contributed works. But since about 1965 the company has tended more towards the classical repertoire.

The inter-war period also saw the formation of several societies and organisations specifically for the promotion of contemporary music. The fruitful period at the Royal College of Music following 1920 was made possible by the official endowment known as the Patron's Fund, which was used for the purpose of orchestral rehearsals, and thus for the very direct benefit of composers. This therefore is, in effect, the first official contemporary music society.

In 1903, Sir Ernest Palmer, later Lord Palmer of Reading, presented to the Royal College of Music (founded thirty years previously) the sum of £27,000, which was later increased, for the specific purpose (among others) of 'the selection and performance of works by British composers under forty years of age'. This exciting and novel project was put into the hands of a committee made up of the staff of the Royal College and the Royal Academy of Music (founded in 1822); and between 1904 and 1914 they administered a series of public concerts, at the Bechstein Hall[1] for chamber music, and the Queen's Hall for orchestral music. The composers normally conducted their own works, and if the list of those included had a strong academic bias, this was, perhaps understandably, because the Committee felt that their first loyalty was to those who were in some way associated with the two main teaching institutions in London. These concerts were thus the first, and official, shop-window of the Establishment. Unfortunately, the public was not yet ready, and a lack of public interest in new music resulted in many empty seats.

The concerts were suspended when war broke out in 1914. When they were resumed in 1919 it was decided, at Hugh Allen's instigation, that public concerts, for which there was no public, should be superseded by public *rehearsals* in the College. The London Symphony Orchestra was engaged, and Adrian Boult conducted. At that particular moment in time the results were highly advantageous for British music; but the same principle was applied later with much less success.[2] It was an innovation which represented an important shift of emphasis. It can by no means justifiably be said that it caused the rift between the composer and the

1. Now the Wigmore Hall.
2. See p. 365.

public, but it was a realistic recognition that such a rift existed—and indeed has continued to exist ever since. Probably in 1919 it was unrealistic to expect a conservative, and largely unaware, public to accept such an exciting and radical conception as Lord Palmer had visualized. Unfortunately, the relegation of the composer to 'public rehearsal' status, while in some ways an admirable expedient, created an impression of second-class musical citizenship which still survives today. There is something of a parallel to these 'public rehearsals' to be seen in Schoenberg's 'Society for private musical performances', which he started in Vienna at about the same time.

In the early years of the twentieth century, several private attempts were made, of an isolated and somewhat disjointed nature, to promote music by British composers. In 1907 Delius and Elgar launched a concert-scheme which they called the League of Music. Granville Bantock and Henry Wood were also associated with it, though Wood's interest must have been slight, as he does not mention it in his autobiography. A somewhat dismal account by Beecham[1] records the work of the League:

> The League struggled through a period of nearly two years of fitful activity, underwent several changes of direction, succeeded in giving one Festival of concerts in the October of 1909, and thereafter sank gently into oblivion.

Composers, however eminent, are not necessarily good administrators. Moreover, the time was not yet ripe. But another musician who privately sponsored a considerable number of concerts out of his own pocket at this time was Balfour Gardiner. Small concerts, often with Charles Kennedy Scott's choir, were given privately, for instance at Lord Leighton's house in Kensington; bigger concerts were promoted at Queen's Hall.

Balfour Gardiner was a wealthy patron, who worked through the Establishment, often with most positive results, as in the case of Holst's *Planets*. But the first effective group-movement came in 1919, when the British Music Society was founded, on the initiative of Dr. A. Eaglefield Hull. This society was intended for the general furtherance of music in this country after the war. It was not to be a society for British music alone, but a British Society for music in general. Its underlying aims were twofold: first, to encourage and promote the general level of musical taste and understanding among concert audiences, who were generally speaking extremely conservative; second, to promote the young and untried composer, who had little or no chance of public performance, except through the Royal College of Music concerts, or abroad at a Festival such as Donaueschingen.

It was the second purpose which proved the more fruitful, and under Edward Dent's presidency there grew the London Contemporary Music

1. *Frederick Delius*, p. 147.

Centre (L.C.M.C.). This was created specifically for the new composer, and it was not only the first, but also the most continuously active and long-lasting branch of the British Music Society. Its outlook was always, and from the start, international, and never limited just to British composers. This fundamental principle is maintained today by its successor, the Institute of Contemporary Arts (I.C.A.).

Another dimension, and one that was to prove of great importance, was added to the work of the L.C.M.C. from an unexpected source. In 1921 a group of Viennese musicians, notably Egon Wellesz and Rudolph Reti, formed the International Society for Contemporary Music (I.S.C.M.); and the first international festival took place in Salzburg the following year. It was intended as an international music forum, the first since the end of the war. Most European countries were represented, as well as America. Performers of various nationalities participated, sometimes in the same work, and the focus was on new music from different countries. It was agreed that sections should be formed in each country, and that festivals would be presented in different cities of various countries in turn. The works played would be chosen by an international jury from those submitted from each country. It was also agreed by a majority of those at Salzburg that London should contain the central office, and so the (then) chairman of the London Contemporary Music Centre, Edwin Evans, undertook that his society would carry out the duties of this central office, and that they would also become the official representatives of the British section of the I.S.C.M.

The original British Music Society dissolved in 1933, but the London Contemporary Music Centre continued very active until 1953, when it amalgamated with the I.C.A. It was responsible for the organization of those I.S.C.M. Festivals that were held in this country in 1931, 1938 and 1946. Edward Clark later became the chairman, and their annual series of concerts, held mainly at the Cowdray, Aeolian or Wigmore Halls, were of the greatest practical help to younger composers, whose works would probably otherwise not have been heard in this country; certainly not in professional public performance.

The inevitable shortcomings of this pioneer society were of less importance than its very real achievement; they were the sort of shortcomings which are inevitable when committees are faced with artistic matters—there is a marked tendency to settle for the lowest consensus of opinion, and to prefer the devil-you-know to the devil-you-do-not-know; particularly if the devil-you-know is present at the same meeting. Certain eminent composers are surprisingly absent from the programmes, while certain others, not so eminent, are noticeably present.

The young fledgling composer needed, and will always continue to need, not only the professional performance of his work at a public

concert, but also the opportunity to hear it and assess it at the rehearsa l
or workshop stage. Ideally, this should form an essential part of any
college or conservatoire curriculum; but the situation in 1930 was—
as it is today—far from ideal in this respect. The work of the newly
established L.C.M.C. was thought by some young musicians to be not
sufficient for the needs of composers, who were beginning at this time to
be a force to be reckoned with. A group of three students at the Royal
College of Music formed, in 1931, a private society to promote young
British composers. Elisabeth Lutyens, later the wife of Edward Clark, was
the originator; her collaborators were Anne Macnaghten and Iris Lemare.
The first series of concerts, known as the Macnaghten Concerts, took
place in December 1931; they strongly favoured, whether fortuitously
or not, works by the fair sex—Elisabeth Lutyens herself, Imogen Holst,
Gustav Holst's daughter, and Elizabeth Maconchy. Other composers
represented in the early years of the Macnaghten Concerts, given in the
Mercury Theatre, Notting Hill Gate, were Benjamin Britten, Alan
Rawsthorne and Arnold Cooke. The concerts have continued ever since,
and the promotion of British music, particularly of lesser known young
composers, has always been, and still remains, their constant policy. In
the first eight years of activity after 1945, works by more than sixty
contemporary British composers were played. But after 1957 there was a
slight shift in emphasis, to match the changing situation in London, and
in the country as a whole. It seemed that more good could be done by
presenting not quite so many new British works, and by ensuring that
those that were presented were assured of as large an audience as possible
by mixing them with works by acknowledged masters—not necessarily
always British. In the choice of foreign works, an effort would be made
always to offer something new to this country. Moreover, there has also
been a marked swing, since about 1968, towards the *avant-garde*.[1]

And so, in summary, the period up to 1939 was a formative, exploratory
one for British music. In orchestral concerts the mainstream of the repertoire was made available to the public, and those British composers whose
works represented the late flowering of romanticism. The more ardently
adventurous had to seek outlets in the smaller societies, particularly the
L.C.M.C.; any broad public acceptance of the more experimental or
outré contemporary trends still lay in the future. But after 1945 a more
adventurous spirit begins to appear.

Meanwhile, the ground had been prepared; the basis from which
composers could work.

1. After 1945 three other societies were added to the number of those whose concern
was to perform contemporary music; these were the Committee (later Society) for the
Promotion of New Music (1943), the Park Lane Group (1956), and the Redcliffe
Concerts of British Music (1964), (see p. 364/7).

C

II

The establishment of a tradition

1 William Walton

The commonest criticism made today of Walton's music is that its style
has remained consistently conservative, and has not 'advanced'; that those
works on which his reputation most securely rests, whose mastery is not
in dispute, were written before the war, and that his compositions after
1945 represent a re-tilling of old ground, rather than a staking out of new.

If there is one who retains his head, when most of those around him are
losing theirs, this may well be disconcerting for his colleagues and contemporaries; and certainly Walton has shown a marked disinclination to
be swayed by the dictates of the 'new music' of the 50's, when serialism
became all the rage. He refused to 'develop', as some would have had him
do; he refused to be swayed by fashion; and this placed him beyond the
critical pale of some journalists.

But the criticism is both slick and specious; its logic is apparent, not
real. It is just as illogical to condemn a work because its composer does
not move with the times as it is to praise it because he does. It implies
that a composer's style *should* 'develop', without specifying for what
purpose, or in which direction, or on what grounds such a fundamental
aesthetic assumption is made. In this case it fails to take into account the
profound and many-sided nature of Walton's style. It is indeed one of the
most striking instances in contemporary journalism of the extent to which
criticism has moved away from a reasoned aesthetic foundation, in favour
of unreasoned, dogmatic assumptions.

There is no law of aesthetics which lays it down that the merit of an
artist's work is to be measured in ratio to his acceptance of current
fashions and contemporary trends. If anything, the reverse is the case;
the acceptance of current fashions will almost inevitably ensure that his
work contains a considerable proportion that is of ephemeral interest only,
which will become outmoded when one fashion gives way to the next.
Anything more lasting calls for a less shifting foundation than fashions or
trends can supply.

Strangely, however, just such a canon has been adopted by several writers and critics, and made to apply to a wide range of composers, chief among whom is Walton. This has resulted in a considerable distortion of artistic judgement, since what is of primary importance is not so much that a composer should adopt this or that particular idiom or technique, but what use he makes of it.

But an aesthetic principle of greater seriousness, and wider importance, is raised by this criticism. To lay down general rules from a particular case can, where art is concerned, cause the severest distortion of view, because it may mean a work is considered from the wrong point of view; that is to say a view other than the artist's intention. Perhaps one of the greatest victims of the musical law-givers has been opera; so Walton was to discover with *Troilus and Cressida*. Its composite, artificial form makes it particularly open to theories, rules, and regulations, and those who have defined the function of opera—what it must do, and what it must not do— range from the French Encyclopaedists to Michael Tippett; from Busoni to Boulez.

It is an essential part of a composer's work that he should define and regulate the purpose of his own work. But this is a very different matter from our taking his working principles as general rules and applying them indiscriminately to other composers. The principles of opera composition that Tippett, for instance, arrives at in *Moving into Aquarius* are of the greatest relevance, and give us a deep insight into Tippett's operas. But to apply them as absolute rules, which are to be obeyed by all opera composers, is a very different matter; and a more than doubtful critical procedure.

Yet one that is frequently followed; and not just in opera. Many indeed are those critics who take it on themselves to lay down what music should or should not do, and then proceed to condemn, or ignore, a composer because he fails to pass through their own hoop. On the contrary, each composer's work can only be adequately considered on its own terms. It is not a question of whether it should do this, or should not do that; such assumptions have nothing to do with aesthetics. Indeed, if a composer only adopts a particular idiom or style because he thinks he ought to, then his integrity is to that extent impaired. What matters is not so much what idiom a composer adopts, as whether it is a suitable vehicle for the full range of his artistic vision.

Walton's idiom has always been tonal. He has worked, generally speaking, slowly and deliberately, with the result that his many-sided imagination was progressively stretched with each succeeding work; and the characteristics of his style, already latent since *Façade*, became gradually more marked. They extended in several directions.

The underlying and strongest feature of his musical thought is its sheer bigness, whether of his original conceptions, or of the overall breadth of phrase, or of his finished structure. The size of his musical ideas not only encompasses a wide range of human emotion, but also inevitably necessitates a large orchestra. Far the greatest part of his output is conceived on grand symphonic lines, and uses the full orchestral resources.

As the table shows, only in nine works does he reduce to double woodwind; only in five works out of twenty-four does he dispense with the tuba, and of these one is a chamber opera and two are ballets for which a reduced orchestra might reasonably be assumed. And even *Façade* was enlarged from a *divertissement* for chamber ensemble, which it was originally, to an orchestral work. Walton's style is large; the range of his ideas is big.

Smaller pieces include songs and chamber music, which taken as a whole form but occasional moments-in-passing between the large works, and represent only one aspect of his style. The songs are 'A song for the Lord Mayor's table', for soprano and piano[1]; 'Anon in love' for tenor and guitar; and three songs with words by Edith Sitwell.

The chamber music works, each of substantial size, are the *String Quartet* (1947), and the *Violin Sonata* (1950). The first of these was written, he says, 'more as an exercise in purification' after the film scores of the war years. Not that these were entirely ephemeral; the Shakespeare films with Laurence Olivier, such as *Henry V* (1943) and *Hamlet* (1947), are unique in combining symphonic technique with the requirements of a film sound-track.

SCORING OF SYMPHONIC WORKS
(in addition to strings)

Year of completion		Woodwind	Brass Horns—Trumpets— Trombones—Tuba	Extras
1925	Portsmouth Point	Triple	4—3—3—1	Timp. Perc. (3)
1928	Sinfonia Concertante	Double (+ piccolo, Cor Anglais)	4—2--3—1	Timp. Perc. (2) Piano
1929	Viola Concerto	Triple (orig.) Double (rev.)	4—3—3—1 4—2—3—0	Timp. Timp. Harp

1. These songs were later (1970) orchestrated, and benefited considerably from the fuller accompaniment.

SCORING OF SYMPHONIC WORKS (*continued*)

(in addition to strings)

Year of completion		Woodwind	Brass Horns—Trumpets— Trombones—Tuba	Extras
1931	Belshazzar's Feast	Triple (+ alto saxophone)	4—3—3—1 (+2 brass bands: 0—3—3—1)	Timp. Perc. (4) 2 Harps Piano Organ
1935	Symphony No. 1	Double	4—3—3—1	2 Timp. 2 Perc.
1937	In honour of the City of London	Double (+ piccolo)	4—3—3—1	Timp. Perc. Harp
	Crown Imperial	Triple	4—3—3—1	Timp. Perc. (2) Harp Organ
1940	Violin Concerto	Double	4—2—3—0	Timp. Perc. (2) Harp
	The Wise Virgins (Ballet)	Double	4—2—3—0	Timp. Harp
1941	Scapino	Triple	4—3—3—1	Timp. Perc. (3) Harp
	Music for Children	Double	4—2—3—1	Timp. Perc. (2) Harp
	The Quest (Ballet)	Double	4—2—3—0	Timp. Perc. (2) Harp Celesta Glockenspiel
1953	Orb and Sceptre	Triple	4—3—3—1	Timp. Perc. (4) Harp Organ
1953	Coronation Te Deum	Triple	4—3—3—1 (optional: 4 trumpet, 3 trom- bone, 4 S.D.)	Timp. Perc. Harp Organ

Year of completion		Woodwind	Brass Horns—Trumpets— Trombones—Tuba	Extras
1954	Troilus and Cressida (Opera)	Triple	4—3—3—1 (+1 horn, 4 t't tenor D, S.D.)	Timp. Perc. (5) 2 Harps Celesta
1956	Johannesburg Festival Overture	Triple	4—3—3—1	Timp. Harp Perc. (3)
	Cello Concerto	Double	4—2—3—1	Timp. Perc. (3) Celesta Harp
1958	Partita	Triple	4—3—3—1	Timp. Perc. (4) Celesta Harp
1960	Symphony No. 2	Triple	4—3—3—1	Piano Celesta 2 Harps Timp. Perc. (4)
1961	Gloria	Triple	4—3—3—1	Timp. Perc. Harp. Organ
1963	Variations on a theme by Hindemith	Triple	4—3—3—1	Timp. Perc. (3) Harp
1967	The Bear (Chamber Opera)	Single	1—1—1—0	Timp. Perc. Harp
1968	Capriccio Burlesco	Triple	4—3—3—1	Piano Timp. Perc. (3) Harp
1970	Improvisations on an Impromptu of Benjamin Britten	Triple	4—3—3—1	Timp. Perc. (3) Harp

Numbers in brackets denote number
of percussion players called for.

Active tradition is his mainspring. He inclined more by both instinct and environment to the tradition of Elgar than to that of Vaughan Williams; not only do some of his occasional pieces, such as the two Coronation Marches *Crown Imperial* (1937) and *Orb and Sceptre* (1953), sound directly with the same Elgarian ceremony and swagger, but the sequential nature of his thematic construction is also highly similar to that of the elder composer. Moreover, the output of the two is strikingly similar; like Elgar, Walton wrote an outstanding work in each of the larger categories, such as the concerto or overture, or orchestral variations; two symphonies; no piano pieces worth mentioning, and a handful of songs; a small amount of chamber music, an orchestral suite for children. Like Elgar, Walton is almost entirely self-taught. He is, moreover, like his friend Constant Lambert, quite uninterested in folk-song. Just as Walton's idiom is wide, so is his appeal.

His music is the sort of music that the broad mass of English people expect an English composer to write; its appeal is therefore deep, instinctive, unwitting; and this partly explains the heartfelt disenchantment with which some of the more esoteric latter-day critics have turned on him; or, which amounts to the same thing, turned away from him. They know that his music represents so much of the many-sided aspects of the English genius that they feel such a sense of disappointment, amounting almost to outrage, that he should show such a regrettable lack of interest in competing in today's *avant-garde* stakes, whose foremost runners, they maintain, are alone worth their serious consideration.

Two primary factors colour Walton's innate romanticism, curb it, and so prevent it from running riot with the music. The first is a toughness of fibre, which may be evident either in the form of that rhythmical tautness which is such an instantly noticeable feature of his style, or in a strictness of control of even the most apparently loose and lyrical phrase; the long sentence for the soloist, with which each of the three string concertos opens, is an example.

The second factor is a sense of fun and wit; the jazz-inspired parody of *Façade;* the pungent *malizia,* the vivid *scherzando,* that occurs at many points in his mature works. There was nothing particularly remarkable about the frivolous and disrespectful antics of the 20's; everyone was doing it; indeed you were expected to, if you did not wish to be considered hopelessly academic and out of touch. Walton's wit, however, is something altogether deeper, and matches his strongly lyrical instinct.

But there is a wider range to his style than can be seen from either its chief outward characteristics or his assimilation of external influences. He is a predominantly orchestral composer; he thinks in terms of the instruments, and he makes the orchestra speak with greater fluency, and

more compelling urgency, than most other symphonists of his generation.
The trombone music at the opening of *Belshazzar's Feast* is an example
of sheer physical urgency. He relies on nothing outside the music; the
process of thematic development is his second nature (in this respect he
is at the opposite pole to Britten, whose music is a reaction to an external
stimulus), and it gives the finished work its virility and urgency, both in
the minutest details of nuance and colour, and in the overall design of a
movement or of a whole work. Phrase answers phrase in a logical sequence.
They grow like branches of a tree. There is a bigness, a spaciousness and
a depth about his symphonic design which is by definition denied to the
composer who adopts the more fragmented methods of serialism, or the
more experimental, emotionally shallower, styles of the *avant-garde*.
Walton's style is emotionally involved, at many different levels, which
makes it open to varying interpretation by different conductors, all
equally valid: the lyricism peculiar to the English, the rhythm of the
20's, following Stravinsky's works after *The Rite of Spring*, the incisiveness
of Bartok, the nobility of Elgar; a mastery of symphonic form, and an
orchestral virtuosity second to none among contemporary British
composers.

William Walton was born in 1902 at Oldham in Lancashire; in 1912
he went as a chorister to the Choir School of Christ Church, Oxford,
and in the following years began his first tentative efforts in composition.
His precocious talent was brought to early fruition in the atmosphere of
the English Cathedral tradition, and his early works included a *Piano
Quartet*. He did not, however, proceed to become a Bachelor of Music[1],
as he was sent down from the university for not passing Responsions,
before he submitted an exercise. So, leaving Oxford, he went instead to
Chelsea, where he was given a room in the house of the Sitwells; he had
met Sacheverell Sitwell at Oxford. Thus began a remarkably productive
association.

Following the extraordinary early success of *Façade*,[2] which was the
first-fruits of his association with the Sitwells, Walton's early works were
played at I.S.C.M. concerts; an early *String Quartet* (1923), the overture
Portsmouth Point (1926). Through his close association at this time with
Constant Lambert, who wrote a ballet for Diaghilev's company, Walton

1. Another composer who was a somewhat reluctant student at Christ Church, Oxford,
at about this time, and who left after only one year, on the outbreak of war in August,
1914, was Philip Heseltine/Peter Warlock; he was Walton's senior by eight years. For
an account of Warlock's year at Oxford by his student-contemporary Robert Nichols,
see Cecil Gray, *Peter Warlock*, pp. 61–92.
2. Osbert Sitwell fully describes the events surrounding its first performance in
Laughter in the Next Room, pp. 168–198.

explored the possibility of himself doing likewise, particularly as Diaghilev had attended a performance of *Façade*. But nothing came of this, and the *Sinfonia Concertante*, originally intended as a ballet score for piano duet, became an orchestral piece, with piano obligato.

But it was with the *Viola Concerto* (1929) that the series of master-works begins, each developing from the previous one, each a unique composition, forging its own fresh tradition as it went. *Belshazzer's Feast* followed in 1931, whose sheer physical energy dealt a mortal blow to the old traditional English oratorio, and opened the way for the replacing of it by the more vital tradition of opera, particularly since 1945. Walton himself benefited from this development, and contributed two important works in this category, one grand opera in the traditional manner, *Troilus and Cressida* (1954), and a one-act chamber opera, in the Aldeburgh manner, *The Bear* (1967).

The *First Symphony*[1] occupied his attention for four years (1932–35), and broke new ground on practically every count, except in its four-movement structure. The first movement, sustained, intense, proliferating with detail and rhythmically complex, is the testimonial of his tonal idiom. Walton accepted tonality because his music was to be broadly based, and capable of the widest range of romantic expression. He did not extend tonality, as Bartok did, and (later) Alan Rawsthorne; rather his work is an individual application of existing tonality, whose implications he accepted. These implications were chiefly that notes should be related according to their function in the tonal scale (tonic, dominant and so on), that move-ments should be constructed on the principle of thematic and harmonic contrast, and that the logical movement of the music should be decided mainly by the harmony, and the answering of phrase with phrase.

The contrast in the symphony's first movement is extreme: between the steadily moving minim metre, and a highly detailed, finely calculated pattern of rhythmically articulated small notes; between changing chromaticism in the upper parts, and an unchanging, anchor-like bass line, largely built round pedal points. There is no key signature.

Both in this symphony and in other major works, Walton reflects the influence of those two composers whose work was chiefly respected by the leading musical thinkers of the 30's, namely Sibelius and Berlioz.[2] The terse, episodic nature of the thematic construction of Walton's first symphony, as well as its prevailingly sombre mood, derive from Sibelius.

1. First performed, including the finale, on 6 November 1935.
2. Cecil Gray wrote a biography of Sibelius, and visited the composer in order to do this task adequately. His admiration for Berlioz is frequently attested in his other writings. Ernest Newman also wrote a study of Berlioz, in spite of his ardent Wagnerian bias.

The use of brass bands in *Belshazzar's Feast* is derived from the Berlioz of the *Requiem*.

Straight away the opening indicates something on a big scale, like the beginning of Beethoven's ninth symphony. The interval that pervades the movement, as indeed the whole symphony, is that of the seventh, or its inversion the second. This decides not only the shape of the principal themes, and the sombre light they cast on the twin prevailing moods of melancholy and savagery, but also the tonal relationship between the main sections, namely B flat minor and C. The opening oboe theme concentrates a wealth of expression into a handful of notes; it is balanced melodically, rhythmically and harmonically in a way that Walton never surpassed; it germinates the later parts of the symphony.[1] Themes there are in plenty; or rather an abundance of thematic ideas, which the thirty-year-old composer develops with a bewildering profusion of contrasts. Walton has never exceeded the first movement of this symphony for music of a concentrated, dramatic intensity. It is highly instructive to notice the impressions of two musicians[2], which are so different, and so largely contradictory, as to cause doubt whether they refer to the same work. Even allowing for the fact that Mr. Howes writes as a somewhat didactic critic, while Mr. Shore writes as a heavily-involved orchestral player, the truth perhaps may be deduced from these two accounts, that the music is so varied, and so detailed, that it presents a different aspect from differing viewpoints. Both accounts are valid, and not so much contradictory as complementary.

If the first movement is a conflict of moods, of which the themes are a reflection, the second scherzo movement is a conflict of rhythm, in a tonality (E) a tritone away from that of the first movement. The unison theme at [51] is a distorted, maniacal version of the original oboe theme at the opening of the first movement; this, and the brilliant frenzy of the orchestration, recall Berlioz's *Symphonie Fantastique*.

The melancholy that was implicit in the opening is next made explicit in the slow movement. The extreme agitation and incisive frenzy of the scherzo are now replaced by a melody with a slow rate of harmonic change, over a static pedal-point bass note (C sharp), and an accompaniment of open fifths or sevenths, as in the first movement. The development is more contrapuntal than the preceding scherzo, while the mood remains one of resignation, melancholy, highly expressive of its period.

1. It has been copied, whether consciously or unconsciously, by many another composer. For instance Herbert Howells uses it in his *Saraband for the Morning of Easter*, bar 47 following; Francis Chagrin uses it in the first movement of his symphony.

2. Frank Howes, *The Music of William Walton* (pp. 23–40). Bernard Shore, *Sixteen Symphonies* (pp. 372–387).

Hardly, however, a suitable ending for a work on this scale, even in the 'devil's decade' of the 30's. The finale, as is well known, was not finished until nearly a year after the first three movements had been publicly performed.[1] It was sketched out as far as the fugal section, when the composer allowed himself to be persuaded, by Hamilton Harty and Hubert Foss, into letting the three movements be performed, when it became obvious that the finale was not going to be finished in time for the announced date. Walton now considers that this was a mistake.

In deciding on a fugal structure, Walton used the other main device of the classical composers, not already used in this symphony. The subject is taken from the B flat minor oboe theme at the opening, but varied into the major, and introduced with a bolder, fanfare-like upbeat in fourths. The climax inherent in fugal writing is preceded and followed by a *maestoso* prologue and epilogue, which bring the work to a grand, ceremonious close.

It was twenty-five years before Walton wrote his next symphony, which was first heard at the Edinburgh Festival on 2nd September 1960. Meanwhile the musical scene had changed radically. This was the time when serialism was the fashion in this country, and general critical opinion was coloured by that fact. Expectedly, therefore, the new symphony was greeted with less fulsome enthusiasm than it would have enjoyed even ten years earlier; the general comments were that this work was characteristic of its composer, but that he had unfortunately failed to 'advance' in his style. It was then brilliantly recorded by an American orchestra;[2] the same orchestra which had commissioned the *Partita* two years earlier, and first played it on 30th January 1958; the same orchestra, also, which premiered the *Violin Concerto* with Heifetz as soloist, and Arthur Rodzinski conducting, on 7th December 1939. Then it was realized that this symphony was in fact a feat of orchestral virtuosity which few, if any, British composers could equal. The texture is lighter than that of the first symphony, yet no lessening of brilliance or tension ensues; on the contrary, Walton's style has now mellowed. The savage incisiveness is very much still there; and something else besides. The work is a most decided advance on the first symphony—but not in the way that some were expecting. It is more refined technically and structurally, more thematically integrated, and more fluid harmonically; this partly is due to there being fewer pedal-points, which occur only occasionally.[3]

The G minor tonality of the first movement is coloured with C sharp, and the totally chromatic first subject uses, in the course of its exposition,

1. In December 1934, under Hamilton Harty.
2. The Cleveland (Ohio) Orchestra, conducted by George Szell.
3. For instance I, bars 317–323; II bars 129–152; or III bars 225–244.

all twelve notes, distributed over a gradual episodic build-up of short phrases, marked *sospirando,* and echoed between wind and strings; the interval chiefly used is the major seventh. After a climax (bars 51–59), worked out of the last few notes of this composite theme, the texture is gradually reduced to a single line, to make way for the second subject, whose melody is shared between violas and clarinet, with a lighter, more sustained accompaniment. The melody is confined to six notes (B flat–A–F sharp–G–E flat–D) which are the first six of the 12-note passacaglia theme that is to come later; and this gives the music greater repose, in contrast with the first subject. Thus Walton makes the twelve-note scale subservient to the expressive requirements of the music; his tonal idiom is broadly enough based to admit this chromatic element. A trivial little accompaniment figure, which leads into this subject

is contracted rhythmically into a characteristic ostinato at bar 95:

This propels the music forwards through forty bars of *agitato* (bars 92–133) into the all-important development section which follows. Here the first and second subject material is combined and built up from a quiet contrapuntal beginning (bar 139) into a highly characteristic and brilliant climax (bar 201). This figure,

which contains the central germ of both themes, as well as the ostinato rhythm of bar 95, is treated sequentially; orchestral virtuosity is an integral part of Walton's technique, and the climax sections are less complex, less laboured than in the first symphony.

At bar 217 the first theme is recapitulated, but shorter than before, a fifth higher, though with similar texture. Once again an orchestral climax is followed by reduction to a single line (bar 249), to introduce the second subject. This appears a major sixth higher than in the exposition, and allotted to the first violins, instead of the more sombre violas. The *agitato* section follows once more (bar 276), and the ostinato rhythm leads the music forward, this time to a short, brilliant section, such as only Walton could have written. The original tonality (G minor) returns for a coda (bar 338)[1], with the first phrase of the first subject recalled several times.

Walton dispenses with a *scherzo* as such, and goes straight to the slow movement. Notes 7–12 of the passacaglia theme of the finale direct the tonality of the second movement towards B major, which thus complements the second subject of the first movement. This slow movement rests on two themes (starting at bar 7 and bar 42), which occur twice, and are followed through, rather than developed. As in the first movement, the interval of the seventh is much in evidence, for instance in the slow violin theme at bar 19; set against this is the series of fourths, with which the movement opens, and which, in spite of its strong B major tonality, give the harmony a certain neutral colour.

The final passacaglia returns to G minor; and since the two halves of its 12-note theme have already been referred to in the previous movements, a thematic continuity is thus automatically established. Moreover, the shortening of the symphony from four movements to three enables Walton to embody some of the missing scherzo into the finale, which consists of three sections, *Passacaglia* (theme and variations), *Fugato*, and *Coda* (scherzando).

The composer has his tongue resolutely in his cheek as the full orchestra struts its way, in a solemn and pompous unison, through the 12-note theme. Trills add to the mock-serious nature of the occasion. The first five variations are straightforward, with the theme set, like some mediaeval *cantus firmus*, against varying counter-subjects in different sections of the orchestra. In the sixth variation it is shared between the brass instruments, while in the seventh Walton subjects it to the serial technique of retrograde inversion. He is as capable as the next man of musical carpentry. The speed has meanwhile gradually quickened, but the tension is relaxed in the eighth, the pace slackened in the ninth, while the theme undergoes more transformation; it returns in its original form in the tenth variation, which acts as a brilliant lead-in to the *fugato* section of the movement.

---

1. Not really bar 330, as Mr. Howes suggests.

The fugal subject, which consists of the notes of the passacaglia theme reset, is highly characteristic of Walton, and contains many points of resemblance with the equivalent fugue in the first symphony. But its working out is much less elaborate.

Ex.3.

Walton
Symphony No.2
Third movement Bar 166

The fugato section is quite short (166–227), and in the Coda that follows the pace quickens up to *presto* (bar 257). As in the first symphony, there is a ceremonious broadening out as the work nears its end. It concludes with twelve bars of reiterated chords of G major.

Walton's next orchestral work, which followed the *Second Symphony*, is the *Variations on a theme by Hindemith*.[1] Here he draws attention to, and publicly acknowledges, the obligation of friendship that existed between the two composers, ever since they met in August 1923 in Salzburg, when Walton's early quartet was played. Later, in 1929, when the English violist Lionel Tertis had turned down the *Viola Concerto*, it was to Hindemith that Walton turned; and turned successfully. The Concerto was performed[2] with Hindemith as soloist, Walton conducting. Now Walton repays the debt; and includes Gertrud Hindemith in the dedication, which both recipients found deeply touching. Hindemith particularly respected Walton's workmanship in this piece. The theme is from the beginning of the second movement of Hindemith's *Concerto for Cello and Orchestra* (1940):

Ex.4 Tema
Andante con moto

Walton
Variations on a theme by Hindemith

The principle of deriving a tonality from the notes of a series, which Walton had developed in the *Second Symphony* is carried one stage further in this work, in which each of the nine variations takes its tonal direction and destination from the successive notes of Hindemith's theme.

1. First heard conducted by the composer at a Royal Philharmonic Society concert on its 150th anniversary, 8 March 1963.
2. On 3 October 1929, at a Henry Wood Promenade Concert.

D

The customary fugal finale finishes on E major, the original starting-point. Thus the scheme of the work is as follows:

Theme Andante con moto, E tonality (36 bars)

Var. I	Vivace, G sharp tonality
Var. II	Allegramente, F sharp tonality
Var. III	Larghetto, B tonality
Var. IV	Moto perpetuo, C sharp tonality
Var. V	Andante con moto, D tonality
Var. VI	Scherzando, A tonality
Var. VII	Lento molto, C tonality
Var. VIII	Vivacissimo, B flat tonality
Var. IX	Maestoso, F tonality
Finale	Allegro molto, E tonality

Variation VII also includes, at a climax moment towards the end, a quotation from Hindemith's opera *Mathis der Maler*[1], which bears a striking similarity to the theme of this work, bars 29–32. The essence of the passage is a pattern of descending triads (E–C–A flat–E), each a major third apart. This colours the end of Walton's work, if not the whole of it, which is thus somewhat more harmonically inhibited than the symphonies, though written with no less brilliance of orchestration.

Among Walton's four concertos, the least characteristic, also the earliest, is the *Sinfonia Concertante*. But the other three, for viola, violin and cello respectively, all occupy a unique place in the international repertoire, comparable with the concertos of Elgar. In each of these three works Walton has been fortunate in his soloists; the most recent concerto, that for cello, was written in 1956 for Gregor Piatigorsky, who first played it in Boston, U.S.A.[2]

Like the *Viola Concerto* and the *Violin Concerto*, it opens with a long, lyrical sentence for the soloist. The orchestral accompaniment to this melody is built round a chord which Walton used again at the beginning of the *Second Symphony*, written three years later; moreover the texture and layout of the two are remarkably similar.

Ex. 5   Walton   Orchestral accompaniment; basic chords
(a) *Symphony No.2*   (b) *Violoncello Concerto*

1. Page 221 of the piano score, at [47] –4.
2. On 25 January 1957.

As a whole the work is restrained, lyrical, elegiac, like Elgar's cello concerto. It contains little of the *vivo* of the *Viola Concerto*, or the *presto capriccioso* of the *Violin Concerto;* and the virtuoso solo writing of the second movement, or of the two cadenzas in the third, is overcast by that dark colour proper to the cello, and by the chromatic, prevailingly minor tonality. The same basic material is used in all three movements, and its main features are the contrast between fourths and triads; the scoring is generally speaking light. So in many ways the work is unique in comparison with Walton's other works.

The first movement is one continuous *cantabile*, made up of seven lyrical sentences for the cellist, each separated by two or three bars of orchestral accompaniment. The sixth sentence is a recapitulation of the first, a tritone higher.

The second movement is the most *concertante* of the three; an integrated conversation between soloist and orchestra, with brilliant solo writing, including harmonics and throwing-bow technique, at a fast speed (*allegro appassionato*).

Each section of the third movement is derived, however remotely, from the opening 16-bar cello solo, to which the movement as a whole thus stands in the distant relationship of an improvisation to its parent theme. The opening is slow, and the central section of the movement is supported by two cadenzas. The first ('Brioso') heralds the only brilliant *ff* section in the entire work, an outburst for orchestra alone, which however is short, and soon gives way to the soloist's second cadenza ('Rapsodicamente'). To conclude the work Walton recalls the opening of the first movement.

Of his three concert overtures, the first two, *Portsmouth Point* (1925) and *Scapino* (1941), are tone-poems, based on pictures; the third, *Johannesburg Festival Overture* (1956), is not.

Portsmouth Point is a light-hearted musical illustration of a print by the eighteenth-century cartoonist Thomas Rowlandson; this depicts a variety of activities, reputable and not-so-reputable, taking place on the quay of Portsmouth harbour. Walton's score uses rhythmic devices inherited from Stravinsky, much as *Façade* had been an English adaptation of Schoenberg's *Pierrot Lunaire*; and the overture is a high-spirited parody by the twenty-three-year-old composer of all things solemn, bourgeois and stuffily English.

Scapino makes a fitting partner to it. This comedy overture was commissioned in 1940 by the Chicago Symphony Orchestra for its fiftieth anniversary. Its model was an etching by the seventeenth-century French engraver Jacques Callot, in *Balli di Sfessania* (1622). Scapino is one of the less familiar characters of the Commedia dell'Arte; the hero of Molière's *Les Fourberies de Scapin*, who may figure in the complicated ancestry of Figaro. From him we derive the word 'escapade', which accurately describes his function; he was the servant who planned his master's escapades, especially those of an amorous nature. This aspect of his work is strongly suggested by the more legato cello theme, starting at bar 132, which forms the central section of the piece, preceded and followed by a highly characteristic Waltonian *vivace*.

The *Johannesburg Festival Overture* is more of a symphonic composition in its own right, and is cast in the form of a rondo. Also unlike the other two overtures it contains no metrical intricacies of any kind, and the quickness of the opening (*presto capriccioso*) is maintained unchecked throughout. Very much in the same high-spirited vein as the three concert overtures is the 7-minute *Capriccio Burlesco*, written in 1968 for the 125th anniversary of the New York Philharmonic.

If the overtures, particularly the first two, are of primarily rhythmical interest, the two operas are primarily lyrical. They are entirely contrasted, the one being directed at the large-scale, international tradition of grand opera; the other at the newly established English chamber opera, associated with Britten's English Opera Group.

Troilus and Cressida was first produced at Covent Garden on 3rd December 1954. It is a romantic opera, true to most of the traditions of romantic opera; a love story in the grand manner; Christopher Hassall's libretto presented the composer with considerable scope for broad strokes of character study, as the strands of the plot interlock. Troilus, son of Priam, King of Troy, is enamoured of Cressida, daughter of Calkas, the Trojan High Priest, who deserts to the Greeks. Meanwhile his brother Pandarus provides comic relief, as he arranges for the lovers to meet. The folds of the plot thicken, however, when Cressida is handed over to the Greeks in return for Antenor, a young Trojan officer captured in battle. While in captivity, a Greek prince Diomede wins her over. Troilus then gets through the lines during a truce, and the ensuing confrontation leads the opera to its tragic climax.

The central theme is thus a love story; the Trojan war provides the military background against which the action takes place. Walton's opera thus differs radically from Tippett's *King Priam*, which also deals with the Trojan war. Walton has provided a singer's opera, in broad melodic lines, with very little orchestral development; the entr'acte between the two scenes of the second act is the only example,[1] and this serves the double purpose of representing the passage of time between the two

1. [73] — [82]

scenes, and of showing the fulfilment of those amorous emotions just expressed in the love-duet.

But in writing lyrically Walton was dependent on the words for both mood and shape of the melodic line. He does not hesitate to use melisma or word repetition if the musical organization requires it. In the wider context, whereas the structural climax of the orchestral works is thematic, and the composer's symphonic imagination is given full play, in *Troilus and Cressida* the working out is dramatic; the composer's thematic invention is directed towards pointing an already existing mood or character; the climax is built into the libretto, and thus the composer's characteristic symphonic style is not called fully into play. There was no room in such a lyrical work for that ferocity, that physical dynamism with which for instance *Belshazzar's Feast* had broken apart the bonds of conventional oratorio. The idiom of *Troilus and Cressida* is no less advanced than *Belshazzar's Feast;* but the composer's aim is different.

With *The Bear* Walton entered still fresher territory. This one-act 'Extravaganza' was first heard at Aldeburgh on 3rd June 1967, performed by the English Opera Group. The librettist was Paul Dehn,[1] who wrote rhyming lyrics, and adapted Anton Chekhov's 'vaudeville' in collaboration with the composer. Chekhov's original play *The Bear* (1888) was sub-titled 'A jest in one act'; and so both composer and librettist went about their task with a high-spirited enthusiasm that shows on every page of the brilliant score. The clue to the work, its mainspring, is parody, which was not unfamiliar to the composer of *Façade*, and caricature, which was inherent in Chekhov's comedy.

Walton has defined caricature as 'so accurate an exaggeration of the real thing as to be funny'. It is also good-natured, because parody is affectionate; this distinguishes it from satire, which is aggressive. And so Walton's musical parodies match Chekhov's character parodies.

The comedy is one of manners, not of plot. Indeed the story round which it is built is threadbare and (in the true sense) farcical, and can be stated in one sentence: Popova, a pretty widow, and faithful to the memory of her late and unfaithful husband, is confronted by one of his more persistent creditors, Smirnov; but when after a quarrel they point pistols at each other, they are unable to fire as they have meanwhile fallen irretrievably in love. A third character, the servant Luka, completes the cast. The comedy consists in the comparison of their apparent with their real natures. Popova is outwardly genteel, inwardly passionate; Smirnov is outwardly boorish, inwardly sentimental; Luka is outwardly servile, inwardly resentful. Walton's score makes explicit all these facets that are implicit in the text. It thus differs radically from *Troilus and Cressida*.

1. Who was also Lennox Berkeley's librettist for *The Castaway* and *A Dinner Engagement.*

There is one other side to Walton's work which is not so much to do with his style as with the function he has been called on to fulfil; this is the provision of music suitable for official celebrations. Two choral works were commissioned for ceremonial occasions; the *Te Deum* for the Coronation on 2nd June 1953; the *Gloria* for the 125th anniversary of the Huddersfield Choral Society. In each work, certainly in the first, Walton was required to be the spokesman for an already exciting mood of official pomp and splendour. Both works cover a big expanse of sound, and use the breadth that comes from the antiphonal use of two choirs; both works use the characteristic tonality based on the seventh. The *Te Deum* is the simpler, less dissonant, of the two, but it stands out as riches indeed in comparison with most of the other music sung on the famous occasion of its première.

Two other smaller sacred works are no less characteristic, though their range is more confined; first, the anthem *The Twelve*, to words by W. H. Auden, which Walton wrote in 1965 for his old Oxford College, Christ Church; second, the *Missa Brevis*, written for Coventry Cathedral. Thus in addition to the wide range over which Walton's music extends, he does not lose sight of the cathedral choral tradition, which was his starting point.

2   Alan Rawsthorne

Though he was born in the same year as Tippett, Rawsthorne's music shows markedly different characteristics of style, reflecting their difference of artistic personality. Rawsthorne's style is less complex, less visionary; his idiom has been forged from instrumental and symphonic compositions, which make up by far the greater part of his large output. Works for voices form but a small proportion; he has not been drawn to opera as Tippett has, and he has been more prolific than the other composer, who may well spend several years' concentrated work on one project, such as an opera.

Not until his early twenties did Rawsthorne decide to pursue composition seriously and permanently. He studied at Manchester, and later on the continent, where he specialised in the piano, under Busoni's most renowned disciple, Egon Petri. Writing for the piano is a central part of Rawsthorne's work, whether he uses it as a solo instrument, as part of a chamber ensemble, or as a concerto instrument. A fondness for and an understanding of the piano is rare among contemporary composers. It is not surprising that he has written several pieces specifically for that most virtuoso of contemporary pianists, John Ogdon; such works include the *Ballade*, and the *Concerto for two pianos* (with Brenda Lucas, Ogdon's wife).

The first works to bring Rawsthorne's name before the public were the *Theme and Variations* for two violins (1937), the *Bagatelle* for piano (1938), and more especially the *Symphonic Studies* (1938), which were first heard in Warsaw in 1939.

The Symphonic Studies (1938), dedicated to John Ireland, is a continuous twenty-minute movement, whose sections are built up from one thematic motto, given out at the opening. This motto is not so much varied as presented in different guises, whether harmonic, contrapuntal or textural. The sections are: Introduction–*Maestoso*; (i) *Allegro di bravura*; (ii) *Allegretto*; (iii) *Allegro di bravura*; (iv) *Lento*; (v) *Allegro*

43

piacevole. Section (iii) is largely a repetition of section (i), and the opening *Maestoso* is used again at the end of the 1st and 5th sections.

The importance of the work is threefold; first, the use of orchestral sonorities; second, the treatment of the somewhat angular theme; third, the highly individual exploitation of tonality.

As the title implies, the piece is a study in orchestral sonority. In the first *Allegro*, wind and strings are used antiphonally; the next section contains much colourful contrast, with bars for full orchestra alternating with bars for quiet strings and harp. The cor anglais melody (at [11]+7) is highly characteristic of that instrument, while for the brass there is a fugue in the final section (starting at [48]), against a colourful background of *tremolo* strings and percussion.

The thematic motto is stated at the opening.

Ex.6   motto   Rawsthorne *Symphonic Studies*

Simple variants of it are obtained by altering the note order,

Ex.7(a)   Rawsthorne *Symphonic Studies*

First simple variant

Ex.7(b)   Rawsthorne *Symphonic Studies*

Second simple variant   [11]+5

and by transposition. The first simple variant is used freely in the oboe part at [25], at [4]+3 in the bass part, and in numerous other places throughout; the second appears at [11]+5/6 in the bass part (see also Ex. 10).

Chromatic variants are obtained by altering the inflection of one of the notes.

Ex.8(a)   Rawsthorne *Symphonic Studies*

First chromatic variant   [48]   etc.   [11]   etc.

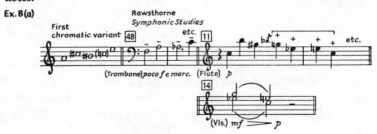

Ex.8(b)

Second chromatic variant

Ex.8(c)

Third chromatic variant

The first chromatic variant appears in many places; it forms the fugue subject at [48]; it appears with the notes in reverse order at [11]; it is used chordally at [14]; the note order is altered at [11]+7

Ex.9

Rawsthorne
Symphonic Studies

The second chromatic variant occurs, among other places at [36]; the third at [35]+4.

Rawsthorne's highly individual idiom is the result of his exploitation of tonality. He makes use not so much of the somewhat obvious device of the simultaneous sounding of conflicting keys, or bitonality, as of the suggestion of various tonal centres. Two examples will illustrate this. The opening motto is stated boldly.

Ex.10

Rawsthorne
Symphonic Studies

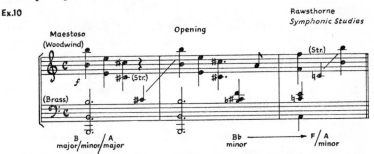

Clearly the note B natural is tonally important; indeed the work ends with a B major chord. Yet the tonality of B is by no means unambiguous, and several tonal centres are suggested in the opening bars. At [11]+7

the solo clearly indicates E minor, of which B would be the dominant, as the tonality of the *Allegretto* section. The A flat/G sharp is due, as we have seen, to the fact that the notes of the melody are a chromatic variant of the motto. But apart from this, numerous shifting tonalities are suggested by the highly colourful harmonic movement of the flute part against the static, continuo-like chord of the horns and bassoons.

Rawthorne's orchestral output continued with the first of his two piano concertos, which originally appeared in 1939, then in its final form in 1942. Its deliberate intention was to be accessible to a wide general public. The *Second Piano Concerto*, which is better known, was written for Clifford Curzon for the Festival of Britain celebrations in 1951, and immediately gained considerable popularity. It is more virtuoso a work, less *concertante* than the first. It has frequently been performed, and twice recorded. Outwardly romantic, after the manner of the traditional piano concerto, it nevertheless combines virtuoso piano writing with an important part for percussion.

His orchestral overtures include *Street Corner* (1944), *Cortèges* (1945), *Hallé* (1958) and *Overture for Farnham* (1967). The last two, as their names imply, were written with specific occasions in mind; the second, which the composer describes as a Fantasy Overture, is the most elaborate, and the most effective, of his pieces in this genre.

The chamber orchestra and string orchestra have by no means been ignored by Rawsthorne. The early concertos for clarinet and strings (1936) and oboe and strings (1947) led to the *Concerto for string orchestra* (1949) and the *Concerto Pastorale* (1951) for flute, horn and strings. Later works in this vein include the *Divertimento* for chamber orchestra (1962), and the *Elegiac Rhapsody* for strings (1964).

But for the apex of Rawsthorne's orchestral music we must turn to the symphonies; and in particular the third symphony, which is more of an integrated symphonic structure than the first two.

The *First Symphony* was written for the Royal Philharmonic Society in 1950; the *Second* (Pastoral) was commissioned by the John Feeney Charitable Trust, and first heard in Birmingham in 1959. The first uses the customary four movements, as well as conventional formal structures; the second also uses four movements, but is in many ways unconventional, even unsymphonic, and relies on folk-like material. The third movement is a scherzo in the form of a country dance, while the short finale is a setting of a poem by the sixteenth century Henry Howard, Earl of Surrey, in praise of summer. The whole conception of the symphony is slight; too slight indeed for what it carries.

Very different in both conception and execution is the *Third Symphony* (see plates 2 and 3), which was first heard on 8th July 1964 at a Cheltenham

Festival concert. In no work is the composer's highly individual idiom
put to a severer test than in this; and in no work does it prove more equal
to the demands made of it.

Using the standard large orchestra, Rawsthorne has no recourse to
tricks or gimmicks to build up a large-scale symphonic structure. The
music lives solely through the vigour and variety of the musical utterance.
He looks on the instrumental groups as contrasted tone-blocks, which he
deploys with mastery, each section of the orchestra being fully exploited
both in chorus and in solo use. Winding, sinuous passages of imitative
woodwind, chords for full brass, often with a brilliant rhythmical articulation, and great variety in the use of the strings, are just some of
Rawsthorne's hallmarks.

The symphony is based on an E tonality, and is built not so much on
contrasting themes or subjects, as the classical procedure was, as on the
varied presentation of a tonal idea. As with the *Symphonic Studies*, this
idea is contained in embryonic form in the motto with which the work
opens.

Ex11(*a*)

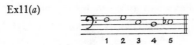

Very quietly, in quick semiquavers, the suggestive figure is introduced
in a 12-note series assigned to the low woodwind and 'cellos. Melodically
it contains a certain tonal ambiguity, set up between E and E flat,

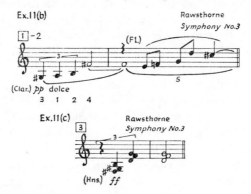

which appears in different guises throughout the first movement, and
forms the central core of the whole work; the pearl in the oyster. It is
hammered out by the strings in octaves ([4]+9), echoed by the brass
([5]+6); it gives rise to more lyrical counterpoint ([6]+4), and a somewhat nostalgic comment, after the tumult has temporarily died away, by
a solo violin ([7]+7).

The harmonic-chromatic scale implied in the motto is made explicit by the harp (after [9]), and by the horns (just before [11]). Finally, all the tonal implications of the motto are brought together in a resounding climax-chord, *fff* (at [15]).

Based on this structure of tonal contrast and variety, the music moves logically. After the initial semiquaver movement has spent itself and run its course, a gentler rhythm of crochets and minims takes over. This leads to a lyrical counterpoint between cellos and violas which, out of all his music, contains the very essence of Rawsthorne's art.

The middle section of the movement, corresponding to the development section in Sonata form, changes the metre to 3/8, and the shorter phrases lead to the culminating climax (at [15]) already mentioned. In the ensuing long-drawn-out calm, we wait for the semiquaver movement of the opening to recur. But Rawsthorne does little more than suggest this before allowing the music to die away. The underlying tonal ambiguity remains unresolved.

The slow movement is a ternary structure, the first and third sections consisting of melodic variants of the motto, over a pedal E. The movement takes up where the previous one left off; indeed it begins with exactly the same chord. The middle section, beginning at [28], uses more rapid string passages, and more brilliant brass writing. At the beginning of the third section the principal theme recurs, again over a pedal E, but this time in canon between oboe and clarinet.

The scherzo is a brilliant display of orchestral virtuosity. Lightly scored, and at a low dynamic level, the whole movement is all of a piece, homogeneous; there is no trio section. The melodic content is slight; what there is, is derived from the first movement; and the rhythm of the opening bars is ambiguous up to [35]. The strings move together, largely in thirds and sixths, which tends to reduce the tonal ambiguity. In all respects this movement is the perfect foil for the rest of the work. Scurrying semiquavers for the strings and woodwind; occasional chords and snatches of rhythmic figures elsewhere in the orchestra. But there is still no suggestion of a resolving of that tension that has been created since the beginning of the work. The composer is concerned, as he says, 'more with hints than statements'; it is as if we are holding our breath for the finale.

This, when it comes, consists of violent orchestral outbursts, which give way to a more tranquil mood in a contrasting tonality. An ordinary enough principle, to be sure; yet Rawsthorne uses his material in a fresh and anything-but-ordinary way. Brilliance is achieved by the quick 3-in-a-bar metre, by the wide, strutting figuration of the string writing ('obstreporous, emphatic and a little vulgar' are the composer's words), by the strings being used largely in unison or octaves, by the more obvious use of sequences.

The first quiet section, starting with the woodwind at [60], is over a D pedal; the second one, at [67], is built up from the same material, and given to a solo string quartet. The last outburst, starting at [70]+4, leads to the final brilliant resolution of that E/E flat tension that has haunted the whole symphony. Now at last the E tonality is allowed to reach its fulfilment as E major.

But still Rawsthorne adds a coda ([77]–end). It is as if he wishes to glance back at the journey covered since the opening. Now echoes of E flat are heard, and the metre reverts to a duple one, as it was originally; but once the major tonality has been firmly established, the effect of such nostalgic echoes is to make us even more aware of it. The work dies away on a note of secure and confident serenity.

Rawsthorne's interpretation of those two chief and related concerns of the contemporary composer, tonality and serialism, is made explicit in this symphony. Composition for him is a conditioned instinct, and tonality is inherently part of that conditioning. Why seek to avoid it? Why should one write negatively, to avoid? Tonality is the source of one of the most basic of all musical sensations, namely preparation-tension-relaxation. Musical structures have their origin in this sensation, which is indispensable.

Serialism, on the other hand, provides not so much a set of rules as a set of principles. The idea of serialism is important for Rawsthorne rather than its mechanics. The strict observance of serial procedures limits the composer's scope rather than enlarges his expressive range. Yet there are several instances in his works, of which the opening of the *Third Symphony* is one, where he makes use of serial devices in order to achieve effects which would not be possible by simply tonal means. Another instance is the *Quintet for piano and wind*, in which the scherzo is serial.[1] But the total and committed adoption of serialism would, Rawsthorne considers, limit the expressive range of his music.

Rawsthorne has always had a strong predilection for the violin, the traditionally lyrical yet at the same time most versatile of instruments. The first of his two violin concertos was dedicated to Walton, and was heard at Cheltenham in 1948. Its two movements are played without a break. The first is marked by an intense lyricism, and an impassioned orchestral *tutti* forms the centre of the movement. Gradually the pace slackens, and after a cadenza the opening mood is recaptured. The second movement contains considerable orchestral development, which is some-

---

1. Apart from the piano scales.

what at variance with the solo nature of a concerto. But in the words of one critic,[1] 'the new work made an immediate and deep impression on the audience'; it was to be followed by a much more successful second concerto eight years later.

The *Second Violin Concerto* is more characteristic of its composer than the first. In the opening bars, a tonal spell is cast over the music. As in the case of the *Third Symphony*, E is juxtaposed with E flat. In this case it is the solo violin that spells out the simple melodic material of the work in two long phrases, of which the second is an inversion of the first. The tonality of the concerto is E, and its style is richly lyrical, with a dramatic and declamatory slow movement centred round an A tonality. The theme of the finale, which is in the form of a Theme and Variations, is set against an accompaniment made up of material from the slow movement. This finale was enlarged formally after the first performance, and another variation added.

Particularly noteworthy among the lighter works for chamber orchestra is *Improvisations on a theme of Constant Lambert*, which was written for the Northern Sinfonia, and first played by them on 11 January 1961. The theme is from Lambert's ballet *Tiresias*, which was heard at Covent Garden in 1951, the year of his death, and after the theme the six improvisations follow continuously, to finish very quietly and expressively. The work is dedicated to Rawsthorne's wife, Isabel, who was Lambert's widow.

Rawsthorne's idiom is instrumentally derived, tonally chromatic, personal and subtle. It is thus perfectly suited to the intimate medium of chamber music. Not surprisingly, he has written numerous works in this category for different combinations of instruments; two piano quintets, one for wind, one for strings; sonatas for all three stringed instruments, among which that for violin and piano, written for Szigeti, is a particularly clear example of a unified structure built up by the most simple means from a motivating tonal idea—in this case the adjacent triads of D and E flat minor. The extreme difficulty of the *toccata* movement probably limits its performances. Other works include an oboe quartet; a clarinet quartet; a piano trio; a sonatina for flute, oboe and piano; and, to crown his endeavours in this field, three string quartets. These aptly summarise the various phases of his development. The first (1939) is a theme and six variations, which vary in pace, texture and diffuseness of harmony. The *Second Quartet* (1954) demonstrates Rawsthorne's personal use of the established large-scale structures. One of his favourite devices is the shortening of a theme at its recapitulation; another is his fondness for the

1. *The Times*, 2 July 1948

variation principle, which he uses in the last of this quartet's four movements.

The *Third Quartet* (1965) followed the third symphony, and stands in the same relationsjip to his chamber music as that work does to his orchestral music. It represents a culminating point of achievement.

This work was commissioned by the Harlow Arts Council, and first played at that town on 18 July 1965. It is in four continuous sections, preceded as usual by an introductory motto of six bars (*allegro deciso*), in which the material, with its various possibilities of development, is first stated; rising fourths a semitone apart, stated melodically by the second violin, as bold intervals by the first;

Ex.12   Rawsthorne
                                                             Third String Quartet

also the thematic use of the major seventh and minor second. The first movement, which uses 6/8 metre, develops the melodic potential of the material; the second, in common time, combines its tonal and rhythmic potential; the third opens with eleven bars of quiet, chordal introduction before the viola gives out the seven-bar chaconne theme, which is derived, needless to say, from the opening. The theme switches to the cello, and the music grows to an impassioned climax before the chordal passage ends the movement as it began. The finale is a brilliant gigue, in which juxtaposed fourths, spelt out staccato, pp, make a glittering texture of multiple tonalities. As a whole, the quartet is proof of the many-sidedness of Rawsthorne's idiom, and its capability in many different directions.

Vocal and choral music forms but a small part of Rawsthorne's output, which is predominantly instrumental. Indeed most of his vocal compositions use instrumental accompaniment of some kind. Songs for voice and piano are practically non-existent; the French nursery songs, for instance, are early (1938) and un-typical.

His first vocal piece was late (1952)—*A Canticle of Man* for baritone and choir, accompanied by flute and strings. This was an occasional piece, written for a summer school. Various small choral works followed; the *Canzonet* (1953) was Rawsthorne's contribution to that official collection of part-songs, *A Garland for the Queen*, which was a somewhat self-conscious, entirely unspontaneous attempt to celebrate the coronation of

Queen Elizabeth II—much as the famous *Triumphs of Oriana* had celebrated her Tudor forbear.

Pieces for the conventional mixed choir include *Four Seasonal Songs*
(1956), *Lament for a Sparrow*, after Catullus (1962), *A Rose for Lidice*,
and the short carol, to words by Hardy, *The Oxen*.

Pieces requiring larger resources include the *Mediaeval Diptych* for
baritone and orchestra (1962); *Tankas of the Four Seasons* for tenor and
instrumental quintet (1965); *The God in the Cave* for chorus and orchestra
(1967). But the most substantial choral work is the *Carmen Vitale*,
or 'Song of Life', for soprano, chorus and orchestra. First heard in
London on 16 October 1963, it is an oratorio in two parts to words by
anonymous mediaeval poets. Its theme is life, starting from Christ's
nativity. Two arias for solo soprano, and two pieces for the orchestra
(fugue and chaconne), are offset by the choral sections, some of which
use plainsong to Latin words. The composer's purpose was more to
capture the mood of the text than to set the words. But certain inconsis-
tencies deprive this work of that sureness of touch which is so essential
to a large-scale structure. Not only is Rawsthorne's idiom instrumentally
conceived—which tends to make the orchestral writing more interesting
than the choral—but the modalism of the plainchant with which the
work opens, and which is quoted elsewhere in it, is at variance with the
harmonic movement.

More fundamentally, the place of oratorio had been for a long time
open to question, particularly since 1945. The old-style oratorio, which
had been for many years the staple fare of many a festival or choral society
since the nineteenth century, had already begun to show signs of change
in the 1920's; it suffered a mortal blow in 1931, with Walton's *Belshazzar's
Feast*. Audiences asked for colour, movement, drama; the attention of
composers accordingly switched to opera.

This is not to say that the oratorio tradition died overnight; but
although works continued to be written in the former mould—such as
Howell's *Hymnus Paradisi*, or Ferguson's *The Dream of the Rood*—the
medium had ceased to have that artistic vitality which an art-form must
have if it is to make an impact on an audience. The stuffing had gone out
of it. Indeed, the meaning of religion, and of Christianity, was in the
process of acquiring a new kind of relevance; the mysticism of a Cardinal
Newman, which had so inspired Elgar, was being replaced by a more
realistic theology, such as is shown by Dietrich Bonhoeffer or Pope
John XXIII.

Therefore, if a post-war composer was to write an oratorio, he would
need a particularly urgent message, which could not be communicated
in any other way, such as by means of opera. He would find audiences

particularly critical of this genre; it might have a distinguished, if perhaps slightly academic, past; it was highly doubtful after 1945 whether it would have a future. Indeed the post-war scene is plentifully strewn with the numerous wrecks of not-quite-successful oratorios: Goehr's *Sutter's Gold*; Reizenstein's *Voices of Night*, Crosse's *Changes*, and many more. All these works, while in no way perpetuating the old tradition, lacked that urgency which would inspire a contemporary audience.

Exceptional works prove this general principle. Tippett's *A Child of our Time* lives through the composer's concern and compassion for the underprivileged. Milner's *The Water and the Fire* is a unique expression of the meaning of Christianity today, and the work lives as a result. More ephemerally, Britten's *War Requiem* exactly caught the widespread anti-war feeling of the time (1962).

Seen against this background of an evolving form, Rawsthorne's work seems to be poised midway between the old and the new, and it lacks that driving urgency which is suggested by his theme. While the urgency of his orchestral and chamber music is derived mainly from his technique and idiom, which is instrumentally conceived, in an oratorio this urgency can only come through the words; the instrumental writing is, to some extent, secondary. In the case of *Carmen Vitale* the words are not sufficiently telling to impress an audience.

In considering his work as a whole, Rawsthorne does not immediately impress the listener with striking thematic ideas; nor does he indulge in outrageous experiments. The listener is invited to seek for himself, to pay the closest attention. Rawsthorne's art is an intimate one, but his idiom is richly varied, and suitable for all occasions of instrumental music, whether a full-length symphonic work, or a smaller chamber piece. Though forged from traditional materials, it is anything but derivative. Practically alone of his generation, he has followed through the implications of a developed form of tonality in the basic types of instrumental music, and has successfully solved the many problems of form and style that confronted him. He is concerned with artistic achievement, not with trends and fashions, which have nothing to do with art.

He sees several distinct streams of musical development in the contemporary situation, all of which are as valid as they are independent; one is the 12-note/serialist/*avant garde* stream; which leaves him, on the whole, unimpressed. Another is the Liszt/Busoni/Bartok stream, to which he has a much closer affinity. Indeed if there is one composer who has exercised more influence over Rawsthorne than any other, that composer is Bartok. Bartok's evolution of tonality, particularly in the works written during the middle years of his life, may be aptly compared with Rawsthorne's. And though Rawsthorne did not consciously model his string

E

quartets on those of Bartok, those of the elder composer were present at the back of his mind, as part of his general experience. Many are the works of Bartok that Rawsthorne admires, and occasionally he models his own on a particular one; the *Divertimento* is a case in point.

The road of music has many different paths. As far as British music is concerned, Rawsthorne stands in the direct line of Elgar, Walton, Constant Lambert (who was a close friend in early life), and Tippett. There is no doubt that his influence on later composers will prove immense.

3 William Alwyn

William Alwyn, who was born in 1905, is an unashamed, if unfashionable romantic. Not for him the new, the experimental or the untried; he has sought to make his music live with the traditional means of the symphony orchestra, and with recourse to nothing apart from the sheer quality of his craft. For him the key of C major has not yet been fully exploited, and there is a great deal still waiting to be said with the ordinary orchestra as we know it.

His extremely full professional life started on the bandstand on the sea-front at Broadstairs. From there it took him as a flautist to the London Symphony Orchestra in 1927, when he played under Elgar and Vaughan Williams during the heyday of the Three Choirs Festival. He has appeared as conductor, not merely of his own works, though opportunities for this have been infrequent. He has been unstinting in carrying out those more menial tasks that sometimes befall musicians; from 1926 to 1956 he taught at the Royal Academy of Music in London; he has also undertaken more than his fair share of advisory panels and committees. There is no contradiction in this. The busy practicalities of everyday life are the necessary checks and balances against which the concentrated work of composition is done. This is Alwyn's personal solution to the question that every composer has to answer, today more than ever—the extent to which he must commute between the ivory tower and the market place; both are equally important, and yet neither by itself is sufficient.

Not until he was forty-four did he undertake his first symphony; but it was by no means his first composition. As a student, when he was under Sir John McEwen at the Royal Academy of Music, he had written a piano concerto, which his student-contemporary Clifford Curzon played at a concert in Bournemouth, under the composer's direction. Several early manuscripts were discarded, including a second piano concerto, and a violin concerto; and as early as 1927, when he was only twenty-two,

Henry Wood had introduced his *Five Preludes for Orchestra* at a Promenade Concert. From his student days onwards, Alwyn retained the greatest respect for Wood, whom he described as 'the focus of my musical life'. Then again, in 1940, his *Divertimento* for solo flute had been played at an I.S.C.M. Festival in New York.

He is chiefly known, like his colleague Malcolm Arnold, as a composer of film music; yet to let it go at that, with the implied disapproval that the words 'film composer' usually call forth, would be both unfair and inadequate. Certainly the film studio represents a lucrative economic haven for the composer, which makes it immediately suspect to those who consider commerce and art to be irreconcilable. Certainly the film composer is required to work as a member of a team, and therefore to accept a role of artistic dependence to some extent on the wishes of others, such as the director of the film; this again causes raised eyebrows among those musicians to whom entire independence and personal choice are an article of faith.

Yet there can be more to it than that. No composer has done more than Alwyn to explore the serious possibilities of the use of composed music by established composers in films, which led to such notable successes as Walton's score for *Henry V*, and Vaughan Williams' score for *Scott of the Antarctic*. Alwyn's most notable films were *Odd Man Out* and *The Fallen Idol*, which he made for Carol Reed. His treatment of music in these and his many other film scores was as something dramatic rather than as something merely programmatic or descriptive; and this sharpening of his dramatic sense in the film studio led directly later on to his writing his opera *The Libertine*. Moreover, the film composer can occasionally find scope and outlet for orchestral experiment of the sort that Busoni used to imagine; and this was particularly the case with the documentary films made in the 30's.

Among his smaller compositions, greater scope is given to his characteristic style by the shorter tone-poems, whose central feature is instrumental colour, rather than by those more conventional chamber-music works, whose main structural prop is traditional counterpoint, which does not appeal to him. Examples in the first category, which belong in the tradition of Delius or Arnold Bax, are *The Magic Island* (1952) for orchestra, and *Autumn Legend* (1956) for cor anglais and strings. Examples in the second category are the *String Quartet* (1954) in D minor, and the *String Trio* (1963), the last of which, however, the composer values highly. A characteristic occasional work is the *Concerto Grosso No. 3*, written in 1964, after the fourth symphony, to 'the ever-living memory of Henry Wood', and played at a Promenade Concert on the twentieth anniversary of Wood's death. The three movements use brass, woodwind and strings respectively, and the third movement is an elegy.

But the core of his output consists of four symphonies. The first, in D, was completed in July 1949, and played by the Hallé Orchestra under Barbirolli at a Cheltenham Festival concert the following year. It is conventional in more ways than one; a symphony in the grand manner, which proclaims its composer's allegiance without qualification, and stands in direct line with the tradition of Tchaikowsky or Richard Strauss. This romanticism strongly appealed to Barbirolli. In thus displaying his orchestral prowess, Alwyn displays a remarkable craftsman-ship. Though the symphony is diffuse in its material, it shows already certain features, such as pedal-points and brass writing, which are permanent characteristics of his style. The themes are firmly diatonic, the texture luxuriant; there is also a suggestion of the cyclic technique, which he was to develop later. But taken as a whole the work sums up the past, as Alwyn had experienced it, rather than points to the future.

The *Second Symphony* marks a turning point. It was completed in April 1953, and followed the highly colourful symphonic prelude *The Magic Island* (1952). The symphony is in two parts, as against the customary four; the first part is slow, elegiac, characterised by falling, chromatic intervals, particularly the augmented second. The material of this part has close affinities with *The Magic Island*.

The second part is entirely contrasted; quick, impetuous, brilliant, with spacious phrasing. The material is the same as that of the first part, but it is differently applied, and the *scherzando* momentum of the opening bars is never lost sight of; even in the slow, trio-like middle section, the main pace is felt to be present, though beneath the surface of the music. Moreover, the structure of the movement is clearly delineated and genuinely symphonic; those parts that are thematic are differentiated from those that are merely subsidiary, or links. The point towards which the music moves is a transformation into D major of the F/D minor material from the opening of the first part. The work closes with a coda, recalling the mood of the first part.

The introduction of more chromatic progressions, the evolution of a thematic pattern over a held pedal-note, or repeated pedal-point, the distribution of homogeneous thematic material over the symphony as a whole, are all features which indicate the direction in which Alwyn's symphonic thought was developing, and which anticipate his individual contribution to this *genre*, which was to become fully apparent in his next symphony.

This was written in 1955/6, and played by the BBC Orchestra under Beecham on October 10th 1956. Barbirolli, who was to have conducted the work, was taken ill some time before. The year spent in writing this symphony has been described by the composer in his diary *Ariel to Miranda*,[1] which is not only the self-portrait of an artist at fifty, but is also the record of his work on the symphony, interspersed as it was with the innumerable distractions of a working musician in London; his thoughts, his observations about his colleagues, about his art generally, and indeed about humanity at large.

Several smaller works separate the second from the third symphony; the D minor *String Quartet*, the highly characteristic and colourful *Fantasy-Waltzes* for piano, the concerto for harp and strings *Lyra Angelica*, and a little piece for solo harp, *Crépuscule*. The last piece was a deliberate and highly productive exercise in self-discipline and limitation of material—a device that was to be applied again in the middle movement of the third symphony, as well as elsewhere. Alwyn himself says,[2] 'My new system of founding the harmonies on a short scale pattern consisting of a few selected notes and working within these limits is proving as stimulating here as it does in the symphony. The discipline is neither restrictive nor irksome; on the contrary it seems to ease the mental process, and by limiting the palette, paradoxically suggests new colours.'

The rough sketch of the *Third Symphony*,[3] which the composer saw, with justification, as 'a fresh chapter in my symphonic output', was completed by 29 September 1955, and played through to the conductor John Hollingsworth. Two weeks later, it was commissioned by the BBC, and is therefore dedicated to its then head of music Richard Howgill. Work on various film scores (*Safari*, *Black Tent*) interrupted work on the symphony, as well as a book on film music.[4] Orchestration began in March 1956. The first movement was finished by 8th May; the slow movement by 14th May; the whole work by 11th June.

The symphonic principle first developed by Alwyn in this work was the division of the twelve notes of the chromatic scale into two groups, of eight notes and four notes respectively, which would be so contrasted that their melodic and harmonic content would provide the forces of conflicting tonality from which the whole symphony would spring. This was a personal adaptation of the 12-note style into the tonal structure of a large-scale work. The first group includes the tonality round which the symphony is chiefly centred, E flat; the second group

1. Published in *Adam*, International Review, Nos. 316–17–18 (1967).
2. *Ariel to Miranda*, 3 November.
3. Published by Alfred Lengnick & Co.
4. *The Technique of Film Music* (Focal Press, 1957).

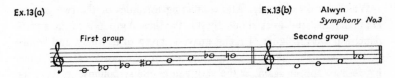

Ex.13(a)   Ex.13(b)   Alwyn
                                                                 Symphony No.3

contains the contrasting, conflicting elements, centred above and below
the note F. Of the three movements of the symphony, the first is built
from the notes of the first group, the second is built from just the four
notes of the second group, while the third is built from a bringing together,
and a consequent working-out, of the two groups. A rhythmic ostinato,
with which the symphony opens, is associated with the first group, and
thus occurs, in varying guises, in the first and third movements; but in
fact, as Ex. 14 shows, the themes and rhythms of each movement are
closely related.

Ex.14   Alwyn
                                                              Symphony No.3

The first movement consists of the presentation of various thematic
patterns and fragments formed from the notes of the first group; these
are fitted into a freely modified sonata-form structure. The second
movement consists of the exploitation of the melodic and harmonic
possibilities contained in the four notes of the second group. Thus the
chord of the tritone pervades the movement, and the tonality veers
between D minor and F minor. 'The closing bars,' says the composer,
'should sound strangely remote.' The acceptance of the self-imposed
limitation in this movement is highly suggestive, partly because of the
contrast with the first movement—extreme slowness compared with
extreme speed; the insistence on one chord compared with frequent
directional changes of harmony—partly also because of the sense of
foreboding that the listener feels, subconsciously; a sense that the calm
of this movement is not to be permanent; that it is the calm before the
storm of the finale.

Which breaks abruptly. The conflicting tonalities of the two groups are juxtaposed and worked out. By [Q] the second group is in the ascendant; a powerful figure of rising quavers, given to trumpets and trombones, marks the apex of the development of this movement; the same figure is to appear again, at the very end of the symphony, to mark its exciting fulfilment, when the E flat tonality of the first group finally triumphs. This conclusion is forecast at [W], when the note linking the two groups, B flat, is at last established. From this moment onwards the end is inevitable, since B flat, the dominant of E flat, attracts the music irresistibly towards that tonality. But first Alwyn recalls the corresponding moment just towards the end of the first movement (after [Z]), with a quiet violin theme in E flat.

Once more in this symphony, the characteristics of Alwyn's orchestral style are amply represented: plentiful writing for the brass; fondness for *ostinato* phrases, and expressive use of orchestral colour; the conception of music as a succession of contrasting episodes, marked by bursts of climax, and based on the primary musical elements, such as loud contrasted with soft, strings contrasted with wind, *con tutta forza* contrasted with *molto calmato*, and so on. But the symphonic principle of the conflict and working out of tonalities derived from two complementary parts of the 12-note scale, is both a highly individual technique, and recognisably a valid development of traditional symphonic practice.

The same principle is carried one stage further in the next symphony, the fourth[1], which was first heard played by the Hallé Orchestra under Barbirolli at a Promenade Concert in 1959. It is more subdued a work than the third, which is illustrated by the fact that the composer dispenses with the percussion that he has hitherto used in the first three symphonies, and uses only timpani. The twelve notes are again divided into two groups, of eight and four notes respectively.

Ex.15(a)   Ex.15(b)   Alwyn
                                                                      Symphony No.4

The first group is scalic, centring round F sharp; the tonality encompassed is therefore that of D major, or F sharp minor. The second group is intervallic, chiefly consisting of fourths and fifths, and centring on the tonalities of B flat and E flat. The tonal contrast and conflict between the groups is thus very marked, and the composer proceeds to exploit this

1. Published by Alfred Lengnick & Co.

in the course of the symphony. Generally speaking, the first group is
used to create rhythmic movement and thematic life at the opening of
phrases, and at the beginning of sections of the symphony, and to
project the music forwards; the second group provides the converse of
this, and is used to mark the cadences at the end of phrases, to conclude
sections, and indeed to provide the end of the symphony as a whole,
which is on B flat.

After an introduction in which the two groups are carefully spelt out,
the one by the woodwind, the other by the cellos and basses, the first
theme, consisting of the first group, is given to strings and woodwind
together. An afterthought to it is allotted to a solo cello, over a pedal F
sharp, which is the note in common to both tonalities of the first group
(Ex. 16 (a) and (b)).

Ex.16(a)   Alwyn
                                                             Symphony No.4

B (1st subject)

Ex.16(b)   Alwyn
                                                             Symphony No.4

C +7 (Subsid.theme)

(Solo Cello)
mp   mf

The conflicting tonality of the second group is immediately juxtaposed,
by horns and bassoons, which makes also for contrast of timbre, and the
resulting clash leads to the first moment of climax, in D major, propelled
forward by a rhythmic ostinato, derived from the first theme. Again the
music comes to rest on F sharp, high up this time in the violins. A gradual
quickening leads into the next *Allegro*, and the ostinato forms the link
with the following section. The tonalities combine for the second subject,
which first appears in the muted brass,

Ex.17   Alwyn
                                                            Symphony No.4

Flutes and
J Trumpets,
con sord.

p   mf

but is soon exploited and developed by the strings. The strings maintain a restless assertion of the first group, and just when the music is
moving towards this, the horns in unison (*ff, con tutta forza*) proclaim
their dissent, and succeed in veering the music towards the B flat tonality

of the second group. The bass instruments however remain loyal to the first group, and are not won over until the next, and last, moment of climax (at [S]). Once this has happened, a B flat pedal-point is maintained until the end of the movement, while the timpani sustain the rhythmic ostinato.

The brilliant second movement follows the conventional symphonic form of scherzo and trio. After the scherzo rhythm (3+3+2) has been established, on the single note D (after the manner of the opening of the third symphony), the scale-notes of the first group are used as a thematic pattern on which the movement is built. The notes of the second group are used either melodically or chordally to offset the tonality of the first group. They are interjected, first by the trumpet, later by the brass generally. Inevitably the first passage comes to rest on F sharp, and soon the first-group scale appears in that tonality, sung out by a solo oboe, while muted trombones interject the second-group notes as a chord. At the repeat of the scherzo, this solo is allotted to a violin, with the indication 'roughly'. It is just the sort of country-fiddle theme that Aaron Copland might have written.

When the strings and woodwind change, at [N], from the bright tonality and swinging rhythm of the first-group theme, and assume the more ponderous gait of the second, we know that the end of the first scherzo section is not far off. The slower middle section combines the notes of both groups in a theme given first to violins alone, then to two bassoons in canon. All the tension and excitement of the scherzo is released, and the thematic pattern is given a free rein for it to move to a full, romantic climax for the whole orchestra in unison (at [W]). After the repeat of the scherzo, the music comes to rest on F natural (at [LL]), and the first-group scale is then transposed, inverted and developed, with the two theme-groups jostling for supremacy.

The slow movement, with which the symphony ends, is in the form of a free passacaglia. It takes up where the second movement left off, with both theme-groups side by side,

Ex.18   Alwyn
                                                         Symphony No.4

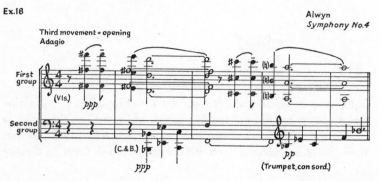

and the music making use of the characteristics of each; the phrases begin with those of the first group, and end with those of the second. There are two points of climax; the first, built round a passage of Elgarian luxuriance, leads up to [N], where a quickening of the pace recalls the rhythm (3+3+2) of the scherzo, and the brass once again blare out the second-group tonality in an attempt to pull the rest of the orchestra away from that of the first group. The attempt this time is unsuccessful, and the music flickers away and reverts to the mood and pace of the opening.

The second climax maintains the pace of the opening, but builds a gradual crescendo, while the violins start the theme in E flat minor, an augmented second lower than the first time, at [S]. The intensity increases, but when all the strings change to the second-group tonality, after an allargando at [U], the conclusion of the symphony is felt to be inevitable.

Alwyn's four symphonies form a musical unity. The first represents the introduction, the second the development, the third the climax, and the fourth the finale. They epitomise what might be called the romantic principle of composition; ideas are conceived, and freely followed through, in terms of the instruments for which they are written. Orchestral climaxes, often of shattering proportions, are the result of an increase of nervous and emotional tension, and are usually marked by a variation of speed and dynamics. As the composer's style is both tonal and thematic, the listener's attention cannot but focus on to the themes themselves, which carry most of the weight of the musical argument; and Alwyn is entirely unafraid of the big line, the broad sequence, the grandiose gesture. That such a style is in danger of becoming cliché-ridden is obvious.

The most positive feature of Alwyn's style is his mastery of the orchestra. His study of orchestration, both as conductor, performer and composer, has been wide-ranging, his most recent being an analysis of Berg's *Wozzeck*. His acquaintance with the symphonic and operatic repertoire is very wide. He is preoccupied with orchestral technique, the layout of instruments, the distribution of an orchestral climax. Three parts, he feels, give a clearer effect than four. Each must be heard effectively, each instrument so placed as to make its best contribution to the orchestral *tutti*. Alwyn's brass climaxes sound louder and more brilliant than in other composers' scores not because he uses more instruments, nor because the players blow harder, but because the layout of the chords is such that each instrument is heard to contribute in the most telling way to the overall effect, like the upper harmonics of an organ mixture-stop.

Another not-so-positive feature is the general lack of counterpoint. This results in a high proportion of writing that is filling-in, repetitive, or purely accompanimental. There is an absence of that dynamic, inner growth that only comes from contrapuntal writing, and for which mere loudness is no substitute. In a sense, the use of *ostinati*, or repetition of a figure, coupled with an unwavering ear for orchestral colour, goes some way to compensating for this, and to providing the music with that momentum and drive that would otherwise be obtained by means of counterpoint; but too frequent a use of the pedal-point, or *ostinato* pedal, tends to halt the harmonic movement. A theme which evolves and unfolds over a static bass-note is one of the commonest features of Alwyn's style. But for him symphonic orchestral technique is all important; in particular the development of symphonic structure. This holds his attention more than counterpoint, which he considers has become gradually less important since Bach's day.

Analysis and description of a score give, in the case of most composers, only a partial view of the nature of the music. This is particularly so with Alwyn, whose artistic personality is compounded of many parts, and is somewhat enigmatic. What is unusual today, he holds to a personal ideal of artistic beauty; what is practically unknown today, he admits to such an ideal. His view is Platonic; beauty exists as an ideal goal to which art approximates to a greater or lesser extent. It follows that the two basic requirements of the artist are, first, that he should express what is in him, and only what is in him; second, that his technique should be good enough to enable him to communicate fully and adequately. Integrity is essential, which means that the artist can give the listener only what he himself has heard and experienced. Thus he differs from the *avant-garde* composer, who gives the listener what is new, or what he thinks he (the composer) ought to be experiencing. Moreover, the artist must aim at the complete expression of his ideas, and this for Alwyn is not possible with musical means alone. Literature and the visual arts can express and describe in a way that music cannot. Alwyn's artistry is versatile. He is acquainted with many fields of writing, particularly French poetry and novels, such as the work of Nathalie Sarraute, and different schools of painting. He is himself a painter; he has also selected and translated an anthology of 20th century French poetry.[1]

His literary bent and his composition have combined with his dramatic sense in his biggest venture yet, his only opera *The Libertine*, which so far has taken four years to write, and is only awaiting the chance of performance for its final completion. Alwyn has never set poems to

1. Published by Chatto & Windus (1969).

music; his fondness for poetry may have something to do with his
reluctance to add another dimension to a poem, which, if it is a good
poem, is an already-complete artwork. But word-setting is something he
enjoys; he had already written a radio opera *Farewell Companions;* it
was a logical continuation to write a full-length work for the theatre.

Two great figures of literature, which almost amount to archetypal
images, have always dominated his imagination; one is Don Juan, the
other is St. Joan. He is well-read on each, and in selecting the first as the
subject of his opera, his reason was that Don Juan was a theme about
which he felt he could write an individual interpretation, which would
be relevant for today, yet which had an age-long connection with both
the theatre, and literature generally—to say nothing of opera itself. St.
Joan, on the other hand, had been the subject of powerful interpretations
by Bernard Shaw and Jean Anouilh.

So he decided to use the Don Juan story, and set about writing his
three-act opera *The Libertine*. The libretto, which took him a year to
write, is in verse, some of it rhyming, and is based on James Elroy
Flecker's play *Don Juan*, as well as on Byron, Baudelaire, Molière, Shaw
and Nietzsche. The plot, in the true operatic tradition, is more than
slightly ridiculous, and is set in 'the not too distant future'. What is
implied is just as important as what is said. Don Juan returns from hell
to this country, where he pursues his ideal life of happiness and pleasure,
and proceeds to kill the prime minister, who was contemplating a war.
The prime minister had two daughters, Anna and Isobel, both of whom,
needless to say, are the recipients of Don Juan's attention, and both of
whom he also eventually murders. A statue of the prime minister had
been put up by an admiring and grateful nation, much to the convenience
of the story, and as an integral part of the Don Juan legend; and this not
unexpectedly comes in to pronounce judgement. Don Juan is then
banished for ever whence he came.

The opening caused the composer much thought. Originally he
visualised a Prologue depicting a storm at sea, and shipwreck; this idea
then evolved into an orchestral Prologue of storm-music; but finally
both these possibilities were discarded in favour of a much more direct
and simple beginning; the curtain rises to the grey of a spring dawn over
the sea. A very short introduction leads to a climax, in bar 10, which
contains the 'magic' chord of the opera (Eb and A major combined), to
depict Juan's ability to cast spells over people.

The first scene[1] is set on the rocky coast of Cornwall. Haidie, a young
girl, comes down the cliff and stands naked, ready for her morning swim,

---

1. The first act was completed in April 1968.

when she sees two bodies washed ashore on the beach, after the storm of
the previous night. They are Juan and his servant Owen Jones. This first
scene is one of innocent, idyllic love, simple and dreamlike; a background
experience; Byron tells[1] how Juan recalls his meeting with Haidie as
something far-off, ideal, visionary. Over an ostinato figure, Alwyn gives
Haidie a simple folk-like tune, while the music leads forward to the climax
of the 'magic' chord. A romantic duet, lyrical and simple, marks the
innocence of this idyll; then, as the sea comes in, Haidie and Owen carry
Juan's body up the cliff.

The next scene takes place a month later, in early summer. The love
affair of Juan and Haidie has flourished as it should, but selfishness has
asserted itself. Simplicity proved boring, and a note of bravado is soon
to spoil it. The dream *motif* recurs in Haidie's music, but the first
discordant note is struck when workmen rush in who are on strike, and in
pursuit of one of their workmates, whom they call a 'traitor' and 'blackleg'.
The violins have a 12-note theme at the word 'traitor', and the more
chromatic writing, over a ground, breaks into and destroys the love-idyll.
The men want to kill Lord Framlingham, the President of the English
Republic, for political reasons. But the carefree Juan was a close friend of
Framlingham, and so he turns the workmen's argument on to himself,
and allows the blackleg to escape. 'What of the poets?', he asks; 'what
of our dreams?' The 'magic' chord recalls us to the beginning-point
once more.

A swaggering line accompanies his words 'blow up parliament', and a
hint of a fugal section works up to a climax, with shouts of 'blackleg'.
This gradually dies away as the crowd disperses, and we see Juan left
pointing his revolver not at the crowd but at his own father, Don Pedro,
the Spanish Ambassador in London, who suddenly appears. The
'father' theme dominates the music of this next section. Juan meanwhile
has forgotten Haidie—but then he remembers her. His father, however,
urges him to leave Haidie and go to London. This he decides to do; he is
driven, as we know, by a force stronger than his own will. The only
explanation he can give Haidie is that, however much he values her love,
he values his own freedom more. So he chooses to leave the dreamlike
innocence of the love-idyll for the selfish course which is to lead to his
own destruction.

The second act takes place in late July two months later, in Juan's
London flat. Framlingham is planning to declare war, to general popular
acclamation; and this necessitates intervention by the individual, if
disaster is to be averted. A dance is in progress; we hear a tango off-stage,
but the dance band is interrupted by orchestral interjections. Juan and

1. *Don Juan* (Canto 2).

Framlingham's younger daughter Isobel dance to a quick, scherzando waltz, symbolising their passionate relationship. Inevitably the music culminates in a love duet. Anna, the other daughter, enters to a slow waltz. As the windows shut, the dance band is shut out, just as the political action of this scene shuts out the background of Juan's amorous activities. Anna, we learn, beneath a cold and passionless exterior is in fact on fire with love and jealousy for Juan. After Juan and Isobel go out there is a moment of repose—that dramatically essential calm before the next stormy moments of action.

Framlingham enters with the other guests, and announces war; whereupon Juan entreats him against this course, in a biting dialogue: 'In war no man is free'. When Framlingham is deaf to all arguments, Juan plans to murder him; and so he arranges to meet him 'by the cool of the river, by Cleopatra's Needle'. The scene closes; meanwhile, as before he had forgotten Haidie, so now Juan forgets Isobel. But Anna is told that Juan has gone out, and thinking, not entirely unreasonably, that he has made yet another amorous assignation, follows him angrily.

At this point in the opera Alwyn had originally inserted another scene, as Juan shoots Framlingham by the river. This however was discarded because he felt it would be too melodramatic, 'too operatic', and not really necessary for the understanding of the story.

The third act[1] takes place a year later. Once again it starts with the dawn, and the 'magic' chord marks Juan's soliloquy. The rising sun evokes memories of Haidie and a lost innocence. When Owen enters, their dialogue hints at mystery, and the murder of Framlingham. Owen, the strange servant, alias Leporello, tries to hypnotise Juan, who gradually comes under the spell. 'Who was your mother? Who are you?' asks Owen (quoting Byron). The climax is reached with the words 'I am Don Juan', and Haidie's first folk-song theme is heard through the haze, like the voice of Juan's conscience. Suddenly the sun is blotted out, and, as if from the past, Haidie appears; but her voice is dull, meek; all joy has gone out of her; and the retrospective scene recalls earlier phrases. Their duet moves to a climax of intensity, and as Owen leads Haidie away, the scene closes with Owen's strange promise about 'the night of the falling stars'. Thereupon the sun reappears, as the curtain falls.

A short intermezzo takes us back to the purity of Haidie's love scene, before the final scene. The statue is an integral part of the legend; it occurs in both Da Ponte and Molière; Alwyn gives a fresh twist to the tradition by making the statue that of the hero, Juan's friend. A chromatic orchestral figure represents the crowd and after the opening dialogue between Don Pedro and Juan there is a knock at the door which reduces

1. The scoring of the third act is incomplete.

Don Pedro to terror. We expect the statue—but instead Anna comes in.
Her theme returns, and the ensuing duet becomes gradually more
passionate and retrospective. Juan is shown to evolve in the course of the
opera, as his power, which is his undoing, gradually increases. The
climax of this duet occurs with a swaggering tune for his words 'Then I
am God', which prove too much for Anna, who succumbs to him—as
she had all along intended to do.

Enter Isobel, to a nagging, persistent accompaniment theme. The
love theme of Juan and Isobel dominates the next section as Juan denies
Anna, until, at the very point of climax, when Juan says, somewhat
unconvincingly, 'I have always been loyal', Anna breaks in, to reveal
what she saw that night a year before, at Cleopatra's Needle. Mad with
jealousy, she puts on Juan's cloak—the one he wore for the murder—
and dances round to a macabre, distorted waltz. At the climax of her
narrative, with the words 'I was there', pistol shots sound in the orchestra.
So Isobel realizes that Juan has murdered her father. There follows the
only explanatory part of the opera, as Juan tells why he killed Framlingham. This is spoken, for the uniquely special effect, after the climax of
the previous section.

Now Anna has nothing to live for; but too afraid to kill herself, she
asks Juan to do it for her. Having murdered once, it is easier for him to
murder twice; and he shoots Anna.

What now of Isobel's love? Eventually, even in spite of the two
murders, her passion proves stronger than her reason. The music now
becomes more lyrical, and they eventually kiss and embrace. Can guilty
love endure if innocent love was rejected? 'Put out the light, then we can
see the stars.' The room is now in darkness, with only a glimmer of light
from the window. 'What care we for the stars?' they say. 'Are they
falling? Let them fall—they cannot destroy our love.' Gradually, inevitably, strange music; footsteps; a knocking at the door—three times,
unrhythmic. Then at last the statue of Framlingham does enter, eerie
and luminous. Juan shoots—but kills Isobel instead. There follows a
duet in fugue, based on Framlingham's theme, as the statue pronounces
judgement and punishment, and Juan attempts to explain himself. Juan
goes out, to a rain of fire. A pedal D in the orchestra sustains a violently
clashing and imitative passage, based on the Framlingham theme. Then
the door closes, and the statue disappears. Only the starlight remains—
'the night of the falling stars'— as Don Pedro nervously comes in, turns
on the light. Just one chord sounds, as he whispers to himself in horror,
'Santa Maria'.

Alwyn's opera is conceived in line with the grand operatic tradition of
Debussy and Puccini, just as his symphonies continued the romantic

orchestral tradition. His romanticism knows no half measures; in this lies its strength. Moreover, his stagecraft is calculated down to the finest points of action and movement. Details of production are as important as the music. Film work was the best possible training in this respect. But the impact of this work is due to two main factors; first, the inevitability of the plot's development and growth; second, the use of an archetypal image, which the composer has originally and successfully realised in contemporary terms. The Don Juan theme is not only one of the most basic of all stories; it is also highly relevant to the present day, in the hands of an understanding interpreter. Thus Tippett interpreted Paris in *King Priam*, and Berg interpreted *Lulu*. As far as English opera is concerned, the opera nearest in mood to Alwyn's, though their idiom differs widely, is Delius's *A Village Romeo and Juliet*. Both operas introduce symbolism; in both the business of the world is contrasted with the function of the individual, dreams with reality, innocence with self-interest. In both the place of the individual is shown to be supremely important; in both there is a certain carefree quality, as the lovers journey to where human corruption cannot touch them in their spiritual exile; their goal is the same, whether it be 'towards the setting sun—the Paradise Garden' of Delius's imagination, or 'beyond heaven and hell', as Isobel says in *The Libertine*.

Alwyn's instinct not to portray the murder of Framlingham on the stage is a true one; also to leave out the storm at the beginning of the opera. It would have been inconsistent to introduce such realism. Operatic action is suggestive and symbolic, not realistic and representative, as numerous composers have pointed out.[1] The libretto of *The Libertine* never explains events; but opera as Alwyn sees it is closely akin to drama, and so he avoids melisma or word repetition, and aims instead to achieve a flow of words as if they were spoken, while the orchestra supplies the lyricism.

But you cannot avoid convention in opera, particularly in romantic opera. If you do not, to some extent at least, accept the conventions, you should not write an opera. Alwyn's work is more in the line of Berg and Tippett than of Britten. *The Libertine* is a complex, composite work, uniting many facets of the composer's many-sided romantic personality. His imaginative experience is a collective and traditional one, in the sense that the material of a Greek tragedy was collective and traditional; he is keenly aware of contemporary drama and literature, and so his development of the Don Juan theme is markedly original. All of which suggest that, although the work is still not completely scored, when it is eventually produced it will make a remarkable impact in the theatre.

1. For instance, Peter Warlock in *Delius*, and Busoni in *Entwurf einer neuen Aesthetik der Tonkunst*.

4   Edmund Rubbra

There are two main kinds of progressive, whether in music or in other fields of human activity. The first are those who are entirely disenchanted with the continued relevance of established methods and past traditions; they therefore seek to do away with them, and to replace them with something else; something fresh, untraditional. The second are those who do not discard past traditions, but seek instead to reinterpret them, and to apply them in a fresh context as they see fit.

The first kind, who may be described as the ideological iconoclasts, are far more readily noticeable than the second. It is indeed one of the prime requisites, if you are going to put forward new methods and fresh styles, that your gestures should be both strikingly novel, if possible outrageous, and immediately recognizable. Thus the *avant-garde* aesthetic is a simple one. But the severe risk run by those who subscribe to it is twofold; partly that means may be mistaken for ends—the striking of a fresh posture, the adoption of an untried process, may be mistaken in itself for an art-work, which it is not; and partly that, by thus shifting the scale of values, the concept of permanent validity in the finished work becomes relative. Your novelty one week may well be made redundant by someone else's more radical novelty the next, if you have no other yardstick by which to measure it than the fact of its 'progressiveness'.

The second kind of progressives run risks as well, though of a different, more subtle, nature. They may be overlooked as merely 'traditional', and their work not understood for what it is. Because they do not sever all links with the past, as the other kind do, but on the contrary accept the past and try to relate it to the present, their relevance for the present may be questioned. In the eyes of the first kind they will probably appear as 'blacklegs', who have, by compromising with tradition, forfeited any right to be called 'progressive' at all.

And yet the self-styled revolutionaries, of whom several adorn the history of music—much as heretics adorn the history of the Christian Church—rarely reach beyond the ephemeral stage. At most they succeed in focusing attention on to a particular idea, which others may then pursue and develop. Art reaches a more than ephemeral validity only when its creator takes a wider view of tradition than the narrowly revolutionary one.

But both kinds of composers, the revolutionary progressive and the traditional progressive, have the same means at their disposal as their starting-point; the same orchestral or choral resources; in the long run, the same public. One of the first questions therefore that each kind of composer has to solve is his use of, and attitude to, the contemporary musical resources. Is he, for instance, to take the symphony orchestra as we know it today, which is a highly sophisticated musical tool, and develop it or modify it according to his taste; or accept it as it is, and fit his ideas within this existing mould?

One composer who has accepted and worked within the scope of the existing musical means is Edmund Rubbra, who was born in Northampton in 1901. His is just the sort of musicianship that, because of its traditional, even ordinary, appearance, may well pass unnoticed. He does not discover new sounds; he does not extend the aural frontiers in breadth; instead he exploits the existing ones in greater depth. He has worked, broadly speaking, within the established traditions. If that were all, there would indeed be scant grounds for going further. But his claim to be considered progressive rests on two grounds: a personal, mystical interpretation of Christianity, which is rare among contemporary composers (only Anthony Milner invites comparison), and a reasoned, consistent and refined attitude to tonality. Both factors combine to give some of his choral work a mediaeval, timeless flavour, which for its very simplicity is practically unique in contemporary British music.

He is a traditionalist—yet in twentieth-century terms. He sees the confusion of the present scene as a rift between on the one hand those who accept the traditional concept of music as a gradual development over the centuries, and on the other hand those who destroy existing traditions for ideological reasons. He has aligned himself without any qualification on the side of the first; and once he found his path, he has been quite uninfluenced by external pressures, and the swing of fashion away from him. The groundwork of his thought is concerned with harmony, and in this he shares the company of Debussy, Schoenberg, Scriabin, and some of the English composers of the early twentieth century, such as Cyril Scott; but his solution was not to reject tonality so much as to view it in a different way.

He had happened to pick up in Paris in the 20's, at a second-hand bookstall, a treatise on harmony by none other than Ezra Pound.[1] Set in

1. *Antheil and the Treatise on Harmony* (Three Mountains Press, Paris 1924).

the form of a somewhat flippant dialogue between master and pupil, it
nevertheless managed to make some searching comments. For instance,
it pointed out that what happens *between* sounds had been neglected by
composers. This was putting, in somewhat non-musicianly language,
what was generally being questioned by musicians at this time. Debussy,
for instance, found out for himself the possibilities inherent in various
scale-formations; and this in turn led to many fruitful developments by
later French composers, particularly Messiaen.

Rubbra's approach was the same in principle. He sees the composer's
art as the use of common, ordinarily accepted sounds in an uncommon,
poetic way. This is analogous to a poet's use of words; Henry Vaughan
for instance puts together common words in an uncommon way to
describe a sunrise: *The unthrift sun shot vital gold.* Similarly Rubbra's
use of one very ordinary chord, the dominant seventh, in an unexpected
context, is shown in this example from the first *Tenebrae* setting, Op. 72
no. 1[1]:—

('The spirit indeed is ready')

So the composer, according to Rubbra, must objectify the sounds, and
thus explore the frontiers of aural experience in depth. He builds bridges
between chords, sets up relationships between tonalities, and thus by a
logical unfolding of the music, in time, he creates form. Music for
Rubbra is the tonal art. He has consistently eschewed anything resembling
radicalism, sensationalism or novelty.

By such stressing of the overriding importance of harmony and
tonality, this kind of creative thinking tends to leave out of account other
primary elements, such as rhythm, and thematic development. But
Rubbra built up gradually on experiences gained during his formative
years. He was first a private pupil of Cyril Scott; later, at Reading
University and at the Royal College of Music, he was under Gustav
Holst. Both these were diatonic composers, both showed an exotic,
Eastern influence, but Scott was freer in his use of chromaticism. Another
highly fruitful study for Rubbra was that of Elizabethan counterpoint

1. Another use of this chord, and Rubbra's fondness for it in the Fourth Symphony, is
noticed by W. Mellers in *Studies in Contemporary Music.*

under the scholar-musician, R. O. Morris.[1] There is no composer today
who makes more direct application of the techniques of sixteenth century
counterpoint than Rubbra; he also shares something of the romantic
spirit, and the theological fervour of the sixteenth century.

His output is large; over a hundred and thirty works with Opus
numbers. One of the earliest (1925) was the little carol *Dormi Jesu*[2]. Its
style is the modal one of the period, established by Vaughan Williams
and Holst, and it is very similar to Holst's cradle-song *Lullay my liking*,
written a few years earlier.

In the early 30's Rubbra moved gradually out of his formative stage
into a more personal harmonic style, with such a work as the *First Violin
Sonata*, Op. 31. The foundation of this work is a harmonic one, though it
contains some counterpoint. Thereafter the balance became tilted towards
counterpoint, starting with the next work, the *Four Mediaeval Latin
Lyrics*, Op. 32, for baritone and string orchestra.

The instrumental works that followed were the *First String Quartet*,
Op. 35, and the *Sinfonia Concertante*, Op. 38, for piano and orchestra.
This latter was written in 1934, just after Holst died, and was taken from
a discarded piano concerto; both works contain traces of an earlier
exoticism, which was partly innate, partly inherited from Holst and
Cyril Scott. The *saltarello* in the *Sinfonia Concertante* is an example of
this.

Thus Rubbra gradually enlarged the range and size of his structures,
with each work slightly larger than the one before. The logical result was
the *First Symphony* (1935)[3], which built up a symphonic design of
forceful, extrovert intensity. He followed this almost immediately with
the *Second Symphony*, which was more austere, primarily contrapuntal.
The *Third Symphony* (1938) developed the lyrical content, while the
Fourth Symphony (1941) was more concerned with harmony, less with
counterpoint. Thus in his symphonic works up to the war an evolution
can be traced. Each succeeding symphony shows a contrast of reaction
to the previous one, as the composer feels his way towards that structure
which is logical for his idiom. Of these four symphonies it is the third,
first heard at a Hallé concert in Manchester in December 1940, which
chiefly clarifies Rubbra's symphonic technique up to the war. The
concern of the composer to write long, melodic lines, with plentiful use
of sequence, canon and ostinato, and a Brahmsian breadth of phrase,

1. His *Contrapuntal Technique in the 16th Century* (1922) and *Foundations of Practical
Harmony and Counterpoint* (1925) are standard.
2. *Oxford Book of Carols* No. 175.
3. 1935 was something of an *annus mirabilis* of British symphonies; Bax's third, Walton's
first, Vaughan Williams' fourth.

makes for a somewhat static quality in the harmony, which is mainly triadic. The material of each movement is homogeneous, and the scherzo theme was unconsciously derived from the rhythm of the first movement.

As far as rhythm is concerned, this is derived from the crossing of contrapuntal parts; it is the rhythm that results from the absence of a bar-line, and it is thus not immediately obvious.

The outbreak of war interrupted Rubbra's composition and he served in the army. However, the war years were not entirely without music for him, as he was able to form a trio with himself as pianist, William Pleeth (cello) and Joshua Glazier (violin)[1], and to tour camps giving concerts. Their repertoire was largely classical; Haydn, Mozart and Beethoven. This work started in 1942. Rubbra has always been a highly accomplished pianist, though, unlike Reizenstein, his playing took second place to his composition. He was active in the 30's as a pianist, and played a wide range of music, some of it unfamiliar, and largely for radio recitals. His trio achieved such success with the wartime concerts that it continued afterwards, and not until 1956 did pressure of other engagements compel Rubbra to give it up. Immediately after the war another opportunity came his way when the first Professor of the newly-formed Music Faculty at Oxford, J. A. Westrup, invited him to join the academic staff of that university. He remained a member of it from 1947 until 1968, and thereafter he continued teaching at the Guildhall School of Music in London, which he had first joined in 1961.

Immediately after the war Rubbra picked up the broken thread of his composition, with a Mass for Canterbury Cathedral, the *Missa Cantuariensis*, Op. 59; also the G minor *Cello Sonata*, Op. 60, written for William Pleeth, for whom he had already composed the *Soliloquy* for 'Cello and Strings, Op. 57. The Sonata continues where the *Third Symphony* had left off; it is an intensely lyrical work, and, like the symphony, finishes with a Theme and Variations, and Fugue. But in the meantime he had worked extensively with his trio, and the beneficial effects of this chamber music experience resulted in several improvements; much greater lightness of texture, and greater thematic and rhythmic variety. Moreover, the reduction from four movements to three leads to greater tautness; and it is far less harmonically static. This process continues with the *Fifth Symphony* (1949), which differs from its predecessors chiefly in its chamber music texture. This was followed the next year by the only work written for his trio, the *Trio in one movement*, Op. 68.

Two symphonies and two concertos mark his orchestral works of the

---

1. Later Glazier's place was taken first by Norbert Brainin, then by Erich Gruenberg.

50's; the *Sixth Symphony* (1954), and the *Seventh Symphony*[1] (1957); the *Viola Concerto* (1954), and the *Piano Concerto* (1958).

The *Viola Concerto* is an elegiac work, written for William Primrose; it is sometimes known as the 'musical necklace' (*collana musicale*) after the composer's title of the third movement; and by the time he came to write the *Sixth Symphony* the following year, Rubbra had worked out the chamber music influence. The symphony is unusual in that the movement which he wrote first, finished with such finality that it could only be placed at the end; so the composer had to work backwards. He took the first four notes of the Cor Anglais solo (E-F-A-B), with which the movement begins, and used them as a motivic germ for the other three movements; thus E-F-A open the first movement, E-A (an open fifth on the horns) open the slow (*canto*) second movement, and E-F begin the scherzo. In the next symphony, the seventh, Rubbra developed greater freedom and more proliferation of ideas.

Other instrumental works include three *Violin Sonatas*, three *String Quartets*, and various smaller pieces; some with solo voice, such as the *Three Psalms* for contralto and piano (1947), or *The Jade Mountain* for high voice and harp (1963). In these five songs from the Chinese, Rubbra achieved a miniature structure, and a highly characteristic intimacy of expression. The harp attracted him, and the *Pezzo Ostinato* for solo harp (1959) was an essay in an Eastern mode of thought; the music revolves, with ametrical rhythms, round Raga-like material, like an Indian improvisation. The pedals, once fixed, remain unaltered throughout the piece.

Apart from a few folk-song settings, far the greater part of Rubbra's choral output is of a religious nature. This, and the modal style, coupled with the instinct for polyphonic growth, give it a mediaeval flavour. He also has a marked preference for minor tonalities, even in short part-songs, such as Christopher Hassall's *Salutation*, Op. 82[2], or the Elizabethan-derived *Madrigals*, Op. 51 and 52.

His religious choral music includes motets, anthems, cantatas, and ranges from show pieces of an exuberant and extrovert nature, such as the *Festival Te Deum*, written for the Festival of Britain, or *Festival Gloria*, Op. 94, to works of a practical, liturgical nature, such as the *Magnificat and Nunc Dimittis* in A flat, or the 3-part *Mass*, Op. 98; or works for various specific functions, often of not great difficulty, such as the *Three Motets*, Op. 76, or the two *Suites* for voices and orchestra, Op. 122 and 129.

1. Of which Panufnik conducted the first performance at a Birmingham concert on 1st October, 1957 (See p. 191).
2. Included in *A Garland for the Queen*, to mark the Coronation of 1953.

The same pattern of evolution is shown in the choral as in the symphonic works. The early ones are shorter, confined to one idea; the later ones are more expansive. An outstanding example of a symphonic structure applied to an unaccompanied choral work is the motet for soprano and baritone soli and double choir, *Lauda Sion*, Op. 110 (1960/61). The Latin text is a hymn of praise by St. Thomas Aquinas, and a rondo structure gives the work strength and cohesion. Rubbra has never surpassed this, which was his largest *a capella* work up to that point, and whose merits can be viewed from many different angles: it is a major work of grandeur and dignity; the mood of the text, which is an all-embracing poem of great power, is entirely integrated with the thematic material; and the growth and development of each run parallel. The polyphonic writing is masterly, and considerably more original than the use of a triadic idiom sometimes implies. The counterpoint is in places a chordal counterpoint; for instance, at the words 'Sub utraque specie'[1] the canon between two 3-part chords results in a harmonic saturation, which is a unique characteristic of Rubbra's style. This recalls the opening of *The Song of the Soul*, where a similar effect is achieved orchestrally, by juxtaposed triads. The harmony arises naturally and majestically from the counterpoint in a way that has few parallels in contemporary music. He followed this in 1962 with another large festive (as distinct from liturgical) piece for unaccompanied 8-part choir, the *Te Deum*, Op. 115, which continues the same development as *Lauda Sion*. But the motet marks a summit of achievement; its successor will probably not come until the 9th Symphony.[2]

Meanwhile his next choral works were suites with orchestral accompaniment. He had already written[3] the highly characteristic *Song of the Soul*, Op. 78, which is a slow but short setting of words by St. John of the Cross, translated by Roy Campbell, 'Oh Flamma de amor viva': the full title is 'Song of the Soul in intimate communication and union with the love of God'. And just before *Lauda Sion* he had written the *Cantata di Camera*, Op. 111 (*Crucifixus pro nobis*), whose strange instrumentation was stipulated by the New York Church for which it was written.

The first choral suite, *Inscape*, Op. 122, is a setting of Gerard Manley Hopkins, and falls into four sections with a 'Gloria' epilogue. The second suite, *In die et nocte canticum*, Op. 129, is a Latin setting of early Christian texts, and falls into three sections, with an orchestral prologue ('Aubade') and epilogue ('Nocturne').

But it is in works for unaccompanied choir that Rubbra achieves his

1. p. 27/28 Lengnick Edition.
2. See p. 79.
3. For Paul Steinitz and the London Bach Society, in 1953.

most characteristic results; the religious fervour, the free movement of modal tonality, the growth of harmony from the contrapuntal lines, the full development of his polyphonic style. *Lauda Sion* is his most characteristic major *a capella* work; the equivalent smaller works are the nine short *Tenebrae* settings, Op. 72, which are a masterly concentration of the *a capella* style. The parts move mainly homophonically in block chords, in a way which is reminiscent of the sombre chord-spacing of Monteverdi, as this, Rubbra feels, is most aptly suited to the solemnity of Holy Week. The first three *Tenebrae* settings, which constitute the First Nocturne, Op. 72, nos. 1–3, were written in 1954; the remaining six, the Second and Third Nocturnes, Op. 72, nos. 4–9, followed later, in 1963, after *Lauda Sion*, and about the same time as the *Te Deum*. Again, the use of chordal canon occurs, in no. 4 (*amicus meus*). There is little independent contrapuntal movement. Rubbra has provided a striking contemporary illustration of a traditional theme.

His idiom is a tonal one, and has always been consistently so. Though he has never consciously tried to imitate other composers, he was in his formative years immersed in the piano works of Debussy, which he played; so he had a thorough insight into Debussy's individual harmonic style. Debussy had been the first composer of undisputed stature to differentiate between key and tonality. He could use the chord of C major without necessarily involving the key of C major; but he also derived strength and colour from the forces at work in the French artistic tradition as a whole, which defined, and gave direction to, his activity.

Although Rubbra worked within a different tradition, with different forces at work, and although his solution is different, nevertheless the same harmonic principles may be seen in the work of both composers. Rubbra works from a tonal centre, which differs from a key-centre in that it does not imply or include all the other notes of the key; he develops instead a harmonic fluidity, which may develop greater or less saturation, according to the number of notes specifically sounding round any given tonal centre. Nowhere does he reach greater mastery of this extremely elusive technique than in the *Eight Symphony*, Op. 132, which is the culminating point of his instrumental works, corresponding to *Lauda Sion* among the choral works.

The work was written in 1966–67[1], ten years after the *Seventh Symphony*, and in it the goals that he has set of breadth of phrase, melodic continuity, harmonic fluidity and structural strength, are achieved to a greater extent than in any previous symphony. The sequences are less

---

1. MS dated 28th December 1967.

exact, the sonorities are more original, while the expansive eloquence of
the slow third movement is unsurpassed. In it Rubbra adopts a new
approach to texture, in that intervals are made the decisive protagonists
in the themes throughout the work. He dispenses with key signatures
for the first time. The first subject, at the opening of the first movement,
is made of interlocking fourths, while the second subject is made up of
thirds. Both come together at [4]—6

Ex.20

where the characteristic 2-part chordal counterpoint leads to harmonic
fluidity round the tonal centre of B.

The material of the scherzo second movement is made up of thirds,
and it gathers up themes as it goes along, like a snowball. The slow
third movement is the finale, and is built round the second and sixth
combined. The symphony thus includes all the intervals, as these two
(the second and the sixth) together make the seventh, as the opening of
the finale shows.

Ex.21

Here Rubbra achieves that poise between harmony and counterpoint
that had sometimes eluded him in earlier works. One instance of this
among many is the violin figure at [56], which is a retrograde version, in

diminution, of the viola and cello part in the previous three bars. This little figure reappears as a flute solo at the very end of the symphony.

Thus both his symphonic and his choral output have reached their respective culminating points. The composer's intention is now to unite them, and write a symphony with voices: his projected *Ninth Symphony*, which is still only at the imagined stage, is visualised as a choral symphony, a *Sinfonia Sacra* on the theme of the Resurrection. In such a concept, Rubbra's symphonic and choral styles, coupled with his strong Christian convictions, will have come full circle.

5   Arnold Cooke

Arnold Cooke is a contemporary of Rawsthorne and Tippett; yet both his music and his career have taken a very different path from either of these two. His music lacks the complexity, to say nothing of the mytho-logical fervour, of Tippett; nor does it exploit the possibilities of extended tonality, as Rawsthorne's does; instead, a simple approach to tonality, inherited from a conventional English background, is overlaid with a certain piquancy, and an unfailing craftsmanship derived from his teacher Hindemith. Cooke is not a stylistic originator; indeed his style is the result of his following where others have led—which would appear to make him, in the opinion of one writer, a bad artist[1]; and certainly, if style were everything, then Cooke would probably have to give place to more original minds than his. But if style is one aspect of creativity, artistic purpose is another, equally important. To whom does the composer direct his music? Cooke's lack of executive ability (though he played the cello at an early age) denies to his music that virtuoso quality which characterises the work of his master Hindemith, or his fellow-student, Reizenstein; the music is, generally speaking, simple, easy to play, accessible; in a word, *Gebrauchsmusik*.

In an article[2] Cooke has described the underlying intentions behind Hindemith's conception of *Gebrauchsmusik*. If we read between the lines, he is describing his own intention as a composer. The literal translation, 'Utility Music', gives a very misleading impression. Hindemith originally intended the term to apply to music written for a specific purpose, particularly music for amateurs and schools. He first suggested the term in a discussion at a festival in the late 20's, and immediately the word was taken up; it became a *Schlagwort*, a slogan. Everybody was suddenly writing *Gebrauchsmusik*; school and amateur music became the fashion, and the word, *mutatis mutandis*, was attached to Hindemith as

1. Hans Keller, writing in *Music Survey* Autumn 1949 (Vol. II No. 2), produces this characteristic aphorism: 'The bad artist is created by his time. The mediocre creates for his time. The better artist creates for posterity. The great creates posterity.'
2. *Music Survey* 1949, Vol II No. 1.

if it applied to all his music. In one sense, everything written clearly has some purpose in mind; and though Cooke reserves the term *Gebrauchsmusik* for those works written for special purposes—not only music for schools and amateurs, but music for theatre, films, radio, and other occasional music—he considers that all his scores should meet the fundamental requirement of being serviceable to musicians in general.

With the growth of complexity and abstruseness in composition, a large amount of contemporary music is beyond the scope of the musician of average ability, whether in the school, the home or the church; a cleavage has developed between music which is capable of being rehearsed and played by reasonably talented amateurs, and music which was conceived to be rehearsed and performed by professionals on the concert platform. What school orchestral society would, or could, consider Schoenberg's Violin Concerto for its end-of-term concert? What local festival would invite its young competitors to compete in playing one of Stockhausen's Klavierstücke? Or what local operatic society would attempt Berg's *Wozzeck*?

It is highly probable that an absence of any clear thought on this dichotomy of interest in contemporary music has lain at the root of a considerable number of still-born developments, certainly in the contemporary English musical tradition, and probably in others as well. The English genius for compromise, in a misguided attempt to please everybody, is particularly obvious in the larger and more official festivals. If you attempt without discrimination to mix the professional and the amateur, you satisfy neither; new wine has a way of bursting old bottles.

So, far from *Gebrauchsmusik* being in some way inferior to concert music, it is in reality complementary and essential to it. The clear recognition and acceptance of a limitation, whether musical or social, is the breath of life to the true artist, and his work depends for its validity on a complete absence of pretence on each side. The purpose of *Gebrauchsmusik* is not that the composer should 'write down' for the benefit of less-gifted performers. On the contrary, if his idiom has integrity it should not need to be changed—merely simplified. By the same token, the function and achievement of *Gebrauchsmusik* is different from concert music—neither better nor worse, but simply different. Music that invites participation by musicians of not more than moderate ability has a different purpose, and therefore its result will be different, from music which presupposes expert or virtuoso performance.

The provision of *Gebrauchsmusik* has been the concern of many British composers. Anyone who has ever written an oratorio or cantata for performance by an amateur choir has experienced something of what it means. He treats the technical or emotional limitations of his performers in just the same positive, artistic way as he deals with the limitations of range and timbre of the orchestral instruments. The best-known example today is that of Britten, whose numerous works written for children and less experienced performers form such a large proportion of his output.[1]

Cooke's desire for 'serviceable' music is largely the product of the Cambridge environment from which he set out. He has always intended that his musical ideas should be easily and readily accessible, whether to the listener or to the performer. These ideas are almost invariably tonal, often diatonic; only once has he written a serial work, Op. 65 *Theme and Variations* for recorder solo. Most of his eighty-odd compositions were written with specific performers in mind, which undoubtedly accounts for his unfailing sense of what is possible.

He was born near Bradford in Yorkshire in 1906, and after a conventional public school education (Repton), he went to Cambridge to study music (1925–1929). The musical environment of Cambridge at this time was mainly choral and operatic; instrumental music was more amateur and secondary. Boris Ord at King's College was re-discovering the great wealth of Tudor polyphony, and in his hands the King's Chapel choir reached a state of professional excellence, apt for sixteenth century polyphony; it became the equivalent, for choral *a capella* singing, of an orchestra for the symphonic repertoire. This was something quite new in English music, and was to have far-reaching results later;[2] Ord's successor in 1954 was David Willcocks.

The rediscovery of opera at Cambridge was due mainly to Dennis Arundell,[3] and the Professor of Music, Edward J. Dent, who in addition to being a fine scholar[4] had a wider, more international outlook than most other musicians in the country at the time. As President of the I.S.C.M. he travelled widely in Europe, and was both attentive and sympathetic to events taking place there. He regularly introduced the new works of the day, such as Honegger's *King David* or Kodaly's *Psalmus Hungaricus*. The more academic and local aspect of Cambridge music was in the hands of Cyril Rootham, while invaluable practical experience of performing and hearing music, largely chamber music, was provided by the Thursday Club.[5]

1. See p. 213.
2. See p. 13/14.
3. Handel's *Semele* and Purcell's *King Arthur* were two of his many productions.
4. His translations of Mozart's operas are standard.
5. This club was originally the Informal Music Club, started in about 1920 by Mrs. Hackforth, whose husband was a classics don at Selwyn College. Informal concerts were held on Wednesdays at the Masonic Hall during the inter-war period. After the war they have been held fortnightly on Thursdays at the University Music School in Downing Place, with occasional larger concerts in the Guildhall. The 1969/70 season was the 50th anniversary.

Thus Cooke found plenty of opportunity for music-making in numerous chamber music ensembles. Meanwhile, the effective, officially approved background of English music, against which all this activity took place, was provided by Vaughan Williams, Elgar and Delius.

It was due to Dent that Cooke went to study at the Berlin Hochschule under Hindemith. Another Cambridge musician, Walter Leigh (also a pupil of Dent), had recently done the same, though English pupils were a rarity in Hindemith's class.[1] While in Berlin (1929–1932) Cooke met a fellow-pupil, Franz Reizenstein, who was later to perform several of his works.

The international flavour of Berlin during the years of the Weimar Republic ensured for Cooke's music a fresh dimension, in total contrast to the academic and provincial English environment from which he had sprung, and to which he was shortly to return.

One of Hindemith's earliest and most fundamental lessons was the importance of 2-part writing. He would take a song of Brahms, and show how just the melodic line and the bass line fitted in 2-part counterpoint; no amount of detail in the inner parts could disguise or conceal the inadequacy that resulted if these fundamental parts were not well constructed. Hindemith's exercises in counterpoint, which were freely chromatic, not strict in the old academic sense, started in two parts, then progressed to three, then more. This strictness of training and cleanness of line, particularly in 2-part writing[2], is one of the chief characteristics of Cooke's style.

Also, certain of his harmonic and melodic progressions, as well as theories of structure, were directly inherited from Hindemith, particularly in his early works; for instance in Op. 1 (1931), which was originally an octet for four wind and four stringed instruments. The only other work that survives from his student days in Berlin is the *Harp Quintet*, Op. 2, which was played at the London Contemporary Music Centre in November 1932 by Maria Korchinska.

Returning to Cambridge in 1932, Cooke worked for a short time at the Cambridge Festival Theatre, where he succeeded Walter Leigh. The following year he was appointed, on Dent's recommendation, to the staff of the Manchester College of Music, and he taught at that institution until 1938, when he moved to London.[3] After a period of naval service in the war, he joined the staff of Trinity College of Music in London, where he has remained ever since.

His compositions up to the war show a gradual development of style.

1. The Australian Stanley Bate was another.
2. Described by Hindemith in *The Craft of Musical Composition*.
3. His successor was Richard Hall. See p. 230.

Early pieces, such as the *First String Quartet*, are clearly influenced by Hindemith; after the war a more mature style appears, notably in the *First Symphony*. The first piece of substance which achieved success was the *Sonato for two pianos, Op. 8*. This work, though influenced by the composer's hearing Stravinsky's Concerto for two pianos, is nevertheless quite individual and has a mature sureness of touch as well as contrapuntal mastery. The piece was suggested by Adolph Hallis, a South African pianist who was active in promoting contemporary music concerts in London before the war, largely at the Wigmore Hall. The two players of Cooke's sonata were Hallis himself and Franz Reizenstein.[1]

Hallis also suggested that Cooke should compose a piano concerto, and this was duly written in 1940 (Op. 11); though not played until 1943, when Hallis was no longer active in London, and the soloist was Louis Kentner. This was his largest work up to that moment.

Opportunities for the performance of new works by British composers were hard to come by for an 'outsider' in the years before the war; and the years immediately following 1945 were by no means easy. It is only since about 1960 that some of the obstacles facing the composer have been at least partially removed.[2]

Of Cooke's seventy-six main compositions, fifty-seven are for chamber groups (whether instrumental or vocal) or solo instruments; sixteen are orchestral; the remaining three are essays in the accepted extended forms, and consist of one opera, *Mary Barton*, Op. 27, which has not yet been performed; one ballet, *Jabez and the Devil*, Op. 50, which was commissioned by the Royal Ballet on the suggestion of Cooke's friend Denis ApIvor, and performed at Covent Garden on 15th September 1961; its success, however, was only a qualified one; and one oratorio, Pope's *Ode on St. Cecilia's Day*, Op. 57, which was performed by Cambridge students on 20th February 1968.

Cooke's style shows most of the positive features of good chamber music writing; clean contrapuntal lines, a sense of thematic symmetry and balance. He has never experimented rhythmically, and his metres are invariably regular and constant. His acceptance of tonality has meant that he has not been beset by those formal, structural problems which automatically face the atonal, serial or *avant-garde* composer.

His chamber-music works cover most of the orchestral instruments, of which all Hindemith pupils were obliged to have at least a working knowledge. He has also written for the guitar and the recorder, while his keyboard compositions, apart from the piano, include the harpsichord and the organ. His composing for the organ places him in a minority

1. Hallis concert, March 1937, Wigmore Hall.
2. See p. 21 (footnote).

among composers: apart from amateur or student works, this is not an instrument that has attracted British composers. And while his lesser organ pieces, such as *Prelude, Aria and Finale* and *Fugal Adventures*, were requested by publishers, and fall into the category of easy *Gebrauchs-musik*, his larger works, such as the the *Fantasia*, Op. 60, or the *Toccata and Aria*, Op. 70, were commissioned by his pupil Peter Marr, and are more substantial. The *Fantasia* was written for the opening, in September 1964, of a two-manual organ, built on classical principles, at Shinfield, Berks. The built-up chords of the introduction are used in arpeggio form in the first main section, and triplets are used over long pedal notes. The middle section develops a new theme by imitation and augmentation, and allotting it to the pedals leaves the manuals free for increasingly intensified chord patterns, trio treatment, and stretto. After a return to the material of the first section, the work ends with a coda, which starts with a flourish derived from the middle section.

The *Toccata and Aria* was written for a recital at the church of St. Giles, Reading.[1] The *Toccata* uses recurring material, like a rondo, while the *Aria* is in three sections, of which the middle one develops into an *arioso* before the recapitulation; the third section is a coloured version of the first.

The positive features of his style, which make these works an important addition to the almost non-existent school of contemporary British organ music, are an ability to write contrapuntally, an ability to colour the melodic structures with a considered use of harmonic dissonance, and a feeling for the nature of the organ as it has developed in recent years in Europe and North America.

His style is based on an acceptance of classical practices, though it is not 'neo-classical' in the sense in which that term is used to describe Stravinsky or the French school of the inter-war years; that is to say Cooke does not simply take the classical formulae of harmony, melody or cadence and apply them in a new context. Two works which most fully illustrate his acceptance of classical influences are the *Sinfonietta for Eleven Instruments*, Op. 31, and the *Concerto for Small Orchestra*, Op. 48. The first of these, written in 1954 and played at a Macnaghten Concert the following year, makes use of the conventional four movements (Allegro—Scherzo, vivace—Lento—Allegro), and is scored for woodwind quartet, string quartet, trumpet and horn. Its tonality is Bb, with the inner movements in related keys.

The second work was commissioned for the Bath Festival 1960, and played on 20th May that year. The tonality is E flat and the three movements, appropriate for such a concerto, are *Allegro Vivace—Andante—*

1. See *The Organ*, January 1967.

G

Molto Allegro. The writing for each group of instruments brings out its characteristics in a work whose mood is light and straightforward; it is competent, serviceable music.

If Cooke's work does not call for the deepest emotional response, or excite the profoundest involvement by the listener, it rarely, if ever, falls below a serviceable level of competence. As with all thematic styles, the listener's attention can hardly avoid focussing on the themes themselves, since they sustain the weight of the musical argument. Cooke's themes are similar to those of many other composers who have pursued a traditional ideal, whether neo-classical or not; in his case it was an ideal handed down from Hindemith. Moreover, Cooke has never felt the necessity for changing or modifying his idiom; his ideas are in the main melodic, diatonic, and have always been consistently so. He seeks no other means of expression.

His natural medium is instrumental music, whether chamber or orchestral. Far the majority of his works, seventy-three out of seventy-six, are for standard groupings of instrumental or choral forces. Of the remaining three works—one ballet, one oratorio, one opera—the largest and most ambitious by far is the opera *Mary Barton*, op. 27.

He began it as a result of a competition sponsored by the Arts Council in 1949; and though Cooke was unsuccessful in obtaining an award, he went on to write the opera over a period of five years (1949–54), a longer time than he spent on any other of his compositions.

The libretto is by W. A. Rathkey, from the novel by Mrs. Gaskell, and the scene is set in Manchester in 1840; the industrial North at the time of the Chartist movement, before the establishment of Trade Unions. The plot concerns the effects of oppressive working conditions, labour unrest, managerial complacency.

Carson, a mill-owner, has lost his mill in a fire, which the work-people suspect was his own doing. As a result fifty men lose their jobs, and the ensuing unrest focusses round their spokesman John Barton, a Chartist leader. His daughter Mary, who looks after him, considers marriage to Harry Carson, the mill-owner's son, as this will enable her to provide for her father and his friends. Jem Wilson, a foreman mechanic, proposes to her unsuccessfully; though we soon learn that Mary's love really rests on him rather than on Harry Carson, whom she rejects.

The idle leisure of the Carson family is shown in stark contrast to the wretchedness of the work-people. Harry Carson is then confronted by Jem Wilson, who strikes him to the ground.

This personal conflict is pursued in a wider context when the Masters meet the Men in Oddfellow's Hall. When the work-people's demands are entirely rejected, and the employers leave angrily, the men draw lots to decide who shall strike a violent blow against the employers, particularly Harry Carson, who insulted the men during the meeting by drawing a sketch showing them in rags. They swear the Chartist oath of secrecy, and the scene closes with the result of the ballot unknown.

The light-hearted triviality of the Carson girls at home is interrupted by the news that their brother Harry has been shot. Carson himself immediately swears revenge. Jem Wilson is arrested for the murder, and Mary Barton in distress assumes that he killed Harry Carson for her sake. However evidence is soon produced which shows her that it was her father who committed the crime. Her dilemma is then very acute; her father is a murderer, and the man she loves is likely to be hanged for it. Jem Wilson, however, is tried and acquitted at Liverpool Assizes, and returns to Mary. John Barton is oppressed with guilt for his crime, and describes to Mary and Jem what led him to do it. He is ready to face trial, though Carson enters, still seeking vengeance. John Barton then dies, and Mary and Jem decide to emigrate to Canada to start a new life. The off-stage Chartists' chorus closes the opera.

This is an opera of contrasts, simply, sometimes naïvely, presented; good versus bad; the idle frivolities of the rich versus the agonised struggle of the poor. The plot unfolds melodramatically, so that the issues of good and bad are personified, and somewhat simplified, into 'goodies' and 'baddies', and the dramatic conclusion is so manipulated that personal involvement by the audience is superfluous. One needs only to observe the events happening; the author has fixed them all; one in particular, the death of John Barton, though no doubt convenient, is dramatically feeble, and releases most of the carefully prepared tension. But this is by no means more ridiculous or irrational a plot than that of many other operas, and certainly Cooke's libretto develops genuine dramatic momentum. The subject is topical today, and concerned with everyday matters. If we are to accept Dent's classification of opera into mythical, heroic and comic, this opera aspires to the second category. It is certainly neither mythical nor comic.

It is romantic in that Cooke provides at all times a prominent vocal line. He conceives opera as primarily something to be sung; the singers lead, not the orchestra, as Dent had advised, and his highly organised scenes are divided on classical principle into arias, ensembles, choruses and orchestral interludes. The musical contrasts between the characters are clearly defined, and folk-song material is added occasionally for particular purposes; for instance, Mary's nostalgic song in Act I includes the nursery rhyme 'Polly put the kettle on', to recall an un-recallable childhood before her mother died; also the Chartists' hymn, 'May the Rose of England never blow'. Moreover, the mill fire with which the opera opens was suggested by memories of such an event which the composer saw as a boy near Batley in Yorkshire. Cooke's particular tonal style is capable of great flexibility. It has a directness, a simplicity which admirably matches the clear line of the story. The opera has not yet been performed.

The development
of a tradition

6 Humphrey Searle

Humphrey Searle's music is coloured, and limited, by his creative alignment with the 12-note style of Schoenberg. His was a conscious and deliberate choice. It is only partly true to say that his work is derivative from his Viennese models; but it is more, or less successful in performance in proportion to the degree to which he has assimilated the underlying artistic purposes which motivated Schoenberg, Webern or (later) Boulez.

Born in 1915, Searle's training was conventional, and entirely within the academic English tradition. After Oxford, where he read Greats, and associated with such unexceptionable figures as Sir Isaiah Berlin and Sir Hugh Allen, he proceeded to the Royal College of Music in London, where he studied, somewhat hesitantly, with John Ireland. In trying to discover a sense of artistic discipline, his attention was drawn in several directions; towards Paris, for instance, where Nadia Boulanger was attracting large numbers of distinguished and shortly-to-become-distinguished pupils with her exposition of the neoclassical style. Eventually, after consulting other musicians, such as Walton, Humphrey Searle went for a six-month visit to Webern in Vienna. This gave him an insight into that composer's outlook, as well as a sense of purpose for the future. Though he has not written in the style of Webern, except for some parts of the fifth symphony, he gained an invaluable knowledge of music from the Viennese point of view, as well as an insight into Webern's technique; the importance Webern laid on every note, for instance, which is a different matter altogether from the mathematical approach adopted by some of Webern's self-styled successors.

During this formative period (1937) Searle had no doubt that the path indicated by Schoenberg was the one that music was destined to take. But the musical atmosphere in England before 1939 was, he considered, parochial. Not till after the war did any continental influence begin to be felt, though already in the 20's the Sitwell family had worked towards an internationalism of music, and away from the narrowness of the established English academic style: they associated with musicians such as Diaghilev, Busoni, Ansermet, and the English composers who chiefly felt the benefit of their patronage were Walton and Lambert. What appeared first in the 20's as frivolous antics were later to be taken for granted; the 30's, however, were a sadder period, with the shadow of fascism and war looming ever larger.

Searle was dissatisfied with the academic traditionalism that was rife in England at the time. Tradition was one thing, certainly; but one could be aware of, and even respect, tradition, without necessarily abiding by it; and the sort of Establishment attitude that was all too often the concomitant of it could practically be relied on to stifle artistic progress. Fresh air could only be admitted from outside; and although Searle was to some extent swayed by the other magnetic forces of Bartok and Stravinsky, particularly as far as rhythm and colour were concerned, it was to the Viennese school that he turned for his most constant and most fundamental guide-lines.

Returning to London from Vienna, he resumed study at the College. The war then intervened, and six years' service in the army delayed his start as a composer, though a few works date from the early 40's. He found early champions in his friend and colleague Constant Lambert, as well as the conductor Walter Goehr, both of whom performed several of his early works during the war years. Later he met René Leibowitz, the chief protagonist of the 12-note style, who taught in Paris after 1945, and who asked him for a 12-note piece. The result was the *Intermezzo for 11 instruments*, Op. 8 (1946). Various small pieces followed, until in 1949 he wrote *Gold Coast Customs*, Op. 15, for a radio performance. This was his first large-scale 12-note work. It was an ambitious setting of a poem by Edith Sitwell, for speakers, male chorus and orchestra. It was the first piece of a trilogy for speaker and orchestra; the other two works were *The Riverrun*, Op. 20 (1951), with words by James Joyce, and *The Shadow of Cain*, Op. 22 (1952), with words once again by Edith Sitwell.

Gold Coast Customs was first performed by Edith Sitwell and Constant Lambert. The basic series of it is built in alternating fourths and semitones; from it two other series are derived, by taking every third and sixth note respectively. These are used to point certain aspects of the poetry; the lyrical content for one thing, with which the poet occasionally interrupts the social satire, and the symbolic and satirically treated figure of the rich Lady Bamburgher.

In this trilogy Searle used the words to supply the inevitability of movement, and coherence of structure, that he felt to be endangered by his chosen style. However interesting the orchestral sounds might be, they did not necessarily have any sense of purposive direction. Themes and structures derived from key-relationships had been done away with; how then could the music move convincingly, and not merely consist of a succession of static sound-patterns? In this matter Searle anticipated very accurately an inherent quality of serialism that Boulez and his school were later to wrestle with.

Searle sought a solution in the use of words. Word-patterns and images supplied just that underlying movement and structure that was needed, particularly in a large-scale work. In a sense the music becomes secondary, like sound-effects; Edith Sitwell's verse itself possesses a musical structure—first idea, second idea, conflict, climax, coda. Moreover, words are used as much for their sound as for their meaning. Searle could hardly have chosen better for his first large-scale work.

The Riverrun is rather different. It is a setting of the final section of Joyce's *Finnegans Wake*; the underlying basis of the piece is therefore literary. Joyce introduces an element that Sitwell does not; namely, Irish humour. Anna Livia, a river, flows to her grave, the sea; the words tell the sequence of her thoughts.

After this trilogy, Searle set about the task of applying his style to two principal categories of work: large-scale orchestral pieces and opera. What mattered, he felt, was not that a composer should adopt a particular style or technique, but the use to which he put it. It must be moulded to the particular personality of the individual composer. There was nothing doctrinaire about Schoenberg, and Searle has had no hesitation in admitting a tonal influence if he wishes to, as Berg did.

Five symphonies and two piano concertos are interspersed with various smaller pieces. Of the piano concertos, the first is an early, romantic piece (Op. 5, 1944); the second is lighter in mood, blatant and percussive in style, somewhat reminiscent of Bartok, and very much influenced by Liszt, for whose music Searle has always had the greatest admiration. Indeed his study of Liszt[1] puts forward the hypothesis that Liszt in his later works anticipated the 12-note style. Naturally the influence of Liszt is most markedly felt in piano compositions, such as (apart from the concertos) the *Ballade*, Op. 10 (1947), and the *Sonata*, Op. 21 (1951), which was written for a concert on Liszt's anniversary. The *Second Piano Concerto*, Op. 27, which was first heard at Cheltenham in 1955, is not so much 12-note as freely atonal; its movements are continuous.

Of the symphonies, the first, Op. 23, was written in 1953 for Scherchen, and was cast in a traditional mould. The first movement, for instance,

1. *The Music of Liszt* (Williams and Norgate, 1954).

uses sonata form. The series is that of Webern's String Quartet, Op. 28, and consists of a succession of rising thirds, which give the harmony a tonal flavour. The four movements (*Lento-Allegro deciso*; *Adagio*; *Quasi l'stesso tempo—Allegro molto*) are played without a break.

The *Second Symphony*, Op. 33, followed five years later, in 1958. Its three movements are *Maestoso-Allegro molto*; *Lento*; *Allegro molto-Lento, solenne*. The work ends as it began, and also shows some typical Searle characteristics, such as the gradual build-up of complex chords, which are then sustained and repeated with increasing force. But the contradictions and problems inherent in constructing a large-scale form, such as a symphony, with a style such as Schoenberg's are here very apparent. A note-row is by no means the same thing as a theme; there is little distinction between primary and secondary material; and the overriding importance paid to harmony, which was Schoenberg's starting point, not only leads, curiously, to a monotonous chromaticism, which makes a poor substitute for the tonal contrast of the classical sonata form, but also makes for unrelieved heaviness of texture.

The next two symphonies followed at two-year intervals. The *Third*, Op. 36 (1960), was programmatic; the *Fourth*, Op. 38 (1962), was fragmentary, after the manner of Boulez. Both are transitional, somewhat exploratory works. It was not until the *Fifth Symphony*, Op. 43 (1964), that Searle reached that height of achievement towards which he had hitherto been tending. This piece, which was written continuously over a period of three months, June-September 1964, is in memory of Anton Webern, and its sections are illustrative of the different moments in his career. The slow opening (*Andante*) recalls Webern's youth in the Austrian mountains, and the ensuing *Allegro* follows his career up to 1914. There is a short Intermezzo, from bar 148—bar 212, to depict his war service, when he undertook a variety of jobs; this is followed by another quick section (*Allegro deciso*) for that period when he resumed work again, up till the tragic climax of his death. The symphony ends with an *Adagio* epilogue, balancing the slow introduction.

The symphony succeeds because its effect is consistent with its means. The use of pointillism makes for greater rhythmic interest as well as lighter texture, and great contrast is provided by the serial treatment of the parameters. The composer here exploits those aspects of orchestral composition, particularly tone colour, which are proper and legitimate to his serial style, and avoids those that are foreign to it. In his use of the 12-note style in orchestral composition, a comparison of Searle with Gerhard is highly instructive. Whereas Searle derived his style from his use of the 12-note technique, Gerhard imposed his style on the material, within his chosen context of serialism. Moreover Gerhard moved beyond just pitch-serialism to a much greater extent than Searle.

Searle's first ballet score, *The Great Peacock*, Op. 34a, was based on his *Variations and Finale* for ten instruments, Op. 34. Each of the ten variations that make up this work shows off one of the instruments, and was written for a particular member of the Virtuoso Chamber Ensemble. The finale brings them together. The ballet was performed at Edinburgh in 1958. Five years later, in 1963 at Wiesbaden, there appeared his next ballet, *Dualities*, modelled to some extent on Stravinsky's *Scènes de Ballet*.

But it is in opera that Searle's other main achievement lies, apart from the symphonies. His first opera, *The Diary of a Madman*, Op. 35, was presented by the indefatigable Hermann Scherchen at the 1958 Berlin Festival. It has since been staged in this country. It is in one act, after the story by the nineteenth-century Russian writer Nikolai Gogol, whose grotesque style is in keeping with the serial idiom. This opera is a grim fantasy, starting with a correspondence between two dogs, and finishing in a lunatic asylum. As with his trilogy for speaker and orchestra, Searle looks to words not just for their direct meaning, or realism, but for their atmosphere and symbolic association. The composer's underlying thought in this and ensuing works is the position of the individual in society. The effects of madness and unreality are further achieved in this work by the use of pre-recorded sound effects.

His next opera, *The Photo of the Colonel*, Op. 41, is a full-length three-act opera. The composer wrote his own libretto, after the story by Eugene Ionesco. The work was given a radio performance in this country in 1964, and a stage première in Frankfurt in June of the same year. As in the earlier opera, there is symbolism in plenty, though it is sometimes obscure. For instance we can assume, though we are not told, that the killer stands either for death, or an enemy of society, or both.

The composer's total avoidance of key, and total chromaticism, are consistent both in this work, and with the style of his previous opera. He looks to the subconscious world of the imagination as a match for the 12-note style. The words say one thing, mean another, and imply still another. The orchestral accompaniment is entirely subservient to, and independent of, the voices, and consists for the most part of colourful sound-effects, supplemented by the occasional use of pre-recorded sounds, such as breaking glass, traffic noises, water splashing, and so on. Occasionally Searle uses directly representational music, such as the distorted playing of the pub-pianist in the bistro scenes. He experiments with rhythmic speech (the architect), *portamento* (the drunkard), and a sort of wordless musical chuckle (the killer). The vocal lines are angular, after the manner of serialism, and in the case of the principal character, Bérenger, monotonously so; not till the final scene with the killer does Searle allow the 12-note series, which consists of three groups of four adjacent semitones, to be used step-wise in this crucially important vocal part.

Unfortunately this effect of long-awaited musical relaxation runs directly counter to the dramatic movement, which works up to its climax at that very moment when Bérenger meets the killer; indeed it continues its built-up momentum until after the final curtain.

His third and most ambitious opera, *Hamlet*, was first seen in Hamburg in 1968. In adapting Shakespeare, Searle has made his Hamlet into a dreamer rather than a revenge-seeker; an interpretation derived from Goethe's *Wilhelm Meister*.

Clearly everyone has his own idea of Hamlet: and equally clearly no one could turn the whole of Shakespeare's play into an opera. Searle has kept the main lines of the play, omitting a few scenes—the opening ghost scene is replaced by a prelude, with the curtain up, showing the platform—and he has also left out the scene between Polonius and Reynaldo, and the scene where Hamlet rehearses the Players. The scene where Hamlet appears to Ophelia and looks at her for a long time without speaking, is shown in mime, rather than being related by Ophelia; and the scene where Hamlet replaces the King's letter to England, carried by Rosencrantz and Guildenstern, with one of his own, is also shown on stage and becomes part of the scene in which Hamlet encounters Fortinbras' army. Otherwise Shakespeare's scenes remain as they are, though of course much reduced in length.

Searle does not see Hamlet as mad: he pretends to be mad to deceive Polonius and the King, and he is liable to fits of ungovernable rage, as in the 'nunnery' scene and the scene where he leaps into Ophelia's grave and struggles with Laertes. He ranges widely in mood, for instance from the elation of 'The play's the thing' to his next appearance with 'To be or not to be', where he is clearly contemplating suicide, even though he knows that the play is to be put on before the King. And from this mood he turns to the sudden fury of the 'nunnery' scene with Ophelia: Searle has followed Dover Wilson's suggestion that in the previous scene Hamlet has overheard the King's plot to set Ophelia at him while the King and Polonius watch the encounter, and this explains his rage against Ophelia. A modern psychologist might call Hamlet cyclothymic.

Searle sees Polonius not just as a tiresome old fool but as a dangerous man, dangerous because stupid and wholly devoted to the King's cause. Similarly he feels that Ophelia should be shown with as much character as possible, and she gradually grows in dramatic power through 'O what a noble mind is here o'erthrown' to the mad scene, in which she is not just the 'airy-fairy' mad girl of some productions but is attacking the other characters, particularly the King and Queen, in revenge for the loss of her father and of Hamlet's love. Rosencrantz and Guildenstern again are not just comic characters: Hamlet is genuinely pleased to see them at first, and only turns against them when he realizes that they, like Ophelia, are being used by the King.

The music is based on a single note-row, which was suggested by the setting of 'To be or not to be'. From this, several themes are derived and associated with the different characters: Hamlet has at least two, as well as a figure on the brass which appears in his moments of rage. The Queen also has two themes, one representing how she sees herself, and the inversion of this which shows how Hamlet sees her, and is connected with the ideas of lechery, incest and 'country matters'. Hamlet's and the Queen's themes appear in the Prelude: the King's theme first appears at the beginning of the opening Court scene on the bass clarinet, and Laertes' and Polonius' themes are heard soon afterwards. Ophelia's theme first appears on the oboe at the beginning of her scene with Laertes: Horatio's theme is heard on the violas in the previous scene. It bears some resemblance to the Fortinbras theme, though the latter is of course of a more military character. In Ophelia's mad scene Searle has not given her roulades and cadenzas but music more in the style of folksongs in a modern idiom, which is more suitable to the words. He has set the text in English, but it has been possible to adapt Schlegel's well-known translation to the music without too many changes. The language of the Play Scene, and also of the First Player's speech in Act I, was archaic for Shakespeare's time, and therefore he has written the music for these scenes in a late romantic idiom which is different from that of the rest of the music. In general the orchestration is restrained, with occasional outbursts, and there is little doubling. Hamlet's four chief monologues are each treated in a different way: 'O that this too too solid flesh would melt' is an outburst against the King and Queen when Hamlet is left alone for the first time; 'O what a rogue and peasant slave am I' takes the form of a triple crescendo; 'To be or not to be' is naturally mostly quiet; while 'How all occasions do inform against me' has a more military atmosphere, with Fortinbras' troops passing in the background. There are some moments of parody, as in the Osric scene, and when Hamlet addresses Yorick's skull we hear the faint music of parties long ago.

Searle was, with Elisabeth Lutyens, the first British composer to put into effect the 12-note teaching of the Viennese school. In his work we see clearly the limitations of that school; particularly the limitations of form and structure. He has never moved far beyond the serialisation of pitch that Schoenberg put forward; other elements, such as rhythm, remain very simple in Searle's music; he has certainly never been a follower of Boulez or the later Cologne School, who would say that the style of pitch-serialism is now outmoded. Such is the price of fashion.

Variations of theme and tonality, which the classical composers practised, is replaced in 12-note music by variation of texture, colour, instrumentation. It is in the smaller works, where the possibilities of variety are comparatively limited, that the 12-note composer is starkly confronted with the irreducible raw materials of his art, which admit of no short cuts or gimmicks. A characteristic example of a smaller work is the *Three Songs of Jocelyn Brooke*, Op. 25, for voice and piano. These songs are atonal, not serial, and the melodic line has all the appearance of a theme except the melodic content; this is a deficiency which no amount of manipulation can disguise. Instead of the richness of the rejected tonal idiom, with its multiplicity of devices for effect and contrast, Searle substitutes the grey, anonymous tones of the standard European composer of the 50's. This feature is not so obvious (though it still exists) in the arrangement of the songs with Chamber Ensemble; nor in other smaller works, such as *Oxus*, Op. 47, which is a setting of Matthew Arnold's poem, for voice and orchestra. In this piece the semitonal groups which make up the series are given the extra dimension of orchestral colour, and appear as build-up chords, or clusters, at varying dynamic levels. But the fundamental vocal lines are remarkably similar between the two sets of songs. They are typical of the orthodox 12-note style, and, not surprisingly, contain several points in common

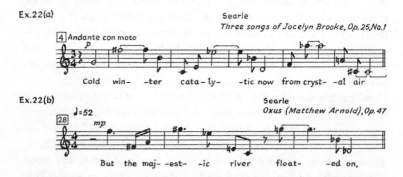

Ex.22(a)

Searle
Three songs of Jocelyn Brooke, Op. 25, No.1

Cold   win-   -ter   cata-ly-   -tic now   from cryst-   -al air

Ex.22(b)

Searle
Oxus (Matthew Arnold), Op. 47

But   the maj-   -est-   -ic   river   float-   -ed on,

When he abandons the strict path of orthodoxy, and admits the warmth, colour and contrast of tonality, Searle reaches the highest level of artistry in small-scale compositions. An example of such a work is *The Canticle of the Rose*, Op. 46, a setting for unaccompanied mixed chorus of the poem by Edith Sitwell, and written in memory of that poet, to whom he owed so much. Edith Sitwell wrote *The Canticle of the Rose* when she read that vegetation was beginning to grow at Hiroshima[1].

Apart from his composition, Searle has been extremely active. Since 1965 he has taught at the Royal College of Music, and numbers several promising composers among his pupils. He has been a prolific writer; apart from writing three books, he has translated several more, and contributed articles to Grove's Dictionary on Schoenberg. Webern and Liszt. He benefited to some extent from the swing in fashion in the early 60's, and a number of his works have had radio performance in mind. The theme of *the individual in society*, which runs through all the operas, extends also to his latest work, a setting of Blake's *Jerusalem*; a prophetic vision of the ideal society, written during the industrial revolution. Searle has attempted to apply the 12-note style to every category of piece, large or small; and also, as Schoenberg did, to bring his composition into a wider context of human experience than a purely musical one.

1. Edith Sitwell *Selected letters*, p. 154.

7 Denis ApIvor

Denis ApIvor's work provides a striking and dramatic contrast to that
of Walton. Like him he began his musical studies as a chorister; like him
he began to compose at an early age; like him he benefitted greatly from
his friendship with Edward Clark and Constant Lambert. But there the
similarities abruptly end. Whereas Walton's style was gradually evolved,
many-sided, and not to be swayed by the winds of fashion, ApIvor
responded readily and radically to the trends of the moment; also to the
social and political atmosphere. First he responded to the 12-note style
in the 50's, then to post-Webern serialism in the 60's. But Fashion's
reward to her most obedient servant has been, significantly, both fickle
and perverse; for whereas Walton's music is internationally renowned,
and his popularity apparently unassailable, Denis ApIvor's name is
scarcely known, even in this country, and his music is almost totally
ignored.

He was born in Eire in 1916, and after starting as a chorister at Christ
Church, Oxford, he went to Hereford Cathedral School, where his
father was chaplain. His first musical experiences were provided by the
choral tradition of the Three Choirs Festival; the instruments he
studied were the organ and the clarinet. In 1935 he entered London
University as a medical student, but serious composition study, first
under Patrick Hadley[1], later under Alan Rawsthorne, caused him to
abandon medicine. He suffered a serious set-back, however, in his
development as a composer with the outbreak of war in 1939; for the
next six years both the study and the performance of music were impossible, though he did start an opera libretto; and this, just at a decisive
moment in his formative phase, was a most serious handicap to him.

His first compositions were songs, in the chromatic/diatonic style of
Warlock and Van Dieren. ApIvor is thus practically the only successor

1. Later Professor of Music at Cambridge.

to that remarkable group of musicians of the inter-war years, whose activity was so intense yet whose influence has proved so far so surprisingly slight. Their spokesman was the critic Cecil Gray, who not only introduced ApIvor to Constant Lambert, which led directly to his composing ballets for Covent Garden, but also helped him financially. He was also helped by Edward Clark, who was the pioneer of contemporary music at the administrative level, and was President of the I.S.C.M. Through Clark he became interested in serialism.

ApIvor's Op. 1, *Chaucer Songs* (1936) (dedicated to the memory of Van Dieren, who died the previous year) and Op. 2, *Alas parting*—five Elizabethan songs (1937), are scored for voice and string quartet, after the manner of their period.

His early pre-war works reach their highest point in Op. 5, *The Hollow Men* (1939), a cantata to words by T. S. Eliot, for baritone solo, male voice chorus and orchestra. Its five highly condensed, colourful sections betray an originality of outlook in the twenty-three-year-old composer comparable with Walton's *Façade*. It was not performed, however, until 1950, when Constant Lambert conducted a radio performance[1]. ApIvor introduces a high-pitched, nasal form of speech, while the harmony, basically diatonic, is coloured by the use of the interval of the second, and by the use of open fifths at the opening. The mood is both sad and serious, reflecting its period, with satirical echoes of an earlier jollity reminiscent of Kurt Weill. The very opening, for muted trumpet, is a twisted version of 'Here we go round the mulberry bush'; the second section ('Eyes I dare not meet') is in the spirit of the Blues, based on sequences of sevenths; this texture also provides the background for the traditional chorale, *Ein' Feste Burg*, played on three trombones (at bar 231); the words however are anything but Lutheran:

> *Here we go round the prickly pear*
> *Prickly pear, prickly pear.*
> *Here we go round the prickly pear*
> *At five o'clock in the morning.*

ApIvor thus anticipates by some thirty years the use of children's rhymes in an unexpected context by some of today's *avant-garde*. The choice of T. S. Eliot's words was also remarkable; surprisingly few composers have been drawn to this most prophetic of poets; ApIvor was to return to him again, in *Children's Songs*, Op. 11, and *Landscapes*,

---

1. On 21st February 1950, when it created something of a sensation. In the same concert Lambert also included Gerhard's Ballet Suite *Pandora*.

Op. 15. Indeed he was the only composer in the 30's to be drawn to these words, which finish with the familiar

> *This is the way the world ends*
> *Not with a bang but a whimper.*

He resumed composition after the war with two chamber works; the *Violin Sonata*, Op. 6, which was played at an I.S.C.M. concert in London the following year (1946), and the *Concertante* for clarinet, piano and percussion, written for Frederick Thurston, and played several times, including another I.S.C.M. concert in 1951. It was later orchestrated in the form of a *Clarinet Concerto*. During these years he embarked on the first of the stage works that form so far the greater part of his output; this was a light, neo-classical 'opera buffa', with a libretto by the composer taken from the play by Oliver Goldsmith, *She Stoops to Conquer* (Op. 12). It was written over four years (1943–47), and ApIvor was thus reflecting the trend of which Stravinsky was the best known pace-setter in his *The Rake's Progress*. But the work had no performance in mind, and has not yet been produced.

The creative impulse that triggered it off was a production of Donizetti's *Don Pasquale* at the Cambridge Theatre. Van Dieren had pointed out[1] how little-known was Donizetti's wit; and it so happened that ApIvor was concerned at this time with the possibilities of comic opera, and somewhat disenchanted with the style and operatic conventions of most contemporary works, such as *Wozzeck* or *Doktor Faust*. So, along with many another composer, he became a pasticheur; he tried to recapture the Donizetti mood, and the fast pace which is essential to it. This mood appears again later in the finale of the *First Symphony*, in spite of the 12-note style of that work; also another example of ApIvor's interest in Donizetti is his scoring of some of that composer's pieces, under the title *Veneziana* (1953). In the case of his first opera, it appeared to ApIvor that the atmosphere of lightness and gaiety, for which he was aiming, was ready-made in Goldsmith's eighteenth-century story.

This opera was followed by the *Piano Concerto*, Op. 13 (1948), first performed ten years later at a Promenade Concert in London. Here the first foretaste of a 12-note style appears, though very much within a diatonic context. The themes are based on 12-note rows, but their subsequent handling is diatonic/chromatic. ApIvor suggests a 12-note style, without developing it to the full; indeed, the use of twelve notes leads mainly to bitonality. This work, therefore, may be said to mark the close of ApIvor's first, formative phase as a composer.

1. In *Down among the Dead Men*, p. 115.

The second phase lasted for ten years, and the works composed during this time use a 12-note style; but tonal devices occur, such as the use of triads derived from the row, or the rotation of parts of the row to emphasize tonal possibilities. ApIvor was attracted more by Schoenberg the theorist than by Schoenberg the composer, whose works appeared to him frequently awkward, their texture opaque.

The works of this second period were heralded by the *Seven Piano Pieces*, Op. 14 (1949), which were played at a Macnaghten Concert in 1952. Apart from the *First Symphony*, Op. 22, the chief works of this period are for the stage, and culminate in the opera *Yerma*, Op. 28, finished in 1958.

But two guitar works written about this time are among the very few of ApIvor's published scores. As with Roberto Gerhard, so with ApIvor; the guitar might be said to be 'his' instrument, as apart from these works he uses it frequently elsewhere (in *Overtones* and *Crystals*, for instance), and learnt how to play the instrument, so that he knew at first hand how to write effectively for it. The *Concertino*[1] for guitar and orchestra, Op. 26 (1954), is a straightforward three-movement work, in a tonal idiom, as befits this instrument. The *Variations* for solo guitar are somewhat more complex, and call for virtuoso performance. They were written for Julian Bream,[2] who has been very largely responsible for the recent re-introduction of the guitar as a 'respectable' concert instrument in this country. *Discanti* was written for the Italian guitarist Angelo Gilardino.

Shortly before his death in 1951, Constant Lambert had suggested ApIvor's name to the Royal Opera House, with a view to a ballet commission. The result was *A Mirror for Witches*, Op. 19, which was first played at Covent Garden in 1952. At about this time ApIvor also wrote another short ballet, *The Goodman of Paris* (Le Mènagier de Paris), Op. 18, produced in 1953 at the Princes Theatre with the same choreographer, Andrée Howard. This score was composed also as a *Piano Concertino* for concert use; in the event, Andrée Howard jettisoned the dramatic content, and used the score simply as an abstract ballet, like *Symphonic Variations*. From *A Mirror for Witches* the composer also took an orchestral suite, Op. 19a.

The success of his first Covent Garden score led to several commissions by the Royal Ballet. *Blood Wedding*[3], Op. 23, followed in 1953, *Saudades*,

1. Published by Schott & Co.
2. Though not played by him.
3. The German composer Wolfgang Fortner has also set *Blood Wedding* as an opera (1959).

Op. 27, based on an old Portuguese legend, in 1955. The first of these, to
a scenario by the composer based on the play of Lorca, was first played
by the Sadlers Wells Ballet, whereupon it was taken into the repertoire
of many other companies, notably the Royal Danish Ballet, several
German companies, and those of Ankara, Santiago and Cape Town.
Thus with this work ApIvor achieved his first international recognition.

In 1955 he was again commissioned by the Sadlers Wells Trust, to
compose his next opera *Yerma*, Op. 28. The libretto was by Montagu
Slater, based on the tragedy by Lorca. The work, which was written
largely in the West Indies, was finished by 1958; but in 1959 the Sadlers
Wells Theatre took the unusual step of refusing to perform the work.
This major rebuff, for which no reason was officially given, caused very
great concern to the composer, and to other musicians who spoke for
him. His only consolation was a studio performance of the work by the
BBC, at the suggestion of Edward Clark. The opera, by far the most
important of his works up to this time, marks the culminating point of
ApIvor's second period. In choosing the work of the Andalusian poet
and dramatist Federico Garcia Lorca, ApIvor was once more responding
to the influence of his environment, particularly the mood of the late
30's. He had already translated and set Lorca's *Thamar and Amnon*, and
set Lorca's songs, to say nothing of *Blood Wedding*. Lorca was assassinated
in the early days of the Spanish Civil War, at the early age of thirty-eight,
and his death somehow symbolised the popular movement against
dictatorships, and made an impression on the sensibility of the intelligentsia. Lorca was more a popular dramatist than a political one. As a
young playwright he took the theatre to the people, travelling round the
country with his company of players, in a way that has few parallels
today; perhaps only Arnold Wesker invites any sort of comparison in
this country, with his 'Centre 42'.

Lorca was closely connected with music. Not only did he himself
study it for a while, but he was associated with Falla in folk-festivals in
the early 20's. His personality was a compound of poetry and music;[1]
his nature contemplative, idealistic; and the theme of death occurs
frequently in his poems, of which his best known is the *Lament for the
death of a bullfighter*. Another was 'on a child drowned in a well'; this
theme is used in *Yerma* as a background fantasy, symbolising the child
that the heroine never had. His dramatic output reached its highest point
in three tragedies. *Bodas de Sangre* (1933) and *Yerma* (1934) were gypsy
plays, which juxtaposed freedom and convention, life and anti-life,

1. See Roy Campbell, *Lorca: an appreciation of his poetry.*

outward reputation and inner integrity; the same theme also recurred in
La Casa de Bernarda Alba[1] (1936).

Montagu Slater adapted *Yerma* into an opera libretto of three acts,
each divided into two scenes. Some of the verse is in rhyming couplets.
The story was ready-made theatre, full-blooded, dark-toned, romantic,
while the poetic, slightly unreal nature of the theme made it well suited
to operatic treatment.

The first scene is set on a summer's evening in a Spanish village. The
beautiful Yerma is awakened from her dreamy sleep by the Angelus, to
prepare a meal for her husband Juan, a hard-working smallholder and
sheep farmer, who comes home tired from work in the fields. After two
years of marriage Yerma still longs for a child; but Juan appears indifferent, and urges her to be patient. He is preoccupied with his work.
As a street band goes by, and the bustle of village life is heard, Juan is
contemptuous of those who have nothing better to do but stand and
watch.

Left alone, Yerma is visited by an old school-friend, Maria, and
though her apparent sterility makes her envy the child Maria is about to
have, she agrees to help make the baby-clothes. While she starts this,
another sheep-farmer, Victor, a childhood friend from the village, comes
to sell Juan a prize ram, and seeing Yerma at work happily thinks this
means a son is to be born to her. On finding his mistake he tries to cheer
Yerma by telling her she will have a child before long. Juan overhears
and mis-judges this, and threatens Yerma that his two sisters should
come to live with them to watch her. Yerma is distraught at this bleak
prospect and, left alone, she longs for the child who fills all her dreams.
(Thus we are given the first insight into Yerma's character.)

Scene two takes place a year later, during work in the olive groves,
some of the women are carrying food for their husbands; others are
gossiping as usual. Yerma confides to a gay old woman, who has fourteen
children, how she longs for a child, but how she feels little or no sympathy
for her husband Juan. Only Victor used to thrill her with his embrace
when they were younger. The old woman's coarse rejoinder is, however,
repugnant to Yerma. 'Your world, not mine,' she sings. (Thus we have
the second insight into her character.) A crazy girl, also childless, tells
her that in the autumn she and others are going to pray to the saint of
fertility; and that her mother, Dolores, is a woman wise in the use of
herbs. Victor and Yerma then meet by chance; they are drawing close
together, and she almost offers herself to him, but being a man of integrity

---

1. Kenneth MacMillan adapted *La Casa* into a ballet to the music of Frank Martin's
Harpsichord Concerto.

he does not take the opportunity. Yerma is then distraught by hallucinations of a drowning child ('the child drowned in a well' of Lorca's earlier poem)—'I heard a child crying'—and she clings to Victor hysterically. (This is the third insight into Yerma's character.) Juan enters and, suspecting his wife of infidelity, upbraids her bitterly. They part in opposite directions.

In the second act, Yerma's home has become a prison to her; Juan's sisters watch over her like wardens; her mind gradually begins to give way under the strain. The women, washing clothes in a mountain stream, indulge in their customary gossip about Yerma, while Maria does what she can to discourage them. Juan warns Victor that childhood loves are best forgotten, and says he should leave the village, where he is causing trouble. Victor decides to go.

In the distance the shepherds are rounding up their sheep, while the women only stop gossiping to watch Juan's black-clothed sisters, and to greet Yerma with their ribald singing.

In the second scene Juan, returning home in the evening, finds that Yerma has again escaped his sisters' watch over her, and warns her once more of gossip. Left alone, Yerma hears Maria passing. Maria allows her to nurse her baby. The crazy girl comes to take Yerma to see her mother, the wise woman Dolores, with her powers of black-magic and invocation of spirits. Victor comes to say goodbye, and Yerma tries to remind him of the past. He has sold his flock to Juan, who sees him on his way. Yerma then rushes out with the crazy girl to find the mother, leaving Juan's sisters calling for her in the empty house. In extreme agitation they go out to find Juan.

During the night, Dolores and two neighbours have conducted a seance for Yerma in the churchyard. The third act opens with Yerma back at her house just before daylight. She promises that her prayers will give Yerma a child. But just at dawn, when Yerma is about to leave, Juan and his sisters arrive, as usual suspecting Yerma of infidelity with Victor. She pleads her love for him, and thinks there is something in her blood that prevents her having the children she longs for. But Juan in a passionate scene throws her to the floor, leaving Dolores and the two neighbours to comfort her in her wild, insane despair. 'Now I am entering the deepest pit', she sings. (The final insight into her character.)

In the second scene, an autumn fiesta takes place in the hills, and outside the hermitage a crowd gathers, and street sellers are standing in wait for the women pilgrims, who have come to beg the saint for children in the coming year. But there is another less saintly side to the celebration, with dancing and drinking, and girls being carried off by young men, who have come for that very purpose. Maria tells a neighbour she fears that

Yerma is somewhere there; then, as the hermit greets the pilgrims, Yerma joins them. She has come in great distress to pray to the saint for fertility.

There follows a choral ballet, as the crowd break into a vigorous dance, urged on by some maskers representing the Devil (or Horned God) and his Wife, who simulate the eternal pursuit of man and woman. As the dance reaches its climax, Yerma comes out of the chapel, only to be accosted by the old woman (of Act I), whose advice she had earlier rejected. She learns from her that her childlessness comes from her husband's family, not from her. But when the old woman thereupon offers her own son to Yerma, if she will only leave Juan, Yerma is again outraged. She spurns the old woman's offer, and is in turn taunted with her barrenness.

Juan once again overhears this conversation, but has no kind words for his wife, telling her to be content with childlessness. The hallucination of the drowning child returns, the child crying to be born. Nevertheless, he is drawn by her beauty, and goes to embrace her so eagerly that in revulsion she grasps his throat. The thin fibre of her sanity snaps, and in a sudden access of maniacal strength she strangles him; and with him the child that could never be hers.

As dawn breaks, the festival ends with a hymn to the Trinity by the unsuspecting suppliants in the background. The first rays of sunlight reveal Yerma prostrate beside the body of Juan, trying to raise it. She cries aloud, as with horror she realizes that in killing her husband she has condemned herself to final sterility. 'Do not approach me, for I have killed my son.'

The earlier Lorca ballet, *Blood Wedding*, centred round the theme of a dominating mother; the opera brings to the surface the animal instincts and frustrations of a woman who is denied motherhood. Latin-American society, dominated by Catholicism, is matriarchal. ApIvor felt that the psychological depths of a character can best be explored by means of opera, and expressed in a more complete way through music. For instance, the water of Lorca's 'child drowned in a well' symbolizes the unconscious, the separation from someone you love—and fear. Music alone has the quality of association to convey these depths of meaning.

Lorca's story was ready-made opera. Only one scene had to be interpolated which was not in the original: this was the scene between Juan and Victor (Act II, Sc. 1), which replaced a scene of anguish by Yerma; this seemed superfluous, and indeed harmful to the movement of the opera.

The dramatic movement of the opera is the working out of Yerma's
private grief. She is like a female Wozzeck, and the murder of Juan is the
inevitable point of climax. ApIvor's 12-note style, as with other works of
his second period, has a pronounced tonal bias; the melodic lines use
a composite tonality, frequently triadic. The underlying theme of the
opera is the overwhelming nature of Yerma's grief, and this gradually
increases as the opera proceeds. It is paralleled by the increasing chromaticism of the melodic writing. The musical centre of the opera is the
dramatic lyricism of the chief soprano line.[1] Yerma's grief is shown in
relation to other people: To her immediate circle, such as Juan and
Maria—the one indifferent, the other sympathetic; next, to those less
immediate, such as the old woman, and the witch Dolores; finally, to the
crowd of bystanders. For two brief moments it is shown turned inwards
towards Yerma herself, as she suffers the hallucinations of the mentally
unstable. This is suggested by the composer by means of a shimmering
texture of chromatic brilliance, rather than by specific themes. This opera
displays one of the most original and expressive uses of a 12-note style.
The idiom of Yerma derives from a highly individual melodic use of
several basic sets. The work is based on three 12-note rows, of which the
first is:

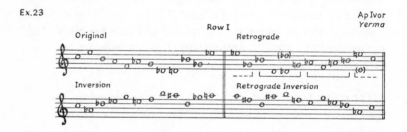

Ex.23   Ap Ivor
                                    Row I   Yerma
        Original   Retrograde

        Inversion   Retrograde Inversion

This is derived thematically directly from Yerma's love-song with
Victor (Act. I, Sc. 2), at the words 'Why shepherd sleep alone'.[2] This
original form of the first row also appears at the beginning of the opera,
in the orchestral introduction, and represents Yerma's longing for a
child. So the first scene is written round it. From the Retrograde Inversion
of this row is derived Victor's music; for instance at [47], 'I have a ram
whose horns will curl'. This is square-cut, deliberately tonal, to distinguish Victor's guileless, bluff nature.

1. Brilliantly sung at the studio performance by Joan Hammond.
Fig. 2. [106] + 6.

Two other note-rows are then derived from the first. The second row is a simple transmutation of the notes within the 4-note groupings of the Retrograde of the first row:

Ex.24

Ap Ivor
Yerma

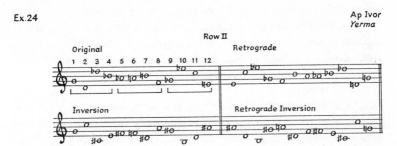

The value of this second row lies in its properties of tension and emotion; almost the whole opera is based on it, from the second scene onwards. In that scene, at [65], the 'music in the fields' is given a tonal flavour by an orchestral accompaniment consisting of a quick downward scale, which is made up of 3-note chords from the Inversion of the second row. Examples of its use in the second set include Juan's 'jealousy' motif at [25], and Maria's lullaby theme at [41]. In the third act, examples of its use include the Retrograde version for the 'fertility rite' section at [36]; and (perhaps the most expressive uses of the series in the whole opera) notes 6–9 of the Inversion depict Yerma's obsession with the drowning child at [118]; while notes 4–12 of the original form express Yerma's despair, at the end of the opera, after the murder of Juan.

Ex.25

Ap Ivor
Yerma, Act III, Sc.2

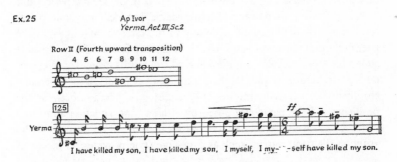

For the chorus of priests, with which the work closes, the modal character which the composer wanted was obtained by dividing the row into two tonally-inclined sections; the first section (notes 1, 8, 2, 11, 4, 6) starting on A (the eleventh downward transposition of the row); the second section (notes 3, 7, 5, 9, 12, 10) starting on E flat.

For the simpler 'peasant' scene (Act II, scene 1) this second row was not entirely suitable; so ApIvor manufactured a third row by taking every other note of the first row (C-B-F-G etc.). It so happened that the three resulting 4-note groups of this third row have tonal characteristics, which aptly suit the pipes and horn-calls of the shepherds.

The chorus is carefully integrated into the action; not only does it separate scenes from each other, but it is given a dramatically expressive role, starting off-stage in Act I, Scene I, gradually becoming more prominent, until with the pilgrims' procession and the choral ballet of Act III it occupies the stage. By this time Yerma's mood and character have been fully presented in their several aspects, and the composer can therefore afford to draw the contrast effectively between this and the *fiesta* mood which pervades the final scene, interspersed like a recurring rondo theme.

In spite of the non-acceptance of this remarkable opera, and the apparent loss of five years' work, ApIvor pursued his composition, and continued in the direction which seemed to him inevitable and logical. His is a remarkable example of artistic integrity and moral courage.

The third period started in 1960. Like the second it was also heralded by *Seven Piano Pieces*, Op. 30, and may be described as post-Webern. ApIvor's style now gradually becomes non-thematic, and the principle of 'perpetual variation' is rigorously applied. ApIvor himself considers this period to be the only logical continuation of the second, which was in a sense formative and preparatory. The serial works of this third period tend to be short, epigrammatic, and the orchestra tends to consist of solo performers. The tonal bias of the works of the second period give way, in the third, to a non-tonal, non-thematic, but melodic counterpoint; the linear style of the opera gives way to the rarefied pointillism of the later orchestral works. For ApIvor this is the way forward from a 12-note style; the multimelodic counterpoint which results from his Webern-derived technique is the contemporary equivalent of Bach's diatonic/chromatic counterpoint. Indeed ApIvor sees close parallels between the problems and the paradoxes posed by today's fluid situation and those which obtained in Bach's day. He has no time for those musicians who abandon the organization, such as a 12-note style provides, in favour of anarchy or total aleatoricism, which he considers to be little more than neo-Dadaism, or non-art like that of Marcel Duchamp. However much he might be attracted, politically or instinctively, to these negative manifestations of *avant-garde* art, to accept them philosophically would mean for him an end to art itself; and ApIvor is both too intelligent and too optimistic a composer to countenance any such conclusion. The composer, he feels, matters, and is more important than some might suggest who tend to polarize music—thus allotting 'pop' music to the low-brow, Stockhausen and Cage to the high-brow. He rejects electronic music, though retaining a profound respect for a composer such as Gerhard who uses electronic effects, and who has had the courage in his late works to build an entirely new serial world, quite different from his earlier one. This is in effect what ApIvor has also achieved, to interpret serialism for himself. The free, aleatoric randomness of a Cage is philosophically unacceptable to him, because it destroys the basis of composition as such. For this reason chiefly, he sees himself out of touch with many contemporary musicians, since although he has always been temperamentally allied to the *avant-garde*, he is not in agreement with certain developments that have been shown by the *avant-garde* school of Cardew or Bedford. This may have something to do with his non-acceptance today: 'tous réaction est vrai'. Following Webern, ApIvor reacted against a homophonic, harmonic style, and explored counterpoint. Now yet another reaction has set in, more quickly this time, against contrapuntal complexity.

Whereas the focus of his works during the second period was on the theatre, it was widened in the third period to include more instrumental and orchestral works. ApIvor wrote, however, two dramatic works in this period: first, a satirical *avant-garde* opera in three acts, *Ubu Roi*, Op. 40 (1965-6), with a libretto by the composer based on a horror-play of Alfred Jarry; second, a forty-five minute ballet, *Corporal Jan*, Op. 42, which was commissioned by BBC Television, and screened in 1968.

Ubu Roi, which was ApIvor's third opera, summed up the serial works in all forms composed during the preceding five years. It married the theatrical with the musical *avant-garde*. The play by the twenty-three-year-old French writer Alfred Jarry, which had scandalised audiences in 1896, is accepted today as simply the first of many works making up the *avant-garde* theatre. It was a radical, satirical, anarchical, absurd take-off of everything connected with established society, and anything resembling theatrical convention. Père Ubu, coarse, vicious, pompous, entirely amoral, and extremely funny, is the prototype of the contemporary anti-hero of many a present-day novel. To that extent the work has considerable relevance now;[1] and if Tippett is right when he says that opera is ultimately dependent on the contemporary theatre, then ApIvor's choice of this work was well-judged.

The intention was the same as that which blended the serious with the absurd in *The Hollow Men*; that combination of the profound with the

1. It was produced at the Royal Court Theatre, London, in 1966.

banal—'*Ein' Feste Burg*' with 'Here we go round the mulberry bush';[1] in this case the introduction, as the chief character of an opera, of the prototype of an anti-hero; no Boris, or Grimes, but a popular revolutionary figure, so familiar in recent years; ignorant, cowardly, whose rule is deceit, and whose sceptre is a lavatory brush. Such a figure features as one of the few representative myths of the twentieth century.

ApIvor wrote the libretto himself, and divided each act into several short scenes, like revue sketches.

I

Scene 1 Mère Ubu emulates Lady Macbeth. But it is difficult to persuade the fat Ubu to assassinate the King.

Scene 2 & 3 The Ubus believe in doing business over dinner. But there is something very much the matter with the dinner. Captain Bordure agrees to join the plot. But the future looks bleak to his men.

Scene 4 King Wenceslas makes Ubu a Count; but Ubu is not impressed.

Scene 5 The plot is hatched, and everyone has his or her own favourite method of assassination.

Scene 6 The Queen has a dream, but the King ignores her warning. The dream comes true, and the King and his sons are all killed, except the young Bougrelas, who escapes with the Queen.

Scene 7 The fugitive Queen and her son find a convenient cave, where she dies. Bougrelas receives reassuring news from the Beyond.

Scene 8 Ubu is King; be the people never so ungrateful. It is a shock to him to find that he cannot keep all the money. Some has to be used to bribe his way to popularity.

Scene 9 He initiates the Ubu Roi Financial Stakes, with a prize of real, free money. His reign gets off to a good start. Ubu makes another popular move and proclaims an Orgy. Much shouting and breaking of glass.

II

Scene 1 Ubu has chained up all the aristocrats, and double-crossed his friend and co-conspirator, Captain Bordure. This situation has Mère Ubu worried.

Scene 2 Ubu has a hangover; but he gets to work just the same. One by one the aristocracy are fed into the patent Ubu Sausage Machine in the basement; but not before the Financiers predict devaluation, and the Judiciary predict chaos.

Scene 3 Ubu goes out collecting taxes. But the peasants don't like paying, particularly twice a year.

Scene 4 Bordure pays a short visit to the Czar of Russia, who disapproves of him. But the Czar does not object to making war against Poland.

Scene 5 Ubu learns how things are going on the home front. Bordure writes a threatening letter to him, and everyone is happy that this means war; war will

1. The same intention motivates a large amount of Peter Maxwell Davies's work (see p. 240).

solve unemployment and boost profits. But they all agree not to raise the pay of she troops.

Scene 6 Ubu goes to war arrayed in unconventional armour. But it is harder than he thought to mount a horse. He announces a terrible fate for cowards, and takes the key of the Treasury with him. Mère Ubu meanwhile has her own plan; she will steal the gold from the Royal Tombs, and decamp with it to the West.

III

Scene 1 Mère Ubu robs the Tomb of the Polish Kings. A voice from the Tomb sounds very angry.

Scene 2 Bougrelas starts a counter-revolution. Everyone agrees, and Mère Ubu is driven out of the palace by flying rubbish.

Scene 3 Ubu meets the Russian Army on the plain. He puts his Master Plan into operation, and is instantly defeated.

Scene 4 Ubu takes refuge in a cave occupied by a bear. He repeats the Lord's Prayer while his friends kill the bear.

Scene 5 Retribution, in the shape of Mère Ubu, catches up with Ubu in his cave. Soon Bougrelas and his men catch up with both of them. Later they are seen toiling across the snows of Livonia. Ubu is not sorry they are going; as he says, 'It's not much fun being a king'.

Scene 6 Ubu attempts to teach the ship's captain his job, as they sail across the Baltic. Disaster is narrowly averted. No-one knows where they are going, but it certainly will not be as nice as Poland; besides, as Ubu says, 'If there wasn't any Poland there wouldn't be any Poles'.

Ubu is fierce satire, not pantomime or farce. The non-thematic, 12-note style of the score is therefore quite unremitting. There are no thematic links, or expressive lines, as in *Yerma*. Melody does not exist; indeed, the expressiveness of the work lies elsewhere than in the vocal lines. The opera abounds in concerted writing and writing for the chorus, and spoken dialogue is used to link the scenes. The parts are more concentrated, and more strictly derived from the original row, than in the case of *Yerma*; and whereas the earlier opera was intense, tragic, melodic, *Ubu* is violent and uncompromising in its savagery. Though it has not yet been performed, it is the direct precursor of Birtwistle's *Punch and Judy*.[1]

Starting in 1960 Aplvor deliberately explored abstract serialism, in works for solo instruments as well as in works for fuller resources. Short piano works include the *Seven Piano Pieces*, Op. 30, *Animalcules*, Op. 35, and *The Lyre-playing Idol*, Op. 45, whose five sections make up his longest composition for this instrument.

1. See p. 315.

Other small solo works include *Mutations* for cello and piano, Op. 34, *Harp, Piano, Piano-Harp*, Op. 41, and *Ten-String Design*, Op. 44. The piano-harp is an upright piano with the key-action removed; the player sounds the strings in various ways, ranging from a finger-glissando to the use of xylophone beaters. ApIvor used this again in *Corporal Jan* the following year (1967) and in *Neumes* (1963). *Ten-String Design* is an elaborate three-movement work for violin and guitar, constructed along very strict lines. The first movement, *Antiphony*, consists of periods of 2, 4, 8, 16 and 32 bars, interlocking with periods of 32, 16, 8, 4 and 2 bars. The metre moves 4 3 2 3 4.

Guitar	2	4	8	16	32	
Violin	32	16	8	4	2	
Metre	4/4	3/4	2/4	3/4	4/4	

The second movement, *Monody and resonances*, consists of a melodic line for the violin supported by serially derived chords, or 'resonances', for the guitar. Both instruments resume their democratic relationship for the finale, whose structure is contrapuntal and closely organised according to the technique of perpetual variation.

More conventional chamber music compositions of this period, though very different from each other, are the *Wind Quintet*, Op. 31, and the *String Quartet*, Op. 37. A not-so-conventional work is *Crystals*, Op. 39, which consists of six short movements for percussion instruments, supported by a Hammond organ, guitar and double-bass.

In the four years that separate the *Wind Quintet* from the *String Quartet*, ApIvor had moved a considerable distance along his chosen path. The technique of athematic melody and fragmentation, that is the goal of the post-Webern serialist, was slowly won. the *Wind Quintet* is a hesitant work, and does not shake off traces of his former, more linear, thematic style. It resembles Gerhard's early *Quintet*. Moreover, the sharply differentiated character of the five instruments does not make for homogeneity; on the contrary, the one-ness of the material draws attention to the disparity of the texture. This does not apply to the *String Quartet*; by this time (1964) ApIvor had a clearer picture of the sort of abstract structure that is appropriate to a serial idiom. The tonal similarity of the four instruments also helps towards this end. The result is that the hesitancy of the earlier work is replaced by greater conviction, bolder strokes, and the music stands in its own right, independent of any poetic, theatrical or architectural points of reference. The Prologue and Epilogue, twenty-five bars long, are each a palindrome of the other; the three central movements, about fifty-five bars each, can be played in any order. Thus the musical 'object' can be viewed from three directions. As Lambert used to say of Satie's *Gymnopédies*, the three movements are three views of the same object. This device was also used in *Mutation* for cello, Op. 34. The music has no thematic or dramatic climax, no pictorial or philosophical meaning; it simply begins and ends, and displays a high degree of organization in between.

Apart from the opera *Ubu Roi*, ApIvor has written two choral works in his third period; the Dylan Thomas *Cantata*, Op. 32 ('Altarwise by owl light'), and *Chorales, The Secret Sea*, Op. 38. The *Cantata* (1960) was the earlier and is scored for soloists, chorus and orchestra, and each of its ten sections uses a different combination of twelve instruments: the selection is aleatoric. The poems are savage, the imagery terrifying, with the universe seen as a factory of destruction; so the vocal style is acute, and the choral writing combines speech with a syllabic vocalization similar to that used by the Italian *avant-garde*, Berio and Nono. *Chorales* is gentler. In Hugo Manning's text, man discovers his divine nature; so the style is altogether more restful.

Unlike the chamber works, some of the orchestral works of this period have pictorial or literary points of reference. The earliest is *Overtones*, Op. 33 (1961/2). This is the title of a work by Paul Klee. In the composer's words:

The word also indicates the relationship between these nine short pieces and the paintings or drawings of Paul Klee on which they are based. Most of the works are only semi-representational, and one of them, the 'uncomposed object in space', completely abstract. This forms the ninth, and last, orchestral piece. They all combine fantasy and whimsical humour.

Fragmentary points of orchestral colour, like shafts of sunlight, coupled with virtuosity of scoring, combine to bring these impressionist pieces to life; contrasts of pitch, dynamics, timbre and texture are most marked, which come easily to an operatic composer. For instance, the very short, fragmentary first piece ('Dance with the veil'), built largely round string harmonics and trills, is immediately followed by the more linear second piece ('Dance of the sad child'), which uses wind, with vibraphone and xylophone, and the lugubrious alto saxophone for intensification of mood. The predominantly high pitch of the third piece ('Fragment of a ballet for Aeolian harp') is followed by the predominantly low pitch of the fourth ('Animals at full moon'); and so on (see plate 4).

The *Second Symphony*, Op. 36 (1963), is Webernian, though not a 'chamber symphony'. Scored for solo instruments with harp, piano, guitar and mandolin, it lasts thirteen and a half minutes. The middle movement consists of variations, with only five players in each variation—starting with the 'sharp', high instruments (flute, trumpet, xylophone), and working down.

The *Concerto for String Trio and Orchestra*, called *String Abstract*, Op. 43 (1967), which was commissioned by, and performed at, the Cheltenham Festival in 1968 is the prelude to his most ambitious orchestral work so far, the variations for chamber orchestra, *Tarot*, Op. 46 (1968).

The Tarot is a book of 'ageless wisdom', said to have originated in Alexandria and Fez in the thirteenth century. Through its study the wise man aspired to higher things, psychologically and spiritually; he was brought into harmony with the cosmic purpose. The twenty-two 'major trumps' correspond to the twenty-two letters of the Hebrew alphabet, and like them have a cabalistic significance.

The twenty-two variations of this work correspond to these twenty-two 'major trumps', and the music employs the twenty-two tones of an 11-note row and its inversion. Eleven of the twenty-two performers are employed at a time, the choice being made by chance. The work may be played with or without back-projection of the Trumps, and choreographic interpretations of the various numbers.

Examples of the esoteric significance of the various Trumps are shown in No. 12 and No. 13, *The Hanged Man* and *Death*. The Hanged Man, mentioned in T. S. Eliot's *The Waste Land*, is hanging by one foot; his personality is dependent on the All (symbolised by the Tree from which he hangs), and in gaining psychic freedom he will be involved in an act of surrender, and be viewed by the rest of the world as having his values upside down, contrary to the worldly standard of orientation. The letter Nun, of No. 13, signifies a fish, and means movement, transformation, death of the self, leading from the narrow, personal consciousness to a universal or cosmic consciousness. Thus the symbolism is not one of death and ruin, but of transformation, leading to a new life, at one with the cosmic order of things.

With this work ApIvor reached an impasse. Serialism presented him with a profoundly disturbing choice. To continue along its course would lead him to ever-increasing complexity and abstraction; moreover he had the example before him of several composers, such as Boulez, who had followed this path only to find that it could lead to a *cul de sac*. Serialism without a personal sense of direction and artistic purpose might well prove to be artistically arid; there was little point in following that path unless you wished to discover a new sound-world; as Gerhard had done in his later works. Moreover the use of twelve notes does not necessarily provide the composer with a ready-made architecture for a piece; this is also something that he needs to discover anew with each work.

So in his next work *Neumes,* Op. 47 (1969), ApIvor struck out afresh, and abandoned serial organisation as an end in itself. The 12-note row became superfluous, because by this time Schoenberg's principle of non-repetition, as well as the avoidance of tonal procedures of composition, had become ingrained into his style. This work, a set of ten orchestral variations, is based on the shape of each of the ten symbols, which is transferred into a direction of melody, rather than on any thematic variation.

ApIvor's work shows an unceasing progress, a voyage of discovery, of both style and mood; from the jazz-inspired 30's to the abstract 60's; from the tonality of the first period to the serialism of the third; from the sombre fatalism of the 30's, with anger rising over Spain and Munich, to the despair of the 60's, over Cuba and Vietnam. ApIvor is a composer who is deeply aware of all these issues; which makes his almost total rejection by his contemporaries even harder to understand. His output includes three operas, five ballets, songs, song-cycles, piano pieces, chamber music, choral works, and orchestral compositions; yet very little indeed of this considerable achievement is heard in this country, and only a tiny fragment is published.

List of compositions by Denis ApIvor

1st period

Date	Op. No.	Chamber Works	Orchestral, Opera, Ballet, Choral
1936/8	1	Chaucer Songs	arr. Busoni's *Fantasia Contrappuntistica*
	2	'Alas Parting'—five songs	Veneziana
	3	Songs	
	4	Fantasia for Strings on a Song of Diego Pisador	
1939	5		The Hollow Men (T. S. Eliot)
1944/5	6	Violin Sonata	
	7	Concertante for Clarinet, Piano & Percussion	
	7a		Concertante for Clarinet & Orchestra (1959)
1946	8	Lorca Songs (Tr. ApIvor)	
	10		Estella Marina (Pierre de Corbillan)
	11	Children's Songs (T. S. Eliot)	
1947	12		She Stoops to Conquer (beg. 1943)
1948	13		Piano Concerto

2nd period
(12-note)

1949	14	Seven piano pieces	
1950	15	Landscapes (T. S. Eliot)	
	16		Concerto for Violin & 15 instruments
1951	18		The Goodman of Paris—ballet
	18a		Piano Concertino from the ballet
	19		A Mirror for Witches—ballet
	19a		Suite from the ballet

Date	*Op. No.*	*Chamber Works*	*Orchestral, Opera, Ballet, Choral*
1952	22		Symphony No. 1
1953	23		Blood Wedding—ballet (Lorca)
	24	Songs of T. L. Beddoes	
	25		Thamar & Amnon (Lorca)
	26		Concertino for guitar & orchestra
1954	27		Saudades—ballet
1954/8	28		Yerma (Lorca)
	29	Variations for solo guitar	

3rd period
(post-Webern)

1960	30	Seven piano pieces	
	31	Wind Quintet	
	32		Cantata (Dylan Thomas)
1961	33		Overtones
1962	34	Mutations for cello and piano	
	35	Twelve piano pieces— 'Animalcules'	
1963	36		Symphony No. 2
1964/5	37	String Quartet	
	38	Five Chorales—'The Secret Sea' (Hugo Manning)	
	39	Crystals	
1965/6	40		Ubu Roi
	41	Harp, Piano, Piano— Harp	
1967	42		Corporal Jan (Television Ballet)
	43		String Abstract
	44		Ten String Design
1968	45	Five piano pieces	
	46		Tarot—Orchestral Variations
1969	47		Neumes—Orchestral Variations
1970	48	'Discanti' Five pieces for solo guitar	

8   Thea Musgrave

It is an accepted *datum*, common to all post-Schoenberg composers, that style is a result of choice. Instead of the acceptance of a common tradition, Schoenberg substituted the necessity of the individual composer's own choosing. This is therefore the starting point from which those younger representatives of the 'new music' set out whose formative years occurred after about the mid-50's, when the newly-discovered serialism exerted an almost irresistible force. Thea Musgrave's style has been one of steady and continuous movement, first towards serialism, then away from it, and with variants of style in succeeding works. She was born in Edinburgh in 1928, and after reading music at Edinburgh University, where she was firmly grounded in the classical tradition under Sidney Newman, and received early lessons under Hans Gal, she went for four years (1950–1954) to Nadia Boulanger in Paris—one of the comparatively few British composers to do so. Indeed the 'Boulangerie' was not where you went if you wanted the very latest in serialism or *avant-garde* experiment. That remarkable teacher, whose pupils include most of the best-known American and European composers and musicians, did not indulge in such things; she was concerned with traditions, with technique, with attention to detail; also, perhaps justifiably, with the most distinguished horse from her stable, Stravinsky, who had not yet defected to the serial ranks. It was a period for Musgrave of artistic awakening.

In her search for a style that would fully suit her idiom, Thea Musgrave tended to 'let it happen'. The means adopted are, after all, of less importance than the end towards which they are directed; the finished art-work is what matters. Nevertheless, one is not possible without the other, and her style resulted from various and continuing influences. Her early works were tonal, and mainly vocal; songs such as the *Five Songs* for baritone, which occupied six months of her student years; the *Cantata for a Summer's Day*, the *Suite o' Bairnsangs*. The exception to this was a two-act ballet *A Tale for Thieves*, from which the composer extracted an orchestral suite; straightforward, Stravinskyan, abounding in *ostinato* figures, yet showing an unspoilt freshness.

Another influence was felt in 1953, when she attended a Summer School at Dartington Hall, organized by William Glock. She found Glock a persuasive lecturer and teacher, and through him became acquainted with Schoenberg, Webern, and the American composer, Charles Ives. So gradually her style became more chromatic; in the chamber opera *The Abbot of Drimock* (1955) key signatures are dispensed with, and though the vocal parts are still quite simple, certain complexities begin to appear, such as Schoenbergian *sprechstimme*. This tendency is pursued in the *Divertimento for Strings* (1957) and *Obliques* (1958), which feel their way tentatively towards a 12-note style. The second of these works, in the form of orchestral variations, happened to coincide with a visit to Tanglewood in 1958, when her meeting Aaron Copland and Milton Babbitt resulted in an even stronger pull towards serialism. The first works to adopt it were the *Song for Christmas* (1958) and *Triptych* (1959) for tenor and orchestra. In this score, which is a setting of Chaucer's *Merciles Beaute*, those precise instructions, so familiar in serial scores, are used for the first time by Musgrave; they would have been unthinkable five years previously in the ballet suite. Also the orchestral percussion section, swollen as it was for *Obliques*, becomes even more swollen to include claves, crotales, and bongos, as well as the inevitable vibraphone. Moreover the metre, hitherto regular, now becomes fragmented; irregular patterns, with rapid upbeat figurations, begin to colour the score. Another somewhat experimental work of this period was the *String Quartet*, commissioned by Glasgow University, in which one idea appears in different guises, and of which the style is an indeterminate chromaticism.

The process is pursued in *Colloquy*, for violin and piano, and the *Trio* for flute, oboe and piano. Both were condensed pieces, for which short *motifs* were appropriate; both were written in 1960. The first is a study after the manner of Webern, while the second is more concerned with the textural problem of academic serialism. In her search for that style which will please her technically and aesthetically she is highly susceptible to the influences around her that are strongest felt; but she has not yet fully discovered that marriage of idiom, style and structure that is the mark of mature artistry.

Nor does she discover it in the *Sinfonia* (1963), a somewhat transitional piece, which was written to a commission from the Cheltenham Festival, and in which she used a serial style for the last time. She found the fragmentation technique, and the use of small motives, though suitable for small-scale pieces, a limitation in a bigger work; so the phrases

become longer, more legato. This is particularly felt in the second
movement, where she harks back to that scherzando style of *A Tale for
Thieves* which is inconsistent with the serial principle, but which was
naturally hers, and to which she had already reverted in the *Scottish
Dance Suite* (1959), as well as in the *Serenade* (1961). She was beginning to
find herself, and to reconcile that freedom of expression, which was
instinctive, with that strictness of technique, which she was persuaded
was proper to the composer of the 60's. In *The Phoenix and the Turtle*
she reverts from serialism, and searches for a more lyrical, flexible,
intense quality. This was followed by two large works. First was *The
Five Ages of Man* (1963), a setting for choir and orchestra of parts of
Hesiod's *Works and Days*. The melodic lines are longer, more legato;
though still angular and chromatic. In accepting the commission from
the Norfolk and Norwich Festival, the composer wrote a work within
the recognizable confines of the old oratorio tradition. There are no
soloists, but the choir is divided into chorus and semi-chorus. The
choice of a Greek poem of the eighth century B.C. is somewhat surprising.
It is really a treatise on farming, plentifully interspersed with moralizing
maxims about the progressive decline of the human race, as illustrated
by the social and economic distress of Boeotia, where the poet lived. The
'five ages' represent this gradual declension—golden, silver, bronze,
heroic, iron—with proportionately increasing gloom and misery. It is a
pagan account of the Fall of Man, and the composer found it not merely
powerful, but disturbingly relevant to the present day. Her score concentrates on the drama and colour of the mainly descriptive text. The
work, which lasts twenty-seven minutes, is sung without a break, and the
sections fall approximately into those of a symphonic work: introduction—
quick, scherzo—slow—quick, finale. Chromatic lyricism pervades the
choral writing, and a certain rhythmic restlessness, such as an avoidance
of the first beat of the bar, which is one of Walton's chief characteristics.
Like the text, the music is descriptive, and allows for performance by
good amateurs by means of orchestral doubling of the main leads.

The chorus also predominates in the next major work, the opera
The Decision (1964/5), which is a continuation on a larger scale of the
style and trend of *The Five Ages of Man*. The libretto by Maurice Lindsay
is about a miner, John Brown, who was trapped for twenty-three days in
Kilgrammie coalpit, Ayrshire, in 1833. He was taken out alive, in full
possession of his mental faculties, and lived for three days after. The
'decision' was whether or not to rescue the trapped miner, a decision
which was complicated by the fact that Katie, the wife of the pit-foreman,
had been his lover, and died after giving birth to his child. Like *The Five
Ages of Man*, the opera shows a gradual decline in fortune, starting with

past memories of possible happiness and finishing with Brown's death. These memories are shown in flashback, which has the effect of interfering somewhat with the opera's momentum. Furthermore the cumbersome, unwieldy nature of the plot presented the composer with formidable problems of structure and balance. The work lacks dramatic working-out, and consists of a succession of scenes, whose unifying feature is their unrelieved and overwhelming gloom. Again the music is mainly descriptive, right from the opening, where a repeated quaver movement suggests the turning of the wheel at the head of the mine-shaft.

But after the opera Musgrave entered a new phase, and wrote a succession of highly characteristic instrumental compositions, which have earned her a deserved recognition. The *Chamber Concertos* Nos. 2 and 3 (1966), the *Concerto for Orchestra* (1967), and the *Clarinet Concerto* (1968). (The first *Chamber Concerto* dated from 1962, and is not quite so individual a work.) It is as if, like Britten, after long years of exploration, she has found that true style consistent with the many requirements of her artistic personality; her need for freedom, dramatic content, lyricism, length of phrase, continuity, simplicity, discipline. The more chromatic and fragmented her style became, the less memorable had been the themes; something else was needed to hold the listener's attention, and this was provided by a dramatic content. The opera is variable in its effect, in proportion as the dramatic tension ebbs and flows. But in the works that follow the opera, this dramatic content was expressed in purely musical terms, and integrated into her style. She thinks dramatically. All these later works are in one continuous movement, divided into sections; they are conceived as one span, in a growing, cumulative form, with a gradual quickening of pace towards the end.

The *Second Chamber Concerto*, which uses the same players as Schoenberg's *Pierrot Lunaire*, is indebted chiefly to Charles Ives, whose music Musgrave had studied. It introduces metrical freedom for the players. Different tempi are placed together, with cue-lines to facilitate performance; in this way *rubato* and lyrical playing are possible, as well as the simultaneous playing of different speeds. Musgrave also incorporates popular tunes, after the manner of Ives; tunes of firmly diatonic simplicity, such as 'The Keel-row', 'Swanee River' and 'All things bright and beautiful', which are in total, bland contrast to their dissonant surroundings.

The *Third Chamber Concerto* uses the same instruments as the Schubert Octet—for obvious reasons of concert-giving.[1] It is dedicated to Nadia

1. Other composers have also written octets with Schubert's instrumentation; Howard Ferguson and John Joubert, for instance.

Boulanger for her eightieth birthday, 16th September, 1967, and begins with a motto, like the Berg *Chamber Concerto*. As it was commissioned by the Anglo-Austrian Music Society, Musgrave had recourse to the academic parlour-game of translating the letters of composers' names into notes. The first and second Viennese Schools thus appear thematically:

*Hay*d*n* Mozart	*Beet*h*oven* *Sc*h*u*bert	(on the clarinet)
H = B	*A*r*n*o*ld Sc*h*oenberg*	(on the viola)
B = B flat	*A*n*t*on W*eberg*	(on the bassoon)
S = E flat	*Alba*n *Berg*	(on the horn)

Thus are derived the basic thematic outlines of the material. The same freedom of construction is followed as in the *Second Chamber Concerto*, but in addition the players are required in turn to stand to play their cadenzas.

The *Concerto for Orchestra*, commissioned by the Feeney Trust, extends the notational innovation into orchestral terms; thus the vertical effect is made subservient to the horizontal lines. Different speeds are possible, and the free repetition of fixed patterns; at the same time control is not lost. Again, the players are required to stand for solo passages, like jazz musicians. The work as a whole is a contrast between solo and *tutti* sections, as different groups take over the solo function.

This principle is carried logically forward in the *Clarinet Concerto*, commissioned by the Royal Philharmonic Society, in which the soloist moves from one group of the orchestra to another. The clarinet can combine satisfactorily with all the different sections, and by this technique not only are independent leads possible, apart from the conductor, but the correct balance can be ensured. Also the somewhat extrovert personality of the original soloist, Gervase de Peyer, was a positive factor in the composer's mind. Thus it is the dramatic structure, more than the thematic material, which holds the concerto together; and this is a, if not the, saving grace for a style that has such strong links with established traditional procedures.

9 Don Banks

Numerous musicians have come from Australia since 1945 to live and work in London. Among composers, the best known are Don Banks and Malcolm Williamson. Their work differs widely, in both achievement and intent (though undoubtedly these two aspects are related, since what you do is largely dictated by what you set out to do). Williamson has the greater facility, and has directed his pieces towards the widest possible public, with the idiom appropriate for each occasion, and with widely varying results; now an opera, now a hymn-tune in the 'popular style', now a piece for children, now something instrumental. There are few more active or versatile composers than Malcolm Williamson.

Don Banks operates on an altogether different level; he is more concerned with pursuing the sort of music that for him rings true than with seeking popularity. He has worked to synthesize his style from a wide range of influences, which makes it more durable and valid; and to aim at nothing short of perfection, which, as Busoni once said, is the only mark of the true artist.

A composer coming to Europe at his formative stage, unfettered by traditions, whether good or bad, and with something of the creative curiosity of a Stravinsky, would be in a highly advantageous position as far as his own style was concerned. The contemporary situation is such that each composer is bound to exercise choice; to interpret the welter of conflicting idioms and influences that makes up the musical mosaic of today, and to exercise what Stravinsky has described as 'creative volition'. Integrity demands of the artist that before making this choice, and asserting his artistic personality, it is necessary to understand the full nature of what is being chosen, and not to be swayed by considerations other than musical ones.

Don Banks was born in Melbourne in 1923. Both parents were Australian, though he can trace to his grandparents some Irish, Swedish and Scottish descent. His father was a professional jazz musician, who led his own band, and played the trombone, alto saxophone and percussion. Thus the young Don acquired not only a liking for, and familiarity with, jazz at an early age, but also an ability to play the numerous instruments that lay about the house. This enthusiasm for jazz, which was his earliest and strongest influence, has never diminished. He himself played piano and trombone with various bands, worked in a night-club, and gained early experience of practical music-making by acting as orchestrator and arranger.

His official musical studies were of a conventional nature, and after obtaining various diplomas, in 1949 he came to England. Here he began detailed study of composition under Matyas Seiber, who provided the next and decisive influence on him. As Banks has put it, 'he opened my eyes to a whole new world of possibilities in composition'.

Though in his own compositions Seiber was an apostle of Schoenberg's 12-note style, as a teacher he did not adhere to any one system. His many pupils included Fricker and Milner. He laid emphasis on analysis, in depth, of music from Bach to the present day, 'to look at the atoms and cells, and see how a kind of life-process goes on like in any living tissue'. He would show the possibilities of harmonic movement, for instance in chorales; he stressed the importance of respect for the musical material, and of economy; the need to cut waste notes, to keep texture clean and disciplined, to keep a sense of progress and proportion, and never to be satisfied with first thoughts. He called for constant examination of the possibilities of any musical material. As he said, 'if you can't see all the possibilities of a *motif*, how can you select what are the best ones?' He taught, in a word, the craft of composition.

So did Luigi Dallapiccola, to whom Banks went subsequently, in 1952/3. Like Seiber, he was not concerned about what style or idiom a composer chose; only how well he wrote within it. Banks found him 'a most sensitive pair of ears', and made a particular study at this time of canonic techniques, of which Dallapiccola was such a skilled exponent. That aspect of composition which is concerned with the minute gradation of musical sounds, also received close attention; the effect, on the sound, of register, weight, relationship to its surroundings, colour and intensity; the difference between the timbre of different instruments playing the same note; and so on. This aspect of his study was to bear much fruit later. The intense curiosity and care lavished on musical sound *per se* is a part of Banks' technique which was fostered by his work under Dallapiccola.

Various other external influences affected him strongly and positively in these formative years. Chief among them was the 12-note style, which he attempted to use in one of his earliest compositions, the *Duo* for violin and cello (1951). Another was the advanced serial thinking of the American musician Milton Babbitt, whose theory of 'combinatorial sets', particularly as it affects the composer's ability to manage and control sound, appeals strongly to Banks.

And so, with his inquisitive, international outlook, sharpened by years of study, Banks embarked at the age of thirty on his career as a composer. His first published work was the *Violin Sonata* (1953), and since then some twenty-five works have appeared, the majority of them instrumental or orchestral, of which the largest and most important is the *Violin Concerto* (1968).

His earliest published compositions include many for conventional chamber-music groupings, which show clearly the characteristics inherent in serialism; the *Three Studies* for cello and piano (1954), for which he had Nelson Cooke in mind; or the *Pezzo dramatico* for solo piano (1956), which he wrote for Margaret Kitchin. Banks is not a strict serialist, and he allows for that element of musicianly common-sense usually called intuition. Indeed he rejects total serialism, and can see no inherent merit in an ability to count from 1 to 12. On the other hand discipline, from whatever source, is essential. The *Pezzo dramatico*, for instance, only 106 bars long, is a thing of contrasts, of marked rhythms, of concentration in depth rather than expansion in length. Its atonal sonorities are exploited at a speed which is, on average, slow—a general characteristic of Banks's music.

The nature of serialism is incompatible with a *scherzando* style, as he found in the *Sonata da Camera* for eight instruments, written in 1961 in memory of Matyas Seiber, and played at a Cheltenham Festival concert that year. The second of its three movements is actually marked *scherzando*, but the lightness of rhythm is short-lived, and it is not long before the music reverts to that fragmentation of the series, and that somewhat self-conscious brooding over the sonorities, that is the mark of the style of many a serial composer at this time. It is not in such works as these that Banks's individuality is most marked.

Nor, quite, in the two horn works which he has written for his fellow-Australian, Barry Tuckwell: the *Horn Trio* (1962) and the *Horn Concerto* (1965). The first uses an 8-note cell, and is not serially organised; the second is. But he would be a bold man who could claim to detect any difference. Banks tends instinctively towards atonalism, and follows his material through to whatever conclusion it may lead him. Both works begin romantically, with a melodic *legato* line; this is practically unavoidable with an instrument of such strong romantic associations as the horn. Again, both works exploit the interval of the fourth. But the concerto is a more developed work than the trio; whereas the trio falls into three

recognisably conventional movements, the concerto consists of eight
contrasted sections, played continuously. The series used leads to a
characteristic chord, which acts as the motto of the whole work, and
consists of a fourth superimposed on an augmented fourth.[1] This
appears at the beginning of each section, differently scored and in
varying guises, which gives the piece a structural unity; it also concludes
the work. Moreover, the nature of the horn, and the different sounds of
which it is capable, are much more fully exploited in the concerto than
they are in the trio.

Already in the middle piece of the *Three Studies* Banks is aware of the
subtlety of sound, and his stylistic development springs from this
awareness. Style for him is the process of refining the use of sounds;
he is concerned with every aspect of the subtle nature of their use. So
his work branches out in two main directions; one is towards an ever-
increasing refinement in his use of the standard instruments of the
orchestra, in those works which call for them; the other direction is
towards the integrated use of newly-found styles and ideas, such as jazz,
avant-garde experiments, and electronic effects.

His approach to electronic sounds, as with others, is both direct and
primitive. His interest is instinctive, but he needs to discover his own,
and to work them into his own experience. He is interested in the
possibility of using instruments and tapes together, much as Mario
Davidovsky has in *Synchronisms*, and the first result of this appears in
Intersections for electronic sounds and orchestra (1969).

His reaching out towards these exploratory regions has already led to
some striking results, such as *Equation I* (1963/4) and *Equation II* (1969),
Settings from Roget (1966) and *Tirade* (1968). The first three of these are
an attempt to fuse together jazz and orchestral music, in what the
American composer Gunther Schuller has called 'Third Stream'. The
precedent for this was provided in Seiber's *Jazzolets* and *Improvisation*.
In Bank's *Equation* the antithesis of quick-moving jazz music and slow-
moving music for orchestral instruments produces a strange mixture of
contrasted associations, of familiar effects in unfamiliar contexts.

Again, in the *Settings from Roget*, he mixes serialism with jazz, notably
in the first two Settings. The problem of combining the free-feeling of
jazz with the strictness of serialism is largely overcome by his use of a
12-note series which divides into three four-part chords with tonal
implications. In the final piece a series is not used: here he considered
pitch control much less important, and it is more of a 'sound piece',
although an 8-note *trope* is used as the basis of both improvised and
written sections. In fact the characteristic vitality of jazz, combined with

1. The war-chord used by Tippett in *King Priam*. (see p. 287.)

the intellectual content of serialism, and the exploration into new sounds, together produce a musical mosaic that is both original and highly representative of the present age. It is as much a reflection of the 60's as Walton's *Façade* was of the 20's.

Banks' reasoned explanation of the use of jazz in a composed score is that, whereas American composers have a legitimate jazz background against which to work, this is not necessarily shared by composers of other traditions. But as he sees it, the charm of jazz is that it allows for a musician's invention over a basis that is fixed. Take that away, and dispense with the compositional process, and the music becomes merely repetitive. A later piece in this category is *Meeting Place* (1970), for chamber ensemble, jazz group, and electronic sound synthesiser.

Tirade does not use jazz; it falls instead, without any qualification, into the category of the *avant-garde*. Three poems by the Australian Peter Porter set the Australian scene through three aspects of time, present, past, and present-future. The third poem is a protest against the commercial exploitation of the country's natural beauty. The work is for mezzo-soprano, piano, harp, and three percussion players, each of whom operates about fifteen assorted instruments. Again Banks introduces an alternation of opposites; this time speech as opposed to a vocal line—which, by itself, is a very simple vocal line, in inverse proportion to the complexity of the ensemble effects. The musical and psychological climax of the piece comes in the third song, with the words

'one day there'll be no inch we haven't raped'

p ———————— *f* ———————— molto *fff* (shriek)

Here the composer deliberately sets up a free situation, since to notate such an expression of frenzy would be a most complex and vain undertaking. All three percussion players improvise (*ff*); the piano plays free forearm clusters on all keys (*ff*); the controlling element is provided by an electronic siren, which gradually rises, then falls. Only the harp abandons the unequal struggle. By this means the climax built round the idea of frenzy is both limited in duration and controlled in intensity.

The other main direction in which Banks has progressed has been towards the ever more refined way of handling orchestral instruments. *Tirade* was written for his friend Keith Humble, who directed a French ensemble, the *Centre de Musique*. When earlier Humble was appointed to the Melbourne Conservatorium of Music, he asked Banks for a piece for the students to play; the result was the orchestral piece *Assemblies* (1966), which gives the impression of being tonal in conception, but actually uses a number of quasi-serial devices centred around the 'polarity' of a particular 4-part chord. Banks intended this piece as an introduction to students of some contemporary orchestral techniques, so one finds, for example, instruments being invited to improvise on a series of fixed pitches grouped within boxes. His earlier *Divisions for Orchestra* (1964/5) is more conventionally conceived and its musical material is derived from a basic hexachord developed into a 'combinatorial set'.[1]

But the culminating work of his purely orchestral output so far, and the one which most fully represents his mature style, is the *Violin Concerto* (1968). The striking originality of this work springs from its combination of a reasonably traditional background with the new-found control of sound-complexes resulting from the composer's individual interpretation of serial discipline. He starts from a cell, which can expand thematically; at the same time, all serial organization is made subject to the musical thought. He allows the material to go its own way, and to develop in its own right. For instance, the concerto was originally to have been in one movement, like the *Horn Concerto*; but it soon became clear to Banks that the music needed more room to move. Also, the second movement, which he found the most difficult to write, was more complicated than the simple opening material would suggest. The structure of the concerto thus arose consciously, step by step, from the nature of the material. The work contains nothing experimental; the effects fall within the framework of normally accepted violin technique, and the soloist is not called on to subject his instrument to any of those experimental procedures so characteristic of the *avant-garde*; nor is there any rhythmical experiment. The soloist at the first performance, which was at a 1968 Promenade Concert, was Wolfgang Marschner, who had asked for 'something to play', as distinct from something to tap, scrape, scratch or knock. Soloists of standing, who probably own a Stradivarius or Guarnerius, are understandably reluctant to subject their instruments to treatment which may well result in damage or defacement.

Banks's concerto falls broadly within the classical concerto tradition; that is to say it has three movements, a basic tonality of D, a cadenza, a melodically prominent solo part, which contrasts yet integrates with its surroundings. At the same time the composer's individuality is apparent from the very opening bars. The soloist does not make a dramatic entry, but instead starts with nothing more startling than an open-string D; this is then juxtaposed with a stopped D on the G string. So begins the complex build-up of sounds; and the characteristic of the chosen series is such that it allows for a central hexachord which remains constant when the series is inverted, while the other hexachord is split into two

[1] A term coined by the American, Milton Babbitt.

outer groups of three notes, which are re-grouped for the second and third movements

Ex.26

Banks
Violin Concerto

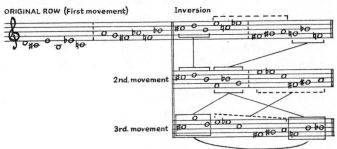

ORIGINAL ROW (First movement)   Inversion

2nd. movement

3rd. movement

The two hexachords give rise to clusters, which may appear as articulated glissandi, as rhythmic pizzicato, or as forceful attacks in orchestral *tutti* passages.

Again, the work may be seen as a study in the different relationships between soloist and orchestra. In the first movement, which the composer has called an 'interrupted cadenza', the soloist dominates. In the second movement, soloist and orchestra conduct a dialogue. In the finale, which contains the climax of the work, the two collaborate.

First movement   *Lento–Allegro*

Nine sections make up the first movement; four important solo sections are interspersed with five others.

Section i   (bars 1–18) Over a static solo D, the orchestra states the three main accompaniment figures. These are:
    a) A quiet, descending cluster (bar 2)
    b) A short, dramatic gesture, ending in a cluster (bar 3–4)
    c) A decorative pattern, given to percussion, piano and harp (bar 5–7)
After this the soloist opens out from the sustained D, with a hint of the *Allegro* that is to come.

Section ii   (bars 19–26) First solo cadenza, leading by quiet clusters to
Section iii (bars 27–56) *Allegro*
The soloist is accompanied by the full orchestra, which leads to a climax (bar 55)

Section iv   (bars 56–69) Second solo cadenza, lightly accompanied, introducing an important semiquaver figure, *accelerando*.

Section v   (bars 69–77) The percussion, piano and harp figure from the first section is developed. The violin has a static A, corresponding to the D of the opening.

Section vi (bars 77–87) Third solo cadenza, with echoes in the orchestra.

Section vii (bars 87–130) An orchestral cadenza, based on the first two accompaniment figures from the first section. The soloist enters at bar 107, and against a glittering backdrop of harmonic clusters in the strings, has fierce double-stoppings and attacks *au talon*. A final burst of protest (bar 121) gradually dissolves into the next section.

Section viii (bars 131–144) Fourth solo cadenza, reminiscent of previous sections, and lightly accompanied.

Section ix (bars 145–144) The soloist centres round D, as at the opening, while the orchestra recalls previous material retrospectively. The ending is very quiet.

Second movement   Andante cantabile   Allegro

Although this movement has certain rondo features (A–BC–A–D–A), it is equally as much a slow movement, a pastorale, a scherzo. It is more harmonic in conception than the first movement, and does not contain clusters. Moreover, to underline the structure, notes 4, 5 and 6 of the series are alloted to bells, horns and harp, to mark the end of the sections, of which there are six:

Section i (bars 1–15) A repeated-semitone figure, accompanied by chords, gives rise to flowing woodwind lines. The soloist is silent.

Section ii (bars 16–46) The violin starts with figuration similar to the opening woodwind passage; but this soon develops into a free cadenza, terminated once again by bell and harp.

Section iii (bars 47–111) Solo and orchestra combine in this central section, which is one of movement and development, leading to a big climax. The violin soars above the rest, then gradually sinks back, after the orchestra has died away.

Section iv (bars 111–136) A return to the opening semitone figure, but this time the violin takes part. Bell and horn again mark the end, whereupon a short bridge leads to

Section v (bars 137–162) The metre changes to $\frac{12}{8}$, *Allegro*, in the style of a scherzo. The soloist is accompanied mainly by the strings.

Section vi (bars 162–182) Coda. The semitone figure returns. The soloist finishes the movement, first with another free cadenza, then (for the first time) the semitone figure. Notes 1–6 of the series appear as an afterthought.

Third movement   Risoluto–Lento–Risoluto

The structure of this finale, as the tempo headings suggest, is a simple ternary one; its nature is that of a forceful and dramatic climax.

Section i   (bars 1–45) *Risoluto*
Semi-clusters in the orchestra alternate with sections of violin solo; these then combine contrapuntally, and develop. After the tension has dropped, the music leads into the next section.

Section ii   (bars 46–62) *Lento*
This section represents the slow movement of the concerto. Banks wished to refer back to the first movement clusters, but with greater subtlety. So a long, unfolding melody for the soloist is picked out, and echoed, by bass-clarinet and clarinet; the strings also follow the solo line, and gradually build up a four-octave cluster. The violin continues, but pursued this time by the piano, which eventually catches up (bar 58); whereupon, bit by bit, the string clusters dissolve.

Section iii (bars 62–112) *Risoluto*
A return to the mood of the beginning of the movement is marked by semi-clusters, and another solo cadenza; thereafter soloist and all the violins are in unison as they approach the biggest climax of the work. A concluding solo statement, followed by quick chords in answer from the orchestra, terminates the concerto.

An analysis such as this shows the means whereby Banks produces a work of originality with basically traditional means. And from his works up to this moment certain general conclusions can be drawn. One is that his musical personality has a strong romantic leaning, frequently apparent in his instrumental and orchestral works. The beginning of the finale of the *Violin Concerto*, for instance, and several points in the two horn works, are strongly romantic, however much this tendency is overlaid by serialism.

Two other features recur in his music. One is a fondness for slow speeds. It is as though he is always anxious to give the music time to breathe, and room to move. Moreover, not only does a complex, contrapuntal style, such as his, preclude very swift movement, but also, as already mentioned, the serial style itself is opposed to the light, *scherzando* touch. Another feature is his habit of taking up a new phrase on the same note on which the previous phrase finished.

His impulse to compose is absolute; his work has no programmatic content. Moreover, although he lives in England, his outlook is anything but narrowly English; it is international. Though he had heard the music of Walton, Bliss and Britten in Australia, his arrival in England introduced him to the music of the second Viennese school and also to such

K

pieces as Seiber's *Ulysses*, which affected him deeply. So the influences which were strongest with him were Central European, not English.

However, he has a strong sense of the duty of musicians to pay back into the common pool something of the assets of their experience. He has contributed a great deal in committee work of one sort or another, chiefly with the Society for the Promotion of New Music. His chairmanship of this society[1] coincided with that difficult period when their being left a large legacy meant that their constitution and function had to be re-thought. Banks sees the function of the Society as not only providing a platform for the performance of music by young composers, but also helping to provide for them many of the facilities they lack at present. With this in mind the S.P.N.M. helped to form in February 1969 a new Society—the British Society for Electronic Music—which aims at establishing a national studio for electronic music in this country. He is one of the founder-members of this society, and plays an active part in its organization. In September 1968 he was given charge of Adult Education in music at Goldsmith's College, London.

1. (see p. 365.)

IV

British by choice. The influence of other traditions

10 Franz Reizenstein

Franz Reizenstein was born in Nuremberg on 7th June 1911. His father, a doctor, was interested in painting and other artistic matters, and provided his family with a helpful and sympathetic background. Franz's sister was artistic, his brother was an amateur violinist, while he himself, from an early age, displayed remarkable gifts as a pianist and composer. He also possessed perfect pitch. So it seems likely that, in different circumstances, he might well have made his mark as a child prodigy. And it was not just a case of his being a composer who also played the piano. His technique was capable of the biggest works in the piano repertoire, and throughout his life the twin pursuits of piano playing and composition made up the two equal halves of his musical personality, and were inextricably bound together, each influencing the other.

In 1930 Reizenstein went to the State Academy of Music in Berlin, where he studied composition with Hindemith, piano with Leonid Kreutzer.

Hindemith required of his pupils that they should acquire at least a working knowledge of all the standard orchestral instruments. As Reizenstein said:

He arranged for his students to take up different wind and stringed instruments in turn. . . We played together regularly and provided most of the music by composing it ourselves. We would not let anyone listen to the ghastly noises we produced—not that anybody wanted to—but we did learn how to write for the various instruments.

Hindemith thought most highly of him, and three guiding principles established during his years of study were never lost sight of later. First, a sense of tradition as being something present, active and growing. He became closely, intimately acquainted with the classical and romantic repertoire, and saw his function as a composer in terms of a continuation of that tradition. Second, a strictness and a discipline in composition, particularly as far as counterpoint was concerned. Third, a rejection of dodecaphony, atonalism, serialism, and all other *avant-garde* experiments. He aligned himself artistically with the established norms of tonal composition, as far as idiom and structure are concerned, and worked from that basis without reservations. His knowledge and love of the standard nineteenth century repertoire were too profound to admit of their being usurped by an allegiance to one of the more experimental schools of thought that began to be rife in Europe in the 20's and 30's, and have grown since.

An article on Hindemith[1] summarises his teacher's, and his own, aesthetic standpoint:

In all branches of the arts there exists a desire to delve into decadence and revel in the macabre, both things far removed from Hindemith's ideals. Vociferous advocates of surrealism, who proudly proclaim that they have freed music from the shackles of tonality, tend to minimise Hindemith's great achievements because he had the courage to expose the basic errors of their doctrine. Any music cast in traditional form or idiom is suspect in their eyes, even if it is of first-rate craftsmanship. They may continue their delicious dance around the serial golden calf indefinitely; this is of little consequence to the general public, who will decide in the long run which kind of twentieth century music it wants to hear. Some irresponsible critics, over-anxious to jump on the *avant-garde* bandwagon, present a false picture of Hindemith's position in present-day music, but most musicians agree that his music will live for a long time to come.

As soon as Hitler came to power in Germany, Reizenstein realized the evils of Nazism, particularly for those of Jewish birth; and so in 1934, at the age of twenty-three, he left and came to England—the first contemporary composer to do so. His choice was helped by the fact that an uncle on his mother's side lived at Kingston. He continued his studies at the Royal College of Music in London; composition with Vaughan Williams, and (later) piano with Solomon.

He never subsequently lost his respect for, nor the influence of, Hindemith, in spite of the very different influence exerted by his new teacher. He found Vaughan Williams much freer, less rigid; just as influential, but in a different way, as his was a dominating personality, both musically and spiritually. Other pupils found this to be the case, that Vaughan Williams was overwhelming as a teacher to all but the strongest; but in the case of Reizenstein it is difficult to think of anyone in England at this time who could have provided him with a more inspiring contrast to Hindemith, or who could better have introduced him to the nascent English tradition, which was from now onwards to form the background to his work.

1. In *The Listener*, 20th March 1964.

From Solomon, who revolutionized his attitude to the piano, he
learned insistence on tone-quality in piano playing, and on the greatest
control of touch, in so far as touch is the chief means of varying tone
quality. Control of tone, particularly at a pianissimo dynamic level, and
mastery of legato—a sense of melodic continuity, in spite of the up-and-
down movement of the keys and hammers—were the cornerstones of this
technical approach, which Reizenstein derived from Solomon. And
technique arose from the music itself.

Later (1958) Reizenstein was given a post at the Royal Academy of
Music as teacher of piano; and later still (1964) at the Royal Manchester
College. He was never appointed to teach composition at any of the
official music colleges in this country; and he only did so on a more
humble, semi-amateur basis, in evening classes at the Hendon Music
Centre and, much later, in America.

The later 30's were years of difficulty for him, of struggle and privation.
He was entirely involved in music, dedicated and professional. Both
then and subsequently, composition and recitals were his life; but not,
to start with, his livelihood. All his energy went into music-making, yet
he was never saturated. It was inevitable that sooner or later he would
triumph; but this was not to be before he had undergone considerable
hardship. On the outbreak of war in 1939 he was interned on the Isle of
Man, along with many others of non-British birth whose naturalisation
papers were not quite in order. In Reizenstein's case, a concert tour of
South America in 1937/8[1] had interrupted the continuity of his residence
in this country. However during his internment he was active in arranging concerts and performing in them.

Throughout this period Vaughan Williams helped him as much as he
could; by writing on his behalf during his internment, by putting work
in his way, such as piano arrangements or editing. Later in the war
Reizenstein volunteered for the army, but was not accepted owing to his
poor eyesight. He was given a job as a railway clerk for a while—and he
even managed to write part of his *Violin Sonata*, Op. 20, during this
period.

Just as his musicianship was made up of two equal halves—piano
playing and composition—so his personality displayed two chief features,
the serious and the funny; the romantic and the impish. As he took
pleasure in observing, he was born under Gemini. He took great delight
in jokes, whether musical or practical; and these found a natural outlet in
the diversions of Gerard Hoffnung in the 50's, which were a much-
needed counterbalance to the overwhelming seriousness that came over

1. With the Violinist Roman Totenberg, who later played in his Boston concerts, 1966
(see p. 148).

British music at this time. For these extravaganzas Reizenstein contributed specifically humorous scores (a notoriously difficult task), such as '*Lets fake an opera*', or '*Concerto populare*'. He also introduced a light note into more solemn surroundings; for instance into his choral work *Voices of Night*. Moreover, an element of fun formed an important part of his personal relationships. But he also liked peace, and the beauty of nature, which he found particularly conducive to composition.

Of his forty-eight compositions with Opus numbers, three-quarters consist of piano and chamber music. This was the medium in which his romanticism found the most apt expression. His pleasure in chamber music was the pleasure that comes from intelligent, cultured discourse between colleagues. He was fortunate in finding excellent musicians to perform his works, a fact which is itself an eloquent testimony to their worth: Max Rostal, Leslie Parnas and Maria Lidka, who was a regular member of his Trio.[1]

Reizenstein's first published work (1936) was the *Piano Suite*, Op. 6; but the first piece that brought him wide acclaim was the *Prologue, Variations and Finale*, Op. 12, for violin and piano, written for Max Rostal (1937–8), and later re-written for violin and orchestra, Op. 12a. The first ideas for this piece came during the South American tour in 1937, between Buenos Aires and Santiago de Chile; the finale is based on South American rhythms, 'en forme d'une Danse Fantasque'. The movements follow without a break, and are characterized by a brilliantly rhapsodic virtuosity, and an insight into instrumental technique, shown by a knowledge of fingering, free use of harmonics and so on, not often found among English composers. The form is cyclic; that is to say, four themes are heard throughout, first stated in the Prologue and developed in the Variations. The range of mood is wide, the texture highly varied.

After leaving Hindemith, he gave rein to his romanticism; which is to say that the effect of the music comes from the way its movement is controlled—at what dynamic, pitch or volume; with what degree and rapidity of harmonic consonance or dissonance—rather than from any theoretical organisation of the musical elements abstracted from, and independent of, their resulting sound.

Another outstanding piece for violin and piano is the *G sharp Sonata*, Op. 20, written for Maria Lidka. This has greater tonal freedom than the earlier piece. If the combination of major and minor modes may be traced to Vaughan Williams, and the prevalence of the interval of the fourth to Hindemith, the overall style is considerably more than the sum of these two constituent parts. The opening movement, in strict sonata

1. Franz Reizenstein (Piano), Maria Lidka (Violin), Rohan de Saram (Cello). (Also Derek Simpson and Christopher Bunting in earlier years).

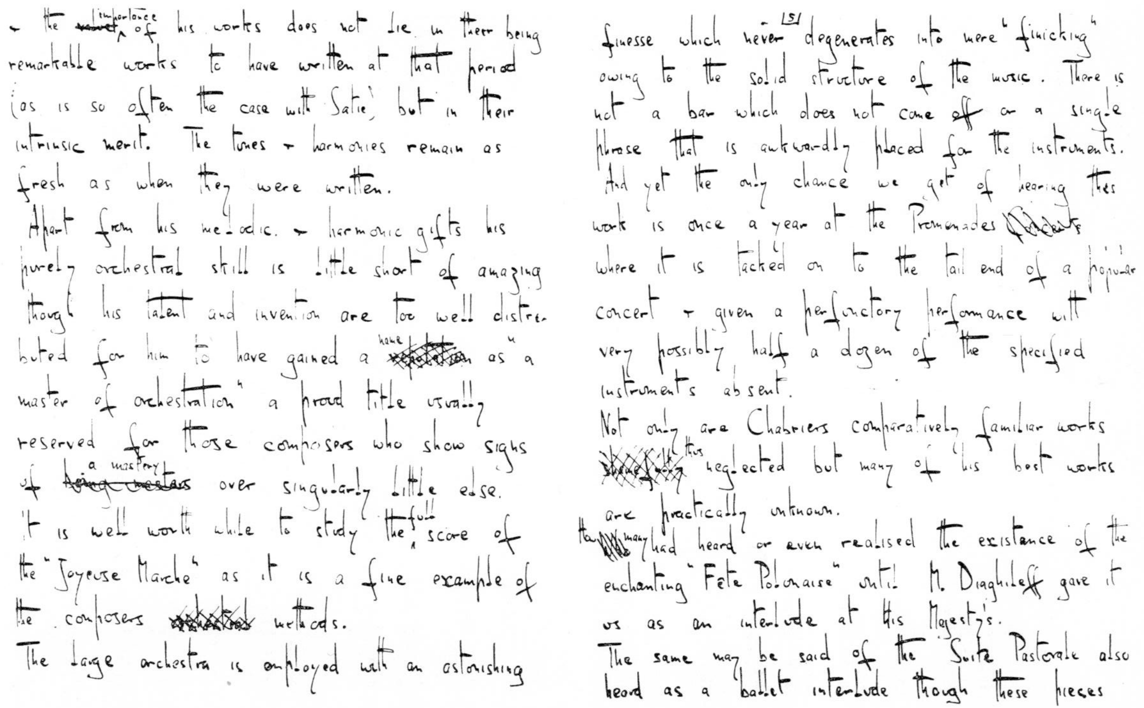

Plate I. Extract from an article on Chabrier by Constant Lambert, which appeared in *Apollo*, October 1926. *Author's manuscript: reproduced by permission.*

Plate 2. The opening page of Alan Rawsthorne's *Third Symphony*, showing the dedication to his wife. *Composer's manuscript; reproduced by permission* © *1965 by Oxford University Press*

Plate 3. Extract from the first movement of Alan Rawsthorne's *Third Symphony*, showing the approach to the climax-chord at [15]. *Composer's manuscript; reproduced by permission*

© 1965 by Oxford University Press

All instruments sound as written (except for octave transpositions

e.g. ContraBass, contrafagott°)

Plate 4. Extract from No. 6 of Denis ApIvor's *Overtones*. This piece is called after the Klee painting 'Sonnen und Mond Blumen' ('Sun and Moon flowers'). The two sections of the orchestra play, and are grouped, antiphonally; the soprano section (Orch. I) is associated with the idea 'Moon-flower', the bass section (Orch. II) with the idea 'Sun-flower'. *Composer's manuscript; reproduced by permission.*

Plate 5. The opening page of Roberto Gerhard's *Violin Concerto*, showing the dedication to a Cambridge scientist and his wife, friends of the composer. The bold directions pp, and rit . . . Io, are a conductor's blue-pencil marking. *Composer's manuscript ; reproduced by permission*

Plate 6. Extract from the first movement of Roberto Gerhard's *Violin Concerto*, showing some of the composer's characteristic corrections and cuts in the printed score. This forms part of the *Molto vivace con spirito* section following the cadenza and includes a reference to the violinist Yfrah Newman, who was the soloist for the recording of this work. *Reproduced by permission.*

© *Copyright 1960 by Mills Music Ltd.*

Plate 7. Extract from Andrzej Panufnik's *Universal Prayer*, showing the end
of the 12th verse of Alexander Pope's poem, set for Bass solo, and the organ
solo leading to the last verse. The key signature for the harps indicate the
pedal-settings, which remain unaltered throughout the work.

Composer's manuscript; reproduced by permission.

© *Copyright 1970 by Boosey & Hawkes Music Publishers Ltd.*

form, develops great warmth in its long-sustained arch-like phrases, a marked characteristic of this composer; and this is admirably balanced by the second movement, which is a scherzo in all but name, and which contains Spanish rhythms, such as the *jota*, and passages which recall the strumming of a guitar. The finale juxtaposes a slow violin *cantilena*, which has a *misterioso* piano background, suggestive of the rustling of trees in the wind, against a more vigorous, more contrapuntal section, in which the instruments discourse on equal terms. The main subject of the first movement returns, and the work concludes in a blaze of romantic glory.

This work marks the end of the first phase of his work, and there followed a two year gap (1945–47), partly devoted to film work, before he embarked on the central, most productive period of his life. This began with the *Scherzo*, Op. 21, and ended with the *Second Piano Concerto*, Op. 37; between these two works are included most of the large compositions by which he is chiefly known. First come two outstandingly successful pieces, the *Cello Sonata*, Op. 22, and the *Piano Quintet*, Op. 23. With the *Cello Sonata* Reizenstein emerges from his two-year silence with increased stature, and with greater command of his individual style of poly-tonality. Within the accepted limits of sonata form, implicit in a tonal idiom, he develops greater freedom of line than in works of the earlier period. Both instruments are used in virtuoso manner, and the characteristic juxtaposition of contrasted moods occurs in the second (scherzo) movement, in which a *vivace* theme, built in fourths, is followed by a poignant, rhapsodic, *cantabile* theme (*lento*), full of tonal ambiguity and contrast of colour—the *sine qua non* of romanticism. The finale is graded in excitement; an *adagio* introduction, which contains most of the material to follow, leads to the main A major theme (*allegro amabile*), which in turn develops into *agitato*.

The *Piano Quintet*, which was his favourite, is the largest of Reizenstein's chamber music compositions, and most fully sums up his contribution to this branch of music. Refined, polished, its four movements firmly grounded in the classical sonata structure, the work can justifiably be placed beside the great chamber works of the past. In his development of the melodic-harmonic-tonal methods of the nineteenth century, and within the context of the English tradition, Reizenstein discovered his characteristic polytonal idiom. And the slow second movement of this Quintet, in which by definition the pace of harmonic change is comparatively slow, is an excellent illustration of the fresh discoveries that lay in store in 1948 for a composer who was able to pursue a path that, according to some, was played out. The chromaticism after [o] is complete, and the twelve notes are used freely; yet never once is the tonal control lost. This section of the slow movement also contains much rhythmic and contrapuntal development, yet always within the framework of a regular underlying metre, so fundamental to the chamber music style.

The scherzo movement gains in brilliance from the larger ensemble. The material, taken from what has gone before, is shared between the instruments with a sense of gay abandon which Reizenstein never surpassed. There is no contrasted mood in this long movement, but nor is there any need for it; the momentum, once established, runs its appointed course. Not till the finale do we encounter any slackening of intensity; starting *andante sostenuto*, the music builds up, as in the Violin Sonata, to *allegro vivace*, then *agitato*. After considerable contrapuntal work, canonic imitation and so on, the instruments come together on the final page for a brilliant conclusion.

To this middle group of works also belongs Reizenstein's small but important output of choral compositions. The first of these, the cantata *Voices of Night*, Op. 27, was written in 1950/1, and first heard in June 1952. The appeal of this work immediately led to two more commissions—the radio opera *Anna Kraus*, Op. 30, and the oratorio *Genesis*, Op. 35, which was first heard at a Three Choirs Festival in 1958. The librettist for all these works was Reizenstein's close friend, the poet Christopher Hassall, who also collaborated with Walton (*Troilus and Cressida*) and Bliss (*Tobias and the Angel*).

Both *Voices of Night* and *Genesis* suffer to some extent from the swing away from the old oratorio tradition that has already been referred to, though *Voices of Night* suffered less than the other work in this respect, since its subject is not specifically religious; moreover the composer's sensitivity to the English language helped to make it a popular success. The work is a sequence of poems invoking night, starting with the onset of night, finishing with the dawn. When the poetry is romantic, contemplative, the composer achieves a most apt result. Such moments occur on No. 1 ('How lovely is the heaven of this night') and No. 10 ('On thy cold shore, O Death'); the music and the words develop in true partnership. But in the poems whose mood is less reflective, the function of the music can only be to add colour to the words; and in such circumstances, with banality just around the corner, Reizenstein's characteristic idiom needed to be held severely in check to avoid inconsistency between words and music. No. 3 ('Sweet Suffolk Owle') and No. 4 ('The bread is all baked') are examples of this more objective sort of word-setting. The composer's model for this aspect of his work was Vaughan Williams' *Five Tudor Portraits*; it is no surprise to hear that Vaughan Williams approved of Reizenstein's vocal style. But such word-painting, verging

sometimes on naïveté, implies a lessening of the role of music in relation
to the poetry; and this was precisely one of the reasons contributing to
the decline of the old English oratorio.

Reizenstein's second choral work, the oratorio *Genesis*, consists of the
story of the Creation, as related in Genesis, interspersed with poems
from various sources to add imagery to the original story. As well as
arranging the text, Hassall contributed one poem, in which he sets forth
the tendency of our age to risk the negation of God's creative work
through the misuse of man's knowledge; other poets represented are
Blake, Milton, George Herbert. The soloists are the same as in the other
choral work—soprano and baritone. Curiously, however, the oratorio is in
many ways more successful than the cantata; the composer himself
preferred it. Though it attempts less, it is better integrated, and more
developed a work, and though it fits more obviously than the cantata
does into a limited tradition, rooted in the past—the much-vaunted
British choral tradition—it is more consistently compelling than the other
work, whose roots are shallower. Its style is more characteristic of its composer's maturity; the use of the fourth may be traced to Hindemith, the
use of moving triads to Vaughan Williams, but the polytonal counterpoint
is the product of the two, and a marked feature of Reizenstein's idiom.

Can it be that one accepts the somewhat academic convention of
fugal choruses in a specifically sacred work, whose milieu is an English
cathedral, with fewer reservations than one has about such a device in a
work designed for concert use? For instance, the choral writing in No. 3a
of *Genesis* ('And Man became a living soul') may be conventional, but it
is at the same time considerably more evocative, and apt, than the fugal
writing for male chorus in *Voices of Night* with which Reizenstein seeks
to adorn the immortal words:—

> *He who goes to bed, and goes to bed sober,*
> *Falls as the leaves do, and dies in October;*
> *But he who goes to bed, and goes to bed mellow,*
> *Lives as he ought to do, and dies an honest fellow.*

Such an admirable sentiment hardly requires traditional fugal treatment, or indeed musical treatment of any sort (except perhaps satirical)
for its full message, with all its undoubted depth of philosophical insight,
to be conveyed.

But the fugue is an illustration of the lighter, impish side of Reizenstein's personality. It is intended as a joke.

After *Genesis* two further works complete the central group of compositions: *Five Sonnets of Elizabeth Barrett Browning*, for tenor and piano,
Op. 36, and the *Second Piano Concerto*, Op. 37. Then followed the second

gap in his output, lasting from 1960 to 1963, which was at last broken by
two pieces for wind instruments. As all Hindemith pupils were obliged
to write for, and to play, all orchestral instruments, writing for the wind
instruments came naturally to Reizenstein; particularly the clarinet,
which he played with greater application than the others. His last composition was a *Sonatina for clarinet*, Op. 48, of which he had completed
only two movements at the time of his death.[1] This piece was intended
to be as approachable a work as the *Oboe Sonatina*, Op. 11, written over
thirty years earlier.

The last years of his life were prolific, and his compositions included
the three *Solo Sonatas*, the *Concert Fantasy* for viola, the *Second Piano
Sonata* in A flat, Op. 40, and the *Concerto for String Orchestra*, Op. 43.

The *Concert Fantasy*, Op. 42, was finished in 1966 in Boston, U.S.A.
It was written for Elizabeth Holbrook, and in addition to calling for a
virtuoso technique, it is a substantial recital piece, exploiting an instrument whose repertoire is somewhat limited in this respect. It is in one
continuous movement, whose various sections alternate slow with fast.
The tonal scheme is classical, while some material (at [G]) introduces a
new display technique for the viola. It is possible that Reizenstein was
influenced in this work by the Walton concerto; the two composers
were on friendly terms, and Reizenstein admired Walton's music.
This was his first composition for the viola; and he followed it the next
year with another major work, the *Solo Sonata* Op. 45, also written for
Elizabeth Holbrook (see plate 8).

It is perhaps surprising that his natural bent for the piano, combined
with his innately romantic temperament, did not result in more compositions for that instrument. But such works as exist are big pieces, and
they repay the closest study. The *Twelve Preludes and Fugues*, Op. 32
are a brilliant exposition of that polytonal idiom, made up of the coupling
together of the major and minor modes in a contrapuntal texture.
The whole composition is dedicated, very appropriately, to Hindemith,
since the order of the keys is that of Series 1 evolved by Hindemith as
the foundation of his theory in *The Craft of Musical Composition*. The
Series presents the notes in the order of their relationship to the nucleus
tone C. It is also used as the main theme of the first Prelude. Unity is
achieved between each pair by introducing the Fugue subject into the
Prelude, though sometimes in a disguised form; in some of the pairs,
there is no break between the Prelude and its accompanying Fugue.[2]

1. The manuscript is dated July—September, 1968.
2. In Nos. 1, 3, 5, 7, 8, 10, 11. The composer has suggested possible groupings for
performance when it is not possible to play the complete set: 3, 4, 5; 6, 9, 10; 3, 7, 8;
1, 2, 3, 4; 11, 8, 12,; 11, 12.

This composition, with its combination of contrapuntal ingenuity and sheer intellectual toughness, obviously recalls Hindemith's *Ludus Tonalis*.

A nine year gap separates it from the next piano piece, the *Second Sonata*, Op. 40; and indeed twenty years separate the two piano sonatas from each other. The first, dedicated to Walton, had been widely heralded, on its publication in 1948, as one of the most important works of the century; with the second, Reizenstein reached mature fulfilment. If romanticism can be defined, at least in part, as the outpouring of music in terms suited to a particular instrument, then this second sonata is romantic pianism *par excellence*. It is also intellectually and dramatically conceived. It opens with a slow motto (*tranquillo*), partly melodic octaves, partly B–A–C–H[1] harmonized in triads. From this the first movement (*allegro*) is derived. The second movement is in memory of Christopher Hassall, who had died the previous year (1963), and uses material derived from the opening of *Genesis*. The Finale, largely in two parts only, is a brilliant *vivace*, almost a *perpetuum mobile*. The motto theme triumphantly concludes the work.

Reizenstein's last large-scale composition was the *Concerto for String Orchestra*, Op. 43, which was not performed until January 1969, after his death. It is in no sense a virtuoso concerto; neither soloist nor solo group is set against the rest of the orchestra. It is a work of a subdued nature, though calling for strength and urgency in performance, and the four movements are of serenade dimensions, in which the instruments are used in different relationships to each other, whether homophonic or polyphonic. The tonality of the first and last movements is C, while the other two movements use the tonality a minor third lower (A) and a minor third higher (E flat) respectively. The first movement uses a miniature sonata form, with little or no development, and the second theme (*poco meno mosso*) grows as a countersubject over the first. The customary scherzo is highly characteristic of this composer, while the principal theme of the slow movement moves in short, cumulative phrases, and its two appearances are separated by imitative passage-work, starting in two parts. After an introduction in E flat minor, based on the third movement material, the finale starts, inevitably, with a fugue in C. Fourths predominate in the working out, and after a brief interlude (*un poco tranquillo*) the fugue subject is recapitulated, starting on F and in a varied form.

Orchestral composition did not come easily to Reizenstein. Not only did Hindemith's training make it more difficult for him to think, and write, orchestrally, but the linear, contrapuntal style that was so peculiarly his, was not suited to the orchestral medium. His purely orchestral

1. The notes B flat–A–C–B natural.

works are few, and reflect his sense of fun: the concert overture *Cyrano de Bergerac*, for instance, is light in style. He also wrote the *Ballet Suite*, Op. 15, which was commissioned by the Arts Theatre. He started a symphony, but never finished it.

It was in the concertos that he achieved fulfilment as an orchestral composer. In the two piano concertos, particularly, he found in the sheer joy of a virtuoso solo part sufficient compensation for the general absence of that contrapuntal and fugal development which was so central to his style, but which is somewhat out of place in a romantic solo concerto.

In the use of a tonally-centred idiom, such as Reizenstein's, the degree of musical intensity imparted to the listener can be measured by the frequency of change of the tonal centre. Frequent changes, close together, induce a sense of approaching climax with much greater urgency than infrequent changes, more widely spaced out. Clearly an instrumentally-conceived phrase is susceptible of greater rapidity of change than one which is vocally conceived; the human voice can only with difficulty assimilate frequent changes of tonal centre. And it is remarkable that the rate of tonal change in the first piano concerto is greater, generally speaking, than in the second concerto, which came after the choral and vocal compositions, and was influenced by them to some extent.

Reizenstein's true style has an inner vitality, a poetry, which lies in the content of the notes rather than in the notes themselves. The concertos differ from the chamber music works in that they demand a more rhetorical, emotive, exuberant style, which is proper to the romantic concerto, but which can all too easily lead to empty excess, as sections of the violin concerto show.

But his insight into string writing make the cello and violin concertos rewarding, if difficult, to play. The early *Cello Concerto* is perhaps less original a work than the other, and not readily accessible to the ordinary listener, though Reizenstein himself liked the work, and Leslie Parnas, who had played it through with the composer in Boston, during rehearsals for the *Sonata*, performed it for the BBC in 1969[1], and intends to take it into his repertoire.

The salient points of Reizenstein's tonal idiom may be summarized under the time-honoured headings of melody, harmony and rhythm. Among his most frequent melodic characteristics are a breadth of phrase, a symmetry of design; also a fondness for a group of notes (two or more) a semitone apart, followed by a major or minor third, or triad perhaps, either upwards or downwards; by this means the composer combines chromatic and tonal elements in the melodic line. His harmonic style rests

1. Bryden Thomson conducted the BBC Northern Symphony Orchestra.

on two foundations, already mentioned; one, the combination of different tonal centres, to produce an effect of polytonality; the other, the prevalent use of the fourth, which derives from Hindemith's teaching. As far as Reizenstein's rhythmic structure is concerned, a regularity of metre was an intrinsic *datum* of his contrapuntal technique, and his sense of rhythm was an essential part of his unfailing craftsmanship. The *avant-garde* meant nothing to him; he was not so much an innovator as a searcher-out of existing techniques. Furthermore, as already mentioned, his ability to write a genuine *vivace*, *scherzo* movement was inherently part of his style, and singled him out from most English composers. Indeed it was a reflection of his lively personality and sense of humour, which found such witty and pungent outlet in his contributions to Gerard Hoffnung's musical extravaganzas in the 50's.[1]

Of equal importance to him was his highly successful work as a concert pianist, from the moment when he first won recognition in the 30's, right through to the end of his life. He first made his name by his performance of Hindemith's *Ludus tonalis*, as well as of his own works. His last engagement as a pianist was, perhaps appropriately, on Nuremberg Radio, in September 1968, when he played his *Second Sonata* and *Zodiac Suite*, Indeed, at the very moment of his sudden death the following month, he was preparing Hindemith's *Piano Concerto*, *Kammermusik No. 2*, Op. 36, for a broadcast.

Reizenstein was a natural pianist. As well as playing his own works, he was conversant with the broad stream of the classical repertoire. His playing had nobility, and a wide emotional range; he also possessed, in full measure, the composer's urge not merely to analyse what he played, but to investigate for himself the lesser-known byways of music; and his catch included rarities, such as Tchaikowsky's *Concert Fantasy*, Bizet's *Variations Chromatiques*, and Dvorak's incomplete *Piano Concerto*, which he edited, revised and arranged—as Dvorak himself had at one time intended to do.

1. One such work, the *Concerto Populare*, or *Piano Concerto to end all Piano Concertos*, was heard in November 1956. The story behind it is as follows:

   'Once upon a time a pianist and a conductor were engaged to play a concerto with a well-known orchestra. Unfortunately, the management omitted to specify *which* concerto. The pianist came prepared to play the Grieg, but the conductor decided otherwise. It was to be Tchaikovsky's famous First—or none at all! Musicians are naturally temperamental and neither would give way. Eventually after a struggle during which fragments of Greig, Tchaikovsky, Rachmaninoff, Gershwin, Beethoven, popular songs and other oddments were heard flying through the night air, the pianist was overwhelmed by the superior forces. He gave way, not without a gallant attempt to have the last chord.'

   The performance, we are told, was a resounding success in every sense of the word.

Curiously perhaps, Reizenstein had no very high opinion of Hindemith's piano style, which he considered awkward, unpianistic. He did however play his teacher's piano pieces frequently, and *Ludus tonalis* was the model, as we have seen, for his own investigations. He had a great admiration for Bartok's work, particularly as shown in that composer's understanding of the piano; though he never copied the percussive style.[1] The other contemporary composers that chiefly excited his admiration were Walton and Shostakovitch.

His appearances in concerts and radio performances were very frequent; moreover, towards the end of his life, when his name was more known internationally, his services as teacher, lecturer and panel-member began also to be in demand. He spent six months in 1966 (January-June) as visiting professor of composition at Boston University in America, where he went at the invitation of Professor Jean Philips to teach composition, with particular reference to his own works. While there he appeared in two concerts specially devoted to his own compositions. This provides one more instance of the enthusiasm and the readiness with which American musicians acknowledge the proven worth of British composers, which their British colleagues are sometimes very slow to give; Gerhard and Fricker are two further instances of this unfortunate trend. In the case of Reizenstein, a number of fine compositions, particularly in the field of chamber music, and a marked individuality of idiom, place him among the important composers of the contemporary period.

List of compositions by Franz Reizenstein

Year	*Op. no.*	*Piano & Chamber music*	*Orchestral & Choral*
1931	1	Solo Sonata for Cello (later rev. as Op. 44)	
1932	2	Theme, Variations & Fugue for Clarinet Quintet (rev. 1960)	
1933	3	Fantasy for piano	
1934	4	Four Silhouettes for piano	
	5	Wind Quintet	
1936	6	Suite for Piano	
	6a	Three pieces for Violin & Piano (arr. from Op. 6)	
	7	Elegy for Cello and Piano (pub. with Op. 18)	
	8		Cello Concerto (rev. 1948)

1. He once turned the pages for Bartok at a Wigmore Hall concert.

List of compositions by Franz Reizenstein (continued)

Year	Op. no.	Piano & Chamber music	Orchestral & Choral
	9	Divertimento for String Quartet	
1937	9a	Divertimento for Brass Quartet (2 Trumpets. Horn, Tuba)	
	10	Three Concert Pieces for Oboe & Piano	
	11	Sonatina for Oboe & Piano	
1938	12	Prologue, Variations & Finale for Violin & Piano	
	12a		Op. 12, arr. for Violin & Orch.
	13	Partita for Flute & Piano	
	13a	Op. 13 for Flute & String Trio	
	14	Impromptu for Piano	
1940	15		Ballet Suite (pub. 1964)
1941	16		Piano Concerto No. 1
	17	Intermezzo for Piano	
	18	Cantilene for Cello & Piano (pub. with Op. 7)	
1944	19	Sonata No. 1 in B for Piano	
1945	20	Sonata in G sharp for Violin & Piano	
1947	21	Scherzo in A for Piano	
	22	Sonata in A for Cello & Piano	
1948	23	Quintet in D for Piano & Strings	
1949	24	Legend for Piano	
	25	Trio in A for Flute, Oboe & Piano	
1950	26	Scherzo Fantastique for Piano	
1951	27		*Voices of Night* S.&B.soli,Ch.&Orch.
	28		Concert Overture *Cyrano de Bergerac*
	29		Serenade in F
	29a	Serenade in F (for wind instruments)	
1952	30		Radio Opera *Anna Kraus*
1953	31		Violin Concerto
1955	32	Twelve Preludes & Fugues for Piano	
1956	33	Fantasia Concertante for Violin & Piano	
1957	34	Trio in one movement (ded. to Vaughan Williams)	

List of compositions by Franz Reizenstein (continued)

Year	Op. no.	Piano & Chamber music	Orchestral & Choral
1958	35		*Genesis*
1959	36		Oratorio, Soli Ch. Orch. Five Sonnets of E. B. Browning (for Tenor & Piano)
	37		Piano Concerto No. 2
1963	38	Duo for Oboe & Clarinet	
	39	Trio for Flute, Clarinet & Bassoon	
1964	40	Sonata No. 2 in A flat for Piano	
	41	Zodiac—Piano Suite	
1965/6	42	Concert Fantasy for Viola & Piano	
1966/7	43		Concerto for String Orchestra
1967	44	Solo Sonata for Cello (rev. from Op. 1)	
	45	Solo Sonata for Viola	
1968	46	Solo Sonata for Violin	
	47	Arabesques for Clarinet & Piano	
	48	Sonatina for Clarinet & Piano (2 movements only completed)	

other works without Op. No.:

Five imaginative pieces for Piano (1938)
Short educational pieces
Musical Box, for Piano (1952)
Capriccio (1938)
A Jolly Overture (1952)

Scores in collaboration with Gerard Hoffnung:

Concerto Populare (Piano Concerto to end all Piano Concertos)
Lets Fake an Opera (The tales of Hoffnung)
(librettist William Mann)

Film scores include:

Highlights of Farnborough (1951)   The Mummy (1959)
The Sea (1953)   The White Trap (1959)
The House that Jack built (1953) Jessy (1959)
Island of Steel (1955)   Circus of Horrors (1960)

and others

11 Matyas Seiber

Matyas Seiber came to this country to take up residence in 1935, at a time when the broad pattern of the musical life of England consisted of the establishment, and the consolidation, of the standard repertoire, and when the nascent English tradition was just developing, mainly under the benevolent tutelage of Vaughan Williams. The general attitude of most musicians tended to a narrow parochialism; English music as a whole was not yet ready or stable enough to admit the influence of continental developments; few indeed were aware of, or susceptible to, the new paths that were currently being unfolded in Europe and America.

Moreover, when Matyas Seiber came here at the age of thirty, he was unknown; he had not yet achieved distinction, and he lacked those academic or official qualifications which are required of musicians before they are admitted to teach in the established English institutions. Little wonder, therefore that he was to be faced with long years of struggle before any sort of recognition came his way. There is a gap in his serious output after 1935;[1] meanwhile, in order to earn a living, he turned his hand to anything and everything.

But versatility had always been one of his chief characteristics. Broadly speaking, his musical personality may be considered under two main headings: his work as a teacher, and his work as a composer—in that order.

He was born in Budapest in 1905, and studied under Kodaly at the Royal Academy there. By 1925 he had written several highly colourful student works, including the *Sonata de Camera* for violin and cello; then, like his teacher before him, he set out on his travels. He was a remarkably susceptible musician, and wished to discover for himself the

1. Particularly in his 12-note composition, for which there was then no audience in England. The *Second String Quartet*, a strictly serial work, was finished in 1935; not until 1944 did he return to a serial style—and quite a free one this time—with the *Fantasia Concertante* for violin and orchestra, written for Max Rostal.

multifarious strands that made up the fabric of European music between the wars. These strands, some of them mutually incompatible, were chiefly folk music, early music, jazz, popular and light music, serialism.

After leaving Hungary in 1925 he travelled widely, visiting North and South America, as well as many European countries. He eventually settled in Frankfurt, where he taught jazz at the Conservatoire. He stayed there until 1933, when he had to leave Germany under Hitler. During these years his ability as an executive musician also spread in many directions. He was a pianist and conductor; he directed music in a theatre; he formed workers' choruses; he was cellist in a string quartet.[1] When once again, after 1933, he was compelled to move his residence, he eventually, in 1935, settled in England, where he lived for the rest of his life, until he was killed in a car accident in South Africa in October 1960.

If his innate curiosity was to give his compositions a variable quality, it also made him one of the most sought-after teachers in England, catholic in taste, wide-ranging in experience. He was never appointed to the staff of any of the major teaching institutions, yet his ability to inspire pupils placed him in the same category as Hindemith or Nadia Boulanger. His pupils, who came eventually from all over the world, included Francis Chagrin, Malcolm Lipkin, Reginald Smith-Brindle, Peter Racine Fricker, Anthony Milner, Don Banks, Hugh Wood, and many others. Thus was his influence most directly and most strongly felt.[2]

His teaching technique was unorthodox; he was concerned with the writing of music, not academic exercises. His mind was agile, logical, penetrating; yet the personal style of each pupil was never interfered with, nor was the necessity for the individual student to discover his own solutions ever lost sight of. How each pupil went about his craft was his own affair; but he could expect the results of his labours to be scrutinized with minute and often devastating attention to detail, down to the smallest particle.

Seiber's views on teaching were summarized in a talk he gave in 1955:

I believe in a few fundamental principles. First, that learning or teaching composition is a purely *practical* matter (no mystery and no theory). It's like learning to make shoes. Just as a shoemaker learns step by step how to cut the right size of upper soles so as not to pinch, how to make joints which don't creak etc., so the student must learn how to present ideas, how to lead from one to the other, how to make joins.

We all agree that we can't teach inspiration, but we can teach the technique of how to make the most of that inspiration, if there is any.

1. The Lenzewesky Quartet.
2. Particularly in the 1950's. See p. 156.

I believe that composition is a technique which can be best learned by imitation, like other crafts. I think the ideal solution would be to have a sort of 'composing workshop', like some of the great painters had 'painting work-shops'. The composer would be given small tasks, details in the master's works, and then be corrected by the master and shown how *he* would have done it. The composition student, in fact, should be a kind of apprentice.

The second point I believe in is that composition is an entirely traditional discipline. There is no short cut—you have to go through the techniques which your predecessors developed, because these are the entire foundation of our present-day techniques.

Also I believe that one of the essential things in the training of a young composer is analysis; and I mean analysis in depth, down to atoms and cells, discovering how a kind of life-process goes on, like in any living tissue.

His own compositions include every species of music, reflecting the range of his curiosity. Inevitably some of the works are experimental. His Hungarian origin is apparent in a number of pieces, particularly early ones; both specifically, as in the arrangement of Hungarian folk-songs, and indirectly in such a work as the *Elegy for Viola and Chamber Orchestra*. His interest in light music, and the folk music of many countries, usually found an outlet in the commercial world of films, radio or television, which was his chief source of income. His fondness for jazz led to some hybrid attempts to bridge the gap between that idiom and more conventional composition; for instance the *Improvisations for Jazz Band and Symphony Orchestra*, which were written in collabora-tion with John Dankworth; or the *Two Jazzolets* for dance band, which date from his years at Frankfurt, and use a 12-note style in a jazz context. His study of early music led to the two *Besardo Suites* for orchestra, which were based on the music of the sixteenth-century lutenist-composer Jean-Baptiste Besard.[1]

But the greatest scope for the force of his musical intellect was provided by Schoenberg's 12-note style, and serialism, with which he overlaid these other more intuitive characteristics. Serialism, he considered, showed the way music was going; it was the international style, while the other styles were merely national, even local. It was in chamber music, and particularly in the works for violin and piano, that he developed his particular brand of serialism, the use of a permutation technique, based on a small group of notes and intervals. Chief among such chamber works are the *Second* and *Third String Quartets*, and the *Permutazioni a cinque* for wind quintet; his most characteristic violin and piano works are the *Concert Piece* (1954) and the *Sonata* (1960). He was particularly stimulated

1. Particularly the *Thesaurus harmonicus* (1603).

by the combination of two such dissimilar instruments, and the *Concert Piece* is an ingenious, totally chromatic work, based on the permutations of a 4-note group.

In many ways the work recalls Schoenberg's *Fantasy*, Op. 47, which was written only five years previously. Its texture is varied and lucid; its originally conceived sonorities cover the full range of the instruments; both players are treated as equal partners, and the composition as a whole is conceived as a virtuoso showpiece for them.

The 12-note row, on which the piece is based, is made up of three segments, each of which contains the basic *motif* of four notes, in the form of two semitones a tritone apart. This *motif* is then transposed twice. In the course of the composition the three segments change, as well as the sequence of notes within the segments. The structure of the work as a whole is that of a free fantasy, though balanced; the contrasted sections are later repeated in varied form. The first performance of the work, which is dedicated to Tibor Varga, was given by Eli Goren and Peter Wallfisch at a fiftieth birthday concert for the composer at Morley College, on 15th May 1955.

The sonata is similarly severe, and he introduced its first performance with a characteristically detailed analysis of its construction. His concluding words sum up his attitude to composition as a whole:

This sort of analysis might sound too mathematical, too calculated, as if music was put together with the help of a slide-rule. But in my opinion, this is the only way in which a composer may profitably talk on his own work. To talk in vague, aesthetic terms[1] doesn't come into his province.

Such constructive principles, such mathematical regularities as I mentioned, are never preconceived ideas with me. They develop as I go along working on a piece. I still cannot do what so many of my younger colleagues seem to be able to do so successfully, namely to plan out the whole work on the basis of these mathematical or architectonic calculations. For me the act of composing is still a journey of discovery; I *discover* all these possibilities inherent in the material as the piece begins to grow and unfold, and then I draw the consequences from them.

It means re-composing many things, until everything begins to fall into place. I know that this is a much more painful and time-consuming procedure, yet I still cannot bring myself to do otherwise. After all, it is for every composer himself to decide his place between freedom and strictness; he has to learn how to be coherent and organised, without losing the ability to listen to the unexpected, unaccountable and involuntary promptings of his own imagination.

1. The idea that the study of aesthetics is automatically and necessarily equated with 'vagueness' was the common view among most musicians, and is still widely held. See my *Contemporary Music*, p. 2.

In deciding his own personal 'place between freedom and strictness', Seiber opted for freedom. He was more concerned with the development of thematic material than with following any rules. On the other hand, he had studied and knew his Schoenberg, and moreover the force of his own intellect imposed its own strictness; so if his thematic material was mathematically conceived in the first place, as it frequently was, its development could only lie along strict lines. Therefore, if his work were to achieve warmth, this would only come from some other source than serialism.

So his use of this technique was by no means consistent or dogmatic; several pieces were quite traditionally conceived, for instance the *Elegy for viola and string orchestra* or the *Tre Pezzi* for cello and orchestra; while in others an innately lyrical style was placed somewhat inconsistently in a serial context; the *Third String Quartet*, the *Quartetto Lirico*, is a case in point.

Warmth of inspiration and strictness of idiom, however, came together, with the most positive results, in the two works with which he reached his highest point of stability and fulfilment as a composer; these were the two cantata settings of words by James Joyce, *Ulysses* and the *Three Fragments*. The texts of Joyce acted as a peculiarly powerful stimulus to Seiber's imagination, and in one sense supplied that poetic, lyrical and cohesive element that is sometimes missing from his more abstract works.

Seiber's cantata *Ulysses* for tenor solo, chorus and orchestra (1949), is based on passages from the novel of the same name by Joyce. It starts where the hero, Mr. Bloom, contemplates the starlit summer night, with 'the Heaventree of stars hung with humid nightblue fruit'. This leads to a contemplation of the universe, the vastness of space, stars and galaxies of immeasurably remote eons and infinite futures. In antithesis to this, there is the minuteness of some living organisms, the incalculable infinity of molecules contained in a single pinhead. His thoughts turn to eclipses, and the sudden stillness which comes with them. His conclusion is that all this is but a Utopia, and the 'Heaventree' a product of his own imagination.

Never was Seiber more sure that he had to set a passage to music. Like the text, his work is in five main sections, each in question and answer form.

The first section is atmospheric, suggesting the magic of night. A 3-note motive begins the movement, in the low strings, and this becomes the central core of the whole work.

The second movement is a passacaglia, to suggest the gradual build-up of size, the vastness of the universe. The climax comes with the addition of a choral fugue, to the words 'of our system plunging towards the constellation of Hercules'.

The third section, the only quick-moving movement, describes the minuteness of organic existence on earth. The 3-note group is extended into a 12-note fugue theme.

The fourth section, conceived as a Nocturne, recalls the hush of mystery during an eclipse. In this 'Homage à Schoenberg', Seiber took the two opening chords of Schoenberg's piano piece, Op. 19 No. 6, added two more of his own, and thus attempted, in 12-note terms, to express the quietness and remoteness he was seeking.

The fifth section, 'Epilogue', refers back to the 'Heaventree' ideal, and the music reverses the order of the opening section; starting with the bright colour of high strings, it moves gradually down to the low, dark sounds of the beginning, before fading into nothing.

When *Ulysses* was first performed in 1949 it made a considerable impact, and did more than any other of his works to establish Seiber's reputation as a composer.

Nine years later, when the Basel section of the I.S.C.M. commissioned him to write a chamber cantata, he returned to James Joyce for the text of the *Three Fragments* (1958), for speaker, wordless chorus and instrumental ensemble (flute, clarinet, bass clarinet; violin, viola, cello; piano and percussion). This time he chose passages from Joyce's *A Portrait of the Artist as a Young Man*. He explains his reason in these words:

A few passages of lyrical beauty, and of great dramatic power, stuck in my mind ever since I read them, and were, so to speak, ear-marked subconsciously for future use. Now it seemed the appropriate time to make use of them.

The cantata is in three movements. The first starts atmospherically, like *Ulysses*, with the words 'A veiled sunlight lit up faintly the grey sheet of water'. With the words 'He heard a confused music within him', the four voices of the chorus sing in four different tempi, while the orchestra adds further to the general melée with a rhythmical irregularity. Then gradually the sound recedes.

In strong contrast to this, the words of the second movement are a dramatic, terrifying description of a child's vision of the Day of Judgement. The music is wild, jagged, harsh.

The third movement reverts to the mood and material of the first before fading away to nothing.

Seiber's importance on the contemporary English scene lies primarily in his influence over other musicians and composers, particularly his pupils, and through his connection with Morley College. English music lacked a first generation of post-Schoenberg composers; by his precept and example Seiber supplied something of what was lacking, and demonstrated one highly intelligent and reasonable approach to the problems inherent in the 12-note style. If it is improbable that his music will evoke a wide or permanent response—partly because his roots lay elsewhere, partly because his eclecticism was so pronounced—nevertheless, he has without question indicated a path and held up a standard for others to follow.

In a sense, though the character and environment of the two men could hardly have been more contrasted, Seiber fulfilled the function and represented to the serial 50's something of what Walford Davies represented to the far-off and very different 30's. Walford Davies might be described as an intermediary musician, who spelt out what was happening in an evolving situation; his subject was the recently established concert repertoire, as well as the narrowly-defined field of church music. Seiber performed much the same service in the post-Schoenberg 50's. His subject was the contemporary scene, and in particular the narrowly-defined field of serialism.

He himself was well aware of the need for traditional roots if a composer's work is to be of more than ephemeral interest; he was also well aware of his debt to Joyce for the warmth and inspiration of his two cantatas; as he said shortly before his death:

Whether or not I shall have the opportunity of setting more of James Joyce's words I really cannot tell now. But for these two extracts I am eternally grateful to him. They are great literature, beautiful poetry, which has inspired me to write my two favourite works. No matter how often I read these passages, I always feel the same thrill as I felt when I read them for the first time.

12   Egon Wellesz

When Humphrey Searle went to Vienna to study under Webern, he
could hardly have foreseen that in a short time a colleague of Webern, a
composer steeped in the Viennese tradition, was to make his home in this
country; and had he wished to study under him, he would have needed
to travel no further than Oxford, where he had himself once been an
undergraduate.

Egon Wellesz was born in Vienna on 21st October 1885. He was a
fellow-student at that university with Webern, who was two years his
senior, and like him was also a private pupil of Schoenberg;[1] but in his
composition he followed a different path from Schoenberg. Composition
and musical history were the central features of his student period; he
was under Guido Adler for musical history, and eventually took his
doctorate with a thesis on the eighteenth-century Viennese composer
Giuseppe Bonno, whose importance for Wellesz was chiefly that he was
a contemporary of Gluck. Already Wellesz was showing a strong inclination towards opera, which was to occupy his main attention as a composer
for the next thirty years.

It was impossible to live just as a composer; many, such as Mahler,
were also conductors, though this involved many years of back-breaking
work on the provincial circuit. So Wellesz chose another path; his work
has followed the twin pursuits of musicology and composition. Though
they are distinct, the one is for him complementary to the other; he
brings to his composition the full range of his shrewd historical perspective. In the years up to 1938, when he came as a resident to this country,
the highest points of his achievement as a composer were *Alkestis* (1923)
and *Die Bakchantinnen* (1931); and it was the second of these two operas
which first gave him cause to visit England.

With a truly English flair for any and every sort of anniversary,
however remote, the authorities of Oxford University had noticed that
1932 happened to be the two hundredth anniversary of the birth of

1. 1904–1906, when Schoenberg was thirty.

Haydn—who had, on one of his visits to England, been made an honorary Doctor of Music of that university. Would it not be appropriate, therefore, if in 1932 another Viennese composer could be similarly honoured? The thought that this lot might have fallen upon Schoenberg himself is indeed a bizarre conception. However, the success of Wellesz's opera the previous year had been noticed by H. C. Colles, a pillar of the Oxford Establishment; and this, coupled with his earlier success in *Alkestis*, as well as his work as musicologist, was the decisive factor in his favour. As luck would have it, another musician who also received an honorary doctorate at the same time was Edward Dent, the Cambridge professor whom Wellesz had invited to be president of the I.S.C.M. in 1922, after he and Rudolph Reti had formed it in Salzburg the previous year. Wellesz in 1932 had a very considerable reputation, and the words of the official peroration— '*musicae hodiernae dux et signifer*'—were not merely empty rhetoric.

Wellesz sprang from the Viennese tradition, at a time when it reached its flowering in literature and art as well as in music; and the composer who exercised by far the strongest influence over him to start with was Mahler. As a boy of twelve he heard Mahler conduct *The Magic Flute*, *Lohengrin*, *The Flying Dutchman*, for the first time at the Wiener Hofoper; and the impression was indelible. Indeed, the impression of Mahler's performance of *Der Freischütz* was so strong on the young Wellesz that the very next day he himself began to compose. Again, when he first heard Mahler conduct Beethoven's ninth symphony, of which he (Mahler) made his own highly personal reading, and even made alterations to the scoring, the sound of Mahler's version of it was for Wellesz a 'school of orchestration'. Many years later he returned, on 26th June 1960, to the rebuilt Wiener Staatsoper, at the invitation of the conductor Karajan, to speak about the achievement of Mahler as an opera director. This occasion marked the centenary of Mahler's birth, and Wellesz re-lived some of the experience of his youth. The cultural ethos that prevailed at the turn of the century in the Viennese tradition—the spirit of innate conservatism coupled with a certain revolutionary radicalism; also the idealism and perfection that were epitomized by Mahler—was indeed very different from the contemporary situation prevailing today. Yet it has guided Wellesz.

Mahler's ten years' directorship of the Vienna Opera began on 11th May 1897, when he first conducted *Lohengrin* there; later that year he was appointed managing director. He exercised an extraordinary personal magnetism. Everything that he, or his designer Roller, placed on the stage had to 'mean' something; it was not enough for it merely to be there. But the performances in which he rose to the greatest heights were those of the operas of Mozart. Music was for him, according to Wellesz,[1] '. . . a holy art', (*eine heilige Kunst*), and each performance was an experience which would continue with the listener for many days. He was, according to Bruno Walter,[2] who was his assistant, passionately devoted to the stage, and brought the whole house, singers, orchestra and audience alike, under his spell.

This also had the greatest formative effect on the young Wellesz, whose musical background during his early years at Vienna was thus made up of Mahler, Bruckner, Strauss and Schoenberg; beyond them, Ravel, Debussy, Bartok and to some extent Stravinsky; and, later still, Honegger, Milhaud, Poulenc and Hindemith, all of whom were his friends. His immediate colleagues, in a circle that was select and personal, were Berg and Webern; it was the latter who—in 1935—arranged a fiftieth birthday concert for him.

Wellesz heard a great deal of music, but always kept to his own path. After his period at the university, musicology and composition, coupled with the very strong Viennese operatic tradition, combined to focus his attention on opera. He studied the works of Fux, Cavalli, Monteverdi, Cesti, and the nature of seventeenth-century Venetian opera, and produced books on these topics, as well as editions of the scores; thus Wellesz anticipated by fifty years the work of some recent musicologists in this country. He explored the possibilities of the classical tradition, based on Greek antiquity, which was such an integral part of the Viennese opera.

Thus Wellesz the musicologist spurred on Wellesz the composer. When considering the whole history of opera, he considered that a great period had ended with Gluck, the eighteenth-century opera composer, who could be claimed as Viennese until he moved to Paris. After Gluck's departure the Austrian tradition was open to foreign influence; the tradition of Rossini, Donizetti, Bellini was alien to that of Vienna, which was much more truly reflected in Beethoven's *Fidelio*.

The Gluck tradition, however, lived on in France. Within a story of classical simplicity, and with just three characters, Gluck made both words and music entirely subservient to the expression of every shade of feeling experienced by the hero and heroine, and was not interested in mere vocal display, or such stereotyped devices as the *da capo* aria. This was the Greek ideal of dramatic art, that poetry, music and dance should unite in underwriting the drama, whose basic facts were traditional common property. The Gluck ideal was later epitomized in Berlioz's *Les Troyens*.

Wellesz attempted to take up where Gluck left off; and his friend

1. Robert Schollum, *Egon Wellesz*, p. 9.
2. Bruno Walter, *Gustav Mahler*, p.30 foll. (English edition).

Edward Dent adds an interesting footnote, clearly referring to Wellesz, when he says[1] that although Gluck could not serve as a model to be imitated, in spite of some attempts, and although Mozart's operas are free of that technical clumsiness which occasionally spoils Gluck's works on the stage, nevertheless

what was important in Gluck's operas, as in Gluck's own mind, was not the technical method but the moral outlook, and in so far as Gluck had any style of his own, that style could only be imitated by someone with the same philosophical principles. . . . He could only be venerated as the expression of a moral ideal; and for that he still stands even now.

Moreover in the ballets of Gluck, Wellesz saw the first application of the principles of modern dance techniques; and it was this development, rather than, for instance, the French-influenced Russian Ballet, which visited the Wiener Oper in 1914, that influenced Wellesz when he made the dance a very central, and emotional, part of his dramatic expression. His first ballet, *Das Wunder der Diana*, Op. 18, was written in 1914. The libretto was by Béla Balázs, who also wrote those of Bartók's *The Wooden Prince* and *Bluebeard's Castle*; and the story is similar—of temples animated by the moon-goddess, and lovers transfigured; of transportation from an atmosphere of passion into one of other-worldly passionlessness; of serenity as if, by transformation of a boy and a girl, everything unstable has disappeared. This score was a preparation for *Alkestis*, Op. 35; but several other stage works, as well as other compositions, intervened. These included songs, four string quartets, two orchestral pieces, the *Prologue*, Op. 2, and the *Suite*, Op. 16; and piano pieces, such as the *Three Sketches*, Op. 6, which are tonal experiments, like Schoenberg's Op. 11; the stage works were the opera *Die Prinzessin Girnara*, Op. 27 (1919), and the *Persian Ballet*, Op. 30 (1920). This was written for a Russian dancer and choreographer, Ellen Tels, who had come to Vienna with her own small company. Two other intermediate works followed; the one-act ballet *Achilles auf Skyros*, Op. 33, with a libretto by Hofmannsthal, and a piece for coloratura soprano *Aurora*, the material of which was used later in *Alkestis*. *Alkestis* was the work with which Wellesz first successfully established himself as a composer. It continued the rediscovery of the classical Greek tradition of Gluck, which had been already begun in *Achilles auf Skyros*.

The libretto of *Alkestis* was by Hofmannsthal. He had written the play in 1893; now he altered the opening scene, and then suggested that Wellesz should similarly alter, and match, the ending. This change involved a final chorus. Hofmannsthal was fond of insisting that the music needed

1. *Opera*, p. 51 (Pelican edition 1st ed. 1940).

plenty of space; as Goethe said, it needed to be 'widely meshed'. More-over, it also needed the ballet. At the first performance of the work in Mannheim, the ballet was performed by the dancing schools of the town.[1]

It was subsequently produced in ten different opera houses in Germany, including Berlin in 1932. And though it was contemporary with Berg's *Wozzeck*, Wellesz's *Alkestis* could hardly have been a more total contrast.

First, it was 'grand' opera, in the traditional sense of the word, as opera had been for centuries. It belonged in the traditional opera house, just as a work such as *Carmen*, based on daily life, belonged more ap-propriately in the Opéra Comique—where, indeed, it was first performed. But the material of *Alkestis* was mythical, heroic, not everyday. The use of ballet, which also earned Schoenberg's approval, was a logical exten-sion of this principle.

Second, Wellesz was concerned that his style should be linear. He did not so much occupy himself with the theoretical discipline of a 12-note technique, or with the serial fragmentation of the material, as with the achievement of long melodic lines. This characteristic was later to be the hallmark of his symphonic style.

No account of an opera composer working at this time in Vienna would be complete without reference sooner or later to Strauss, who exerted such a great influence over all aspects of music and over many musicians, including Schoenberg and Webern. Wellesz's approach to opera, however, differed markedly from that of Strauss; if it resembled anyone else's it resembled Bartok's. Wellesz adopted a course of daring independence. He was also directly influenced by Hofmannsthal, who was much more to him than just a librettist; he provided a sense of stable literary values in an age of experiment and uncertainty; he represented the Austrian tradition, as distinct from the German tradition of Thomas Mann. Hofmannsthal became estranged from Strauss; and as Wellesz differed so much in outlook from Strauss, his operas could not be done under Strauss. So his next dance-drama, *Die Opferung des Gefangenen* ('The sacrifice of the prisoner'), Op. 40 (1925), was performed in Berlin when Strauss did not wish a performance in Vienna. (Many other composers found the same difficulty, including Berg.)

The story of *Die Opferung*, originally an old Aztec play, describes the Mexican civilization before the arrival of the Spanish; the survival, in the form of tragic drama, of the past grandeur of an old heroic world.[2]

1. By a strange coincidence another *Alkestis* was produced about this time (1922); that of Rutland Boughton at Glastonbury.
2. This theme was also recently (1964) adapted by an English playwright, Peter Schaffer, into *The Royal Hunt of the Sun*, which dealt with the Incas of Peru.

This work was followed by a light, one-act opera, with words taken from Goethe, *Scherz, List und Rache*, Op. 41, which may be approximately translated 'funning, cunning and gunning'. But then in 1929/30 came the fourth and last of the series of 'heroic' operas, *Die Bakchantinnen*, Op. 44, for which Wellesz wrote his own libretto, with Euripides once again as a starting-point.

The series of classical 'heroic' operas is thus as follows:

1. *Achilles auf Skyros*   The young Achilles, awakening to life, chooses the path of a hero.
2. *Alkestis*   The wife of King Admetus, who is ready to suffer death for the idea of kingship.
3. *Die Opferung des Gefangenen*   The young prince who consciously chooses to die, and will be worshipped as a hero after his death.
4. *Die Bakchantinnen*   Pentheus, the man of action, is above the law as king, and sees in the new cult of Dionysus a force that will destroy his tangible world-order. He feels that mysticism, by becoming a practical fact, through a cult, leaves that sphere to which it belongs, and destroys the existing power-structure.

Die Bakchantinnen was his last Viennese opera; it also marked the culminating point of his achievement in that field. It calls for mime as well as chorus-work, and for this the stage-designer Roller agreed to make use of the sixty to seventy members of the ballet company of the Viennese Opera—who sang as well as danced, when it came to the performance. For its first performance in Vienna, on 20th June 1931, the conductor Clemens Krauss required no fewer than sixty chorus rehearsals and twenty orchestral rehearsals. The work made a great impression in Vienna, but could not be repeated in Berlin for political reasons.

After this, until he came to England in 1938, Wellesz's composition took a different turn; songs with orchestra, a piano concerto, a mass; and above all, his first full-length orchestral work (1934–36) *Prosperos Beschwörungen* (Prospero's Incantation[1]), Op. 53; five symphonic pieces based on Shakespeare's *Tempest*.

The style of his works up to *Prospero* may be seen to follow a pattern. His earlier works began somewhat experimentally, but the larger forms that he later worked with required a more linear style. His thought is linear; and just as his interest veered away from Western Gregorian Chant towards the long lines of Byzantine Church Music, so is this reflected in the long, melodic lines of his own works, particularly those for one instrument. A particularly clear example of this characteristic

---

1. 'Prospero's Incantation' is the composer's translation, as it appears on the score. H. C. Colles however insisted that 'Prospero's Spell' is a more exact translation, and more 'Shakespearian'.

occurs in *Die Opferung des Gefangenen*, at the end, just before the prisoner is killed. He has asked to dance once more with his own warriors; but this request is met with silence—that is to say, refusal. There follows a melody for a slow dance, which lasts for fifty-five bars (bars 1200–1255[1]), during which a song of mourning is also heard from the Prince's own people.

This is a very different approach from the pointillism that characterised Schoenberg's style, and the fragmentation of the material, which is one of the chief characteristics of serialism; and whereas Wellesz might use an atonal idiom in smaller works, such as the solo *Violin Sonata*, Op. 36, in which he develops an extended tonality, something more was needed when larger forces were involved. The solution he arrived at was to write in blocks, with the crossing of one melodic line with another to produce varieties of key (polytonality) or varieties of rhythm (polyrhythm). Each line has a distinct character and vitality, while the blocks prevent the work becoming rhapsodic.

An example of this 'emerging tonal complexity' in *Alkestis* (bars 1516–1519), based on the differing tonal implications of combined linear blocks, is quoted by Reti.[2]

His idiom is melodic, and the rhythmic continuity is usually straightforward. He eschews harmonic novelty, and favours instead the substance which comes of contrapuntal treatment of the material. He considers that nothing palls quicker than novelties, and particularly excessive harmonic colouring, of the sort that several late romantic composers indulged in. Indeed, historically speaking, harmonic novelty had reared its head in the works of the sixteenth century Gesualdo, only to be discarded by his successors when they built larger structures. So Wellesz draws a parallel today.

The style of his operas centres round his conception of operatic drama. Whereas a novelist takes his material from life, a dramatist takes his material from the great subjects of antiquity. So opera builds on a traditional foundation. But the fate of an opera, according to Wellesz, is decided on the stage, not in the orchestra pit; the contrasts of mood, which keep an opera moving, are underlined by the music. So for the death of the queen in *Alkestis* (bars 44-77) the characteristic Greek atmosphere is obtained by just clarinet and percussion; the expressive music, noted by Reti for its polytonal character, occurs earlier also at bar 550, for the moment when the women bring flowers after the death of Alkestis; in *Die Opferung* the death of the prince is musically illustrated at bar 1300.

1. Score published by Universal Edition.
2. In *Tonality, Atonality, Pantonality*, p.136.

The chorus forms an integral part in all these operas. As Reti put it,[1] Wellesz achieves 'a blend of inner austerity with the splendour of festive choruses and glittering choreography'.

The first performance of *Prospero* took place on 19th February 1938 in Vienna, under Bruno Walter. A further performance was arranged in Amsterdam on 13th March, by the Concertgebouw Orchestra, also under Walter; and a repeat of this on 16th March in Rotterdam. These performances certainly took place; indeed, Wellesz looks back with characteristic Viennese affection on the concerts; particularly as the violin solo in the third section of *Prospero* ('Ariel's song') was played by Arnold Rosé, the brother-in-law of Mahler.

But on the very day of the Amsterdam concert, 13th March 1938, Hitler entered Vienna, and Austria was annexed to Germany. War was now inevitable in Europe. Thus ended the world that Wellesz knew, and many like him, particularly those of Jewish extraction. There was nothing for him, therefore, but to strike roots elsewhere, and begin afresh—at the age of fifty-three. Ten years later he was to return to Vienna, as a visitor, to be greeted by former students and friends; but this could hardly be foreseen in 1938.

H. C. Colles and Edward Dent arranged for him to come to England. In view of his doctorate, he was made a Fellow of Lincoln College, Oxford; later (1947) a Reader in music; this position he retained until 1957, though he continued to teach after then. It was not Wellesz the composer who was given this academic post, but Wellesz the musicologist; and however distinguished his name might be among international European musicians, there were, so he was told, those at Oxford, and in the more sound-proof ivory towers of this country, to whom his name meant little or nothing. Could he not write a book in order to establish his name in those quarters where it was appropriate that it should be established?

His work as a musicologist had for many years focused on Byzantine Chant, in which he was already known by the 30's as a specialist. He discovered clues to the interpretation of neumatic notation, so that by 1917 the notation of Byzantine Church music was deciphered and transcribed; and gradually it became possible for Western musicians to explore this hitherto unknown territory. In 1931 a conference in Copenhagen brought together those chiefly interested in this work, and it was agreed to set about publishing the texts of Byzantine musical manuscripts. This complete edition, *Monumenta Musicae Byzantinae*, was started in 1935 by the Danish scholar Carsten Hoeg, H. J. W. Tillyard, Professor

1. In *Egon Wellesz, Musician and Scholar* (Musical Quarterly, Vol. 42, No. 1, January 1956).

M

of Greek at Cardiff University, and Wellesz. So when Wellesz came to Oxford, it was arranged that his manuscripts and Byzantine photographs should be brought to this country; whereupon he set about his work. A *History of Byzantine Music and Hymnography* was published ten years later. Wellesz later also became one of the editors of the *New Oxford History of Music*, and of the *History of Music in Sound*.

His arrival in Oxford was followed by a gap of several years in his creative output. The last work that he wrote in Vienna had been a part-song *Quant' e bella giovinezza*, Op. 59. Not till 1944 does Op. 60 appear—his fifth *String Quartet*, 'in memoriam' of former days. Beginning *maestoso*, with a long and violent unison, the work uses a 12-note style. Four more string quartets were to follow. There is a large number of chamber works included in his output, and generally speaking their style is more concise and direct than the larger pieces. Four players can be more agile than forty; and Wellesz frequently precedes bigger works with smaller ones, just as *Aurora* had paved the way for *Alkestis*.

But it was in the next year (1945) that he started on the new path that he has pursued consistently since; that of a symphonist. He has been practically the only composer of the Viennese tradition to develop the symphony since Mahler, and his nine symphonies form the focal point of his output during the period of his residence in Oxford, just as the operas had formed the focal point of the earlier period of his life.[1] The last five symphonies in particular form a group which may be compared with the 'heroic' operas; in them also Wellesz sought an ideal of a new classicism.

The *First Symphony* came about somewhat unexpectedly. In August 1945, when he was staying at Grasmere in the Lake District, he was reminded of the Salzkammergut, the district near Salzburg that he knew so well. A theme occurred to him, which invited symphonic treatment; the next day another theme came to him. Immediately, as if in a trance, he sketched out his *First Symphony* in C, Op. 62, in just three weeks. It was, he says, the most exciting work of his life. The scoring was finished later that year. Its three-movement structure is still classical, for the sake of thematic cohesion, though the development is fugal—a device which he used later in the fifth symphony. The work was performed in 1947 by the Berlin Philharmonic Orchestra under Celibidache, and later, on 22nd June 1948, in Vienna under Josef Krips, for which Wellesz returned to Vienna—for the first time since the war.

The *Second Symphony*, Op. 65 which followed two years later, he called his 'most English' symphony; not only is the character of the

---

1. He wrote an opera, *Incognita*, based on Congreve, which was performed on an amateur basis by the Oxford University Opera Club. It stands in line of descent from Strauss's *Rosenkavalier*.

English landscape portrayed, but the composer's preoccupation at this time with English poetry is also echoed. The four movements have a clearly defined tonality. The work still retains traces of romanticism, and is a blend of heroic and sombre colours. It was performed in this country under Adrian Boult and Walter Goehr; when it was played in Vienna under Karl Rankl, on 21st June 1949, Wellesz returned again for this performance. The following month also his *Octet*, Op. 67, was performed by the Vienna Octet at the Salzburg Festival. It was a busy summer for the composer.

The *Third Symphony*, Op. 68, written between 1949 and 1951, stands somewhat apart from his other symphonic work, since it contains recollections of other Viennese composers, and is the only symphony not published. Very different was the next symphony, the fourth, *Symphonia Austriaca*, Op. 70. A thematic motif, taken from the fourth *String Quartet*, gives the work a unity, like an *idée fixe*. But the composer has now mastered symphonic form; the structure is firm, the contents dramatic.

Thus was the stage set for the five symphonies (5–9) which form the high-point of his orchestral compositions. The *Fifth Symphony*, Op. 75, was written over three years, and finished in Oxford on 2nd September 1956. Meanwhile, in these years Wellesz had travelled widely; to America in 1954, where he was invited to stay at the Byzantine Institute at Dumbarton Oaks, when he lectured at Yale, Princeton and Columbia Universities, travelled all over the country and heard his music played in several places; to Constantinople in 1955, where he addressed a congress on Byzantine music. His name was internationally known; except, strange to say, in England, where he had already been resident for over fifteen years, but where his music was scarcely heard, if at all. But at this time English musicians were just discovering Schoenberg, Berg and Webern; they had not yet alighted upon Wellesz. Not for nearly ten years was his *Fifth Symphony* given its first performance in this country, by Hugo Rignold and the Birmingham Symphony Orchestra, on 21st October 1965. The same orchestra and conductor also performed the sixth and seventh symphonies in the following years.[1] Very slowly the balance began to be restored.

In the *Fifth Symphony* Wellesz goes back to the tonal adventures of his youth; and this time the experiments succeed. What he had aimed at when young, his experience as a composer now enabled him to achieve; a more daring style now becomes tempered with the introversion of age. The solemn but brilliant opening is similar in mood and texture to the opening of the second of the *Three Sketches for piano*, Op. 6, written in

1. The *Sixth Symphony* was first played at Birmingham on 29th September 1966; the *Seventh Symphony* on 21st November 1968.

1911. He adopts a 12-note style, not as a dogma, but in order to give the structure a certain cohesion. The characteristics of his style are all here in abundance; particularly the linear counterpoint over a simple rhythm. The basic tonality of the symphony is D, and the shape of the 8-note row, first sounded in unison, also includes the tonality of E flat; this polytonal implication after its initial, harsh presentation, in bar 5, is worked out in the course of the symphony. At the point of recapitulation in the first movement.[1] after a slower middle section, the speed quickens, and the row is stretched from 8 notes to 12, and is combined with its own retrograde to form a fugue subject.

Ex.27

Wellesz
Symphony No. 5

The second movement, 'Intermezzo', is a short, bright scherzo, also starting in unison, with the row transposed, and with interjections of 5/8 metre into the prevailing pattern of 6/8. A little accompanimental motif, which first occurs towards the end of the *vivace* (at bar 88), forms the connecting link with the next movement, as it gives shape to the 12-note theme, as well as underlying colour to the harmony. The theme is given out *adagio molto* by a solo bass clarinet, and answered by the oboes in retrograde. The development of this movement is contrapuntal, as the theme is first inverted, then treated as a canon between the bass instruments and the brass (starting at bar 29), while the violins develop a brilliant counter-subject. This leads, typically of the composer, to a unison climax. After a more lyrical middle section, the main theme is recapitulated, once more in unison, and the movement ends firmly.

The first three notes of the original 8-note row are inverted to form the bass pattern of the finale. The *maestoso* character of the first movement is here brought to the fore, and the tragic grandeur of the theme takes on the form of a funeral march; muted trombones and tuba (bar 53) enhance this effect. The slower middle section reverts to the material of the first movement, after which the bass-pattern and the funeral march are recapitulated. The symphony finishes grandly, with the expected unison

1. Bar 163; score published by Hans Sikorski, Hamburg.

declamation of the main note-pattern, sounding the E flat and D tonalities round which the work is built.

Wellesz in this work makes a marked contribution to the development of the symphony as a contemporary form. How many composers, indeed, have reached a point of climax with their fifth symphony! Both in the overall conception of the whole, and in the technical execution of detail, he has developed a new form while not losing sight of the classical principles of symphonic contruction. The features—rhythmic, harmonic, melodic—of his initial 8-note row are used variously to give different colour to the themes of each movement, while underlying the work as a whole is a mood of tragic, heroic solemnity, which develops towards the final grandeur of the climax at the end. In his use of the row, Wellesz is contrapuntal rather than serial. He can invert, transpose, and perform the recognized contrapuntal tricks, with considerable deftness; but always the technical procedures are subservient to the expressive needs of the music, and the character of the movement, just as in his operas.

The *Sixth Symphony*, Op. 95, was written nine years later, in 1965, and several important works separated it from the fifth; notably a setting of the first of Rilke's ten *Duineser Elegie*, Op. 90, and also the one-movement *Music for String Orchestra*, Op. 91. The *Sixth Symphony* took only three months, including the scoring (5th April–7th July). It is in three movements, and like the fifth has a basic tonality of D, with a polytonal implication of E flat. It opens, again like a funeral march, slow and heavy in 5/4 metre, with brass and woodwind dominating, and the first movement grows all of a piece from the beginning. The strings enter ff in the seventh bar with the principal theme, a broad and very big, arch-like *cantabile*, whose wide intervals recall Wellesz's early works. The mood is intense, with just occasional moments of contrasting lightness. When the principal theme returns (bar 157) it is not an exact repetition, and after four bars it is suddenly cut off; the mood of the funeral march is recaptured, and the movement ends menacingly. The second movement is light, quick, transparent, scurrying to and fro in triplets and semi-quavers. A more sustained *tranquillo* middle section, for strings only, separates the quick outer parts of the movement.

The third movement, *Adagio*, opens with all the violins quietly and expressively singing their 12-note melody, very differently presented now from the theme in the first movement. Over a rhythmic ostinato in the bass a climax is built up, but in contrast to this theme follows the most delicate part work for solo instruments. The ending is one of peaceful reconciliation.

Wellesz has said of this symphony that it is concerned with one idea, presented in three aspects. It is a contrast more of moods than of thematic presentation of the note-row, as the *Fifth Symphony* was.

The *Seventh Symphony*, Op. 102, is also in three movements, and was written between 11th October 1967 and 21st January 1968. Although it is entitled 'contra torrentem', because Wellesz sees the symphony as being against current trends, nevertheless he has proved himself master of that new classicism in symphonic form that he himself opened up. It continues directly from the point reached in the *Sixth Symphony*, though it is more concise, and covers a wider range of expression, with the greatest intensity. In accordance with his earlier practice, Wellesz derived material from a work written just before; in this case a cantata, *Mirabile Mysterium*, Op. 101, commissioned by the Vienna Radio for the Italia Prize, 1969.

The disposition of the movements of the *Seventh Symphony* is the same as the sixth, with the first and third movements broad, sustained, and acting as a frame for a more lively, joyful middle movement. But this time the violins, largely in unison, develop a feeling of ecstasy, which is theirs alone; the concluding bars consummate this mood:

Ex.28

The sombre character of the music, established at the opening, pervades the work; even the lighter texture of the middle movement is offset by heavy brass chords. The finale is the most extended of the three movements, and the most important, with a resolution of the mood forming the conclusion; beginning and ending with very sustained string writing (*sehr breit*), and quickening in the middle, at [45] -3.

The *Seventh Symphony* was followed by a ten minute symphonic piece, at the request of the Vienna Philharmonic Orchestra. This *Symphonischer Epilog*, Op. 108, which is an intensely concentrated work, might be also described as a tragic epilogue; and once embarked on this course, Wellesz the symphonist could hardly stop. He felt that this work needed a second part; and thus arose the finale of the *Eighth Symphony*, which was written before the other two movements of it.

The *Symphonic Epilogue* was finished on 11th December, 1969; the *Eighth Symphony*, Op. 110, was written between February–June, 1970.

That freedom in the thematic working-out of ideas, which is already apparent in the *Seventh Symphony*, and carried on in the *Epilogue*, is pursued still further in this—and in the next—symphony. A movement is not divided into sections, according to the classical procedure; but the development starts from the very beginning. From the sum of his symphonic experience Wellesz in his maturity took what was essential for the music, and wrote just that; the pure reality of sounds, naked colours, in a lighter surrounding texture, and without full harmonization— the opposite of Strauss, or of Schoenberg. In this sense the music is implicit rather than explicit, and its construction a comparatively free and loose working-out of ideas.

The symphony is in the now customary three movements; sustained outer movements enclose a quicker, scherzo-like section. The third movement, *Molto tranquillo*, which was composed first, is both substantial and complex. It opens with a phrase built round the interval of the second (B flat-A flat), which recalls the funeral music in *Alkestis* (bar 495 foll.). Biting scoring, with flutes and three high oboes (bar 15) leads to an increase of intensity, and the music is characterized by broad lines and wide intervals, spelt out in notes of small value.

Having completed the finale, the other two movements came quickly to Wellesz. The opening *Lento* has a long solo for the trumpets as a leading idea. This is later recalled—not repeated—with mutes, against the static chords of *divisi* strings. The material of this symphony is diverse, yet the work is homogeneous. Here Wellesz has applied the principles of Mozart, that whereas each 2-bar section of an 8-bar sentence may contain material of diverse interest, nevertheless the overall phrase is a unity. In this case, though the juxtaposed *motifs* are different, yet the whole musical experience is coherent. The material is firmly controlled, however loose the structure.

The central *Allegretto*, in triple metre, represents the *scherzo* movement, with just a suggestion of a very short *trio* for flute and oboe. The scoring in this movement is slightly pointillistic, with very short *motifs*, even single notes, distributed between the instruments. The style of the *trio* is picked up at the beginning of the finale.

Following the completion of the *Eighth Symphony*, Wellesz was faced with the congenial task of celebrating his 85th birthday—on 21st October, 1970. To mark the occasion, chamber music concerts were given at the Austrian Institute in London, as well as Oxford, Vienna and elsewhere, by the (Vienna) Philharmonic String Quintet, for whom he wrote *Four pieces for String Quintet*, Op. 109. But already his mind was turned towards the possibility of the next symphony; and this was started in November.

The *Ninth Symphony*, again in three movements, is a continuation of the eighth. Like its predecessors, it was composed over a comparatively short period of uninterrupted work. The speed is remarkable. The sketch of the first movement was finished by 20th December. On Christmas Day the middle movement was sketched out in essentials—and has since remained basically unaltered. The very next day, 26th December, he started work on the final *Adagio*. The entire symphony was scored between 22nd January—6th February, 1971.

By this time the chromatic tendency of the 12-note technique had become so much second nature to Wellesz that, like Schoenberg in *Moses and Aaron*, he no longer concerned himself with the mechanics of it—as he had in some earlier works. Here the composer in his maturity writes what he wants to write, of the sort of symphonic music that by now he had forged for himself from the style of the Second Viennese School.

The first movement, *Andante Moderato*, opens with characteristic vigour, and the music immediately works towards a point of intensity (bar 31). A 3-note *motif*, with a prominent dotted rhythm, acts as a unifying point of climax. It occurs again in bar 137, and at the end. The slight pointillism noticeable in the previous symphony is here carried to a much greater level, and the scoring differs markedly even from bar to bar. Orchestral colour is used more than in earlier symphonies; for instance the horns feature prominently, often in unison; one of the most dramatic and powerful effects, discovered by the 85-year-old composer. Leading *motifs* are given to certain instruments; for instance a falling figure to the harp. As before, the composer is concerned that nothing should overlay or obscure the absolute sounds of his orchestra.

The *scherzo* movement, *Allegretto grazioso*, is of very light texture. The harmonic movement is slow, and static passages alternate with evanescent, shimmering sounds. The central *trio* this time is just hinted at by *tremolo* strings.

The concluding *Adagio* contains the essential Wellesz. Like the finale of the *Eighth Symphony*, it is of complex construction, though free. It opens with a powerful unison violin melody, whose long line, and characteristically wide intervals, gradually rises, then falls. This process is immediately repeated, with rhythmic diminution, and the music grows in intensity to bar 20. The 3-note *motif* of the first movement comes as a contrast, as well as a unifying link in the symphony. The following section, a *hocketus* melody in the woodwind, and a rubato passage, leads to the strings resuming the original tempo at bar 55, with a recollection of the first movement rhythm.

A stricter, more martial pulse, beginning at bar 58, leads inevitably to a powerful section (bar 75–85), when the first movement rhythm becomes again more prominent. The strings recall the beginning of the movement (bar 103), and after bar 115 the woodwind and horns, in 3-part harmony, and equal crotchets, have a simple passage, like a chorale. The final moment of the symphony is heralded by a high note (E flat), by two desks of first violins, which gradually swells up to ff, only to fade.

To the work of the Second Viennese School Wellesz added the symphony. Schoenberg, Berg and Webern had been effectively inhibited from writing symphonies by the overwhelming influence of Mahler; Wellesz forged a new symphonic style, over a remarkably rich 25-year period (1945–1970)—which also exactly coincides with the period covered by the present study.

Between the first and ninth symphonies he never once varied the make-up of the symphony orchestra. Not for him the experimentation of Tippett, or the novelty of Gerhard. This is one illustration of those forgotten ideals, that striving after perfection, that emanated from Mahler, but which now no longer activate the *avant-garde*; it is also entirely consistent with Wellesz's avoidance ot novelty, whether of harmony or sonority.

At his very first lesson with Schoenberg—an unforgettable experience— the latter had shown him the harmonic novelties at the opening of Strauss's *Salome*. Soon however Wellesz noticed that these novelties appeared flat indeed in comparison with the more striking novelties of Schoenberg's own work. Novelty, Wellesz concluded, was a false god; once heard, it ceases to be a novelty. Therefore he did not pursue it.

His achievement in the symphonies particularly since the fifth, has been to take the greatly increased possibilities of expression of today's various musical idioms, and, using only what he needed of them, to fashion a new conception of symphonic form. In many ways the contemporary composer is faced with precisely the opposite situation from that which confronted the classical composers, who first forged the conception of the symphony. They worked from the basis of a fixed key, and an established diatonic scale of seven notes, to which they added the additional expressiveness of the remaining five chromatic notes in whatever proportion and to whatever extent was compatible with the overall tonal scheme. The contemporary composer, however, works from the basis of twelve notes, whose organization may or may not be serial as he sees fit; nor is this licence confined to pitch only.

From such total chromatic freedom, which is clearly inconsistent with the classical principles of symphonic form, Wellesz worked inwards and deduced a structure that was compatible with his chosen idiom. He sees the contemporary situation of the symphony as not unlike what it was prior to its formulation by Haydn, who poured out music, and from the resulting stream fashioned a symphonic structure. Now Wellesz sees the necessity to refashion the symphony; and for structural contrast, corresponding to the classical sonata form, he does not so much introduce a second theme as make use of different melody and varied movement. He has built a new edifice, without losing sight of the old.

13   Roberto Gerhard

Few composers in Britain today have had a richer, fuller artistic life than Roberto Gerhard. After a slow, gradual growth, his compositions increased steadily in later years in both number and range. Artistic vision and intellectual vigour made for his insatiable curiosity about music of many different periods and styles. Indeed, the assimilation of fresh ideas and influences was part and parcel of his creative personality. This particular period of time requires of the composer not just that he should be aware of the forces and influences at work around him, but that he should also interpret them; and Gerhard proved fully equal to this challenge.

The work, no less than the composer himself, can be approached on many different levels, all of which are valid, and any one of which will lead the enquirer into ever more complex and intricate side-turnings; pointers to the working of a daringly original mind. There is, first, the surface-level of a piece, those themes or motifs which give it its cohesion; next the subtler undercurrent of unity, that inner subconscious structure, those details that are implicated in the folds of the texture that make it hang together; this is particularly the case in the later works from 1957 onwards.

Listen, says Gerhard; do not look, or analyse, or follow in a score. So the first impression that reaches the listener is one of the craftsman in sound; and first impressions are often the strongest and most valid. But underlying the sound-craftsmanship is an intellect at once rigorous, tough, all-demanding. The structure, form or shape (call it what you will) must be consistent throughout; if a work is serial, the series must be logical, in both its vertical and linear use. The two hexachords must interlock. Again, underlying all his work was a philosophy at once liberal, compassionate, far-sighted, powerful enough to guide him through the inevitable setbacks and difficulties of a long and varied life. He wrote innumerable lighter pieces, arrangements and settings, largely for

175

economic reasons, including an electronic sound track for a film made by two Cambridge doctors, *Audiomobile No. 2 'DNA'*; yet these he looked on as just as real an artistic experience as his more serious work. He admitted, as we shall see, a number of lighter pieces into the definitive list of his compositions; *Alegrias* for example.

He was born at Valls near Barcelona on 25th September 1896. His mother was French, his father Catalan. His awareness of the upsurge of nationalism in Spanish music that we associate particularly with Albeniz and Granados was increased when he studied the piano with the latter in Barcelona (1915–16). More importantly, he studied composition with Felipe Pedrell, until Pedrell's death in 1922. The eighty-year-old professor would refer to his young pupil as 'Benjamin', and hint, somewhat mysteriously, that he was destined to further his work. And indeed, twenty years later, Gerhard was asked for a single-movement piece to mark the centenary of Pedrell's birth (1841), to be played on the Latin American service of the BBC. This work, though written, was not performed; but the composer had become so caught up in it that he extended it into a three-movement work of symphonic size, and gave it the title *Pedrelliana*. He took material from Pedrell's opera *La Celestina* (1903), which was a sort of Spanish *Tristan and Isolde*, and used it as a starting point for his own work. Curiously enough, Falla, another Pedrell pupil, took the same opera as a basis for a piece; but he quotes it much more directly than Gerhard does. As usual Gerhard became entirely absorbed in the work, and the third movement is about Pedrell himself, whose life Gerhard saw as tragically split between the divided loyalties of musicology on the one hand and composition on the other.

Like Falla, Gerhard looked beyond Spain for that spur to deeper means of expression and a wider sense of artistic direction than provincial Spanish life provided. But whereas his compatriot had travelled no farther than Paris, to the congenial world of Debussy and Ravel, Gerhard travelled to Vienna and Berlin, where for five years (1923–28) he was Schoenberg's pupil.

This was that extremely fruitful time when Schoenberg was just formulating his 12-note technique. 1924 saw the first purely 12-note work of Schoenberg (the *Piano Suite*, Op. 25), and in December of the following year Berg's *Wozzeck* was first produced in Berlin. The young Gerhard could hardly have chosen a more climactic moment; he was witnessing the birth of one of the driving-forces of twentieth-century music.

But he did not immediately adopt Schoenberg's style. Indeed, during these years he wrote little; only the *Wind Quintet* (1928), which though not entirely serial, uses certain serial devices—for instance the Passacaglia bass in the second movement, and the principal melody in the third. This work throws into relief certain problems inherent in the 12-note style, which Gerhard sought to solve for himself; the dichotomy between the principal and the subsidiary parts in a texture of imitative counterpoint; the inconsistency of using such sharply differentiated instruments as flute, oboe, clarinet, horn and bassoon in a style that makes for unity and homogeneity above all else. But Gerhard is an unorthodox Schoenbergian. For instance, his concentration on pattern, one of the most intellectual inventions of the human mind, has nothing to do with the linear series of his teacher. As we shall see, Gerhard was later to make a marked and highly original contribution to the craft of serial composition.

Returning to Barcelona, he became, among other things, head of the Catalan Library, where he edited early Spanish music. He also wrote articles and translations for various magazines. In 1938 he was a member of the I.S.C.M. jury in Warsaw[1], and on his return he found that Barcelona had fallen to Franco in the Civil War, and the Catalan government was exiled to Paris. He therefore remained in Paris until June 1939, and meanwhile enquired of his English friend Edward Dent about the possibility of leaving for England.

As President of the I.S.C.M., Dent was much more in touch with musical developments and continental musicians than the majority of his English colleagues and contemporaries. He and Gerhard had met as early as 1932 at the Vienna Festival, and so now, as Professor of Music at Cambridge, he was able to suggest that his friend be awarded a 'research studentship' at King's College. In 1939 Gerhard moved to Cambridge, where he lived happily until his death on 5th January 1970.

Before 1923 Gerhard's compositions were slight; short piano pieces, a piano trio, some songs; notably *Seven Hai-Kai*, settings from the Japanese for high voice, wind instruments and piano, which were influenced largely by Schoenberg's *Pierrot Lunaire*.

Between 1929 and 1939 his works comprised chiefly a setting of Josep Carner's poem 'L'Alta Naixença del Rei en Jaume', and two ballet scores. The first of these, *Ariel*, was given a concert performance under Hermann Scherchen at the Barcelona Festival of the I.S.C.M. in May, 1936[2]; the second, *Soirées de Barcelone*, was not performed owing to the outbreak of war. Webern conducted his *Cançons Populars Catalanes* at an I.S.C.M. concert in Vienna in 1932.

On his arrival in England in 1939, two more ballet scores immediately occupied his attention. The first, *Don Quixote* (1940), was played first as a concert suite before being staged as a ballet at Covent Garden (1950).

1. Where Alan Rawsthorne's *Symphonic Studies* were first played.
2. When Berg's *Violin Concerto* was first played.

The characters that spring from Don Quixote's feverish mind spurred Gerhard on to one of his most characteristic and colourful stage works. Within the principal Don Quixote theme is included a little tune from Gerhard's home in Spain; this gives rise to a note-row, which is treated serially all through the work. The second ballet, *Divertissement Flamenco*, was Gerhard's response to a commission from the Ballet Rambert. Though Catalan, not Andalusian, he considered that he could write a Flamenco as well as the next man, and the ballet was performed in Birmingham in 1943. It has been made into a concert suite, *Alegrias*, and the style is that of a composer enjoying himself in lighter vein. The libretto concerns a bull fight, and Gerhard has musical fun not only at the expense of the bull but of the choreographer. For instance, in the finale (*Jaleo*) gipsy tunes are used for the dragging off of the corpse, while Chopin's funeral march blares out from the trumpets. For a model, if one is needed, we could turn to Falla's *Three-Cornered Hat*, which is based on Andalusian tunes, or the finales of some of Bartok's String Quartets, which are characteristically Hungarian, but not inconsistently so.

Another ballet was performed in Cambridge the following year, by the Kurt Jooss Company: *Pandora*. If certain qualifications surround this piece—its length, for instance—no such qualifications surround his next and most ambitious stage work: his only opera, *The Duenna* (1945–47).

When his wife Poldi returned home one day with a secondhand copy of Sheridan's famous comedy, which she had bought for sixpence from a bookstall, one glance was enough to persuade the composer that here was a perfect opera libretto; and he began work that very day.

Gerhard's opera is based on artificiality. It is pastiche in a serious setting, partly tonal, partly making use of a free 12-note style. If pastiche may be defined as indulgence in a style that you like, then Gerhard enjoyed writing this neoclassic mimicry. But the important clue to pastiche, he considered, is that the character of the impersonator should not be lost sight of.

Points of resemblance and similarity between Gerhard's *The Duenna* and Stravinsky's *The Rake's Progress* are too close to overlook. These become all the more remarkable when we remember that Stravinsky's work was the later of the two; it was not produced until September 1951, in Venice. Gerhard's work has not yet been produced, though it was given a concert performance in Wiesbaden in 1951.

Both composers chose eighteenth century subject material; both use a hero, a heroine and a villain, cast as tenor, soprano and bass respectively; both use a formalised scheme of arias, recitatives, and so on; both use an

E tonality in Acts I and III, with a contrasting tonality in the middle act; each composer has left his own *persona* distinctly recognizable, however much he relies on earlier material. Stravinsky may have had Mozart or Donizetti in mind,[1] but his fingerprints are clearly impressed all over the score. So with Gerhard.

The set numbers of Sheridan's play fall naturally into strophic songs. These are simply tonal. It is in the connecting, secondary passages that Gerhard introduces more chromatic, contrapuntal texture. Motifs and ostinatos are used to help in establishing characters and relationships; the tritone, for example, the atonal interval *par excellence* (just as the fifth is the tonal interval *par excellence*), is used throughout the work to express any undesirable or awkward turn of events. Such a stylistic oscillation, between tonal and 12-note, could result in inconsistency unless it was welded into an artistic unity by the overriding personality of the composer. And this Gerhard achieves.

As an example of this contrast, the first scene of the second act ends with a drinking trio, in which the composer found to his delight that the words fitted perfectly with a Spanish rhythm; he proceeds to indulge this happy discovery for over three hundred bars, and the mood is jovial:

> *Fill a cheerful glass*
> *And let good humour pass*

Immediately, the opening of the next scene is entirely contrasted, and a sombre 12-note introduction leads into Luisa's somewhat wistful song.

Ex. 29

Gerhard
The Duenna, Act II, Sc. 2 (opening)

Sheridan's play has been set by other composers apart from Gerhard. The author's own father-in-law, the composer Thomas Linley, co-operated with his own son (also Thomas) in setting it, and this piece had a long run at Covent Garden, starting on 21st November 1775. More recently, Prokofiev's opera, *Betrothal in a Nunnery*, (Op. 86), is based on Sheridan's play, with a libretto by the composer. Curiously enough it

1. Particularly *Cosi fan Tutte.* c.f. *Memories and Commentaries*, p. 158.

was first staged in Leningrad on 3rd November 1946, exactly the time when Gerhard was engaged on his version.

After the opera there followed the first of the purely orchestral master works by which Gerhard will be permanently remembered, the *Violin Concerto* (see plates 5 and 6).

This was first performed at the Florence *Maggio Musicale* in 1950, conducted by Scherchen, with Antonio Brosa as soloist. Strictly speaking this work is Gerhard's second violin concerto. An earlier essay in this form, written soon after his arrival in Cambridge, was abandoned just on the point of completion because the composer was dissatisfied with it; yet not so much with its musical material, some of which was used in other works later, as with the solo violin technique, which, so Gerhard held, needed to be one of the main justifications of a solo concerto. If the solo writing does not represent a carrying forward of past achievement for the soloist, why should the work necessarily take the form of a concerto? By this Gerhard did not mean indulgence or exhibitionism on the part of the solo violinist; simply that the spark of creative *necessity* (a Schoenbergian concept) needed to be focused on to the solo writing. Gerhard was his own first and sternest critic, and since his earlier violin concerto did not, in his opinion, pass this test, he decided to abandon it. But the lesson learnt from this was applied in the next concerto, whose very essence, and 'instrumentality' would be unthinkable in any other form than that of a violin concerto.

For the first time the twin problems of structure and sonority are triumphantly and originally solved in an orchestral context. It is serial in part only. After the first movement cadenza at [31] there is a 12-note section, *molto vivace con spirito*. The slow movement uses the 12-note series of Schoenberg's Fourth String Quartet[1], while the last movement is largely autobiographical. The suggestion of the *Marseillaise* at the opening recalls the fall of France in 1940, as well as the composer's French mother; the use of a Catalan folk-tune recalls the Abbey of Montserrat, where his father died.

Two further concertos span an important and formative period of Gerhard's artistic development which then ensued: the *Concerto for Piano and Strings* (1951), and the *Concerto for Harpsichord, Strings and Percussion* (1956). They have common features; both are characteristic of their composer, who makes for simplicity and directness with such devices as regularity of metre, pedal-point (with which the piano concerto opens), repeated figurations, a sustained semiquaver pulse, imitative

---

1. See Rufer, *Composition with twelve notes*, p. 83. Schoenberg had celebrated his seventieth birthday on 13th September 1944.

entries, and so on. The piano concerto starts freely, and later becomes serial, while the series of the harpsichord concerto, with its falling minor thirds, has an inbuilt diminished seventh chord, which makes for awkwardness.

Though written in the same year as the harpsichord concerto, the *Nonet* could hardly be more different. Two quartets of wind, one woodwind, one brass, are linked by a highly original choice of *continuo* instrument, an accordion. Certain sonorities are striking, but the piece as a whole presents the opposite use of the 12-note style to that revealed in the harpsichord concerto. Whereas that was brilliant, glittering in texture, full of contrast, based on tonal exploitation of the note-row, this work is more academic, dense in texture, opaque and heavy in sonority. Its non-thematic construction places all the more burden on the colour of the instruments to save the music from monotony.

During this period (1950–55) Gerhard developed his original conception of a rhythmic series. This he intended should do in the field of time what Schoenberg's note-row did in the field of pitch; and the pivot work, in which he first worked out his idea, was the *First String Quartet*. The first movement of this work was written in 1950, the remainder in 1955. The second movement is a free improvisation, but the third and fourth movements apply the working of a time-series; the third movement (*Grave*) in rallentando, the fourth (*Molto Allegro*) in acceleration, which makes the motifs more easily comprehended.

Some of Gerhard's thoughts about the nature of serialism are summarised in an article written about this time[1], in which he puts forward the hypothesis that the 12-note technique is a new formulation of the principle of tonality. The word tonality, derived from the Greek *tonos*, implies something stretched; but it had hitherto been taken to refer only to pitch. Why confine composition to an imitation of Schoenberg's pitch-serialism? Most rhythm is thematically derived, yet rhythm, though interrelated, is something independent; it governs the temporal order of a piece, the way the music unfolds in time. Boulez had evolved a time-series, for instance in *Structures*, but Gerhard found this unsatisfactory because of the octave relationship between a note and another note twice its value. The essence of Schoenberg's pitch-serialism was that each of the twelve notes was different; and octave displacement did not alter the note itself, any more than in the diatonic system the inversion, or octave displacement, of a chord altered its character.

Gerhard's solution was to construct a numerical rhythmical series using prime numbers, and to interpolate the two groups of six (or three groups of four, or whatever the division of the twelve might be) in just

1. 'Tonality in twelve-tone music' in *The Score*, May 1952.

N

the same way as Schoenberg interpolated the two hexachords of his pitch-series. Thus if one group uses seven beats, another thirteen, and they both start together, they will not coincide again until ninety-one beats later (7×13); how many bars this constitutes will depend on the metre.

This central development in Gerhard's thinking took place between the first and second symphonies. The *First Symphony* (1952–53), which is in three movements, breaks entirely fresh ground in symphonic composition, in that, while retaining certain traditional links, it does away with themes. In place of the classical procedure of thematic form, with its exposition, development and so on, Gerhard substitutes a succession of long, melodic arches, serially constructed, and constantly varying in texture and rhythmic intensity; now the pace is quick, events crowd in on one another; now it is slack, lazy, and the parts have more breathing-space. The work is serial, though the later part of the first movement is somewhat freer, and uses motivic development. The most remarkable characteristic of Gerhard's orchestral writing is his use of the strings. He condenses his original conceptions of orchestral sonority into the string writing, which is at all times highly effective, if occasionally extremely difficult. Moods alter; the music veers now this way, now that. The symphony as a whole can best be compared to a day, from sunrise to sunset, where the constantly shifting rays of light create effects of emphasis, climax and release, in a continuing and unbroken cycle. Interestingly enough, from the *Second Symphony* onwards (1957), all his works are a continuous movement, without breaks which he considered unnatural.

With the *Second Symphony* he completes the separation, not just from the traditional thematic principle, but from his own earlier serial thinking. The numerical series, which, apart from the first String Quartet, is first used in this work, makes for closer coordination of the texture, a more taut temporal order. But the processes of composition are irrelevant for the listener, who is concerned primarily with the sound; it is unfortunate that the sound of this symphony, which is to some extent a transitional work, as it marks the composer's striking out into the more complexly abstract territory of pure sound, is not so characteristic of Gerhard as some other works. It resembles that grey, anonymous Esperanto which was the style adopted in the 50's by innumerable European serialists whose individuality it is almost impossible to pick out; the absence of themes imposes great burdens on the listener's ability for concentrated listening at the intellectual level.

The number of percussion instruments is greater, the number of notes sparser, than in the First Symphony. Seven percussion players are called for, and the various categories of instrument (tom-tom, cymbal, wood-block, Korean block, etc.) are graded into small, medium and large. This was the standard practice of the European *avant-garde*.

In its original form, the second main section of the symphony (*Lento*, bar 471) opens with an ostinato pattern for percussion which twice returns after intermediate sections for other instruments. The dynamic level is extremely low. There follows a little *spiccato* fugal section for strings (*comodamente*), similar to the opening of the *Nonet*; a cymbal-roll leads straight into the *Molto Vivace* final section, whose speed is disguised by the fragmented nature of the texture.

Yet that the *Second Symphony* occupied an important turning-point in his creative growth is proved by the fact that he later subjected it to basic revision. It was re-written under the title *Metamorphoses*[1], of which 181 manuscript pages were finished when the composer died. It is in three movements, compared with the two main sections of the earlier symphony, and these three movements, according to notes left by the composer, represent the final, complete version of the work. It was his last manuscript composition. A projected fifth symphony was not finished.

The *Third Symphony, Collages* (1960), was commissioned by the Koussevitzky Foundation. It introduced yet another technical innovation, magnetic tape. Gerhard had used electronic effects in two earlier pieces: first as background for a radio play *Asylum Diary*, next for a recitation of Lorca's *Lament for the Death of a Bull-Fighter*. In the Third Symphony tape and orchestra were juxtaposed in a way whose results could not be foreseen. The overall programme of the work is, explicitly this time, the span of a day from dawn to night; the sections invoke (in order): the dawn; the silence of plant life; the tumultuous world of man; the world of unconsciousness; re-assuming consciousness; cities in the distance; the calm of night.

Gerhard's individual interpretation of the serial idiom was to reach its mature fulfilment in two orchestral works, the *Concerto for Orchestra* and the *Fourth Symphony*. But three other works intervene: *Concert for 8* (1962), *Hymnody* (1963) for seven instruments, percussion and two pianos, and *The Plague* (1963), adapted from Camus for speaker, mixed chorus and orchestra.

It was in the *Concerto for Orchestra* (1964–65) that Gerhard reached that maturity in the new style which the *Violin Concerto* had in the old. In the *Concerto* for the first time the process of composition without themes, with the work based solely on those intangible, instinctive processes of constantly alternating and varying the timbre, intensity and

1. Published by Mills Music.

duration of sounds of a very wide sound-spectrum, has been fully assimilated. His break with his former style is thus complete. The principles governing Gerhard's serialism, as well as his intentions underlying this key work, are expressed as clearly as they could be by the composer's note at the front of the score:

> The present work is in one single movement. Its form largely depends upon three contrasting types of continuity which, in their alternation, strongly affect our passage-of-time consciousness. The first type is characterized by a high rate of eventuation. *Tone* plays *solo* here, so to speak, and tonal configuration is the leading composition principle.
>
> The second type is represented by almost static yet pulsating constellation-like patterns. Here *time* is playing *solo* and temporal configuration, based on 'time-lattices', is now the leading principle. Pitch is merely subsidiary here and, therefore, free use is made of a number of sounds of indeterminate pitch obtainable on some instruments by unorthodox ways of playing them.
>
> The third type of continuity might be likened to action in very slow motion. Comparatively little happens here, and everything casts long shadows, conjuring up, ideally, the magic sense of *uneventfulness*. A characteristic feature of this type of continuity is the virtual suspension of metre (only preserved for the convenience of notation). This, together with a conspicuous freedom of tempo, is what reminds me of a possibly last, tenuous link with the *ad lib.* spirit of the old cadenza.

The piece, which was first heard in Boston, on 25th April 1965, lasts twenty-one minutes. It carries on where the *Second Symphony* left off; absolute priority is given to sonority, from which Gerhard assumes the structure will automatically be formed. Texture has supplanted thematic repetition as the deciding factor in the shape a piece takes. This is in accordance with the earlier principle of sonata form, which followed naturally from the use of thematic composition, and contrasted keys. The unorthodox ways of playing the instruments that the composer refers to include the strings being played with the finger-nail below the bridge, *col legno* on the tail piece, the finger-tip tapping the belly, and so on.

The achievement of the *Concerto for Orchestra* was further consolidated in the *Fourth Symphony*. This work, more assured in idiom, and stronger in texture than the second, was commissioned by the New York Philharmonic as part of the celebration of its 125th anniversary, and performed in December 1967.

Among the smaller pieces, it remains to mention three short and straightforward piano *Impromptus* (1959), dedicated to Lord and Lady Harewood; also the *Second String Quartet* (1962), which was commissioned by the University of Michigan, following Gerhard's visit there in

1960. This twelve-minute work is remarkable for its fragmenting the series into 9, 8, 7, even 3-note sets; it also anticipates those effects which were later to be used in the *Concerto*.

Gerhard's work is remarkable for many reasons. He was one of the very few British composers of the 60's who, having forged a style within the limits of total serialism, could still call it his own. His musical personality was sufficiently pronounced for his later serial works to reach beyond that technical anonymity that claims most.

He was one of the composers who benefitted directly and positively from the swing towards serialism in the 60's; indeed, without it, and the active support of William Glock, it is more than doubtful, first, whether his music would have flowered as it did in the last decade of his life; next, whether it would have been heard to the extent it was. It was a remarkably productive period for Gerhard in which, having opened up his new serial world, he proceeded to occupy it; not only with the large-scale orchestral works, but with smaller pieces for chamber ensemble. His last three chamber works had astrological titles: *Gemini* (1966), a duo concertante (as it was originally called) for violin and piano; *Libra* (1968) and *Leo* (1969) for various ensembles.

The composer's note to *Gemini* is characteristic:

The work consists of a series of contrasting episodes, whose sequence is more like a braiding of diverse strands than a straight linear development. Except for the concluding episodes, nearly every one recurs more than once, generally in a different context. These recurrences are not like refrains, and do not fulfil anything remotely like the function of the classical refrain.

It is a brittle piece, of alternating movement and stillness for each instrument, and containing many of the *avant-garde* characteristics of piano-playing: cluster chords, *glissando* on the strings, and so on.

Libra, the Balance, was the composer's own Zodiac sign. Like *Gemini* it could also be seen as a series of contrasting episodes, or better, heard as a series of contrasting sonorities. *Leo*, his wife's Zodiac sign, also for chamber ensemble, was the last composition published in his lifetime; and it ends, appropriately, with a long *diminuendo* over a rocking piano bass.

Gerhard, like Stravinsky, travelled a great distance in terms of creative discovery; his style covers a wide spectrum. His artist's curiosity was impelled by philosophical and intellectual energy. Even when expressing himself verbally, which he was sometimes reluctant to do, he took a delight in finding exactly and precisely the correct word or phrase to describe what was probably an abstruse, metaphysical idea. Clarity of speech reflected clarity of thought; nothing was more alien to Gerhard's aesthetic than the imprecise, ill-formed, aleatoric approach to art.

The visitor who was fortunate to engage him, or perhaps overhear him, in conversation, would come away several hours later a considerably richer man. Thought-provoking ideas, paradoxes, aphorisms were carefully enunciated, for later consideration. One writer has noted several[1]; some more are:—

Sound imagined is real; sound heard is reflex.
Composing at the piano removes a dimension of imagination.
The necessity of redundancy . . .
Repetition makes structure (c.f. Paul Klee)
Schoenberg put forward a way of handling pitch; he did not solve formal problems.
The composer feels thoughtfully, thinks feelingly.
Only when sound transcends its material nature does it excite the musical imagination.

Surprisingly, he rarely taught. Since 1939 he neither taught nor lectured at Cambridge, though in 1967 he was made an Hon. D. Mus. of that university. It was an American University (Ann Arbor, Michigan) which in 1960 persuaded him to accept an engagement as 'visiting professor'. He returned to America the following year, to Tanglewood.

Gerhard's aesthetic has a broad, philosophical basis. He felt a kinship with scientists, and the scientific attitude. Music, he maintained, was the pre-eminent art of the nineteenth century; this hegemony then passed to science. He moreover derived much benefit from Paul Valéry, whose research into the multifarious problems connected with the creative process led him to conclusions with which Gerhard was in sympathy.

Apart from the use of a numerical series, his style is dominated by the smaller intervals rather than by the compound intervals which so appealed to Webern; also by his interpretation of serialism according to what he would call 'tonal' principles; chiefly, that is to say, the principle that the hexachords, of which there are sixty, can have permutations also within them. The music as a result grows in many directions, and is full of inner melody. He was fond of quoting the Byzantine definition of the smaller intervals as *somatic*, or substance-forming, and of the wider intervals as *pneumatic*, or insubstantial.

Another characteristic is the ostinato technique. If repetition is the corner-stone of structure, ostinato is the corner-stone of repetition. It is central to Gerhard's style, and to his building of texture. Texture starts for him as imagined sound; composition finishes when the imagined sound has become real, and the moment has become crystallised.

At a rehearsal of the *Fourth Symphony*, a copyist was rash enough to

1. In *The Score* (September 1956).

suggest that a certain passage be cut. The ensuing conversation throws a light on Gerhard's personality as well as his music; an element of seriousness is concealed, in true Anglo-Saxon style, beneath the lightness of the moment:

G.   You are lucky I am not Schoenberg; he would have bitten your head off!
Cop. I knew you would not bite my head off!
G.   You should have said—I am not Schoenberg.
Cop. Perhaps one Schoenberg is enough?
G.   One Schoenberg is more than enough!

14   Andrzej Panufnik

Like Reizenstein, Panufnik combines executive with creative musician-ship. Unlike him, however, he had already attained eminence in both fields, conducting and composing, before leaving his native Poland in 1954.

One of the most remarkable features of the British attitude to musicians from other countries is that while the warmest welcome is extended to visitors, the reception accorded to newly-arrived citizens from other countries is ambivalent, and considerably less fulsome. Composers who have taken up residence in this country, and become British citizens, have found obstacles in their path which are inexplicable to any who do not fully understand the full implications of that ominous and much-quoted phrase 'English reserve'. And so, in the case of Panufnik, who is one of the most gifted composers in Europe today, in spite of his residence here, and his British nationality, his services as a composer and conductor are in demand in every other country of the Western hemisphere except London, where he lives.

He was born in Warsaw in 1914. His father was originally an engineer, but later he devoted himself entirely to making stringed instruments; he was extremely knowledgeable on the early Italian violin, and he con-structed two completely new models of his own, *Antica* and *Polonia*, which became famous. He also wrote scientific books on the art of violin making, which are to be found in the library of the British Museum. Andrzej Panufnik's mother, of partly English origin, was a highly accomplished violinist although she never played in public. After a period at the Warsaw Conservatoire, where he studied the groundwork of composition under Kazimierz Sikorski, he proceeded, in 1937, to the Vienna State Academy, where he studied conducting as one of the very few and rigorously selected pupils of Felix Weingartner, and at the same time, acquainted himself with the 12-note style of Schoenberg and Webern. Panufnik has always considered his work as a conductor to be complementary to his composition; it has brought him into contact with music-making, and it has helped to give him that insight into the use of instruments which every orchestral composer needs. He has never been a career conductor.

He was also a creditable pianist, though he never considered himself as a concert soloist. He rounded off these formative years of study by going first to Paris, then to London. In Paris he concentrated his attention, naturally, on French composers, while continuing to work as a conductor under Philippe Gaubert. In London, which he visited in 1939, he acquainted himself with the early period of English music, largely by research at the British Museum. He also heard several concerts at the Queen's Hall. In short, few musicians in their twenty-fifth year have emerged from their student period better equipped to embark on their life-work.

He returned to Poland in 1939; and almost immediately the war broke out. He remained in Warsaw all through the Nazi occupation, and the difficulties and troubles of those years may well be imagined, on the personal as well as on the musical level. The city of Warsaw was completely destroyed, and the hell and agony of the Polish nation reached its dire climax in the ill-starred uprising of 1944. In such severe conditions, what music could there be, except on a makeshift basis? Orchestral concerts were 'for Germans only', and the performance of Polish music (especially Chopin) and of works by Jewish composers was banned by the Nazis, so music-making often had to be underground. Indeed, that any music was made at all seems miraculous; and yet it was at an underground concert in 1942 that Panufnik's *Tragic Overture* was first heard.

As well as working at his own composition, Panufnik played duets for two pianos with his contemporary, Witold Lutosławski, and for this purpose they made transcriptions of some hundred works, from Bach and Mozart to Stravinsky and Szymanowski, and other banned composers. Tragically and mysteriously, all these transcriptions by both the composers, with the exception of the Lutosławski *Paganini Variations*, were lost in the Warsaw Uprising. But unspeakably more tragic was the loss, also in the 1944 Uprising, of all the music that Panufnik had ever composed; not only that, but his brother Mirosław lost his life as a member of the Polish Underground Resistance Army. What better way had the composer of keeping his brother's name alive than by dedicating the re-written *Tragic Overture* to his memory?

After the war he became conductor of the Cracow Philharmonic, then director of the Warsaw Philharmonic Orchestra. He began to travel extensively as guest conductor to foreign orchestras. He resumed composition, and in the years immediately after 1945 he was free to develop as a composer in whatever direction he saw fit. Gradually, however, political pressure began to be felt more intensely, and the Soviet principles of 'Socialist Realism' were applied more severely. Music, like every other art, was looked on as an instrument of political propaganda; the composer was required to write mass songs and patriotic cantatas; all 'formalism' was proscribed, whether it was that of Debussy, Hindemith and Schoenberg, or of the Impressionist school of painters. This political pressure gradually became a stranglehold, which reached a climax in the years following 1949. Several works were banned, and some composers, including Panufnik, came under official criticism. It was only later, after 1956, that a more liberal atmosphere began to be felt, which was shown in the Warsaw Festival of that year. This liberalisation was the result not only of political events but also of a courageous struggle by the Polish composers; and certainly Panufnik's dramatic protest two years before helped to influence the situation.

Much of the development in contemporary Polish music can only be understood in the light of these events; after 1956 Polish composers at last were able to experiment as regards their musical language, and at the same time, in a subtle manner, they were thus able to demonstrate against the Soviet regime which had so fettered their speech, and to emphasize that their cultural allegiance lay with the West. Therefore, after 1956 they excitedly pursued post-Webern serialism and post-Cage aleatoric devices.

Panufnik, however, followed a different path. For him the heart of the Polish tradition, and thus of his true style, lies in that spiritual, emotional, tragic, heroic feeling that can be traced from Chopin; he has never found any compensating satisfaction in an abstract theory or system, though he was acquainted with the serial technique.

He was highly respected in Poland, and well-known both as a composer and conductor. He was elected, among other things, the Vice-President (jointly with Honegger) of the International Music Council of U.N.E.S.C.O. in Paris. He travelled extensively, and had been to England several times, for instance for the I.S.C.M. Festival in 1946, when his *Five Polish Peasant Songs* were performed.[1] At last, however, in spite of outward success, he could endure the artistic stagnation and the political control in Poland no longer; so in 1954 he decided to leave the country. It was a bold and radical step to take at the age of thirty-nine particularly as he would be leaving behind in Warsaw all his most valued and personal possessions; his manuscripts, and his pricelessly valuable collection of over fifty stringed instruments, old Italian as well as new ones constructed by his father. However, after a concert in

1. On July 12th 1946, by the BBC Chorus, in the Goldsmiths' Hall, London.

Zurich, instead of returning to Warsaw, he came to London. His action and protest, which he made known through every available source, has never been forgiven by the Warsaw Government, and his music is still banned in Poland and all communist countries. He knew no one in England, nor had he any financial backing. Apart from one concert with the Philharmonia Orchestra, his conducting engagements continued to come from abroad. The first year after his arrival was spent, as the list of his works shows, in rescuing and revising his works for publication: such works, that is, as he had managed to bring from Poland. After a few years' residence he did get two BBC commissions,[1] and later he was for two seasons (1957-9) conductor and musical director of the City of Birmingham symphony orchestra. He succeeded Rudolf Schwarz, who had been conductor since 1951, and was succeeded first by Sir Adrian Boult, for just one season, then by Hugo Rignold. But it was one thing to appear as guest conductor on the international circuit; it was quite another to devote a fuller proportion of time to the artistic direction of a provincial English orchestra with a very unadventurous audience and management committee. However, in addition to the standard repertoire, Panufnik introduced the Birmingham audiences to the work of several British composers. He conducted the first performances of Edmund Rubbra's *Seventh Symphony* and Lennox Berkeley's *Second Symphony*, and a Symphonic Prelude, *Polonia*, by no less a composer than Elgar. He presented only four of his own works. Above all, he showed particular interest in early English music: Avison, Arne, Boyce, Byrd and Purcell. Indeed, it is more than probable that he was much better acquainted with the early music of the country of his adoption than most Englishmen.

But he found, as many have, that the demands of composition and those of a conducting career are incompatible. Since leaving Birmingham in 1959 he has devoted the greater part of his time to composition, and confined his conducting to guest appearances. These have been mainly abroad, in such places as Buenos Aires, Lisbon, Paris, Stuttgart and elsewhere.

Of his works nothing survives prior to 1944. These included *Symphonic Variations*, a *Little Overture*, a *Psalm* for soloists, chorus and orchestra, and several chamberworks and piano pieces.

But some other pieces were reconstructed. One in particular, the *Tragic Overture*, was firmly enough imprinted on his mind to be re-written later. Apart from its central position in Panufnik's creative consciousness, it is characteristic of the composer in style, mood and technique; it serves therefore as the best introduction to his music.

1. The *Rhapsody* and *Polonia Suite*.

Panufnik's principles and methods of composition are highly individual, and, more so than with most contemporary composers, are an essential clue to an understanding of his music. Whereas Sartre used to say that 'existence precedes essence', in the case of Panufnik a deep, spiritual feeling, a poetic intuition, precedes creativity. Many lesser composers adopt to music an emotional attitude of one kind or another, whether deep or not, as a substitute for the rigorous discipline of composition; many a hack religious work, for instance, or aleatoric sketch, has been written on this flimsy and threadbare aesthetic basis. Others, again, accept the necessity for strictness, but lack that underlying intensity of feeling which gives warmth and power to the finished structure; many a composer, whether academic or *avant-garde*, has became so mesmerised and preoccupied by technique as to mistake the means for the end of his art.

But Panufnik, like Messiaen (who is only six years his senior), treats each stage as equally indispensable and important. The spiritual content decides the very structure of the composition. First, the emotional involvement, from which derives the innate character of the themes; these in turn dictate the form of the composition; lastly come the progressions, tone-colours, and so on. Thus has Panufnik restored that balance in contemporary music between content and style—between what you say, and how you say it—which is always the first casualty in any war between irreconcilable partisans, of whatever viewpoint. And what snobbery is there that is more fierce, or more irrational and exclusive, than an aesthetic snobbery?

In no piece is Panufnik's method more clearly shown than in the • *Tragic Overture*. A 4-note cell pervades the work like a motto

It accumulates great warmth and strength. The other most apparent features are economy, discipline, tidiness. The structure of the piece approximates to sonata form. The first thematic idea leads to a progressive increase in tension, built up entirely from the 4-note *motif*, which culminates at [8] (Boosey and Hawkes' edition). The second idea consists of a quiet, sustained melody in minims, first given to the flute at [9], while the 4-note *motif* serves an accompanimental purpose. The development consists of the inversion, augmentation and diminution of the *motif* in various sections of the orchestra.

Ex.31   Panufnik
                                                             Tragic Overture

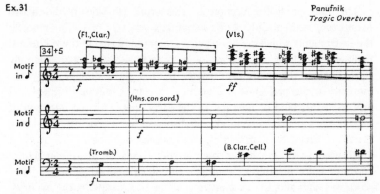

The recapitualation consists of the working of the material up towards a
different kind of culminating moment, at [60], at which point the violins
and woodwind immediately sing out the secondary theme (ff, *cantabile*),
while the accompanimental quavers are given to the brass. When, after
[71], the brass join the other instruments in the sustained minims, the
only section of the orchestra left to hammer out the 4-note *motif* is the
percussion; and so, up to the end, an antiphonal ostinato is maintained
between the side-drum and the bass-drum, with occasional interjections
from the tom-tom and the cymbals.

The 4-note cell, which pervades the work from the first note to the
last, gives it its melodic as well as its rhythmic character. It is also
susceptible of development, and allows greater freedom to expand than a
series which uses all the twelve notes. Another work which is constructed
on similar principles is the *Heroic Overture*, which was written for the
Helsinki Olympic Games, 1952, and was awarded a prize in a competition
in Warsaw that same year.

But the *Tragic Overture* epitomises the two most striking features of
his idiom; these are his use of tonality, which is extended to a highly
individual, chromatic polytonality; and an accumulated intensity of
emotional feeling. These features come together in his favourite device,
the simultaneous use of conflicting degrees of the scale, a major-minor
duality.

Ex.32   Panufnik
                                        Tragic Overture

The first published version of this work (Polskie Wydawnictwo Muzyczne, 1948) already shows Panufnik's new way of writing a score; the instruments which are not playing are not indicated in the traditional manner by a stave, key and rests—a space is left and notation is only started when the instrument comes in, the stave disappearing once more when the performer has nothing to play. Panufnik invented and first used this kind of notation in the early '40s, with the intention of making the score clearer and more transparent for conductors, alleviating the usual necessity of pencilling in additional markings. (Frequently a much-used score which has been in the hands of many conductors becomes quite illegible.) Panufnik's simplified method of writing the score was later adopted by numerous composers, including the majority of today's *avant-garde*.

Panufnik is primarily an orchestral composer. Choral and vocal music does not come easily to him, though one example, *Universal Prayer*, is among his major works. Chief among his orchestral compositions so far are the three symphonies and the piano concerto, while shorter pieces include *Lullaby*, *Landscape*, and more particularly the exquisite *Nocturne*. With all his compositions it is the basic conception that is all-important; in the case of the *Nocturne* this conception was like an arch; the music beginning from nothing, working towards a *tutti*, then returning to nothing, whence it came; the end mirrors the beginning (a side-drum roll). This piece was awarded first prize in a competition in Cracow in 1948.

Some works are inspired by traditional Polish folk-melodies, and are therefore not so characteristic of the originality of the composer. However, his approach to folk-lore is very much his own, and is different from, for example, Szymanowski, Bartok or Vaughan Williams. An example of this is *Hommage à Chopin*, which exists in two forms; one is for soprano and piano, the other is for flute and strings. The work is based on rustic melodies and rhythms from Masovia in central Poland, where Chopin was born. Other works which originated in this way are the *Five Polish Peasant Songs* and the *Polonia Suite*, and some others.

Highly characteristic, however, and of great importance, though they are deceptively slight, are the piano pieces: the *Miniature Studies* and *Reflections*. The studies make the fullest use of piano texture and sonority. Starting in C sharp major-minor, the key of each study moves to a fifth lower than the one before, so that the twelve notes are encompassed in the overall scheme. A quick movement is succeeded by a slow one, loud alternates with soft, until the final study, which starts pp and works a gradual *crescendo* up to ffff, *molto secco*. Each study, needless to say, is built round just one pattern, or *motif*. For originality of conception these pieces are unequalled by the piano compositions of other British composers; only Fricker and Reizenstein invite any kind of comparison.

The nine pieces, also called *microstructures*, which make up *Reflections* use even more economy of technique.

Of Panufnik's symphonies, the first, *Sinfonia Rustica*, is partly based on Polish folk-themes. It divides the strings into two stereophonic groups, each made up in the proportion 7, 6, 5, 4, 3, with the wind in the middle, though without clarinets and percussion. The four movements of the symphony are given markings according to the mood of the music: *con tenerezza, con grazia, con espressione, con vigore*. As a whole, the work shows a fresh, original concept of symphonic writing, which was to bear such excellent fruit later. Although it won yet another first prize, this time in the Chopin competition in Warsaw, 1949, it was violently attacked later that year at a meeting of the Composers' Union, as being 'alien to the great Socialist era', and he was told by the Minister of Culture that his *Sinfonia Rustica* had 'ceased to exist'. This was the crucial period when the regime really started to put very strong pressure on creative artists in all fields, to impose the method of 'socialist realism' and force the composers to write music for the 'broad masses' with a clear political propaganda message. To avoid giving way to this pressure, Panufnik turned to the early Polish music of the sixteenth and seventeenth centuries (which was not proscribed), and finding by research some unused themes of several composers of that period, wrote two works, *Old Polish Suite* and *Concerto in Modo Antico*, without any harmonic or rhythmical distortions, in the style of the period. (Also, fifteen years later, he returned with one work to this style, when he wanted to write a special occasional piece for a concert celebrating Poland's Millennium of Statehood and Christianity in 1966; this was the *Jagiellonian Triptych*).

The second symphony, *Sinfonia Elegiaca*, is constructed in one continuous movement, in three sections: *molto andante, molto allegro, molto andante*. It was first performed in Houston, Texas, by that champion of the contemporary composer, Leopold Stokowski.[1] The first and third sections were later (1957) used for a ballet, *Elegy*, presented in Seattle and New York by the City Center Joffrey Ballet, conducted by Seymour Lipkin. As a symphony, the conception is of a central section of savage and percussive energy, flanked on either side by music of sombre gravity.

Many of Panufnik's works are of symmetrical construction; and none more so than *Autumn Music*, written in memory of a friend who, through a long, incurable illness, 'experienced her last autumn in 1960'. Its three

1. Stokowski also gave the world première of another work, *Katyń Epitaph*, ten years later, 1968, with his American Symphony Orchestra in New York.

main sections (A-B-C) are hinged together like a triptych, by two very short Interludes, and it is of symmetrical construction, with the climax in the middle of the central section, which is itself in a mirror form. The material, athematic and very simple, consists of germ-cells of two intervals. The first section, A, and the second interlude, is based on major and minor seconds; the last section C is based mainly on the minor third and minor second, like the first interlude. In the middle section, B, which is contrasting in character to the others, the telescoped melodic lines in canonic writing are taken from a chord built in thirds only. This stands like an axis in an almost perfect symmetry; the symmetrical construction of the work as a whole is also emphasised by its texture, rhythm, tempo and dynamics.

The following diagram summarizes the whole technical description of this composition:

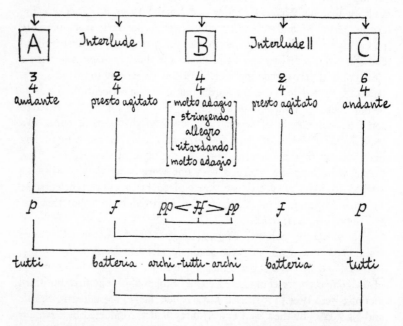

But it is the third symphony, *Sinfonia Sacra*, which calls for chief attention. It was composed, under a grant from the Kósciuszko Foundation, for Poland's Millennium of Christianity and Statehood (1966), and won first prize for Great Britain in the Monaco competition, 1963. This time the source of inspiration demanded that the symphony should be particularly Polish in character, and that it should emphasize the deeply-rooted Catholic tradition of that country. Therefore the composer chose the first known hymn in the Polish language as his starting-point. This is a Gregorian chant called *Bogurodzica* ('Mother of God') (Ex. 33), which represented for the Poles what the Lutheran Chorale represented for the Germans, a secular as well as a sacred hymn, heroic as well as religious; and this duality pervades the symphony.

Ex.33   Panufnik
                                                             Sinfonia Sacra

('Bo-gu-ro-dzi - ca')

Sinfonia Sacra is Panufnik's culminating symphonic work up to now The indefatigable Leopold Stokowski, who gave the first New York performance, described it as 'most powerful, extremely original'; the first London performance was not given until 1968, and even then not by one of the London orchestras.[1] But this symphony has had many performances abroad, including two performances in Paris, one of them televised. The symphony was also used with brilliant success by the choreographer, Kenneth MacMillan, for his ballet *Cain and Abel* at the Deutsche Oper, West Berlin, in November 1968.

The work is in two parts; *Three Visions* and *Hymn*. The Visions, which follow without a break, are strongly contrasted. The first is an extended fanfare, a colloquy built in fourths, between four trumpets which are placed at the four compass-points round the orchestra. The Second Vision uses strings alone to create a mystic, contemplative atmosphere. The material anticipates the melody that is to come later. The Third Vision, far the longest and most dramatic, mounts to a climax of agitation, an orchestral shout of protest, which is suddenly cut off, to be followed immediately by the Hymn. This expresses the adoration and warmth of a simple prayer to the Virgin. It starts with very quiet string harmonics, which gradually dissolve to allow the music to grow gradually, until the *Bogurodzica* melody breaks through in full splendour (Ex. 33), A recall of the opening fanfare brings the work to a climactic end.

As in the *Tragic Overture*, a 4-note cell is used, for instance after [25], where a cross-rhythm is introduced to give both refinement to the movement of the music and excitement to the tension (Ex. 34). Intervals are also used as cells of development; the fourth in Vision 1, the major second in Vision 2, the minor second in Vision 3 (Ex. 33).

1. On 23rd November, 1968, by Constantin Silvestri and the Bournemouth Symphony Orchestra.

o

Ex.34   Panufnik
                                                                         Sinfonia Sacra

But analysis does not give the whole picture; it is a mistake to dwell
too long on the many technical aspects of the work of this most spiritual
and poetic of contemporary composers. Certainly the order and consistency of a piece demand a rigorous discipline; neither the component
motifs, viewed horizontally, nor the use of harmony or tonality, viewed
vertically, can be left to chance; indeed, Panufnik considers that the
aleatoric principle runs contrary to the composer's art, which is anything
but accidental.

The year 1970 was a busy and important one for the composer: not
only did he appear as a conductor for the first time for many years in
London[1], but the year also included three premières. First, on 7th
February, the 'Cantata for young singers and players', *Thames Pageant*,
given by sixteen schools in the Richmond area. Two treble-voice choirs
are placed on either side of the hall, and the orchestra is divided between
the junior players, who play with open strings, simple recorders and
percussion, and the senior players, whose part is more difficult, and
includes four brass instruments. The work is a suite of seven sections,
with words written by the composer's wife, Camilla, descriptive of the
River Thames.

The following month saw a première of a very different sort. Following
the success of *Cain and Abel* to Panufnik's music, the choreographer
Kenneth MacMillan commissioned the composer to write a new ballet
for performance in Stuttgart; and this took place on 8th March. *Miss
Julie*, a ballet in two acts, was based on the Strindberg play, and enjoyed
great success at its first performance.

The third première of this year was on 24th May, in the Cathedral of
St. John the Divine, New York, when the redoubtable Leopold Stokowski
conducted *Universal Prayer* (see plate 7). This conductor had already, as
we have seen, championed Panufnik's work in America; on this occasion
he performed the new work twice to the vast audience that filled the
largest of Anglican cathedrals.

Universal Prayer represents a fresh departure for Panufnik; not only
is his purpose a deeply-felt one, grand and solemn, but his interpretation
of the sense and sound of the words is new. Pope's heartfelt text comes
from his *Essay on Man*, written about 1715, and it seemed perfectly

1. On 11th May, at the Queen Elizabeth Hall. The concert included his *Autumn Music*.

suited to the composer's purpose, which was to write a prayer detached from any religion, but suited to any individual man. Pope's prayer is addressed to the one God of every race, every religion, every age: Jehovah, Jove or Lord. Panufnik finds this inspiring and significant for this age, and his dream is that people of different religions, and of different races, should take part in the performance, through which they will unite their feelings.

The structure of the work is symmetrical in all its aspects: texture, rhythm, tempo and dynamics. There are thirteen verses in the poem, and the seventh verse, musically, represents an axis. The first verse corresponds with the last, the second with the twelfth, the third with the eleventh, and so on. These verses are divided by interludes which are also constructed symmetrically, as are the introduction and coda.

The scoring is for four solo voices, three harps, mixed chorus and organ. It is written stereophonically, on two distinctive levels:

Level I: Four solo voices and three harps. The music is written with precise indications of rhythm and tempo.
Level II: Organ and chorus, written *senza mesure*. Each chorus-singer chooses freely his or her own rhythm on the three words 'Father of all'. The chorus throughout have just one note—B natural—and they also retain independence from each other rhythmically, and make themselves heard as individuals.

The material is most simple, and the whole work is based only on one triad, made up of the notes F-B-E, which is constantly transposed, and used melodically and harmonically, or both simultaneously. This is a new departure in Panufnik's expressive language, simple, yet awesome.

The central feature of his art, which should remain uppermost in our minds, is the poetic content. This is not only the point from which the composer sets out to compose; it is also the source of colour and vitality in the unique, residual impression created by each finished structure; it is that suggestive spark of creative intuition which, the strongest of all weapons in a composer's armoury, most surely strikes a responsive chord in the listener's consciousness.

The works of Andrzej Panufnik

Date*	Category†	Title
1934/1945/1967	1	*Trio, for Piano, Violin, Cello*
1940/1945/1959	2	*Five Polish Peasant Songs* (voices & wind instruments)
1942/1945/1955	1	*Tragic Overture*
1947/1955	2	*Lullaby, for 29 strings, 2 harps*

The works of Andrzej Panufnik (continued)

Date*	Category†	Title
1947/1955	2	*Nocturne, for orchestra*
1947/1955	1	*Twelve miniature studies,* for piano solo
1948/1955	2	*Sinfonia Rustica*
1949/1955	2	*Hommage à Chopin* a) soprano & piano b) flute & string orchestra
1950/1955	3	*Old Polish Suite*
1951/1955	3	*Concerto in modo antico*
1952/1965	1	*Heroic Overture*
1956	2	*Rhapsody, for Orchestra*
1957/1966	1	*Sinfonia Elegiaca*
1959	2	*Polonia—Suite for Orchestra*
1962	1	*Autumn Music, for Orchestra*
1962	1	*Concerto for Piano and Orchestra*
1963	1	*Two Lyric Pieces*
1963	2	*Sinfonia Sacra*
1964/1969	2	*Song to the Virgin Mary* (choir *a cappella*)
1965	2	*Landscape, for String Orchestra*
1966	3	*Jagiellonian Triptych, for strings*
1967	2	*Katyń Epitaph*
1968	1	*Reflections, for piano solo*
1968	1	*Universal Prayer* (Pope), for 4 soli, choir, 3 harps, organ
1969	1	*Thames Pageant* (cantata for young players & singers)

* A second or third year added after the date of a composition indicates the year of its reconstruction or revision.

† The categories into which Panufnik's works fall are:

1. Abstract, independent, composed according to self-imposed discipline, often with whole sections, or even whole works, built out of germ-cells of two or three intervals.

2. Based on, or inspired by, Polish folklore and history; founded on a kind of free tonality, often using a major-minor duality.

3. Composed from themes by Polish composers of the sixteenth and seventeenth centuries.

V

The evolution
of a tradition

15 Benjamin Britten

Like the musical thought of some of his larger works, Britten's career has developed simultaneously on several different levels; whether as composer, pianist, founder of both the English Opera Group and the Aldeburgh Festival, or conductor, his is the most acute musical sensibility; his knowledge and appreciation of literature are formidable; moreover, his music is the best-known and most performed of any contemporary English composer. He has strongly influenced a large number of younger composers, particularly in matters of operatic style. He has received public recognition by being made a Companion of Honour (1953), and being awarded the Order of Merit (1965). In 1964 he received the first Aspen award in America.

He was born in Lowestoft, Suffolk, in 1913, on November 22nd—St. Cecilia's day. His talents appeared early; by 1930 he had already written a large quantity of music, both instrumental and vocal, including well over fifty songs.[1] Looking back at these boyhood works, Britten has said, revealingly: 'The choice of poets was nothing if not catholic. There are more than thirty of them, ranging from the Bible to Kipling, from Shakespeare to an obscure magazine poet "Chanticleer"; there were many settings of Shelley and Burns and Tennyson, of a poem by a schoolmaster friend, songs to texts by Hood, Longfellow, "Anon", and several French poets; and one to the composer's own words ("One day when I went home, I sore a boat on the sands"). In some cases the songs were written so hurriedly that there was no time to write the words in, or even to note the name of the poem or poet. The poet whose name appears most frequently is Walter de la Mare, whose verse caught my fancy very early on. I possessed several of his volumes, but a few poems were evidently copied from inaccurate reprints in anthologies. . . . At any rate, although I hold no claims whatever for the songs' importance or originality, I do feel that the boy's vision has a simplicity and clarity which might have

1. Some were published in 1969 under the title *Tit for Tat.*

203

given a little pleasure to the great poet, with his unique insight into a child's mind.'

He went to Gresham's School, Holt, in Norfolk, and during school holidays Frank Bridge gave him lessons in harmony and counterpoint; a valuable discipline for a precocious youngster. In 1930 he went to the Royal College of Music, where he was under John Ireland for composition, and Arthur Benjamin for piano. His musical horizon broadened during these years, and many valuable contacts were made with other musicians. The first of his long list of works, the *Sinfonietta*, Op. 1, dates from June/July 1932, and was the only one of his student works to be performed at the College; it was written with characteristic speed, in about three weeks, and also was the first work to reach a wider, though specialist, public.[1]

On leaving the College in 1934, Britten was anxious to spend some time in Vienna studying with Alban Berg; but the combined wisdom of his elders advised against such an extreme course. It is interesting, indeed, though perhaps vain, to speculate what effect the composer of *Wozzeck* would have had on the twenty-one-year-old Englishman. Britten at this time was seething with ideas; he had no doubt whatever that he was to be a composer; and yet he was uncertain of that goal towards which his creativity should be directed. Fluency and facility make their own exacting demands.

As he faced the prospects of musical London, two factors helped him: the first was a contract with a publisher, Ralph Hawkes, whose confidence turned out to be handsomely rewarded;[2] the second was a chance to work on documentary films, for the G.P.O. Film Unit. He had already written the title music for a documentary film *Cable Ship* in 1933, and between 1935 and 1939 he wrote seventeen more, as well as a considerable number of other film scores, and incidental music for plays. In this way a very difficult period of his creative life was successfully surmounted. As far as technique and style were concerned, not only did film work require fluency and speed of writing, which have always been his in abundance, but it also developed his ingenuity, and ability to write effectively for small combinations of instruments, a trait which was to be fully realised later.

But he was a long time finding his true musical personality. One

1. At a Macnaghten concert on 31st January 1933.
2. Rarely has a composer been supported by his publisher with more sustained and steady publicity than Britten's publisher, Boosey and Hawkes, accorded him in their house magazine *Tempo*. Starting in September 1946, twenty seven full-length articles appeared, culminating in a fiftieth birthday issue (No. 66/7, Autumn-Winter, 1963).

   Britten's present publisher, Faber Music, are evidently tempting history to repeat itself by offering a contract to another young College student, Douglas Young.

decisive factor was his close friendship with the poet W. H. Auden. Though some years Britten's senior, Auden had also been at Gresham's School, Holt; and it soon became clear that his voice was characteristic of the 30's.[1] His work took him to the theatre; it also took him, as luck would have it, to the G.P.O. Film Unit, which thus became, however unwittingly, the patron of a remarkable artistic partnership. *Coal Face* and *Night Mail* (1936) were the immediate result; but the collaboration between Auden and Britten was extended farther than the film world, into the theatre and beyond. Auden supplied what Britten needed, that poetic impulse and image to which his own creativity could respond. So over the next few years many of Britten's main works were settings of Auden's words: *Our Hunting Fathers*, *On this Island*, *Ballad of Heroes*, and the operetta *Paul Bunyan*.[2] The partnership ended with the *Hymn to St. Cecilia* (1942).

It was largely through Auden that Britten decided to go to America in 1939. The rise of Fascism in Europe, particularly after the Spanish Civil War, and the Munich affair in 1938, made it appear to him that only in the New World could an artistic personality be fully developed. Moreover, travel in itself can be important for a young composer, particularly if English audiences prove frustratingly slow to win over, as they usually do. So in the summer of 1939 Britten and his friend Peter Pears left for America.

After staying with the American composer Aaron Copland[3] in Brooklyn, they went to Amityville, Long Island, which was their home for the next two years. While in America, Britten's services both as pianist and composer were much in demand. Works which date from this time include several works for orchestra, the *Violin Concerto*, the *First String Quartet*, and two song cycles, *Les Illuminations* to French words by Rimbaud, and *Seven Sonnets of Michelangelo* with an Italian text.

The years in America mark the end of his preparatory, formative stage as a composer. Gradually the characteristics of his true style became apparent. His is that highly sensitive form of creativity that responds to an already-existing image, and illustrates it with music. The image may be literary, pictorial, dramatic, religious; the resulting composition is a sequence of colourful sound impressions, rather than the development of purely musical themes. Such a style is clearly much more inclined

---

1. The young poets of the 1930's, whose work was represented in *New Signatures* (1932) are described by Leonard Woolf in his autobiography *Downhill All the Way* pp. 174-6
2. This was performed on 5th May 1941 in New York, but later withdrawn.
3. Copland had been in London in June 1938, when his *El Salon Mexico* was given at an I.S.C.M. concert and met Britten during his stay in England (see *50th Birthday Symposium*).

towards vocal and dramatic works than to symphonic treatment; and indeed, after his return from America, orchestral or instrumental works form a very small part of his output, and give place to the operas. Also, his response to other composers' works makes him the most sensitive of performing artists, whether as pianist or conductor.

His work with Auden in America was centred round the operetta *Paul Bunyan*, which dealt with the early settlers in that country. It was not a success, though it paved the way for what was to come. The image of the American pioneer would strike much more of a response in an American composer; indeed, Copland's *Appalachian Spring* is about just that. Would not an English composer be more inspired by something which he knew from experience in his own country?

And so whereas Auden became an American citizen, Britten did not. He decided to return to England in 1941. But this was no simple matter in wartime, and it was not until March 1942 that a passage was found, on a neutral Swedish cargo boat. The months of waiting were not wasted, however, for they resulted in his meeting Serge Koussevitsky, when the latter performed his *Sinfonia da Requiem* in Boston; this meeting resulted in an advance of $1,000 to the young composer, to enable him to devote time to writing a full-length opera, which would be dedicated to the memory of Koussevitsky's wife Natalie, who had recently died. The result, three years later, was *Peter Grimes*.

Nor were the weeks spent on the voyage home idle ones: the *Hymn to St. Cecilia* and *A Ceremony of Carols* were written on the boat.

On returning to England, he lived at Snape, a few miles from Aldeburgh in Suffolk. Five years later he moved to Aldeburgh itself. Now, starting with the *Serenade* (1943), his work enters a more mature period. He is no longer searching for a sense of artistic direction; now it is a question of finding those images that would inspire him, and be a vehicle for his creativity; his background became the England that he knew. From now on, starting with *Peter Grimes* (1945), the greater part of his output was to consist of opera, and other vocal and choral works.

The initial impact of *Peter Grimes*, its famous première at Sadler's Wells on 7th June 1945, and its instant success, which chiefly enhanced Britten's reputation, led to two far-reaching results: first, the formation of a new opera company, the English Opera Group; next, the establishment of a Festival at Aldeburgh. At this time (1948) music festivals were comparatively rare; their mushroom-like spread came later. Over the coming years the Aldeburgh Festival was to make a most positive contribution to the British musical scene, with a characteristic of its own. Mainly the direct inspiration of Britten and Pears, it nevertheless owed its growth to the work of many other helpers, particularly Imogen Holst and Stephen Reiss. Concerts were given in houses, halls and churches in and around Aldeburgh; at Orford, Blythburgh, Ely and elsewhere. Excellent performances by a small number of artists, and something of the atmosphere of a court—a monarch surrounded by his courtiers— have given the Festival a personal flavour rarely found in the more commercial rough-and-tumble of the concert world; and this matches the highly personal nature of Britten's style as a composer.

The formation of the English Opera Group, which would develop a tradition of British opera, old and new, and tour in this country and abroad, was a natural concomitant to Britten's work as an opera composer, and a logical result of the general artistic direction in which he was facing. Opera has always been a minority cult in England, and in the immediate post-war years the outlook was bleak indeed; the only way to get your work performed was to form your own company, particularly if you wanted it sung in English. For reasons of economics it would have to be numerically small. And so the new company presented itself, at Glynde- bourne on 12th July 1946, in Britten's next opera, *The Rape of Lucretia*. This was the first of his chamber operas, and was followed the next year by another, *Albert Herring;* and in 1948 by an arrangement of *The Beggar's Opera*.

Meanwhile, that year the first Aldeburgh Festival took place, and so the 1949 production was a work designed for the somewhat limited capacity of the local Jubilee Hall in Aldeburgh. *Let's Make an Opera* calls for only a string quartet, piano and percussion, and is described, accura- tely, as an 'entertainment for young people'. It is the prototype of many other such works for children, by younger composers such as Malcolm Williamson, Gordon Crosse, and others.

Gradually the reputations of the English Opera Group and the Aldeburgh Festival spread internationally, along with that of their founder. In 1954 his fourth chamber opera, *The Turn of the Screw*, was produced at the Venice Biennale, while six years later a redesigned Jubilee Hall witnessed the première of *A Midsummer Night's Dream*. A most marked advance in the status of the Aldeburgh Festival was made with the building of a specially designed concert hall at Snape, The Maltings. This provided an opportunity for royal recognition, when it was opened by the Queen during the 1967 Festival. It was specifically made suitable for opera performances, as well as chamber and orchestral concerts, and recording. Unfortunately it was very largely built of wood, and on 7th June 1969 it was destroyed by fire after a concert. However, rebuilding was immediately started, and it was ready in time for the opening of the Festival the following year, on 5th June 1970. Again the Queen attended.

Against such a background of continual and much-varied activity we may consider Britten's output as a composer.

Songs

The image that inspires Britten's songs is mainly, and quite obviously, verbal, literary; of all composers, he is the most aware of, and susceptible to, the poetic image; and the poets that he has chosen to set have for this reason invariably been of the first rank; that is to say, those whose vision is clearest, all-embracing, and whose poetry thus both gives the strongest stimulus and invites the strongest response. Of first importance for him, therefore, in realising the poetic image are the capabilities of the human voice, and the clear enunciation of the words, with that rhythmical flow proper to them. Speed, pitch, interval, dynamic, timbre, that together constitute the melodic line, are made to serve this purpose. Next, the accompaniment, whether piano solo or other instruments, is used to throw into relief the solo line, and by means of an illustrative ostinato-figure, to enhance the meaning and mood of the poet's text. So expressiveness is found in the vocal line; colour in the accompaniment.

Within the framework of a diatonic style, many suggestive devices are used. All too easily can a simple idiom slip into the obvious, the banal. Bitonality and polytonality are two of the commonest ways of avoiding this; that is to say, the simultaneous use of more than one key; also the suggestion of ambiguous tonality by means of a unison accompaniment—a ground-bass, allowing for free variation in the upper parts, is one of Britten's commonest devices; also the introduction of unexpected progressions, and subtleties of metre. In later works, particularly since the *War Requiem*, there is a greater freedom in the vertical combination of different parts, and a greater sense of spaciousness.

The early songs and choral works were not always fully successful in realising the verbal image, though some works, *On This Island* for example, contain hints of the individuality that was to come; and *Ballad of Heroes* is cast in four-movement form, thus foreshadowing the *Spring Symphony*, while *Our Hunting Fathers*, particularly in its skilful handling of the orchestra, suggests the future operatic composer.

But his individual characteristics first appear more markedly in *Les Illuminations* and the *Seven Sonnets of Michelangelo*. In the first of these works particularly, for high voice and strings, there is greater freedom of vocal line, and greater colour in the accompanimental part, which in this case consists of a string orchestra. The bitonal opening uses two keys (E and Bb) a tritone apart, and thus provides the harmonic basis of the work—a procedure which was to be used later in the *War Requiem*. Moreover, the threefold repetition of the refrain, 'I alone hold the key to this savage parade', lends a structural unity to the suite as a whole. Unfortunately the French words of this cycle, and the Italian words of the Michelangelo songs, while no doubt meaningful to the connoisseur, act as an impediment to the ordinary English listener, to that directness of effect, that *rapport* with the mass of the audience, which is the corner- stone of such an idiom and style as Britten's.

But once this obstacle is overcome the songs explore various moods within the limited framework of one poetic idea, in a way that is rather reminiscent of Mahler's *Kindertotenlieder*—an earlier example of an orchestral song-cycle, which does the same.

Britten indeed has said that he has been influenced by Mahler, and it is not difficult to see certain points of similarity; both wrote song-cycles with orchestra, both had an individual interpretation of tonality, both aimed at a quality of intense dramatic lyricism. The underlying difference between them, however, is that whereas Mahler was a symphonic composer, Britten's work has been primarily vocal and operatic; and whereas Mahler's symphonies were set against a symphonic tradition that had been a gradual growth since Haydn, the English operatic tradition was a very fragmentary affair; it is indeed reasonable to say that its start still (1943) lay in the future, with Britten's own work.

Directness of effect is the chief strength of the *Serenade*, that most colourful song-cycle with which he announced his return to England. Unity is achieved round the theme of night—another Mahlerian concept; structurally the work is framed (as the *Ceremony of Carols* had been) by a Prologue and Epilogue; in this case a horn-call, which was modelled on an idea from Aaron Copland's *Music for the Theater*.[1] But the work abounds in individual characteristics, which indicate that pattern of musical expressiveness that he was to build on later;[2] the triadic pattern of the *Pastoral*, with its falling phrase to suggest the peace and calm of evening, and lengthening shadows; the onomatopoea of the bugle in the *Nocturne*; the semitonal inflection of the *Elegy* to suggest sickness, destruction; the repeated vocal part of the *Dirge*, which takes up the closing note of the previous song, and appears against a gradually more complex accompaniment; the duet for voice and horn of the *Hymn*, in which the use of melisma on the word '*Ex*cellently' suggests some extravagant gesture of obeisance before the moon-goddess; the silence of the *Sonnet*, which prepares for its final solo *Epilogue*. Britten's meticulous craftsmanship, whatever the nature of his material, ensures effective performance.

Two strongly individual characteristics of style, particularly in choral

1. The English horn solo in the *Interlude*.
2. See p. 224/5.

works, also first appeared fully about this time; the first is a *vivace* style of writing for voices; the second is the structural use of canon. Both characteristics appear fully for the first time in the *Hymn to St. Cecilia* for unaccompanied voices, which is a simple and effective example of the new virtuoso style that was transforming English choral music. The second section ('I cannot grow') is a particularly clear example of the combination of both these characteristics.

The stylistic advance shown in the *Serenade* was consolidated in the songs that followed, *The Holy Sonnets of John Donne*. Apart from the now-established features of ostinato accompaniment-patterns, bitonality, *vivace* style, and the use of intervals for expressive purposes, these songs also have a virtuoso quality of the sort that composers only achieve after long collaboration with sympathetic performers of equal calibre; in this case Britten had the advantage of working with the tenor, Peter Pears, who has always been his prime interpreter and colleague. The Donne Sonnets are linked by the religious sentiments of a soul approaching death; the gloomy foreboding of the first song (B minor) eventually resolves into the bold confidence of the last (B major).

The thread linking together the five songs that make up *A Charm of Lullabies* is one of mood, while in *Winter Words* Britten was inspired by, among other things, Thomas Hardy's sense of humour. The *ostinati* are, as usual, triadic, and frequently polytonal; again, as in the *Serenade*, a falling phrase represents day-close; but other less subjective ideas present themselves for our consideration—isolated jabs, of two notes a major second apart, represent a creaking table; an accompaniment figure in open fifths represents a violin tuning up.

The first of the three *Canticles* derives its effect from its subdued simplicity, which allows the symbolic words of Francis Quarles to make their impact unimpeded. Melisma is used at phrase-climaxes, and in the middle section the *vivace* style is combined with contrapuntal inversion in the accompaniment ('Nor time, nor place') before the piece reverts to its prevailingly sombre tone.

The *Second Canticle* is limited in vocal range by the plainsong style, which the composer uses to portray the religious situation. It is harmonically static, and relies for its effect on the drama inherent in the Abraham-Isaac relationship, that of a father who is compelled to kill his own much-loved son. God's voice is represented by the two singers (contralto and tenor) singing together, either in unison, or a fourth apart, to suggest early *organum*. Britten reverted to this work later, in the *War Requiem*.

The *Third Canticle*, written in memory of the pianist Noel Mewton-Wood, is altogether more individual a work. Edith Sitwell's poem dictated not merely its nature but also its structure, which is that of a theme ('slow and distant') and six short, very contrasted variations for horn, interspersed with six verses of free recitation for the voice. Horn and voice come together for the last variation, and sound the first and second phrases of the opening theme simultaneously. The motto, 'Still falls the rain', marks the beginning of each verse, while each variation ends on the key-note, B flat, and its material contains the melodic shape of the verse which follows it. The B flat theme is made up of three phrases, of which the second is an inversion of the first; the third is the longest and contains inversion within itself. Thus arises the structural outline of each variation.

The *Songs from the Chinese* for high voice and guitar, with a text made up of characteristically philosophical Chinese proverbs, are slight in content, and simple in style, as befits the nature of the instrument. They act as a light interlude to the two more substantial song-cycles composed the following year (1958), the *Nocturne* and *Six Hölderlin Fragments*.

The *Nocturne* takes up after the *Serenade*, and again uses the image of sleep from which to conjure up musical associations. Strings and seven solo obligato instruments provide the accompaniment; the strings open with the sleep motif, a rocking figure which underlines the work and provides a structural cohesion; each of the ensuing seven songs has a different solo obbligato; for instance Tennyson's Kraken is given a bassoon obbligato, while to Keats' 'Sleep and Poetry' is allotted the flute and clarinet. The mood is dark, tense, in some points approaching nightmare. The work ends with strings and wind together, in an unaccustomedly full texture, for Shakespeare's forty-third sonnet, with strings and voice echoing each other.

Britten's use of intervals, particularly the interval of the semitone to express anguish, tension, darkness (see p. 224/5), is well illustrated in this song-cycle, in which the underlying theme of the night—the contrast and conflict between night and day, sleep and waking, dream and reality—is musically symbolised in the relationship of two keys a semitone apart (C and C flat). The most dramatic expression of this conflict occurs in the Shakespeare sonnet, and so for this poem both keys appear simultaneously. The ending is tonally vague, and suddenly veers into the minor.

It was his friend Prince Ludwig of Hesse and the Rhine who introduced Britten to the poems of Johann Christian Hölderlin (1770–1843). The words of these poems are heavy with ideas, explicit and implicit; they suggest as much as they mean. The *Six Hölderlin Fragments* are given a structural and thematic unity by the use in different guises throughout the work of the material stated at the opening. The pattern of rising fourths, taken from the third variation of the *Third Canticle*, supplies the melodic and harmonic outline, and suggests many tonalities. Another similarity with the Canticle is the use of inversion, for instance in the voice part of the fourth song. Canon is also much in evidence, between the voice and piano in the second song, or between piano parts in the sixth.

The *Songs and Proverbs of William Blake*, written for Dietrich Fischer-Dieskau, with the words selected by Peter Pears, present a different world. Though William Blake (1757–1827) was a contemporary of Hölderlin, there is a world of difference between the two poets. Whereas Hölderlin gently reflects the Romanticism of his day and was very much under the shadow of Goethe, William Blake was a visionary who saw far beyond his own age; he was ablaze with poetic imagery and religious fire. Clearly these two poets present widely differing material to the aspiring composer. Hölderlin's words, like Edith Sitwell's words of the *Third Canticle*, are poetically suggestive, and thus receptive to musical realisation. Blake's words however are powerfully descriptive; their integrated imagery already has an impact unexceeded by any words in the English language, and therefore they are not so open to suggestive or atmospheric music. Such poems as 'The Tyger' and 'The Chimney-Sweeper' are hardly, if at all, enhanced by the ostinato technique of song-writing; indeed the figure allotted to the first of these poems—a quick, scale-like phrase starting at low pitch, very quiet, leading to spread chords—tends to confine the listener's imagination to one specific idea of the tiger, instead of allowing it to roam freely, as the beast itself does, and as the poet invites us to do.

The structure of the Blake songs is broadly similar to that of the *Third Canticle*; the 'proverbs' correspond to the instrumental variations of the earlier work, while the 'songs' correspond to the vocal sections. Moreover the material and basic shape of each proverb is the same, though its presentation differs; and it leads directly into the song which follows it. But whereas the *Canticle* was itself a simple, unified work in several sections, each of Blake's poems is a separate and distinct thing in its own right. There is no unifying thread.

Britten's association with the Russian cellist Mstislav Rostropovich took him to Russia several times, and on one such visit, in August 1965, he wrote *The Poet's Echo* for Rostropovich's wife, Galina Vishnevskaya, who first performed the songs in December at the Moscow Conservatoire. The Pushkin poems, again, have no unifying thread, though there is some connection of thought and mood between the first song (*Echo*) and the fourth (*The Nightingale and the Rose*). As in the Hölderlin songs, the material of each song is derived from material presented at the opening of the first; this consists of two fifths, one augmented, one diminished, which are both played as a chord and used as a melody.

Cantatas and Choral Works

Britten has written numerous works for non-professional performers; *gebrauchsmusik* for churches, school children. The larger choral pieces, *St. Nicholas* for example, are thus somewhat limited in expressive range, and often overwhelmingly obvious; they were written for participation rather than for responseful listening; but the dramatic works for young performers have an extra dimension which the more formal, static choral pieces do not; they are therefore much more interesting. Apart from one or two small choral works which fall into the *gebrauchsmusik* category—such as *Rejoice in the Lamb*, *Festival Te Deum* and *St. Nicholas*—the *Spring Symphony* was the first substantial choral composition since the *Hymn to St. Cecilia*. The term 'symphony' is a misnomer, since the work lacks symphonic growth or development. It is a suite of songs with orchestral accompaniment, on the general topic of spring, culminating in a sort of rustic patriotism, with the Reading Rota thrown in for good measure. An earlier example of such a poetic miscellany, formed into a choral suite, is Arthur Bliss's *Pastoral* (1929), in which the poems deal with the general topic of the countryside. Lambert's *Summer's last will and testament* also falls in this category.

Once again, few choral works followed, apart from small ones; the *Five Flower Songs* for Leonard and Dorothy Elmhirst,[1] and the two little Church works, Op. 56. It was ten years before the next important choral composition appeared, the *Cantata Academica*. This remarkable work was written for the quincentenary of Basel University, and first performed there on 1st July 1960. The Latin words are taken from the University Charter; and however inspiring such a document might be to those well versed in Latin, Britten abandoned his customary procedure, and simply used the words as a peg on which to hang a set of choral variations on a theme. The theme is a 12-note one, but tonal, in the key of G minor, and he brings to bear every academic device he can think of to breath life into this 'row'. The twelve notes dominate each section either harmonically or melodically, and the work as a whole is an abstract study in contrapuntal ingenuity.

Very different, and much more characteristic, is the *Missa Brevis* written for George Malcolm and the boys of Westminster Cathedral that same year (1959). In a sense it is a foretaste of the main work in Britten's choral output so far, which was written two years later, the *War Requiem*.

In this work, as usual, the principal parts are allotted to the singers, whether solo or choral; the orchestras are accompanimental. But the

1. The founders of Dartington Hall in Devon, with whom Britten had stayed.

P

range of mood is wider than hitherto, because the image that this time inspired Britten was two-fold: religious truths on the one hand, expressed in the timeless words of the *Missa pro Defunctis*, and human pity on the other, expressed in the anti-war poems of Wilfred Owen. It was a theme, and an occasion, which affected the composer deeply; he had always been opposed to war, since the 30's when he wrote the *Ballad of Heroes* for those who fought in the Spanish Civil War. Now in 1962, as it turned out, he was accurately reflecting an anti-war mood that was widespread at this time; it was a mood that was reflected in the Campaign for Nuclear Disarmament and the Aldermaston Marches; there was a genuine popular fear that political tension between America and Russia would erupt into open nuclear warfare, as had very nearly happened already in Korea. Moreover the English, with their customary taste for anniversaries, were just approaching the fiftieth one of the outbreak of the Great War in 1914; the realities of warfare were preying on the popular imagination. What could more aptly epitomise this mood than the work of Wilfred Owen, whose poetry had a sudden upsurge in the years up to 1964?

Such was the general background to the *War Requiem*, which was first heard in the rebuilt Coventry Cathedral on 30th May 1962, within sight of the old bombed-out building. The whole performance was intended to be an act of international reconciliation: the soloists were to be a Russian, a German and an Englishman;[1] a true coming-together for an act of collective remembrance and pity.

The work is conceived on three levels. The main sections of the Latin Requiem are allotted to the full chorus and main orchestra; the Owen poems are sung by tenor and baritone soli, accompanied by chamber orchestra; the distant choir of boys' voices are accompanied by a chamber organ. Occasionally two levels overlap, as in the *Agnus Dei*; all three come together for the final pages.

The words of the Requiem provide the overall structure; the Wilfred Owen poems, four of which were textually altered by Britten, are interspersed. Such a principle had been adopted in several previous works and had been used four years previously by Fricker in *The Vision of Judgement*. In this case the two themes are juxtaposed in stark contrast, and the musical material of the solo sections is derived from the music of that part of the Mass to which they are attached. The image that chiefly inspires Britten, to which his music is the response, is pity. To an observer, the results of wars are pitiful; the composer realizes this pitifulness, which he presents, exposes and reflects. How we respond to his art depends on our view of the artistic function. Is it to describe or to explain?

1. The work was recorded with Galina Vishnevskaya, Dietrich Fischer-Dieskau and Peter Pears.

To explore or to interpret? To observe or to prophesy? The larger the theme, the greater the need for creative insight, not merely into the appearance of events, but into their reality.

And how are we to interpret pity? It is a simple matter to dispel any sense of emotional detachment or religious complacency by the rude contrast of the battle-field. Such a dramatic device indeed provides a contrast that is basic, almost primitive. But it does not lead to any conclusion. What is to be our view? Anger? Resignation? If we accept that the artist's function is to interpret suffering, not merely to indicate the fact that it exists, then such dwelling on pity can come very near to self-pity, which is anything but ennobling. Pity is not necessarily the same as compassion. Only the compassion and the prophecy of a great artist can point the way through suffering to a wider goal; but the *War Requiem* stops short at the pity.

Technically speaking, one unifying feature, as it had been in *Les Illuminations*, is the interval of the tritone (C–F sharp), which pervades the work right from the opening. Other familiar technical characteristics are the use of canon, inversion, and ostinati; a not-so-familiar feature is the freer vertical combination of independent levels of sound. Britten is very far from being an aleatoric composer, but the simultaneous sounding together of the different groups and soloists does call for a freedom, a lack of rigidness on the part of both conductors.

Earlier works are suggested, both generally and in particular. The Owen poem 'Bugles sang', which follows the *Dies irae*, and is based on the trumpet fanfare at the beginning of it, inevitably evokes echoes of the *Nocturne* movement in the *Serenade*. The closest quotation of all occurs in the *Offertorium*, which is made up of material from the *Second Canticle*, *Abraham and Isaac*. As before, the divine voice is represented by two singers at the interval of a fourth. This section moreover provides a clear example of Britten's artistic response to the theme of pity. Whereas in the Abraham and Isaac story, Abraham was spared from killing his son Isaac because he had been obedient to God's wish, in Owen's poem, because of disobedience, he does kill him—'and half the seed of Europe, one by one'. The very term *Offertorium* takes on a grimly distorted meaning, which is called to mind immediately by the distant boys' voices, singing 'Hostias et preces tibi Domine laudis offerimus'.

What the composer suggests by this juxtaposition is overwhelming in its potentially tragic implication; but he is content to leave it at that. And so the listener who responds positively to these implications is left suspended as it were in mid-air, because they are not pursued; the theme is stated, not interpreted. Pity is there, but nothing more; if our emotions are roused, they are not purged; and the conclusion of the *Offertorium* section, as indeed of the work as a whole, is simply an inconclusive quietness.

Several critics have suggested a similarity with Verdi's *Requiem*, particularly in the dramatic treatment of the material. But an interesting comparison may also be made between this work of Britten and another highly unorthodox Requiem, written nearly fifty years earlier—that of Delius. At first glance the two works could hardly be more different. Britten's is written from the Christian, that of Delius from an atheistic standpoint; Britten was as responsive to the mood of the 60's as Delius was indifferent to, and remote from, that of the First World War; the result is that the work of the later composer was a spectacular success, whereas that of the earlier was an unqualified and unmitigated failure. That said, however, both works have a common origin—the artist's personal stand against the violence and tyranny of the twentieth century; the aggressive instinct that finds its outlet in nationalism and war. Britten sought to show, through Wilfred Owen and the traditional Requiem, the need for pity; Delius, however, also reacting against the false patriotism and mass hysteria of 1914, sought a solution in an anti-Christian philosophy, based on Nietzsche, which propounded the need for self-reliance, the finality of death, the transitory state of man. His was also a major work, written in 1914/16 as a personal tribute to 'all young artists who sacrificed their lives during the war'. But in 1920, popular memories of the recent slaughter were too fresh to admit the wide acceptance of a work which was based on such a negative philosophy. However fine the music might be—and in places it is very fine—this could not rescue a work whose basic tenets were so out of keeping with the mood of the moment. Only the more permissive, less doctrinally secure, mood of the 60's has allowed Delius's *Requiem* to be listened to again in recent years.

The *War Requiem* did not prove to be, like *Peter Grimes*, the beginning of a new artistic developement in British music; its artistic *raison d'etre* arose from a transitory, popular mood, felt at a specific moment in time, while its structure rested, for all its embellishments, on the foundation of the old oratorio tradition.

Following the *War Requiem*, two smaller works were concerned with the general theme of peace and pity: the *Cantata Misericordium*, and an anthem for the twentieth anniversary of the United Nations (1965), for chorus of men, women and children, *Voices for Today*. The *Cantata Misericordium* is a setting in Latin of the parable of the Good Samaritan; tenor and baritone soloists enact the story, while the choir function rather as the Chorus in a Greek tragedy, and keep the audience informed of the events, as well as comment on them. It was composed for the centenary commemoration of the Red Cross in Geneva, on 1st September 1963. Though much less ambitious a work than the *War Requiem*, and much shorter (twenty minutes as opposed to eighty-five,) it is in many ways more artistically complete. Britten's characteristic style—the immediately arresting ostinato pattern, and the lack of motivic development—is much more applicable to a short work than an extended one; and moreover the dramatic development of the theme of pity, which gives the work momentum, is much more complete in the Cantata; the story is not merely told, it is also interpreted.

And Britten's response to this image, though more orthodox than in the case of the *War Requiem*, is no less compelling. We are reminded of a Bach Cantata. Indeed, his debt to Bach is most strongly felt in the alternation of chorus, arioso and recitative; also in the *molto tranquillo* section at [30], 'Dormi nunc, amice'. The theme of pity is never once lost sight of in the music; the 'compassion' *motif*, with which the work opens, is given to a solo string quartet, and is used throughout the work[1] to point the dramatic tension, and also to depict the passage of time. A falling phrase suggests the suffering of the injured man; a major tonality represents the Samaritan; the end recalls the opening, as was the case in the *Hymn to St. Cecilia*.

The influence of Bach is also very strong in the D major 'Overture with or without chorus,' *The Building of the House*. This was the short, five minute, occasional piece written for the inaugural concert of the Maltings Concert Hall, Snape, at the twentieth Aldeburgh Festival, on 2nd June 1967. The choir declaim Psalm 127 like a chorale against a baroque-style orchestral texture. This was followed by *Children's Crusade*, which stands midway between another children's work, *The Golden Vanity*, and the late Church Parables. The accompaniment combines two pianos, an electronic organ, and a large percussion section.

Operas

In seeking an external stimulus to which to respond, and in enlarging the range of his newly-emerging vocal style, it was inevitable that sooner or later Britten would turn to opera; particularly since for some time oratorio had been a dying form. But what was by no means inevitable in 1942 was the success that lay ahead for his first attempt. Very few operas in England had ever reached beyond their immediate occasion; many were of local interest only; most died on their feet as soon as they appeared. And this fact was not necessarily the fault of the music, which in some cases was excellent; Vaughan Williams and Delius are the chief examples.

1. At [13], [17], [20].

What was lacking were national roots and a vital operatic tradition. A further instance of this need of roots is provided by the American experience: American composers equally lack an operatic tradition, with the result that few indeed of the operas of American composers have held their own on the international stage. One of the very few to do so was Gershwin's *Porgy and Bess* (1935), which drew on a distinctively American experience at first hand.

When Britten returned to England in 1942 with Koussevitsky's commission to write a full-length opera, two main problems faced him. The first was to find a dramatic theme of sufficient substance for a full-length work, which would also provide him with an inspiring image, and which would give scope to his creativity. On this would depend the sort of work he wrote. He only knew that he wanted it to be based on George Crabbe's *The Borough*, which described Aldeburgh in the early nineteenth century. He had read an article about Crabbe by E. M. Forster,[1] and this had made a very strong impression on him. The second problem was to assess accurately the operatic situation in this country and elsewhere, and to balance idealism with feasibility; on this would depend the reception accorded to the work. As events were to prove, he was astonishingly susceptible to the needs and mood of the time, as he was to be again twenty years later when he wrote the *War Requiem*.

He assumed, correctly as it turned out, that the musical public were ready for a fresh start in opera: *Peter Grimes* provided it. Recognizable characters sang in English; the place was geographically localised on the Suffolk coast that Britten knew so well; all traditions have to start in a particular place if they are to start at all. Moreover, as in the case of Gershwin, Britten's simple diatonic idiom was the most likely to appeal to a wide audience at that time. More sophisticated audiences than the English might have expected a more sophisticated style, but Britten's possessed that immediate impact which compelled attention, while the idiom was well within the broad operatic tradition of Verdi, Debussy and Puccini. In addition to this, Britten had an acutely instinctive flair for stage-technique, sharpened by experience in film, theatre and radio work.

The central theme of the opera is a compassionate understanding of Grimes, who is an outsider to his society; running parallel to this is the theme of the sea, and the community who live by it and from it. The action develops on many different levels, while the dramatic effects inherent in Montagu Slater's libretto are realized with simple, bold strokes. The overall three-act structure of the opera is supported by six interludes, which serve not merely the practical purpose of facilitating

1. In *The Listener*, 29th May, 1941.

scene-changing, or marking the passage of time between acts, but also set the scene and describe the characters. In a sense they summarise the opera. The first Interlude evokes the dawn over the coast; the second unleashes the full fury of a storm, which continues with indirect reference through the next scene; the third describes a fine Sunday morning (in A major); the fourth is a Passacaglia, a description of Grimes's divided character, with its visionary quality on the one hand and its violence on the other—the Passacaglia theme is taken from the climax moment in the previous scene, when Grimes strikes Ellen; the fifth is a picture of moonlight on a summer's night, with little ostinati on flute and harp to suggest suffering below the peaceful surface; the sixth shows the mist that has come in from the sea, which is also the symbol of Grimes's despair.

Over the next few years *Peter Grimes* was produced in the opera houses of the world: in Europe, America and the Far East. All of a sudden English opera had begun a fresh phase.

Meanwhile, with his appetite thoroughly whetted, Britten set about his next opera, the first of his chamber operas, *The Rape of Lucretia*. The trend of his musical thought has always been more towards solo instruments than to the full symphony orchestra; the orchestral scoring of *Peter Grimes* had consisted very largely of doubling. It was thus a natural choice, as well as economic necessity, which led him to the use of a chamber orchestra for this and subsequent chamber operas—*Albert Herring* and *The Turn of the Screw*—as well as for his arrangement of *The Beggar's Opera*. This orchestra was twelve strong: wind quartet (flute doubling piccolo and bass flute; oboe doubling cor anglais; clarinet doubling bass clarinet); horn; percussion; harp; string quintet. The recitative was accompanied by a piano.

Once again in *The Rape of Lucretia* a general situation, in this case the political relationship between Romans and Etruscans, forms the background to the personal drama, between Lucretia and Tarquinius. Once again, as in *Peter Grimes*, the events lead to suicide. The tension between the two is reflected in the motifs, which appear in both the vocal parts and their accompanying figures; this tension is further increased by their sexual relationship, which distinguishes this opera from its predecessor.

The other two chamber operas introduce fresh factors: *Albert Herring* introduces the element of humour, while *The Turn of the Screw* is a musical ghost story, after the story by Henry James. Like the *Third Canticle* of the same year, it is constructed in the form of a theme and variations, which are interspersed with vocal sections. The material of the story is tense and neurotic, and Britten responds in kind with a 12-note theme of angular severity. The sustained, unyielding tension is made more marked by the absence of any bass singers; the entire work is at a high tessitura. He was to take another Henry James story later for the television opera *Owen Wingrave*, a study in pacifism, which was first screened on 16th May, 1971.

Britten returned to full-scale opera in 1951 with a work commissioned for the Festival of Britain of that year. *Billy Budd*, which was first given in its original form at Covent Garden on 1st December, was in many respects a reversion to the style and manner of *Peter Grimes*. The libretto, by E. M. Forster and Eric Crozier, was an adaptation of Herman Melville's last novel. Against the background of tough life at sea during the Napoleonic wars, when floggings and the press-gang led to mutiny at Spithead and the Nore, the story tells of how Billy Budd the innocent came to suffer death through injustice. Again, Britten's inspiring image is that of pity. E. M. Forster has described the 'counterpoint' that surrounds a Melville story; the meaning is felt apart from the narrative; no simple explanation of seemingly unintelligible facts is possible. Such material is indeed the breath of life to an opera composer, since he can underwrite the words. And yet this opera lacks something of the impact of *Peter Grimes*. Why? The fulcrum of the plot is the Claggart–Billy relationship, and this is progressively oversimplified beyond the requirements of drama, to the point of melodrama. Claggart is all-bad; Billy is all-good; therefore, we are told, the one had to destroy the other.

Moreover, in spite of his admission that no simple explanation is possible of the events leading to Billy's execution, Forster has put forward just such an explanation in the libretto, by invoking the pre-Christian concept of Fate. The three chief characters all admit to their powerlessness against an overriding force of Fate.

Claggart says: 'O beauty, O handsomeness, would that I never encountered you. Would that I lived in my own world always, in that depravity to which I was born.
Having seen you, what choice remains to me? . . . I am doomed to annihilate you.'

Billy says: 'I had to strike down that Jenny-legs, it's fate. And Captain Vere has had to strike me down, fate.'

Vere says: 'I could have saved him'—but did not.

So with these somewhat unconvincing explanations the characters are reduced to puppets; neither through the drama nor through the music do they come into sharp focus. Indeed, instead of becoming the means whereby the characters live, the music is reduced to the subsidiary role of illustrating the various situations. Whereas in *Peter Grimes* the conflict arose within Peter's personality, in *Billy Budd* the conflict is imposed, and has to be carefully explained, both in the libretto and in the music.

The results of the conflict are thus merely pitiful, not tragic or ennobling. As Britten was to find later in the *War Requiem*, the theme of pity requires more than one dimension for its full interpretation. This work therefore lacks the spontaneous inevitability of the earlier opera. But a direct similarity with *Peter Grimes* is the mist which is symbolic of man's blindness. It also frustrates the action against the French ship, and this underlines the fact that the main theme of the opera is a personal, not a military or naval one.

Two other works also owe their genesis to Covent Garden. The first was *Gloriana*, which in spite of its performance in the presence of the Queen on 8th June, 1953, in honour of her coronation, is one of Britten's rare miscalculations. It is more a masque than an opera. The other was his only ballet score, *The Prince of the Pagodas*. But more characteristic and no less important in his output are the children's operas. *Let's Make an Opera*, an 'Entertainment for Young People,' was the first stage work to be presented at Aldeburgh, in 1949. The next was *Noye's Fludde*, which was given in 1958; third was *The Golden Vanity* 'a vaudeville for boys and piano', which was written for the Vienna Boys' Choir, and given by them at the 1967 Aldeburgh Festival.

But a work which stands somewhat apart from the other operas is *A Midsummer Night's Dream*. Though written for the small Jubilee Hall at Aldeburgh, where it was first heard on 11th June 1960, the work has also been performed at Covent Garden; and it benefits considerably from the larger surroundings. It stands apart because the text was selected from Shakespeare by the composer and Peter Pears. Yet in many ways it is the first significant advance since *Peter Grimes*. The vitality and colour of Shakespeare's magical comedy call forth a corresponding vitality and colour from the composer. Structurally the action takes place on three levels: first, Titania and Oberon, and their estrangement; second Lysander and Hermia, who are fleeing from Athens to avoid an undesirable marriage with Demetrius; third, the group of rustics, Shakespeare's 'rude mechanicals', and their antics. The story is amply suited to musical colour; dreams and night-spells are peculiarly characteristic of this composer. Not that the work is entirely impressionistic. Indeed the whole second act is constructed round a sequence of four chords, which include the twelve notes, but in triadic form, and scored for different instrumental groups—as the chords in *Billy Budd*[1] had been. *A Midsummer Night's Dream* is the happiest operatic score Britten has so far composed, and the most successful since *Peter Grimes*.

1. Between scenes two and three of the second act, as Captain Vere goes to tell Billy of his conviction and sentence.

Very different are the later operatic works, the three 'Parables for Church Performance', *Curlew River*, *The Burning Fiery Furnace* and *The Prodigal Son*, which were all played in Orford Church as part of the Aldeburgh Festivals of 1964, 1966 and 1968 respectively. These represent a quite fresh departure, because the image that this time inspired the composer came from an alien tradition, that of the Japanese Nō-play. He had visited Tokyo in 1956 with his friend Prince Ludwig, who has recorded the effect of the Nō-play;[1] the extreme stylization, the slow-moving pace, archaic music, all-male cast, the extreme formalism of production, even down to the costumes, masks and other effects; the rapt attention of the audience, and absence of applause; indeed this, and the legendary nature of the drama, suggested Greek tragedy. Here was a centuries-old tradition; could it be transplanted Westwards?

Clearly not without radical reappraisal. Such a tradition was quite foreign to the Western theatre; but what about the Church? There was nothing resembling any contemporary Church drama; nothing since the mediaeval mystery plays, which had already sparked off certain works such as the *Second Canticle* and *Noye's Fludde*. Could the old tradition of the mystery play be somehow brought up to date, and made a valid experience to a present-day Western audience?

The particular play that Britten saw was called *Sumidagawa* (Sumida River) and he has described his reaction as follows: 'The whole occasion made a tremendous impression on me: the simple, touching story, the economy of style, the intense slowness of the action, the marvellous skill and control of the performers, the beautiful costumes, the mixture of chanting, speech, singing which, with the three instruments, made up the strange music—it all offered a totally new "operatic" experience.

'There was no conductor—the instrumentalists sat on stage, as did the chorus, and the chief characters made their entrance down a long ramp. The lighting was strictly non-theatrical. The cast was all male, the one female character wearing an exquisite mask which made no attempt to hide the male jowl beneath it.

'The memory of this play has seldom left my mind in the years since. Was there not something—many things—to be learnt from it? The solemn dedication and skill of the performers were a lesson to any singer or actor of any country and any language. Was it not possible to use just such a story—with an English background (for there was no question in any case of a pastiche from the ancient Japanese)? Surely the mediaeval religious drama in England would have had a comparable setting—an all-male cast of ecclesiastics—a simple, austere staging in a church—a very

1. *Fiftieth Birthday Symposium*, (Faber, 1963).

limited instrumental accompaniment—a moral story? And so we came from *Sumidagawa* to *Curlew River* and a church in the Fens, but with the same story and similar characters; and whereas in Tokyo the music was the ancient Japanese music, jealously preserved by successive generations, here I have started the work with that wonderful plainsong hymn 'Te lucis ante terminum', and from it the whole piece may be said to have grown.'

The libretto was by William Plomer, who had already written the libretto of the ill-fated *Gloriana*, and he set the ancient Japanese story in a Christian context. A madwoman comes to be ferried across the river; on the way the Ferryman tells of a child who crossed a year previously only to die of exhaustion on the other side. The woman cries; it is her child; but she is freed from her madness at the voice of her child, and the appearance of his spirit.

The orchestra which Britten had already reduced to twelve for his chamber operas, was now reduced still further to seven; flute, horn, viola, double bass, harp, percussion, chamber organ.

Many familiar features of style occur, as well as many unfamiliar ones. The juxtaposition of different keys, canon, ground-bass are all common; and the plainchant prelude and postlude recall *A Ceremony of Carols*. But there the resemblance ends; the accompaniment patterns are static, more so than in the *Second Canticle*, the pace is extremely slow-moving. The use of chamber organ, and the comparatively free vertical combination of sounds, recall the *War Requiem*; but except for the prelude and postlude the composer dispenses with key signatures, and the tonality is indirect. Moreover, the instrumental parts, which are sparse, are not so characteristically independent of the voices as in other works. Some instrumental association is allowed to creep in, however; a flute *flutter-tongue* heralds the mad-woman, a horn calls our attention to the Ferryman, while a *glissando* represents the movement of the ferry.

The experience gained from *Curlew River* led to *The Burning Fiery Furnace*, which differed in that the story was specifically part of the Judaeo-Christian tradition. The instruments are the same as for the first Parable, with the addition of a trombone, to give a royal colour to the instrumental sonority. Procession, lighting, costumes, movement and gesture are all an integral part of the composition and these hark back to the Japanese original.[1] But more happens than in *Curlew River*, and the plainchant is more integrated into the texture of the music, which otherwise is very slow-moving and similar to that of the earlier work. This begins and ends with a plainchant procession, which as before is the

1. Several composers in the 60's have sought to augment a basically very simple conception with such musical and visual 'overheads'; for instance, John Tavener (see p. 312).

only part of the score bearing a key-signature; the melody *Salus Aeterna* is the basis of the work. As before, an Angel appears at the moment of culmination.

The third Parable, *The Prodigal Son*, like the other two, was also written by William Plomer. Again a familiar theme is chosen, of specifically Christian significance. The work differs from its predecessors chiefly in the fuller use made of the chorus, who represent Servants, Parasites, and Beggars. The trombone of the previous Parable is replaced by a trumpet, and the flute becomes an alto flute, changing to piccolo for the dance finale; otherwise the instrumentation and the sonority are the same. The plainchant basis is *Iam lucis orto sidere*, and the climax of the work this time is one of dancing and rejoicing.

An important difference however between *The Prodigal Son* and the two preceding Parables is that in it greater importance is given to the dramatic working out of the inner conflict. This reaches the climax with the son's decision to return home, while forgiveness and reconciliation are the dramatic conclusion of the work. Instrumental association is used, as before, for the heightening of the expressive power of the music. The trumpet and viola represent the extrovert and introvert sides of the Son's character; harp *glissandi* represent the Tempter; triads (B flat major) represent the stability and security of home.

Taken as one unit, the three Church Parables represent the three Christian virtues: Hope (*Curlew River*), Faith (*The Burning Fiery Furnace*), and Charity (*The Prodigal Son*).

Vocal style

The musical austerity and tonal vagueness of the three Church Parables, though compensated by a certain visual and ritualistic richness, in many ways run contrary to Britten's practice. Distinctiveness of melodic line, strikingly recognizable colour in the accompaniment, and strict attention to the rhythmic accentuation and articulation of words, have hitherto always been the hall-marks of his vocal technique. The colour in the Parables is traditional, religious, associative rather than musical; and their somewhat meagre musical content is austerity indeed for Western ears accustomed to a more substantial diet.

But certain melodic characteristics and use of intervals have already been referred to, which are fundamental to his thought and lend distinctive colour to his vocal style. Two chief examples: the interval of the semitone expresses any sort of tension, anguish, darkness or disorder; instances from the songs include the *Donne Sonnets* (particularly No. 3), the *Second* and *Third Canticles* ('Still falls the rain' consists of Eb—D); instances from the operas include the B—Bb relationship in *Billy Budd*, with which the opera opens, and which is central to the tension of the musical scheme; the storm Interlude in *Peter Grimes* is built round the semitone; also it expresses the mad-woman's grief in *Curlew River* (at [81]). There are other instances too numerous to specify.

Triads, on the other hand, often in root position, are expressive of exactly the opposite: calm, decision, 'heavenly things'. A few from the many possible instances include the last *Donne Sonnet*, which is the final, optimistic conclusion of that cycle. At the end of Scene I of the second Act of *Billy Budd*, Vere sings 'O for the light of clear heaven to separate evil from good', and triads suggest such a light. Later, at the end of the next scene, when he has taken the decision to tell Billy of his conviction, simple triads express this calm resolve, as well as Billy's complete lack of any malicious or dark side to his nature. He is the very opposite of Peter Grimes. An instance from the Parables occurs at the end of *The Burning Fiery Furnace*, where the Angel's music, as he sings with the chorus, assumes the repose of triads. The simplest juxtaposition of the two occurs in the *Missa Brevis*, where the confident mood of the Gloria is illustrated by triads on the organ, whereas the more solemn mood of the *Agnus Dei* is depicted by semitones throughout. This expressive use of intervals lends consistency to Britten's vocal works of whatever period.

Orchestral and symphonic works

As Britten gradually found his characteristic voice, he wrote progressively less orchestral and instrumental music. His is not a symphonic style. The pre-war orchestral pieces, such as the *Variations on a theme of Frank Bridge* and the *Piano Concerto*, belong to his formative years, and display a characteristic fluency and ingenuity; and several orchestral works date from the American period, of which the *Violin Concerto* and the *Sinfonia da Requiem* are chiefly still performed. But in a sense these works simply sum up his achievement as a composer up to then; the *Sinfonia da Requiem*, for instance, used material from *Our Hunting Fathers*.[1]

On his return in 1942, three more instrumental works appeared before *Peter Grimes*; the *Prelude and Fugue for Strings* (1943), which was commissioned by the Boyd Neel orchestra; the *Young Person's Guide to the Orchestra* (1946), which was written for a documentary film for the Crown Film Unit; and the *Second String Quartet* (1945), written for the Zorian Quartet[2], to commemorate the 250th anniversary of Purcell's death.

1. C.f. the *Scherzo* of the symphony with the *Dance of Death* of the earlier work.
2. Olive Zorian later led the English Opera Group Orchestra.

After 1946 a few instrumental works have been written expressly for individual players. Viola, oboe, guitar and harp have been catered for in this way. But these pieces, along with the piece for organ, *Prelude and Fugue on a theme of Vittoria*, count among his slighter works. More substantial, however, are the 'cello works for Rostropovitch: a *Sonata*, two *Suites*, and the *Symphony for Cello and Orchestra* 1963, which was the first orchestral work for almost twenty years since the *Young Person's Guide to the Orchestra*, and which may be said to epitomise the features of his purely instrumental style, his absolute musical thought, unmixed with any literary or dramatic influence.

It was first played in Moscow in March, 1964, by Mstislav Rostropovich. In spite of its title, and its four movements, it is a concerto in all but name, with a virtuoso solo part, including a cadenza. The image that chiefly inspired the work was the artistry of the great Russian cellist, whose style of playing decided the nature of the themes. So the strength of the work lies in the range and colour of the solo writing, while its chief weakness is a lack of thematic or motivic development—which is the structural equivalent in instrumental music of the plot in an opera, or the words in a song.

The scheme of the work is classical; indeed, the first movement is the most extended sonata-form Britten has ever composed; but the idiom is highly chromatic, almost 12-note in places. Within an established tonality (D minor), Britten tends to use ten or eleven of the twelve notes in a phrase or group; the missing note(s) are then given a prominent place in the next phrase. Thus in the first theme of the first movement, A flat is held back until bar 8; in the second theme G is held back until the climax moment of the passage ([7] + 4). Again in the solo theme of the slow movement, eleven notes are used; the missing one (G) forms the pedal-point of the orchestral accompaniment.

The two main themes of the first movement are interrelated, and contain motifs and characteristics from which later passages are derived. Features of the first D minor theme, which consists of 3-part 'cello chords built round a wedge-like pattern of intervals, are the 2-note rhythm in bar 3, the end-of-phrase appoggiaturas from which the second theme is derived, and the prevalence of two intervals, the minor seventh and the minor third. The broad, episodic, sequential phrases lead forward to a climax (at [2]), from which a derivative bridge passage leads to the second theme at [6.] This consists of little more than semitone appoggiaturas in a *parlando* style, in which the blend of upward and downward movement suggests question and answer, like a song without words.

The development section is more of a meditation on the existing material; the mood of agitation and tension is largely the result of the semitone interval. Figures and phrases are repeated, not developed, while for the recapitulation (at [17]) the roles of solo and orchestra are reversed. The main theme is given to the orchestra in F major, the subsidiary part to the cellist. This is maintained for the repeat of the second theme (at [21]); and it is not until the D major coda that the 'cello chords of the opening reappear, overlaid this time with a woodwind countersubject, taken from the first bridge passage (after [4]).

The mood of restless tension continues into the next movement, which is a very short, Mahler-like scherzo, whose scale-like theme is also derived from the minor third interval. Scurrying semiquavers flit past, eerie, ghostlike, and lightning-quick. There is just a suggestion of a more sustained scale-theme ([32]–[34]), which provides a Trio-like contrast.

The timpani provide the rhythmic ground over which the slow movement is worked out. As in the first movement, the first theme is episodic and sequential, and is followed through to its climax (just before [52]). Built round the third, whether major or minor, it generates an elegiac intensity, mainly through chromatic tonality. The theme is offset by a filling-in accompaniment figure on the woodwind, from which in due course is derived the comparatively tenuous and loose middle section. At the recapitulation the soloist and orchestra once again change places, and the main theme is allotted this time to the brass; it gains splendidly in stature as a result, while the soloist has to be content with the somewhat gray and neutral accompaniment figures. The work is after all described as a 'symphony', not a concerto. The climax this time is more powerful than at first, largely because the strings are held back until the last moment ([60]–3).

A short cadenza introduces the Passacaglia finale, whose D major theme is made up of four progressively lengthening phrases. This is first announced by a solo trumpet, and is taken from the middle section of the previous movement (at [53]); there its loose construction and derivative nature were less noticeable because its function and surroundings were subsidiary; but to bring it out into the light of day, as it were, and to give it the much more strenuous task of sustaining six variations of a Passacaglia, is a different matter altogether. Moreover, whether consciously or unconsciously, it bears an uncomfortable resemblance to part of a certain well-known nursery rhyme.[1] All these factors weaken an otherwise ingenious finale. One undaunted critic however, describes it[2] as the 'affirmative resolution' of the tension of the previous movements, which he calls the 'emotional crux' of what is, taken overall, a 'disturbing work'. Some such imaginative *rationale* is needed if the finale is not to leave the

1. 'Three Blind Mice.'
2. Writing in *Tempo* No. 70, Autumn 1964.

listener with a sense of anticlimax, and if the work as a whole is to be brought onto the personal level of the listener's awareness.

[On the strength of Britten's work so far, certain salient points stand out. His music is highly and unusually personal: that is to say, its creative impulse is his individual artistic response to an image; technical considerations, however striking, are secondary. His idiom, based on tonality, is ingenious, not new; he is not interested in novelty, abstraction or serialism, still less in the impersonal experiments of the *avant-garde*. So his music relies for its effect on a direct and personal *rapport* with the listener, at the emotional, neurotic level. If the listener can identify himself with the composer's personal response to a poetic image, then well and good; his acceptance of the music will be total, instinctive. Twice Britten has shown, in *Peter Grimes* and the *War Requiem*, that there can be just such a wide, popular response to a contemporary composer who, judging the temper of the times correctly, speaks with a voice to which the majority can listen.

16 Peter Maxwell Davies

Starting in about the mid-fifties, a fundamental change came over the British musical scene. It arose partly from a dissatisfaction among younger musicians and composers with the traditional leanings of their elders; partly from an excitement at the currently unfolding ideas of Schoenberg, Webern and the continental *avant-garde*, whose work was just beginning to be heard and propagated in England at this time; partly from a desire to discover a new, more cosmopolitan style that owed nothing to neo-modalism, neo-classicism, or any other style previously favoured by English composers. The pendulum of fashion swung markedly and decisively away from the established, the traditional, and towards the new, the *avant-garde*, the experimental.

Starting originally among certain individual composers and teachers, and in small minority pressure groups, such as the S.P.N.M. and Morley College[1], the new trend gradually spread outwards, gathering momentum as it went, until by about 1960 it had reached the critical columns of certain magazine and newspapers, as well as the BBC. One of the London orchestras, the L. P. O., was bold enough to grasp the nettle firmly and to include the newly-discovered music in a series of concerts over several seasons; only to find, after some initial success, that the audiences for it formed but a minority of the concert-going public. Since then a more cautious, traditional policy has been followed.

This trend of fashion had both desirable and undesirable effects on public taste. While undoubtedly a fresh and much-needed stimulus, in the broadest sense, was given to the English musical scene, and a hard blow was delivered against those insular and reactionary members of it to whom any change was anathema, unfortunately at the same time a number of babies were lost with the bathwater. Like most, if not all, fashions, it dwelt on some aspects of the musical art to the exclusion of others; it presented a part of the truth as if it were the whole, and thus

1. See p. 156.

inevitably contained within itself the seeds of its own reaction, which was to come later.

Thus, on the positive side was felt an exciting sense of fresh discovery, development and experiment, and a breaking away from narrow parochialism into a broader, more cosmopolitan context; on the negative side an aggressive intolerance of whatever did not appear to belong within the newly-discovered serial tradition of Schoenberg and Webern. It was a case of all-or-nothing. Cliques grew up, which showed an unawareness of, or indifference to, the need for contact and artistic *rapport* between the composer and his audience. The breakdown of tonality was an unquestioned and assumed *datum*, a starting point from which the composer of 'the new music' set out on his voyage of discovery. The tide of serialism, which was running at its full flood in the mid-50's, duly began to ebb in the 60's, leaving behind as it did so a considerable quantity of musical flotsam and jetsam. Many were left high and dry. The goddess of fashion is indeed a capricious and fickle lady, who makes searching demands on her numerous suitors, and sometimes rewards those who succumb to her charms with nothing more than an ungrateful waywardness.

Prominent among this new school was the 'Manchester Group'—four musicians who happened to be fellow students at Manchester between 1954 and 1956: the composers Peter Maxwell Davies, Alexander Goehr, Harrison Birtwistle, and the pianist John Ogdon. All have since moved in markedly individual directions.

Peter Maxwell Davies was born in Manchester in 1934, and his forty-odd compositions so far have developed along highly original and daring lines. The course of study which he pursued at Manchester University prescribed 1500–1900 as the approved limits of musical history; and this he found irksome. As far as English music was concerned, he had no sympathy for Vaughan Williams or Delius, who were held up as the accepted models. How could any pre-Schoenbergian be considered relevant for the young composer of the 50's? While at Manchester he was enthusiastic about all manifestations of new music, Eastern as well as European, and still acknowledges two works written by him then, the *Trumpet Sonata*, and the *Piano Pieces*, Op. 2, written for John Ogdon. Already in the Sonata he experimented with a rhythmic series, related to the set; while in the *Piano Pieces* he introduced the use of isorhythm. His starting point was Schoenberg, though he is by no means strictly confined to a 12-note series.

His first 12-note piece as such, and also the first one to use a mediaeval source (a Dunstable motet), was *Alma Redemptoris Mater*. This is a short, three-movement study for wind instruments (1957), which has since proved to be a fruitful storehouse, and has even influenced other composers, such as Birtwistle and Crosse.

After Manchester, he went on an Italian Government scholarship to Rome, where he studied with Goffredo Petrassi (1957/8). Here for the first time his technique was thoroughly scrutinised; every note was checked. During this time he continued to assimilate influences from all sources, and also pursued his involvement with old music of the Mediaeval and Renaissance periods, which were shortly to have such a pronounced influence on his work and style. Under Petrassi's tutelage he wrote two student compositions in which he first showed his orchestral paces: the *St. Michael Sonata* for seventeen wind instruments, and a full-length orchestral composition, *Prolation*. Both use mediaeval formal devices, coupled with the serial style. The first piece divides the instruments into two antiphonal choirs, after the Venetian style, though the composer largely nullifies this effect by being more concerned with the horizontal line, with texture, dynamics and *timbre*, than with the vertical effect of the sounds in combination; this results in a coarse, unyielding texture, which occasionally lapses into a strident vulgarity. The second piece was a study in rhythm, and the temporal relationship of note values. Again, it was an attempt to apply mediaeval principles in a contemporary context. Climaxes are carefully graded according to density, dynamics, note values and so on. It is here the interest lies, rather than in the thematic material itself; indeed the motifs are very short-winded, and serve only as vehicles for the technical procedures. According to this aesthetic, what matters is not so much what you say, as how you say it. The work lasts twenty minutes—long by Webern's standards—and was awarded the 1959 Olivetti prize in Rome.[1]

In searching for his musical individuality, Davies started from the orthodox serial principle that the smallest particle should be a microcosmic representation of the complete structure. Though he may use a mediaeval melody, or part of a plainchant, as a starting point for a composition, little trace of the original appears in the finished work. For instance, it would take an acute listener indeed to pick out the Dunstable motet round which *Alma Redemptoris Mater* was conceived; similarly, though the *St. Michael Sonata* derives its material from chants from the Requiem Mass, these become lost in the overall effect.

Returning home, he taught music for three years at Cirencester Grammar School (1959–1962), where by his freshness and directness of approach he enthused even the most philistine among the pupils. Children whose ability in other academic directions might be distinctly limited,

1. For which one of the two judges was Petrassi himself.

found that they could respond in a positive way to this most refreshingly unorthodox of music masters, who invited them to participate, to improvise. This was *gebrauchsmusik* with a difference. The most direct result of Davies' years at Cirencester was the Christmas sequence of carols and instrumental sonatas, *O Magnum Mysterium* (1960). The intention of this work was to write something within the range of children but without compromising his own individual style which was just beginning to be formed. The importance of the work is that it tested the applicability and relevance of the new style; if young people could assimilate it, surely the composer might thence proceed to enlarge the scope of subsequent compositions. The instrumental sections allow for free improvisation within defined limits. The words of the carols are, needless to say, mediaeval. Both the carols and the instrumental sonatas are, by necessity, simple, and though the chordal, melodic nature of the carols is a perfect foil for the more fragmentary part-writing of the sonatas, the real climax of the work does not come until the concluding organ fantasia, which is a powerful piece, built round the first three notes of the carol theme, (F–Gb–Ab), and which builds to a shattering climax, before dying away to nothing on a solitary pedal note. For sheer originality of conception, and exploitation of the resources of the organ, as well as for such technical features as 5-part pedal chords, this work is unique in the English organ repertoire.

The principles of construction worked out in *O Magnum Mysterium* were followed up the following year in another school piece, *Te lucis ante terminum*, in which the verses of the Latin evening hymn are separated by instrumental 'verses'. Also written in 1959 were the *Five Motets*, in which three groups of singers and players are treated antiphonally, with considerable freedom of form and style. Davies has also written several shorter carols and choral pieces which stem from the choral style of the *O Magnum Mysterium* carols: simple, yet markedly individual, which appeal to the unspoilt, unspotted naïveté that is in all of us, however overlaid with sophistication.

All his subsequent works tend to fall into sets of two or three compositions derived from the same basic inspiration; and thus his years at Cirencester also saw three works which owe their initial impulse to Monteverdi's *Vespers of 1610*.

These are the *String Quartet* (1961), the *Leopardi Fragments* (1961) for soprano, contralto and instrumental ensemble, and the *Sinfonia* (1962). Their connection with the Monteverdi original is the same as that of Stravinsky's *Movements* to a Monteverdi madrigal; in other words, distant. In the process of assimilating the numerous influences that make up his composite style, Davies has achieved, in the *String Quartet*, lines of greater length, and a more singing style than in the earlier *St. Michael Sonata*; it is a softer, more lyrical work, based on Monteverdi's *Sonata sopra Sancta Maria*. The *Sinfonia* is concerned with the gradual process of transformation of the material. Davies thinks if not thematically, certainly with ideas of a distinct musical identity, and the two features that concerned him chiefly at this stage were a greater concern with the vertical sound, and the process whereby the contours of the music gradually evolve as the idea develops. A comparison with Stravinsky is by no means inappropriate; not only is Davies particularly impressed by Stravinsky's later serial works, such as *Movements* or *Threni*, but like the elder composer he is highly and enthusiastically receptive to the music of numerous other periods and traditions; particularly the mediaeval, which he does not slavishly copy so much as embody into his own musical thinking. He is a neo-mediaeval composer to the same extent as Stravinsky was a neo-classical composer; the two are precisely analogous.

After leaving Cirencester, Davies went to Princeton (1962–4) on a Harkness Fellowship. This had come about through the instigation of the American composer Aaron Copland, who had heard and liked Davies's early piano pieces, and commissioned the *Ricercar and Doubles* (1959), (on the mediaeval carol 'To many a well') for the Dartmouth Festival in America. The instruments used are wind quintet, viola and 'cello (the same as in *O Magnum Mysterium*), but with cembalo; the work lasts for twelve minutes, in three contrasting sections, and is in direct line of descent from *Alma Redemptoris Mater*.

But these years reach their culmination with the remarkable group of works inspired by the sixteenth century composer John Taverner. The centre-piece of the group is the opera *Taverner*, which was begun as early as 1957. The two-act libretto was written by the composer, and itself makes a very characteristic composition. Each act has a very precise structure; each of its eight scenes is based on a single form, such as Renaissance dances, a motet, or a verse anthem. Apart from the highly dramatic nature of the material—the catholic musician John Taverner, accused of heresy, compromised his belief in order to save himself from the stake—the two acts form a sort of dramatic canon, the events of one being mirrored in the events of the other. While in America, Davies worked on the opera, and found out all he could of the facts about this extraordinary mediaeval musician, who held such a compelling fascination for him. The work needs to be assessed on many different levels, like Joyce's *Ulysses*; there is first the hold of the mediaeval period as a whole over Davies, whose background is that of the industrial North of England; the preoccupation with death, and the archetypal nature of Taverner's experience; the result of compromising one's inherent beliefs, which is inevitably an inner spiritual death, in spite of the continuation of physical life. In Taverner's case his spiritual life was represented by his music, and this died in him after he denied his faith. Just so must any composer, at any time, be true to the music, the creative force, that is in him. In an age such as ours, when doubt is almost a prerequisite for intellectual respectability, the story of John Taverner has a direct and alarming relevance. Davies starts without qualification in the direct line of the Western Christian tradition, and draws parallels between the sixteenth century and our own day. But what gives the work its characteristic and individual colour is the element of parody and blasphemy, as shown in Joking Jesus and the Black Mass.

There is no watering down of the force and impact of the drama with bourgeois respectability; the analogy with Berg's *Wozzeck* is, in this respect, most striking. Musical as well as spiritual parallels are drawn: Davies has identified himself with the mediaeval aesthetic to an extent unparalleled by other British composers; far more, for instance, than Britten has identified himself with Purcell, or, in an earlier generation, Vaughan Williams did with Tallis. For Davies, as for his mediaeval model, the *cantus firmus* is a formal device on which to hang the structure of the work; the composer takes for granted the text associated with the plainsong melody, and interprets the meaning of it. The mediaeval *In Nomine* was based on the plainsong *cantus firmus* 'Gloria Tibi Trinitas', and was a free invention over this thematic/structural foundation. Just so Davies superimposes his free invention; the theme may be varied by fragmentation, by octave displacement, different instrumental colour, by rhythmic alteration, and all the contrapuntist's armoury of resources, of which isorhythm and canon are two of the chief ones.

Round the opera, like satellites round a planet, are grouped three instrumental compositions. The *First Fantasia* on Taverner's *In Nomine* theme was written as a 'preparation' for the opera; the *Second Fantasia*, arose from the music of the first Act, already completed by October 1963, and is a 'comment' on it; the *Third Fantasia* will be taken from the second Act.[1] In addition to this, Davies has compiled a short (thirteen minute) instrumental suite, *Seven In Nomine*, in which three sixteenth-century settings of the plainsong theme are interspersed with free, contrasted settings of his own; a scheme which immediately recalls that of *O Magnum Mysterium*. The various pieces were written over a considerable period, and the Suite is a reflection of larger works of the same time. The last, very slow piece crystallizes and summarizes, in more static form, the harmonic character of the previous six.

1. This projected work is not yet written.

The *First Fantasia* is short, as befits an overture, and is preceded by Taverner's original *In Nomine*, taken from the Mulliner Book. It is the first work in which the composer introduces handbells, which appear frequently in his scores from now on; its style is, of necessity, more dramatic than earlier orchestral works.

The *Second Fantasia* is an altogether different and bigger work; it is of symphonic proportions, the largest conception since *Prolation*, but considerably more mature. The somewhat brash serialism of the student work is here tempered by a sense of freedom, such as is shown by the constantly evolving set, or by the whirling woodwind, starting at bar 539, (see plate 11), which marks the central climax of the work; by a concern for the vertical sound as much as the horizontal melody, which has the effect of making the music structurally less diffuse, more tightly knit; by the deeper assimilation of mediaeval contrapuntal techniques, which are used throughout this highly complex and intricate score; also by a broader more symphonic conception, which is impelled by a dramatic momentum, originating from that highly dramatic crisis facing John Taverner at his trial; this gives the work an urgency.

It lasts forty minutes, and its thirteen sections are played without a break. Sections 1—6 make roughly a sonata-form movement, with an introduction and coda; Sections 8–10 make a Scherzo & Trio.

Second Fantasia on John Taverner's *In Nomine*

An analysis based on the composer's programme-note for the first performance. (References are to the full score published by Boosey and Hawkes Ltd.)

Section 1 (a) *Bars* 1–20 Introduction. The three main melodic figures are heard on solo string quartet in a slow tempo. The first figure is heard on the cello alone; the second on the viola, with a first violin counterpoint, which is its retrograde; the third, after a pause, on the second violin, with a counterpoint on Violin I, which is a varied retrograde of the second figure.

(b) *Bars* 21–127 A development, for full orchestra, of the introduction. The music gradually quickens, to *presto* (bar 113), and culminates in a fanfare for brass, with side-drums, which forms an extended 'up-beat' into

Section 2 *Bars* 128–218 Two timpani strokes herald a unison violin melody. This is followed by a 'secondary group', whose identities emerge from the violin melody. The section closes (bar 204) with a brief recall, varied, of the initial violin melody, with the timpani as before.

Section 3 *Bars* 219–446 The development section—in so far as it is legitimate to refer to 'development' in this work, where the material is always in a state of transformation. First, a rising figure, which starts in low strings, with double bassoon, and finishes with a reference to the Fanfare of Section I; this introduces the development proper, which starts with a chord for 4 horns, D—F sharp—E—G sharp. The intervals of this chord gradually dominate and unify the whole melodic and harmonic structure of the work. The development consists of isorhythm, mensural canon, and the superposition of elaborate musical structures on a *cantus firmus*; the *In Nomine* theme is prominently sung by the oboes (bars 415–442).

Section 4   *Bars* 447–504 A varied recapitulation by inversion of Section 2, starting with timpani and unison violins.

Section 5   *Bars* 505–538 A development of the Fanfare from Section I, on woodwind, brass and side-drum. This leads to the climax of the work so far.

Section 6   *Bars* 539–548 Full orchestral climax with whirling woodwind flourishes; this is an amplification of the quartet of Section 1 (a). The final bars (546–548, *lentissimo*) crystallise the harmonies of the music so far into three essential chords.

Section 7   *Bars* 549–607 A slow transition, with a prominent passage for flutes foreshadowing the material of

Section 8   *Bars* 608–759 Four varied statements of an ever-developing melody, in three parts, given to different solo woodwind instruments, accompanied by pizzicato strings. These four statements are separated by three interludes, on low strings, harp and double-bassoon, of which the chief feature is the *In Nomine* theme played on a solo violin, with gradually increasing width of vibrato.

Section 9   *Bars* 760–865 Prestissimo. Solo strings have long-held 'cantus' notes, referring back to Section I, with quick woodwind figurations, bells and harp. The material is transformed in readiness for Section 10.

Section 10 *Bars* 866–1008 This section corresponds to Section 8, with the interludes omitted, and with transformed material.

Section 11 *Bars* 1009–1021 Transition. The entry, for the first time since Section 6 (very high fff), of four trumpets with bells recalls the flutes' figure in Section 7, which becomes the harmonic basis for Section 12.

Section 12 *Bars* 1022–1201 *Lento molto*, *calmo*. This is the longest section, and is scored for strings only, very quiet, except for built-up brass chords towards the end. It consists of four varied statements of a long melody arising out of the three main figures of Section 1, with increasingly elaborate counterpoint, but always harmonically derived from Section 2. As in Section 8, these statements are separated by three interludes; the first with a solo violin against harmonics in the other strings; the second with denser texture, recalling Section 3; the third adding the harp, somewhat louder and more jagged in outline, recalling Sections 8 and 10. The fourth statement of the long melody (starting at bar 1156) is made climactic by the addition of the brass. This fades out, and leads into

Section 13 *Bars* 1202–1215 This final, and shortest, section is scored for woodwind alone, in pianissimo, and refers back to the opening.

Plate 8. The opening page of Franz Reizenstein's *Sonata for Viola Solo*. The title, and composer's signature, have been taken from the front cover of the manuscript and superimposed. This extract contains a clear example of the composer's characteristic use of harmonics. The work, 'Written for and dedicated to my dear Elizabeth', was composed for Elizabeth Holbrook in the short space of three days (25-7 December 1967). *Composer's manuscript; reproduced by permission.*

200

Plate 9. The opening of the slow movement of Michael Tippett's *Second Symphony. Composer's manuscript; reproduced by permission.*

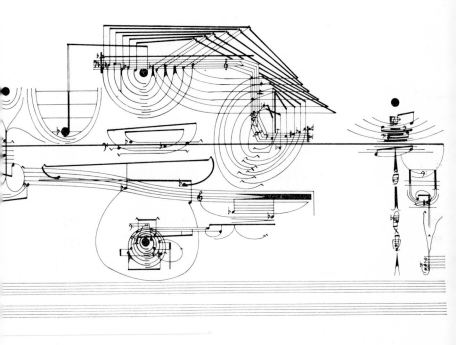

Plate 13. An example of free, graphic notation: a page from Cornelius Cardew's
Treatise. The players whose instruments and numbers are unspecified and
variable, are required to interpret the symbols according to their own conventions. How much of the whole score is performed at any one time is also arbitrary.
This one page could thus form an entity in itself.

Plate 14. The opening page of Priaulx Rainier's *Requiem*, showing the two prefatory quotations. The manuscript is dated 22 February 1956. *Composer's manuscript; reproduced by permission.*

The first performance of this *Fantasia*[1] had to be delayed for a year owing to its difficulty for the orchestra. Its effect in performance is of extreme power, of orchestral virtuosity, though the use of the orchestra is always subservient to the material; the orchestration is entirely functional; the overall effect is of anguish covering a long time-span. The influence of Mahler is pervasive. It is a symphonic elaboration of certain ideas of Act I of the opera *Taverner*, and though the material is derived from the opera, the *Fantasia* has little to do with the dramatic events. The tonal divisions of the orchestra are clearly differentiated; there is for instance a considerable portion for strings only, while the tremendous tension built up round the brass, in Sections 5 and 6, is most carefully graded; yet beyond a certain level of complexity of part writing, and beyond a certain dynamic level, individual part-writing becomes lost in the overall sound.

But the work is a highly individual break-through as far as style is concerned. The post-Webern serialism, which was Davies' somewhat theoretical and forbidding starting-point, has already been left far behind, and has been humanized, personalized, dramatized by the composer's affinity with the mediaeval period. This affinity is on many levels—musical, aesthetic, religious, social. Fantasy, parody, a sense of fun, are as central to Davies's musical thoughts as the strictest attention to contrapuntal detail, and the manipulation of the note-sets are to his technique.

This *Fantasia* sums up his technical advances up to 1964. It is not to be seen as variations on a theme, in the traditional sense; nor even as a free presentation of Taverner's original. Rather is the work built, after the manner of the American school of serial composers, on sets which consist of anything from five to twenty notes. These are in a perpetual state of transformation; definite musical patterns and identities are established gradually, only to disintegrate. Sets are chosen more for their ability to be transformed than for any structural potential. Thus, for instance, a set may be transformed by a given interval throughout, but more often by a series of intervals, sometimes in an elaborate permutation which results in complex curves. The rhythmic cells, as well as the larger isorhythmic units, are subject to a parallel process of consistent modification. So at all times the material is subject to harmonic and rhythmic control, and passes, as it were, through a technical filter. This technique ensures that the music moves quite independently of any preconceived harmonic or rhythmic cliché; the original plainchant establishes the idiom

---

1. By the London Philharmonic under John Pritchard, 30th April 1965. The complaint that scores are too difficult is frequently heard in the dialogue between composers and conductors. Tippett's works afford another example of this (see p. 278).

on a melodic basis, while the common origin of the sets ensures the
consistency of the material. This, at least, was the theory.

The composer's concern was, he says, 'to explore the possibilities of
continuous thematic transformation, so the material is in a constant state
of flux. The musical processes involved are perhaps somewhat analagous
to the literary techniques employed by Hoffman in, say, *Meister Floh*,
where certain people, spirits and plants are shown to be, within the
context of an elaborate "plot", manifestations of the same character
principle, a line of connection sometimes semantic (not a process of
development!) making this clear.'

Also written in America, and somewhat akin to *O Magnum Mysterium*,
was *Veni Sancte Spiritus*. This was for the choir of Princeton High
School, New Jersey, who came to England in July 1964 with their
conductor Thomas Hibbish, and performed the work at a Cheltenham
Festival concert.[1] Though much less complex than the *Second Fantasia*,
it is no less complete a composition, and is a practical application for
schoolchildren of his technique so far. It recalls Stravinsky's *Threni* in
more ways than one, not least in its deceptive simplicity. It is further
simplified by the doubling of voices by the strings. Ex. 35
shows a typical specimen of the texture, and includes hemiola,[1] mirror
canon, inversion, diminution and hocket.

Ex. 35   Peter Maxwell Davies
                                                   Veni Sancte Spiritus

1. The same year as Rawsthorne's *Third Symphony*.
1. 3 against 2.

Note: Words, Soprano and String parts omitted.

During his stay in Princeton, Davies was able to see at first hand something of the musical situation in America, and in particular the isolation of the young American composer from the generality of his society. Certain salient features were particularly apparent to him: that America had inherited the legacy of Schoenberg more than Vienna or any other European country; that Princeton could boast a concentration of talent exceptional even by American standards, epitomized in such musicians as Roger Sessions and his pupil Milton Babbitt; that the 'contemporary problem' facing the young American composer found its two extreme polarities in the mathematical precision of Babbitt on the one hand, and the music-less licence of John Cage on the other, whose notoriety-value is a sure sign of the fundamental decline in the true general musicality of American [and European] society. Davies's comments[1] are both shrewd and highly relevant for the post-Schoenberg English composer, who also faces an unsettling situation.

In spite of offers for him to remain in America, Davies preferred to return to England. He has always been accepted, even by those who are antipathetic to his music, as one of the most prominent, certainly the most articulate composer of his age-group; he has always found his practical services, as lecturer or performer, much in demand. In 1965 he lectured in Europe, Australia and New Zealand, and also contributed to a Summer School at Wardour Castle in Wiltshire. His compositions

1. In *Tempo* No. 72 (Spring 1965).

reflect these various activities; for the Wardour Castle course he wrote
Ecce manus tradentis; for a group of young singers and instrumentalists
in Sydney, Australia, he wrote *The Shepherd's Calendar*.

In 1966 he was Composer in Residence at the University of Adelaide
in Australia; he has also visited Canada and America, appeared in some
television broadcasts to schools, and, most important of all, founded, in
May 1967, together with Harrison Birtwistle, the Pierrot Players, a
highly accomplished group of young instrumentalists.[1] It is specifically
for this group, named after Schoenberg's *Pierrot Lunaire*, that a number
of works have been written since 1967.

The works composed since 1964 exploit those veins previously opened
up, and also discover new ones; for instance, those of parody and distortion, of mediaevalism, of dramatic presentation. Though the influences
interact, a group of compositions whose chief characteristic is that of
dramatic treatment includes *Hymnos* (1967), *Antechrist* (1967) and *Eight
Songs for a Mad King* (1969); a group whose aim is primarily distortion or
parody includes *Revelation and Fall* (1966), *L'Homme armé* (1968), and
the orchestral piece *St Thomas Wake—Foxtrot for orchestra* (1969).
Several lightweight works act as pendants or preludes to the other large
compositions; for instance *Stedman Doubles*, and its partner *Stedman
Caters*; and the Purcell realisations.

Antechrist was played at the beginning of concerts by the Pierrot
Players, like an overture. It stems from the opera *Taverner*, in which the
mediaeval Antechrist concept plays a significant part. Starting with and
from the thirteenth century motet 'Deo confitemini—Domino', the same
'transformation' technique is employed as in the works of the Taverner
group.

Revelation and Fall, however, which was commissioned by the Koussevitzky Foundation, introduces a fresh element. It is more experimental,
more grotesque, more recognisably *avant-garde*, and more reliant on
visual effects than anything previously written. It represents, the composer
says, an 'extension' of his composition technique, and is correspondingly
more complex in form. The sado-masochistic imagery of the German
words by George Trakl, and the specially-made percussion instruments,
all contribute to make this a transitional, experimental work, whose
technical basis is one of progressive distortion. The religious parody
recalls Schoenberg's *Pierrot Lunaire*. Interestingly, the work was declared
unplayable in America, and was first played at a Macnaghten concert in

---

1. Duncan Druce, *violin and viola*; Alan Hacker, *clarinet*;
   Jennifer Ward Clarke, *'cello*; Stephen Pruslin, *piano*;
   Judith Pearce, *flute, piccolo*; Barry Quinn, *percussion*; also Mary Thomas, *soprano*.
   In December, 1970 the ensemble was re-named The Fires of London.

February 1968. It led to *Eight Songs for a Mad King* (see plate 10). This also contains a strong element of parody: but its conception is chiefly dramatic and it continues to exploit certain 'extreme regions of experience' already suggested by *Revelation and Fall*. The flute, clarinet, violin and cello, apart from their independent function, also represent the bullfinches that the mad King, George III, was trying to teach to sing. The percussion represents the King's 'keeper'. Davies, as usual, takes his musical quotations from far and wide, including Handel's *Messiah*. The composer describes his intention in these words:

In some ways, the work is a collection of musical objects borrowed from many sources, functioning as musical 'stage props', around which the reciter's part weaves, lighting them from extraordinary angles, and throwing grotesque and distorted shadows from them, giving the musical 'objects' an unexpected and sometimes sinister significance. For instance, in No. 5, 'The Phantom Queen', an eighteenth-century suite, is intermittently suggested in the instrumental parts, and in the Courante, at the words 'Starve you, strike you', the flute part hurries ahead in a 7:6 rhythmic proportion, the clarinet's rhythms become dotted, and its part displaced by octaves, the effect being schizophrenic. In No. 7, the sense of 'Comfort Ye, My People' is turned inside out by the King's reference to Sin, and the 'Country Dance' of the title becomes a fox-trot. The written-down shape of the music of No. 3 becomes an *object* in fact—it forms a cage, of which the vertical bars are the King's line, and the flute (bullfinch) part moves between and inside these vertical parts.

The climax of the work is the end of No. 7, where the King snatches the violin through the bars of the player's cage and breaks it. This is not just the killing of a bullfinch—it is a giving-in to insanity, and a ritual murder by the King of a part of himself, after which, at the beginning of No. 8, he can announce his own death.

As well as their own instruments, the players have mechanical bird-song devices operated by clockwork, and the percussion player has a collection of bird-call instruments. In No. 6—the only number where a straight parody, rather than a distortion or a transformation, of Handel occurs, he operates a didjeridoo, the simple hollow tubular instrument of the aboriginals of Arnhem Land in Australia, which functions as a downward extension of the timbre of the 'crow'.

L'Homme armé began as an exercise—the completion of an incomplete anonymous fifteenth century Mass on the popular song 'L'homme armé'. While working on this, the composer somewhat disarmingly admits, 'other possibilities suggested themselves'. The work is a progressive splintering of what is extant of the fifteenth century original, with magnification and distortion of each splinter, through many varied stylistic 'mirrors', finishing with a dissolution of it in the last section.

Like *L'Homme armé*, and the earlier *Hymnos* for clarinet and piano, the two works written round a bell-peal also fall into nine sections in groups of three. *Stedman Doubles*, first played at a Redcliffe concert in May 1968, is scored for a fuller instrumental ensemble. The sections in the latter are so short, however, as to be more like a succession of 'points' in a seventeenth-century Fantasia.

The Purcell realizations were a flexing of his orchestral muscles for a large piece to follow, *St. Thomas Wake*. In the case of the Purcell *Fantasia*, the ground bass is allotted to the bass clarinet, while the free upper parts suggest the shrill brilliance of a Baroque chamber organ. In the case of the *Two Pavanes*, this popular sixteen-seventeenth century dance form is re-interpreted in terms of the correspondingly popular dance-form of the twentieth century, the foxtrot. The orchestral work, commissioned by the City of Dortmund and first heard there in June 1969, is a highly characteristic treatment, for orchestra which is set against a small, separate band, of the *St. Thomas Wake* Pavan of the seventeenth-century English composer John Bull.

Worldes Blis, which was first heard at Cheltenham in 1969, also pursues the 'transformation' technique, this time at an extremely slow tempo. But the outstanding work of that year was for dancer and small instrumental group, *Vesalii Icones*. Here Davies combines his Christian mediaevalism, his fondness for parody and pastiche, and for working on different 'levels', with a fresh dimension—that of the modern dance. At the first performance, on 9th December 1969, this was brilliantly realised by William Louther.[1] What is new about this work is not so much the music itself, which is sometimes very simple, but the overall conception, the three 'layers' of meaning and experience.

Davies bought a facsimile edition of *De Humani Corporis Fabrica* (1543) by Andreas Vesalius, and the idea came to him of making a set of fourteen dances, based on the illustrations to this book. Later came the idea of superposing the Vesalius images on the fourteen stations of the Cross (slightly modified to include the Resurrection), and this was the direct stimulus to composing the work.

The processes of working on three levels of musical experience, which he had just used in *St Thomas Wake—Foxtrot for Orchestra*, are in this work not only present in the music, but, more importantly, the dancer has a parallel set of superpositions:

1 The Vesalius illustrations
2 The Stations of the Cross
3 His own body.

1. Who is associated with the London Contemporary Dance Company, an offshoot of the Martha Graham School.

The three levels in the music, namely plainsong, 'popular' music, and Davies's own, derived from the other two, are very much fused together, and rarely emerge as separate identities.

Each dance starts with the body-position of the Vesalius illustration, to the sound of the turning of a wheel of small jingles and bells in the band; a ritual significance of bell-signals occurs in several other works. The dancer then moves to express the parallel 'station', but the dance is not an attempt to act-out the Vesalius drawing or the 'station'; it is an abstract from both, in which the dancer explores the technical possibilities suggested by the Vesalius illustration, in the light of the ritual and emotional experience suggested by the 'station', in terms of his own body. Similarly the music is not an attempt to 'illustrate' in a traditional way the movements or moods of the dancer, but it works out its own inter-relationships and cross-references.

In the last Dance the Christ-story is modified. It is the Antechrist—the dark 'Double' of Christ, of mediaeval legend, indistinguishable from the 'real' Christ—who rises from the tomb, and puts his curse on Christendom to all eternity. Davies's point is a moral one—to distinguish the false from the real, and not to be deceived by appearances.

Vesalii Icones is a particularly clear example of the working of Davies' musical intelligence. To the purely abstract, technical processes of a post-Webern style, he adds the humanizing dimension of the mediaeval tradition—with its fervently personal and ever-present religious beliefs, which Davies has made so much his own—as well as other contemporary ideas of his own devising, such as the dance. Thus he achieves a highly individual, multi-dimensional interpretation of that art-content, which to some extent every composer needs to put into his work, if it is to be relevant to a sophisticated contemporary audience, and not merely of academic interest only, or parasitic on another tradition—which is the case with a high proportion of *avant-garde* works—and without which it will remain coldly clinical, and lack that expressive warmth, for which contrapuntal skill or technical expertise, however excellent, are not by themselves a sufficient substitute.

Thus with each succeeding work Davies encroaches into fresh territory. Taking his works as a whole up to this point, when he is still in his thirties, his first works reached their culminating point in the *Taverner* group, and in particular the *Second Fantasia*. After this his style may be assessed by the extent to which he assimilates the old mediaeval styles; they may be simply laid alongside his own, as in *Seven In Nomine*; or parodied as in *L'Homme armé*; or fused together and integrated as in *Antechrist*; or abandoned in favour of something new, as in *Revelation and Fall*; or blended, by parody and pastiche, with later styles, like a photograph which has been doubly, or trebly exposed, as in *Vesalii Icones*. There is little doubt that sooner or later he will make use of electronic effects as he began to do in *L'Homme armé*; but Davies is anything but an aleatoric composer. Everything he writes is intentional, and thoroughly calculated.

17   Peter Racine Fricker

Few composers have experienced quite such a cruel reversal of fortune as Peter Racine Fricker. Fashion, it would seem, has used him almost as her plaything, to take up or discard at whim. By 1951, the year of the Festival of Britain, Fricker's position already seemed assured; quite remarkably so for a composer just turned thirty. Prizes, performances and commissions came his way in impressive profusion. He was the first young composer to emerge in England after the war with a mature and original technique which all could detect; during the 50's his reputation spread and became international.

Yet within the space of ten years, his name has progressively disappeared from London concerts. In 1964 he left to take up a teaching post at Santa Barbara, California; and when in 1970, in his fiftieth year he was invited by the Redcliffe Concerts to return for a concert of his work—his first visit to England for some six years—the event passed unnoticed except by a handful of friends and former colleagues. To the majority of concertgoers his name meant little or nothing, and his music was unfamiliar. Rarely can a musician of such marked ability have experienced such indifference from his contemporaries, having first been recognised by them.[1]

To describe is easier than to explain. Was his music shallow-rooted? Certainly it would appear that it never laid a firm hold on the public ear. Or did he perhaps pay the price of many pioneers who, having opened new paths, are then required to give place to those who follow? Certainly his name was already established before the fashionable wave of serialism reached its peak in the later 50's. By then he could no longer qualify as a 'young composer'; indeed, the same could be said of his contemporaries, Iain Hamilton and Humphrey Searle. Musicians younger than

1. Apart from several academic honours, he was made an Honorary Doctor of Music of Leeds University (1958), and he was granted the Freedom of the City of London (1962), and the Order of Merit, West Germany (1965).

R

he were already being swept into prominence on that particular flood-
tide. Or again, did he suffer even unwittingly from the lack of any first
generation Schoenbergian composers in this country? He had nothing
to fall back on, as far as that tradition was concerned. Yet his musical
thought has, among other things, a strong element of Schoenberg's
style, particularly in its complex contrapuntal character; and in becoming
Matyas Seiber's pupil he was following his true instinct. Or again, does
his music, serious and well-wrought as it is, and as it was required to be
by the *avant-garde* of the 1950's, for that very reason contain little or no
appeal to the *avant-garde* of the 1960's, whose taste is more inclined to the
experimental, the trivial or the aleatoric?

Born in London in 1920, he was at the Royal College of Music, where
he studied counterpoint and composition under R. O. Morris, and organ
under Ernest Bullock. An interest in the organ has remained with him
ever since, which is unusual among contemporary composers. This
formative period was interrupted by five years' service in the R.A.F.
(1941-6), after which he returned to study privately under Matyas
Seiber (1947-8). By this time his musical curiosity was increasing, his
developing skill as a composer creating a psychological vacuum which
needed to be filled. And Seiber supplied what was needed at this stage,
with his breadth of experience, and his insistence on 'Is this what you
really mean?' Thus, Fricker's naturally thick, richly scored, freely atonal
style became subjected to self-criticism. And the pupil in return helped
his teacher in many other ways, by copying, by assisting with the Dorian
Singers, the choir which Seiber formed. Fricker wrote for them occasionally. It may well be that virtue was culled from necessity in these
early post-war years. Copying and arranging music can provide a very
good groundwork in orchestration; you can learn excellent lessons in
practical instrumentation, in a more direct way than is possible from
more conventional classwork.

Although his first published work was Op. 2, *Four fughettas for two
pianos*, it was the *Wind Quintet* (1947) that first brought his name to a
wide public. Chance played a considerable part in this, since more important than the Clements Memorial Prize, which it won, was the
fortuitous fact that the composer had attended the same school[1] as
Dennis Brain, the horn-player, who broadcast the work with his Ensemble.
The *Quintet* thus gained wider acceptance than would otherwise have
been the case.

Another most important, even decisive factor in Fricker's musical
development was his association with Morley College, which in those
years was one of the most fruitful and active centres of musical activity.

1. St. Paul's School, London.

He met Tippett, who was then its Director of Music. He sang in the choir under Tippett, and occasionally acted as rehearsal pianist for him. He eventually took over as Director from Tippett in 1953. He wrote various pieces for Morley College, such as *The Comedy Overture* (1958) and choral works, and through Morley College he came into contact with a number of eminent and important musicians—notably the conductor Walter Goehr, the violinist Maria Lidka, and the Amadeus Quartet. The latter played his *First String Quartet*, Op. 8 (1947), after its first performance at a C.P.N.M.[1] concert in September 1949, and this work also helped to draw much attention to the composer. In one movement, dedicated to Seiber, it was selected for the Brussels I.S.C.M. Festival in 1950. So it was that, at this time, Fricker appeared as the most promising of young *avant-garde* composers. This impression was further strengthened when his *First Symphony*, Op. 9 (1948-9), was awarded a Koussevitzky Prize. The result of this award was a performance at the official new music forum, the Cheltenham Festival, in 1950, and this was later followed by performances abroad by Schmidt-Isserstedt, Scherchen and various other conductors. Though the first movement is very densely contrapuntal, and includes a 7-part fugal section in its development (a legacy from R. O. Morris), the slow second movement and finale are undeniably effective. With characteristic seriousness of intent and spaciousness of line, Fricker has found his idiom to be suited to symphonic expression, and he has since exploited this fact to the full. He is not among those composers who doubt the validity, and the continued validity, of the symphony orchestra. Not only does his music derive colour from the instruments themselves, but he enjoys working with orchestral musicians. He has frequently conducted his own works. Of his orchestral compositions, the one that has since found the securest place in the concert repertory, and that has been played the most, is the *Dance Scene*, Op. 22. This piece was conceived like a *pas de deux* from an imaginary ballet, and its three sections all use dance rhythm, though no specific dance form.

His music has a toughness which is continental-based, Schoenberg-influenced; a seriousness which recalls Hindemith; yet he belongs to no school. He feels the necessity for melodic lines, and recognizable thematic patterns, though for him the rhythmic impulse matters just as much as the notes. Later he was to evolve not so much a note-row as a pitch-row, particularly in piano pieces.

Two violin works followed the symphony; the *First Violin Concerto*, Op. 11, and the highly concentrated *Violin Sonata*, Op. 12, both written for Maria Lidka. The concerto was awarded an Arts Council Festival of

1. Committee for the Promotion of New Music (see p. 364).

Britain prize in 1951. Again, the composer is quite content to express his ideas, however severe and astringent, within the established three-movement concerto structure. The work started as a double concerto for violin and harp, and indeed the harp still plays a prominent part in the orchestral score.

From this point onwards, Fricker's work was largely decided by commissions. He wrote what was asked for. First came a commission from the City of Liverpool, also in connection with the Festival of Britain, for the *Second Symphony*, Op. 14. This was first played on 26th July 1951, under Hugo Rignold, who has always been the champion of many a British composer.[1] The symphony is unconventional in so far as each of its three movements is a different sort of rondo. It is heavily scored, which benefits the sweeping, driving finale, and while not so contrapuntal as the first symphony, it makes plentiful use of canon; for example, at the opening of the slow movement. The texture is thick, luxuriant, and the impetus of the music is derived solely from the composer's treatment and variation of his themes, and the development of their inherent potential. If it is severely intellectual, based on intervals, it is also polished, refined and warm, full of contrast. He relies on nothing outside the scope of the standard orchestra.

The *Second String Quartet*, Op. 20, like the first, was written for the Amadeus Quartet, and like the sonata it begins and ends with a slow movement. The *Allegro* which forms the first movement is unusual in that an independent subject appears as a fugue in the development section, and combines later with the material of the exposition. The second movement is a scherzo, direct in its effect and unproblematical, while the climax of the third movement is derived from the material of the first. Unusually for Fricker, the work is based on two keys, E flat minor, and F sharp.

Concertos and concertante works followed. The *Concertante No. 2* for three pianos, strings and timpani, a short work, whose four movements follow without a break, was intended as a balance for the three-piano concerto of Bach, and was introduced at a festival at Hovingham in Yorkshire, also in 1951. The composer conducted, as he has in the case of several others of his works; for instance, he conducted his *Litany for double string orchestra*, Op. 26, at a Promenade Concert in 1955, and his *Tenor Cantata*, Op. 37, at an Aldeburgh concert in 1962; there are several other occasions.

1. In the eight seasons (1960–1968) when he directed the Birmingham Orchestra, Rignold made a point of including many British works, of different generations. His premières included works by Hoddinott, Simpson, Maconchy, Whettam, Wellesz, Fricker, Musgrave, and Crosse.

The *Viola Concerto* was written for William Primrose, who first played it at the 1953 Edinburgh Festival; the *Second Violin Concerto* (*Rapsodia Concertate*), which was written for Henryk Szeryng, was first heard at a concert in Rome in 1954. This is richer and more elaborate than the first, and also differs in form. Its first movement is a five-section rondo, its second is a cadenza for the soloist alone, while the finale is a dance, of furious energy, which uses a huge percussion section. The rhythmic element is also particularly prominent in the two concerted works for piano and orchestra. The *Piano Concerto*, Op. 19, written for Harriet Cohen, was first heard in March 1954. Octaves are plentifully used in the outer movements, while the highly pianistic chromaticism of the central movement, an Air and Variations, is built largely in accordance with what fits the hands. Later, the short *Toccata* for piano and orchestra, Op. 33, was commissioned by the Royal Liverpool Philharmonic Orchestra for a piano competition in May 1959, and the composer therefore calls for a display technique. Particularly characteristic of his piano style, as well as of his contrapuntal method of working-out, is the central *Adagio* section.

By the time of the *Third Symphony*, Op. 36, which was commissioned by the London Philharmonic Orchestra, and first heard under John Pritchard in 1960, Fricker's personal characteristics begin to mature and evolve. His style consists primarily of an extreme richness, subtlety and profusion of thematic material, and a contrapuntal chromaticism. In this symphony, however, the composer first uses a process of transformation, whereby the theme-pattern is used not merely as a row of notes, but also as a chord, and a harmonic shape, or pitch-pattern, round which the contrapuntal texture is worked. Intervals are used as links in the structure of the material. Meanwhile the symphony is in other respects more conventional and comparable with the *First Symphony*; its four movements and its orchestration are classical. Apart from the timpani, no percussion appears—a distinct reaction against the trends of the current *avant-garde* in 1960. Each movement is expressive of a single mood; but a mood that is abstract, not personally felt.

This process of transformation of the material is continued in the *Fourth Symphony*, Op. 43, as well as in other works since 1960. Like the *Second Symphony*, it offers a different solution to the symphonic problem. The symphony was commissioned by the Feeney Trust, and played by the Birmingham Orchestra under Hugo Rignold in 1967. It may be less intellectually demanding than its predecessor; its expressive content, however, is more original, more concentrated. This, no doubt, is partly due to its being written in memory of Matyas Seiber, who had died in 1960. Fricker makes partial use of the note-row of his teacher's

Third String Quintet, as well as the chord structure of *Permutazioni a Cinque* for wind quartet, from which he also derived the idea of the pitch-patterns of his soprano songs *O Long Désirs*, Op. 39. This chord is constructed by progressively increasing the intervals between the notes by one semitone, starting with the fourth at the top:

An example of Fricker's use of this principle can be seen in the third and fifth sections of the symphony:

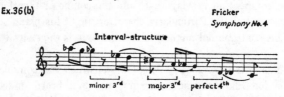

The 3-note groups follow one another at intervals which increase by a semitone each time. The symphony is in one movement, lasting thirty-five minutes, and its continuous line falls into ten contrasting sections round a central *Adagio elegiaco*. This structure had been already used in the finale of the *Third Symphony*, as well as the *Viola Concerto* (1953). These sections alternate fast and slow, and use short cadenzas for solo instruments. Each section expresses one mood, and the material, which is constantly transformed, is taken partly from the interval pattern announced as an introduction at the opening of the symphony,

partly from other thematic ideas in the first few sections. Nowhere is Fricker's use of intervals more clearly shown than in the symphony. Each section presents a different view of the material; the whole work thus has both an internal consistency and an overall unity, which are as original as they are compelling. The central *Adagio* is the longest section.

beginning and ending with a solo oboe, and developing an intensity of considerable force in two climax-points. The final section is also *Adagio*, and the symphony finishes very quietly. It is understandable that Fricker should himself consider this work to be the most satisfactory, from all points of view.

	Formal Structure	Orchestration
First Symphony (1949)	4 movements: 1 Sonata form 2 Slow 3 Scherzo (minuet style) 4 modified sonata form	Orchestra includes piano and harp.
Second Symphony (1951)	3 movements, avoiding sonata form. All the movements are a different sort of rondo.	Fourth trumpet, otherwise normal
Third Symphony (1960)	4 movements: 1 Sonata form 2 Slow 3 Scherzo (*presto*, with a Trio in canon) 4 Sectional, beginning and ending maestoso, with a central *Adagio*.	Classical orchestra, with bass clarinet. Timpani has a solo part.
Fourth Symphony (1966)	1 movement 10 sections, round a central *Adagio* (form derived from finale of *Third Symphony*)	Normal, with possibly extra strings for *solo* and *divisi* parts. Timpani has a solo part.

Fricker's *Fourth Symphony* was finished in California in 1966, two years after his move to America. He had always been an extensive traveller—more so, indeed, than most British composers. During the war he spent three years in India, and after the war, in the 50's, he was a frequent visitor to many countries in Europe. He saw himself as a member of the European musical community. His viewpoint, as well as his style, was thus the reverse of insular. For example, already in 1935 he was acquainted with Berg's *Wozzeck*, as well as works by Krenek, Schoenberg, Stravinsky and others. Moreover, he found the lot of a composer in London far from satisfactory; his work there consisted of a multiplicity of various engagements, which he found unnecessarily time-consuming, apart from leading to an underlying lack of security. He taught at the Royal College of Music from 1955; since 1953 he had directed the music at Morley College; he examined, lectured, conducted, occasionally broadcast. He wrote a number of commercial film scores, and incidental music for radio performances, mainly in the later 50's; also two radio operas. But generally speaking, as far as his acceptance as a composer was concerned, he found that considerable indifference which faced all composers; performances were largely a matter of luck. And so it is not surprising that when he received an offer from the University of California to become a member of the music staff at Santa Barbara, originally for a year, he should be predisposed in its favour. It meant one job in one place; he would be employed specifically as a composer and teacher, and time-consuming activities peripheral to that would thus become unnecessary; he would have plenty of time for the sustained, thoughtful pursuance of his work. Moreover, the Music Faculty contained several excellent performers who would be his working colleagues— which is an almost irresistible bait to any composer.

So in 1964 he moved to America—though he retains a British passport. Starting with the completion of the *Fourth Symphony*, the works of his American period mark a fresh phase. They include several major commissions: the *Three Scenes*, Op. 45, which was written for the California Youth Symphony; the *Magnificat*, Op. 50, for soprano, alto and tenor soli and orchestra; and the *Concertante No. 4*, Op. 52, for flute, oboe, violin and strings, which he conducted himself at Santa Cruz University.

But in addition to these larger works, and as a result of the circumstances prevailing at Santa Barbara, he has also written for solo instrumentalist or duo teams; the *Viola Fantasy*, Op. 44, for Peter Mark; the Piano *Episodes*, Op. 51 and 58, for Landon Young; also the short motet for male voices and piano, *Ave Maris Stella*, Op. 48, and the songs for soprano and harp, *The Day and the Spirits*, Op. 46.

These solo works mark a fresh departure for Fricker. Their thinner texture allows the rich, condensed quality of his characteristic musical thoughts to be more fully expressive than is the case in works involving more instruments. Thickness of contrapuntal writing is subject to its own law of diminishing returns, as far as the directness of expressive quality is concerned. For instance, it is by no means necessarily true to say that a passage which develops a thematic pattern in eight parts is, therefore, eight times as effective as a passage which simply states the theme in a single voice. Rather the reverse: too much density of musical undergrowth may well choke the flower, and prevent it from blossoming naturally, to its fullest extent.

So the solo works of Fricker's American period mark a highly expressive and fruitful phase of development. The orchestral works of this time, starting with the *Fourth Symphony*, also use a thinner texture, and profit as a result. Certain technical innovations are introduced as well. For instance, in the *Three Arguments* for bassoon and cello, Op. 59, a new method of notation is used; one part steady and even, the other variable. The *Episodes* for solo piano also introduce a fresh approach to the use of a pitch-row, and follow on from the earlier *Twelve Studies*, Op. 38—in particular the second study, which uses the intervals of the minor second and fourth. But this remarkable work, more complete than earlier piano pieces, is much more than its title might imply; and though the twelve sections may be analysed technically in terms of canon, inversion, and other contrapuntal tricks of the trade, the whole is much more than the sum of its parts. What is effectively playable on the piano is for Fricker largely determined by the shape of the human hand and by the disposition of the keys, and these two factors always remain constant. Even Stockhausen and the *avant-garde* cannot escape this reality. Fricker's *Twelve Studies* is a rich workshop of pianistic ideas; it contains, in summary form, his method of developing thematic patterns and varied rhythms from progression of intervals; it is bound together by a virtuosity which is entirely original, yet which by no means excludes the traditional techniques associated with the romantic period of piano music; it shows an awareness of piano colour and sonority which few British composers can equal; it was a work containing formative factors on which the composer drew in later works.

After the *Twelve Studies*, the next piano pieces were sets of *Episodes*, written for his colleague at Santa Barbara, Landon Young. *Episodes I* dates from 1967/8, *Episodes II* from 1969. Each makes use of a mosaic form, and is built up from a number of short sections. The first piece, generally delicate in texture, fragments four main sections, and arranges the piece round a central scherzo. The second, more aggressive and dramatic, is constructed from pieces of five sections, and the central sixth one is a recitative.

In addition to the piano works, Fricker's keyboard writing includes several important pieces for the organ. In spite of the closed, narrow view of the organ prevailing in this country, he has always felt an affinity with the instrument; partly as he studied it while a student, partly because the contrapuntal nature of the organ is so much in keeping with his own style. Also, the possibilities of tonal contrasts, echo effects and so on, are much to his liking. An early sonata remains unpublished, but in several short pieces he achieves a marked individuality, notably in the *Pastorale*. Two works written for diametrically opposed instruments, yet both equally effective, are the *Ricercare*, Op. 40, and the *Toccata, Gladius Domini*, Op. 55. The *Ricercare* was first played on the restored Schnitger organ in St. Michaëlskerk, Zwolle, in Holland—one of the historical treasures of Europe, which Fricker once spent a day in discovering for himself. The bright and glittering tone-quality of the full ensemble, and the highly characteristic solo stops, appealed to him most strongly. But the stop-knobs are so inconveniently placed at the side of the player that, without an assistant, alterations of registration in the course of a movement are almost impossible. Therefore, the stops required in the different divisions of the organ have to be set at the beginning of a piece, and then left unaltered. This principle of terraced dynamics was used by Fricker in his *Ricercare*. The *Toccata*, however, was written for Alec Wyton, the organist of St. John's Cathedral, New York, whose enormous instrument, with electric, not mechanical, action, boasts a State Trumpet stop[1], which is duly allowed for by the composer in his brilliant, predominantly chordal, *Toccata*.

His most recent organ piece, finished on Christmas Day, 1969, is the *Praeludium*, Op. 60, which was commissioned by the Anglo-Austrian Music Society, and written for the Viennese organist, Anton Heiller. This virtuoso work, which somewhat belies its title, is as consummate a piece of organ craftsmanship as the *Twelve Studies* was in the case of his piano output. The tonal centre is D, and the structure is that of a continuous suite, whose contrasted sections are evocative of a particular musical mood, derived from the opening motif, or aspect of organ sonority. The motif is an irregular sequence of rising fourths, with implied triadic chord formations. This leads to a chordal section, ff *maestoso*. A quick, barless passage *manualiter*, *Allegro flessibile*, largely with just a single line of notes, leads again to the more measured pulse of the *maestoso* chords; these are then followed by the slow movement, in trio style, with highly expressive antiphonal recitative-like phrases between manuals and pedals. Fricker's use of the material in this section leads to fewer tonal acerbities than in the earlier part.

The scherzo, which follows without a break, is very quiet, though light and quick, and uses an added rhythm technique with a $\frac{1}{16}$ note (semiquaver) metre. Chords, built largely from the fourths of the opening, alternate with staccato, fanfare-like arpeggios. A reprise of the opening (mf) in varied form, gradually builds up again to the *maestoso* chords, ff, which this time are given their head, and the work finishes with full organ, over a D pedal.

His choral output so far centres round two main works; the oratorio, *The Vision of Judgement*, Op. 29, and the *Magnificat*, Op. 50. The first of these was commissioned by the Leeds Centenary Festival, 1958, which may be said to be one of the two remaining bastions of the old oratorio tradition—the other being the Three Choirs Festival. Since Walton's *Belshazzar's Feast* (1931) added a fresh dimension to this tradition,

1. On 100 inches pressure, at the opposite end of the cathedral to the main organ.

namely a dimension of dramatic movement and physical energy, it could hardly continue as before, though there have been many attempts, and several commissions, designed to prolong its life. None has been, or could be, wholly successful, and Fricker's work is no exception. Evolution cannot be halted; the contemporary choral tradition has moved away from the old large-scale oratorio.

That Fricker is himself aware of these developments in the choral tradition, as well as the need for a structural unity, whether of mood or action, is shown in his own writing about *The Vision of Judgement*.[1] His own words are:

I was conscious of the need for a satisfactory overall musical form as well as a logical poetic one. The final shape is of two main movements (or acts, if the work is considered dramatically), divided by an interlude, an unaccompanied chorus.

I have tried to give the work an overall unity by dividing it into scenes and set-pieces in somewhat the same way that Berg did in *Wozzeck*. These scenes are separated from each other either by the piled-up-fifths motive of the beginning, expressive of despair and anguish, or by the Latin interpolations. In only one case are two scenes run together; these are the second and third of the second part, the duet and the final chorus. In addition to sharing thematic material they also share a common tempo. The quaver remains at a constant speed, so that 3/8 (allegro), 3/4 (moderato) and 3/2 (maestoso) are, so to speak, geared together. Most of the 3/4 sections feature a saraband-like rhythm which is intentionally used as a unifying factor.

Fricker was asked for a piece on a big scale, and his oratorio, like Walton's, includes organ and full brass. After working with a choir at Morley College, he knew the capabilities, and the limitations, of choral singers. The text that he chose, which was adapted from 'Christ' by the eighth century Anglo-Saxon, Cynewulf, was one he had known since schooldays. He interspersed the sections of the poem—powerful, dramatic and challenging—with sections of the traditional Latin Requiem, a device that was used by Britten in his *War Requiem* four years later. Throughout the oratorio Fricker uses the orchestra independently of the singers, not merely as accompaniment, and the idiom is tonally simpler than in his instrumental and symphonic works. The other major choral work, the *Magnificat*, Op. 50, dates from his period in America. It was commissioned for the centenary of the University of California, and written in 1968.

Any overall assessment of Fricker's style—if indeed this is possible in the case of a fifty-year-old composer whose creative output is still in full

1. In Hines, '*The Composer's Point of View*', pp. 81–88.

spate—must begin by eliminating those factors which it does not possess. In spite of his Continental orientation, his style is not neo-Bartok, neo-Schoenberg, or neo-Hindemith. Through his connection with Matyas Seiber, it was immediately assumed at one time that he was heavily indebted to Bartok. This is not the case. Seiber did not attempt to force his pupils into the acceptance of any one particular style, or of any single composer; he preferred to discover what each individual pupil appeared to need most in order to develop his own style. Indeed, the strength of Fricker's style, as shown in such works as the *Twelve Studies* or the *Fourth Symphony*, is precisely the personal use of highly chromatic material. He cannot be attached to any school. He is not, for instance, a serialist, though a serial process is involved in certain of his later works, such as the *Episodes* for piano.

Nor does he follow trends or fashions, which exert such a force over many British composers. He has seen several such movements come and go since 1945, but he has remained remarkably consistent in the pursuit of his own idiom and style. Up to about 1950 it was the fashion among those composers whose business it was to be 'contemporary', to write athematic music. This trend soon died out, to be replaced by another. But Fricker has never followed this path, nor swerved from his purpose. Fashions are not, for him, a sufficient basis for a composer's style. After his 1970 London concert it was suggested[1] that his music had no wide appeal because he was writing for the contemporary music audience of twenty years previously, not for that of the present moment. While it is true that he in no way subscribes to the trend of the 1970 *avant-garde*, which is either towards electronic music, or towards aleatoricism, or both, nevertheless it is equally true that neither did he subscribe to the trend of the 1950 *avant-garde*, which was towards athematicism and dodecaphony. His music cannot be so easily categorized, nor so summarily dismissed.

Also to be excluded from his creative thinking are all direct uses of folk-song, and jazz. Unlike his teacher, he has found no use for jazz, though a jazz-derived syncopation is for him a perfectly legitimate rhythmic device. On the other hand, in spite of the intellectually concentrated nature of his musical thought, this does not rule out the existence of certain extra-musical ideas. His music may be assessed not only by the mechanics of its construction, but by its depiction of mood; a certain distilled resignation, controlled anger even, occurs several times. Fricker seeks a direct effect in this way. For instance, the *First String Quartet* resulted from sketches he made after seeing an exhibition in Battersea Park of the work of Henry Moore. His music is partly programme music.

1. In *The Guardian*. 24th April 1970.

But the central feature of his style, which chiefly decides the nature and the overall effect of the finished work, is the process of construction of the thematic patterns, and (later) the transformation of those patterns. Themes, for him, are not purely abstract invention, like note-rows. He is preoccupied with intervals, and the relationship of intervals. Thematic patterns can be derived from intervals, and the line of the melody can then be condensed into a set of chords. His treatment of chromaticism varies. It may be without a key-centre, such as he uses in the piano *Episodes*; it may be held to a key-centre by a background pedal note, such as the repeated A at the opening of the *Third Symphony*, or the D at the beginning and end of the *Praeludium* for organ. But Fricker's style is pure music, he has recourse to nothing outside the twelve notes of the chromatic scale. He has worked consistently towards an idea of an organised, logical tonal procedure in his composition technique, and this logic is for him partly aural, partly structural. If a note belongs in a pitch-row, its position is logical, and its aural effect is therefore correct. In this way the composer can explain to himself why a chord is satisfying or not. Moreover, pitch-rows can have a certain symmetry, as well as logic, in the way they progress. Tonality is the end-product of this progression, not so much the starting point of the composition.

18   Anthony Milner

Like Fricker, though five years his junior, Anthony Milner also proceeded from the Royal College of Music to become a pupil of Matyas Seiber, and was associated with Morley College under Tippett. Unlike Fricker, however, Milner is also a scholar and musicologist as well as a composer; he has been a lecturer at London University since 1965, and has a number of important writings to his credit.

His music falls naturally into two categories, choral and instrumental. The character of his choral music is determined by a glowing, intensely poetic catholicism; a highly personal interpretation of the Christian message in the present-day world; mystical, symbolic, all-demanding. The character of his instrumental music is determined by a restless striving for freshness of effect within a tonal idiom. It is complex, contrapuntal, erudite, reflecting the composer's wide range of musical scholarship. In his orchestral composition he allows the instruments an independence, a striving after adventure, which is not so apparent in his choral works, in which the meaning and implications of the verbal text, usually of a religious significance, are invested with such an urgent and overriding importance.

Instrumental works

Up to the *Chamber Symphony* Op. 25 (1968), nine compositions are for instruments. After the early *Oboe Quartet*, Op. 4 (1953), and the *Rondo Saltato* for organ (1955), Milner's first work of substance was the *Variations for Orchestra*, Op. 14 (1958, revised 1967). The years 1958–1961 were a particularly important and fruitful period of his development, and in this piece a fresh stage of development first becomes apparent.

The theme which forms the subject of the variations is the traditional Advent hymn *Es ist ein Ros' entsprungen*. The fifteen variations fall into three groups of five, played without a break. Each group may be looked on as a symphonic unit, while the theme itself is treated as a note-row, after the manner of the Viennese school; that is to say it appears in its four versions (Original, Retrograde, Inversion and Retrograde Inversion), and is fragmented into its constituent *motifs*.

Group I: 1 *Lento*; 2 *Allegro giocoso*; 3 *Andante quasi una Berceuse*; 4 *Allegro alla marcia*; 5 *Allegro scherzando*.

The D major theme is first heard from a solo muted horn, against a very delicate countersubject by the strings. Throughout the first three variations it is retained in its original form, though fragmented, and treated against a rhythmical countersubject, with a bustling and characteristically irregular metre. Milner uses all the devices of counterpoint to develop a complex texture, in which the original theme is not immediately recognisable. In the fourth variation it is inverted, and in the fifth it is distributed between the wind instruments in long-held notes, after the manner of Schoenberg's *Klangfarbenmelodie*.

Group II: 6 *Lento molto*; 7 *Più mosso*; 8 *Adagio molto*; 9 *L'istesso tempo*; 10 *A tempo*.

Throughout this second group, the theme is used either in its retrograde form, or its retrograde inversion. Milner here exploits orchestral sonorities, for instance in the sixth very short variation, which uses the bottom register of the brass instruments at a low dynamic level (pp). The eighth variation is built over an isorhythmic bass—that principle which may be seen in the work of mediaeval composers such as Pérotin or Machaut. The pattern of notes, which is repeated like a ground bass, consists of two parts, the rhythmic part (*talea*), and the melodic part (*color*). In this case the *color* is the retrograde version of the theme, while the *talea* is itself divided into two, *talea* i and *talea* ii. As will be seen from Ex. 38

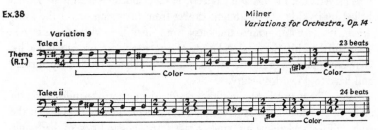

Ex.38

Milner
Variations for Orchestra, Op. 14

the *color* is left incomplete at the end of *talea* ii, and therefore overlaps into the next reappearance of *talea* i. *Talea* i and *talea* ii appear three times, while the *color* appears seven times, with a different rhythmic distribution each time. This distinguishes the isorhythmic technique from that of the ground bass, or passacaglia, of later years. In this case, Milner allots the bass line to the double basses, and gives the cellos free melody, somewhat Elgarian in flavour, with wide leaps, which is repeated and inverted by a solo flute. The ninth variation builds up from pp to a brilliant orchestral climax (ff, *molto brutale*), and the retrograde tune at the end of it is harmonised for wind to form the tenth, very short, variation.

Group III: 11 *Trionfale con moto* (*attacca 12*): 12 *Allegrissimo*; 13 *L'istesso tempo*; 14 *Lento*.

In this third group the theme is restored to its original version, though occasional use is made of its inverted form. Another medi-aeval device, the hocket, characterises the eleventh variation. This is, approximately, a musical hiccough, resulting in the distribution of short fragments of the melody between different instruments, in this case the brass. The very fast rhythm of the middle variations of this group is built round $\frac{1}{15}$ note (semiquaver) movement, mainly in the strings. The thirteenth variation is a double fugue, and the work ends, as it began, with the theme restored to its original melodic form, and given out once more by a solo horn.

In this work Milner's orchestral style first shows certain mature stylistic hallmarks. His conception of variation form is original, while his idiom remains recognisably traditional. He retains a key signature almost throughout, and although certain variations, for example the ninth, are highly chromatic, and use wide leaps and harsh dissonance, he never loses sight of tonality. Complexity, particularly contrapuntal complexity, allied to an irregularity of metre, are intrinsic to his musical thought.

These characteristics mark his subsequent orchestral works, such as the *Divertimento for Strings*, Op. 18 (1961), and the *Chamber Symphony*, Op. 25. The first of these two works, which was commissioned for, and first played at, a Promenade Concert, has a character which is somewhat belied by its title. As one might expect from the composer of the *Variations*, it is a contrapuntal and busy work, in which Milner carries one stage further his personal solution of the problems presented by his characteristically chromatic idiom. These problems are largely formal, and have to do with tonality.

Sonata form had been the direct result, the outward manifestation, of an organized scheme of keys within a movement. The more you blur the edges of key-relationships, and weaken the possibilities of harmonic modulation, the more you undermine not just the distinctive nature of the themes, but the formal cohesion of a scheme such as sonata form. Some alternative is needed, which Milner seeks in the subtle exploitation of tonality. A tonality is by no means the same thing as a key in the diatonic sense; a tonal centre is something altogether more wide-ranging in its implications.

The first movement, *Allegro all danza*, uses the traditional two subjects of sonata form, and is based on a tonality of E, a kind of Phrygian, with modal modulation to introduce chromaticism. The second subject is a chromatic version of an F tonality. The development section is a contrapuntal working out of the material, and builds up to a climax (*frenetico*) before the main theme returns, but this time inverted, augmented and transposed

Ex.39

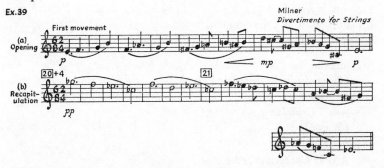

The metre is irregular; $\frac{6}{8}$ juxtaposed with $\frac{2}{4}$.

The short E major second movement, *Moderato*, uses two themes, one in the bass and one in the treble. The second finally ousts the first, which collapses towards the end, after having tried to start in augmentation. The third movement, *Allegrissimo*, again uses two subjects; the first rhythmical, which is treated in fugato style, with Milner's customary irregular pulse; the second lyrical, recalling the opening of the first movement. Not till the very last chord does the C major tonality become finally explicit.

Choral Works

Formal and stylistic problems are not so pressing in Milner's choral compositions. In the first place, the structure of each piece, its overall pattern and nature, is decided primarily by the words themselves; in the second place, the melodic idiom is chiefly influenced by what comes within reach of the human voice. In this respect his instinct is almost unerring, and he is not remotely interested in experiment for its own sake. His choral technique, texture and layout, are remarkably simple, and the music has a correspondingly greater impact and directness. The composer does not hesitate to write for a full chorus in unison if need be; nothing is allowed to impede the meaning of the words that he is seeking to illumine, and the music is in no way inhibited by technical considerations.

Milner's first work, Op. 1, was a choral one, *Salutatio Angelica* (1948), a cantata for contralto solo, small choir (twenty-four voices), and chamber orchestra. The text consists of the ancient devotions known as the Angelus, the Eastertide Antiphon of Our Lady ('*Regina Coeli*'), and the first four verses of Psalm 130. The prefatory quotation gives an essential clue to the composer's underlying purpose: 'For as nothing was done without the Word, so also nothing was done without the Mother of the Word'. The contralto thus suggests the Virgin Mary, and the choir are the faithful who hear the Word and comment on it. The tonality of the work is A at the beginning and end, with excursions into F sharp and C in the middle. But the most striking characteristic is its formal structure, which is as follows:

Ritornello
  Chorus I (duple material: a + b)
Ritornello
  Aria I *Consolatrix afflictorum*
  Chorus II
Ritornello
  Aria II *Causa nostrae laetitiae*
  Chorus III (Material of Chorus I reversed, b + a)
  Aria III, with Chorus, *Mater misericordiae*
Ritornello
  Psalm
Ritornello

The three Arias use the forms of ground bass, fugue and ostinato. In Aria I there is an overlapping of accents between ground bass and solo, while in Aria III the *Sancta Maria* chorus is a diminution of the previous solo line in canon at the tritone, with the sopranos and tenors a quaver ($\frac{1}{8}$ note) later than the altos and basses. Each phrase of the psalm is followed by a phrase of the Ritornello, one of which accompanies the solo verse.

Three years later Milner wrote a short work for choir *a cappella* in which the merits of his choral technique are concentrated with remarkably brilliant effect—the *Mass*, Op. 3, dedicated to his teacher Matyas Seiber. Points of excellence abound in this quite exquisite miniature, which is a *Missa brevis*, without the creed; a characteristically simple and direct choral style; varied metre; varied mood, ranging from the solemnity of the opening, to the vitality of the *Gloria* for double choir; a consistency of idiom, for instance in the use of the semitone throughout.

Midway between the simplicity of these early works and the maturity which was to come, stands a transitional work, the *City of Desolation*,

Op. 7. This, in several senses, is a prophetic composition. Written in 1955, the text is taken from R. A. Knox's translation of the Bible, Psalm 23, and the *Confessions* of St. Augustine. Once again the prefatory quotation gives the clue: '*Fecisti nos ad te, Domine, et irrequietum est cor nostrum, donec requiescat in te*'.

It is a work of direct and vivid expression, built round two contrasting moods, which may be said to correspond approximately to the two subjects of a symphonic movement. The first is a mood of desolation and despair, represented by the semitone, the tritone, and chromatic tonality. This is the mood of the choral introduction, one of the most effectively simple ideas this composer has had. The choir sing, *Lento e molto piangendo*, to a solemn accompaniment of muted brass, and lower strings marked *senza vibrato*: 'Alone she dwells, the city ere while so populous'.

The second mood is one of hope and trust, represented by the whole tone, perfect intervals and major tonality. This is expressed by the choir in unison ('In Him be thy trust'), later by the soloist ('The Lord is my shepherd'). The opening *motif*, and the concluding phrase, of the first choral passage are combined in a theme, given out like an accompanied fugue subject by the flute against a background of strings at [C] + 5. This melody appears again shortly afterwards at [E], inverted in B flat minor, *molto adagio*, before being transformed into the major tonality of A, in which guise it is interspersed between the verses of the psalm, Once again, within the framework of a recognizably traditional idiom. Milner's expression is direct and vivid, his structure highly original and consistent.

There follow two more transitional works, both written in 1956, in which the composer feels his way forward, with varying success, towards the maturity that he was soon to achieve in *The Water and the Fire*. Both these two works, *The Harrowing of Hell* and *St. Francis*, have texts by J. A. Cuddon; Milner is not so much originating a choral structure, as setting words. The first piece was a bold answer to a commission which stipulated a 'substantial *a capella* piece'. Two choirs are used, each with its respective soloist; but curiously, the overall effect is in inverse proportion to the complexity of the choral texture.

The second piece, *St. Francis*, is one of Milner's rare artistic failures. Yet the very reasons for its failure are most illuminating, since they stem from its lack of those features which are the chief positive characteristics of his mature choral style. In this work he was merely setting a text, as distinct from evolving for himself the structure of the composition, its message and import. The composer seems to have been involved only externally; the structure seems to have been ready-made, and the nature of the work pre-determined by someone else. It lacks therefore that burning conviction that such a personal style as Milner's presupposes.

Again, whereas one of his chief sources of strength is a certain simplicity and directness, in this work, as in *The Harrowing of Hell*, he admits more complexity in the choir writing, and this complexity is somewhat derivative; for instance the choral canons recall Tippett's style in *A Child of our Time*. Moreover there is a lack of contrast throughout the work. Only one mood, that of praise, is sustained practically throughout, and this is insufficient to sustain the listener's interest over a large-scale composition. The colourful depiction of the wind and the storm is of momentary, local interest only, while in the third section, the Rondo, which is as long as the other two movements together, the potential vitality of a dotted rhythm is nullified by the laborious tread of the slow-moving metre. In short, Milner is a subjective composer, with a personal, composite style, and he needs a subject in which he can immerse himself, and which he himself can interpret and project.

He found such a theme in *The Water and the Fire*, Op. 16 (1959/60), a work which more than compensates for any shortcomings in earlier transitional compositions, and which contains none of the negative qualities of the previous two works. The composer describes it as a *dramatic oratorio in four scenes*. In it he not only assimilates the new oratorio-style, apparent in British music since 1945, but he sums up the positive aspects of his choral style, and shows greater technical accomplishment than hitherto. Directness of expression is there in abundance, together with maturity of idiom.

The intricate text was selected by the composer from various parts of the Bible, St. Augustine, St. John of the Cross, and the Easter Liturgy. Two quotations at the beginning of the score

> *O vere beata nox*
> *Toute l'immense nuit du corps animé* (Jacques Maritain)

point to the background of the drama; night seen first as the darkness of sin and separation; later as the 'dark night of the soul', and the prelude to resurrection.

The very precise, central intention of the work is suggested by St. Paul's Epistle to the Romans (VI 3-4):

> All of us who have been baptised into Christ were baptised into his death. We were buried therefore with him by baptism into death, so that as Christ was raised from the dead by the glory of the Father, we too might walk in newness of life.

The three soloists are soprano, representing the soul, tenor, a quasi-Evangelist, and baritone, representing Christ. The structure of the work is cumulative and consistent, and the four movements, or scenes, develop an inevitable, overwhelmingly powerful, dramatic momentum, which culminates in the climax of the finale, when the chorus, representing humanity, are drawn into the Easter ritual, and all mankind are united as the redeemed children of God. As the soloists sing, 'My Beloved is mine and I am his'.

In *Scene I, Descent to the Pit*, men and women are separated from their true destiny by sin. They have broken the covenant, and their guilt brings disaster and ruin to cities. In the ensuing storm and flood the human soul feels overwhelmed by darkness and terror. It can only cry out: 'Out of the deep I cry to thee'. But comfort is hard to find: 'Thick darkness covers my face'. The form of this scene is ternary, and an orchestral interlude leads directly into the next scene.

Scene II, Encounter, is dramatically more direct, and thus formally and tonally more simple. It is cast in Rondo form. The chorus and tenor soloist see the Stranger coming in the shadows. He is scarred and bruised, in the image of the suffering servant of the prophet Isaiah. The tenor soloist recognizes the Stranger as Christ. 'Late have I loved thee. Thou didst shine forth and my darkness was scattered.' Can a man bring himself to accept the agony and grief of Christ? Yet by doing this he is healed.

In *Scene III, The Waters by Night*, the soprano sings part of the poem by St John of the Cross, 'Song of the Soul that is glad to know God by Faith'. This short aria represents a pause in the unfolding of the drama, a period symbolizing that interval between Christ's death and resurrection, while the soul waits, patient, yet reliant on the power of the divine grace.

Scene IV, The Easter Fire, starts with a slow, processional interlude for the orchestra, which corresponds structurally with that at the end of Scene I. The shape of the final scene is determined by the Easter Vigil Liturgy, and characterized by the plainchant and antiphonal singing of the Catholic ritual. 'Rejoice, O choirs of angels in the heavens'. The blackness of sin is purged away by the light of the pillar of fire, the new fire of the baptismal font. On the same night when Israel walked through the sea, Christ burst the bonds of death, and rose victorious from the grave.

The shifting and cumulative structure of this highly original conception is aptly matched by the composer's idiom. His personal use of tonality is richly varied and subtle, while the thematic material is integrated throughout the work. The desolate, penitential mood of the opening is represented by ambiguous tonality, and by motifs which grope towards

a tonal centre. At the words 'Out of the deep I cry to Thee', a C tonality
is made more explicit. The interlude joining Scenes I and II is poised
between E and E flat minor; but Scene II opens with an accompaniment
of triads, and the key signature of B flat. The tonality is thus more direct,
and the clash of dissonance more obvious and explicit, than in the first
scene. The word 'peace' (at [24] + 10) is depicted with a plain B flat
major triad. The tonality of scene III is A flat, while that of the final
scene is a free form of C major.

The germ from which the thematic material is derived consists of two
intervals, the semitone (in its two guises of minor second and major
seventh) and the augmented fourth

Ex. 40   Milner
                                                                     The Water and the Fire

Numerous expressive motifs are thus available, which occur throughout
the work. The simple juxtaposition of the two intervals lends a distinctive
flavour to melodic progressions, and matches the spirit of reverence and
awe with which the work opens. This is well illustrated by the motif
with which the chorus first appears, singing starkly in octaves, ff

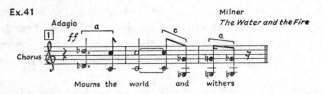

Ex.41   Milner
                                                                     The Water and the Fire

This is dramatically recalled in the final scene by the cellos, p. (at [56] +
3) to introduce the words 'Lord, I am not worthy'. At the very moment
of glory we are bidden to recall the earlier state of sin from which humanity
has been redeemed.

Other instances of the expressive use of these 'motivic' intervals occur
later in the first scene, when the Tenor cries out bleakly and desolately
'I looked and there was no man'

Ex.42   Milner
                                                                     The Water and the Fire

and towards the close of the second scene, at the words 'take up thy cross and follow me'

Ex.43   Milner
                                                   The Water and the Fire

Baritone

Take up thy cross   and   foll-ow   me.

In the first case, the semitone rises, suggesting anguish and tension; in the second case the semitone falls, with exactly the opposite effect.

Used chordally, the semitone interval leads to the clash of tonalities with which scene II opens,

Ex.44   Milner
          Sc.2   *The Water and the Fire*
          Lento molto

while the augmented fourth leads to the climactic chord of C major with which the chorus enter at the opening of scene IV.

Ex.45   Milner
                                                   The Water and the Fire

Choir

          Deo   Grat-   -i-   as

Orch.

Both intervals dominate the instrumental interlude joining scenes I and II. This interlude is ternary in form, the middle section consisting of the 16-bar melody of the first section inverted, and the third section consisting of a repeat of the first, with some decoration, a semitone lower; a subtle use of this interval, and one that is full of expressive power.

The falling semitone is used to form an accompaniment figure in scene I, at [2], to give colour to the word 'guilt', and again in scene II, starting at [20] + 6, where it is developed by the oboe into an independent accompanimental melody. It is referred to again briefly in scene III by the violins. The most striking instance of transformation, which is the hallmark of this work, is the soprano soloist's cry of '*Alleluia*' in the final scene, at [61] + 8, when the notes of the opening of the first scene have lost all their former anguish and torment, and become instead radiant and joyful.

Ex.46

Milner
The Water and the Fire

The opening of the fourth scene is the central moment. Structurally, dramatically, musically and emotionally it represents the centre of gravity of the work, that point towards which the listener has up to now been drawn, and without which a work of these dimensions would be stillborn. The introduction of boys' voices, first as a solo, then as a group, singing the *Lumen Christi* (taken from the procession that follows the blessing of the New Fire in the Vigil rite), provides just that necessary freshness. Three times we hear *Lumen Christi*; first at a great distance, then gradually drawing nearer. Each successive entry is higher in pitch, and louder, while the orchestral passages separating them, representing the slow movement of the procession, are made up of previously heard material. The *Allelluia* chant (from the Vigil Mass) is similarly treated; first by the choir basses, as a background to the happy duet of the tenor and soprano soloists; then somewhat louder, and at a higher pitch, by the choir tenors; then by the full choir.

For the hymn of triumph in the final scene, Milner divides his choir into two, and together with the two soloists, makes a glittering choral texture in ten parts. This outburst is immediately followed by the very quiet sound of boys' and men's voices singing 'as if from a great height', *a cappella*: '*Sanctus, sanctus, sanctus, Dominus Deus Sabaoth,*' They are joined by the full choir for the second phrase: '*Pleni sunt coeli et terra gloria tua. Hosanna in excelsis.*' For this music, Milner uses the *Sanctus* from his earlier *Mass*, Op. 3.

The strength of this work lies in its combining numerous different elements into a single, consistent artistic unit. The ritual of the fourth scene is the consummation of all that has gone before. Though the choral writing is simple, it is varied and highly colourful, with occasionally a high soprano part. The solo parts include every shade of expressive device except *Sprechgesang*, while instrumental colour is used for its association; flutes, for instance, in the final scene for their erotic association, and the organ for its religious association. Milner delights in using the full orchestral colour to depict the floods and the thunder in the first scene, and handbells to add to the ecstasy of the fourth.

After the oratorio, most of Milner's works were for instruments. These include a projected symphony, begun in 1965[1]. Not until 1969 did he write the next large-scale choral work, and this was very different from the oratorio. *Roman Spring*[2] is a three-movement secular cantata, sung in Latin, for soprano, tenor, chorus and chamber orchestra, in praise of love.

A slow introduction (*Largo molto*) with a wordless vocal melisma for the soprano, leads into a setting of the second-century *Pervigilium Veneris*, with its recurring motto, *Cras amet qui nunquam amavit quique amavit cras amet*. The music is jubilant, rhythmically lithe, and the idiom is considerably more chromatic than the oratorio of nine years previously. The vocal line frequently, if unwittingly, encompasses the twelve notes; for instance, the motto which the tenor first sings, *Cras amet*.

The second section is divided between the two soloists. The tenor starts (*moderato flessibile*) with a setting of the Horace ode *Diffugere nives*; after this the chorus and soprano are allotted a more philosophical passage from Lucretius' *De rerum natura*—surely the first time any of this poem has been set to music. Whereas the subject of the first section is the importance of love in the springtime of life, the second section reflects on the common human lot that all good things eventually pass from us.

The third section therefore concludes with the message: enjoy life, and love, while you can! Catullus' famous love-poem to his mistress Lesbia, *Vivamus mea Lesbia atque amemus*, is set as a recitative for the tenor, after which the chorus lead in with a rondo, *Tempus est jocundum*, a thirteenth century poem, in the manuscripts of Benedictbeurn. This brilliant rondo finale has alternating solos, and finishes with the *Cras amet* of the opening.

As well as a composer, Milner is also a lecturer, writer and harpsichordist. His early work with the Morley College choir under Tippett introduced him, at a very formative stage, to the music of many different schools and styles as well as Tippett's own works; to the English madrigal; to Monteverdi's *Vespers*, Purcell's Odes, and Cantatas of Bach and

1. To a commission from the London Symphony Orchestra.
2. Commissioned by the Redcliffe Concerts, and first played on 13th October 1969, at the Queen Elizabeth Hall. The following year it was performed again at the Camden Festival, and at a Promenade Concert.

Buxtehude, which he performed with the soprano Ilse Wolf. The cross-rhythm of the madrigalists fascinated him, while his interest in all aspects of musical history is reflected not only in his own compositions, but in his numerous essays and writings. These deal with the Baroque period, the sixteenth century, the work of Tippett, and the problems connected with present-day Roman Catholic church music, following the decision of the Vatican Council to allow the use of the vernacular.

Milner has been a frequent visitor to America. He was, for instance, the 'composer-in-residence' in 1965 and 1966 at Loyola University, New Orleans, at the summer school of Liturgy and Music.

Like Tippett, Milner's music has more of a long-term importance than an instant popularity. He was, unfortunately, extremely vulnerable to that swing of the pendulum of fashion which took place in England in about 1960; yet his very integrity, to say nothing of his instinct, caused him to discard the more experimental approach of the *avant-garde*, which might have earned him a momentary advantage. Milner is not interested in tricks or gimmicks of any kind; his challenge is the much more formidable one, in that he wrestles with tonality, and seeks out of a traditional idiom to forge a fresh technique, without recourse to any device, except those of whose worth he is convinced.

19 Michael Tippett

The work of Tippett, like that of Stravinsky, is a vital, organic, continuous growth; an astonishingly rich harvest of ideas; a fertile, imaginative synthesis of past tradition and present culture, sustained by a singleness of purpose. His creative thought has a psychological depth which, though it differs from that of Vaughan Williams in many particulars, nevertheless springs from the same source. Both show a firm sense of purpose, a long-term visionary quality, an ecstatic lyricism, which gives their best work a long-term relevance rather than an immediate popularity. Their roots go deep into the English tradition, while their thoughts range beyond the present into a wide view of the future; their tradition is thus nourished. The differences between the two composers are, in one sense, of less importance than their identity of purpose, and are due, in the main, simply to those differences of general outlook that you would expect to occur between one generation and the next. Tippett is post-jazz, post-Schoenberg, post-Jung and post-Vaughan Williams, though he has never adhered to any system or school.

His remarkably penetrating insight into the life of our time has, at all phases, coloured his compositions. The human, though all too rare, attributes of compassion, concern, optimism, which form the channel for his creativity, have their counterpart in that complexity and elaboration of rhythm and melody which have always been so fundamental to his technique. Indeed, complexity is of the essence of his thoughts, whether as a composer or a thinker; his music, like his personality, unfolds gradually, layer upon layer, deeper and deeper. Sometimes different layers interact; sometimes the underlying intention of a work shines through brilliantly and without impediment, and invests the whole composition with a force that burns with its enthusiasm. In *A Child of Our Time*, for instance, the underlying conception of a persecuted minority, is never lost sight of, and the work derives from this a compelling urgency. If the artist may be defined simply as one who is more responsive than others, Tippett is also aware of extra dimensions in contemporary life; the dark side as well as the light, the concealed as well as the apparent.

In purely instrumental works the complexity is more in the nature of the melodic, contrapuntal or rhythmic elaboration of a basically quite simple structure. Sometimes, in for instance the *Third String Quartet* and the *Second Symphony*, there grows out of the music an ecstatic lyricism that is quite unique in British music today.

He was born in 1905 of Cornish stock, and spent his early years at Wetherden in Suffolk. His student days at the Royal College of Music in London were based on the traditional harmonic teaching of the German school, handed down by Charles Wood, and before him by Stanford and Parry. The composer who dominated his student years, however, was Beethoven, particularly the Beethoven of the piano sonatas and string quartets. In addition to Beethoven, his musicality tended more towards that rhythmic drive and vigour, which is not found in the German harmonic approach to composition, but belongs more to the earlier polyphonic period. He also had a particular interest in word-setting, of which the English madrigal, and the songs of Dowland, provided such shining examples. These, however, found no place in the course of studies of the College, and it was the work of a Cambridge musician, also a former College student, Boris Ord, who founded the Cambridge University Madrigal Society in 1922, that gave such an inspiring lead in rediscovering the nature of the English madrigal.

And so, whereas Vaughan Williams had been drawn more to folk-song, on the one hand, and the austere 'one-note-per-syllable' style of the Tudor composers Gibbons and Tallis, on the other, Tippett was much more strongly, more instinctively, drawn to the style of Purcell. Moreover, he felt much more affinity with the neo-classic tendencies of Stravinsky (particularly with the additive rhythm technique of a work such as *Les Noces*) than with the neo-expressionism of the Schoenberg school. He could feel nothing but antipathy for the 'alphabetical' system of the 12-note technique.

Another strong influence in Tippett's musical make-up is that of jazz. He was attracted to it from the start. It seemed to him remarkable that the Blues, which started as such a simple, primitive folk-art, consisting of only twelve bars and three chords, endlessly repeated, should persist and flourish as it has. Here, surely, is proof of sheer artistic stamina and vitality; and the composer's problem is not so much to explain this extraordinary fact—any explanation would really be irrelevant—as to decide how he can adapt and use this means of expression in a purposeful way in his own work, so that it will sustain the emotional weight of his thought. In the Blues is a natural melancholy, decorated with an endless Baroque-style variation in the melodic part. Herein is contained a powerful means of expressing that anguish, which is the essence of the musical voice today; here is found a synthesis of musical styles, melodic and rhythmic, syllabic and melismatic, sophisticated and unsophisticated, which gives the art-form a broadly-based appeal.

As far as folk-song was concerned—that remarkable movement which sprang up simultaneously in many different European countries towards the end of the nineteenth century, and reached its climax about 1930— Tippett was never a field collector, as Vaughan Williams had been; nor did he share the purism of a Cecil Sharp, who dismissed *The Beggar's Opera* as spurious folk-song. Folk-song for Tippett is an art-form in embryo, an artistic principle, which may be perfectly legitimately used if the need arises for 'traditional material'. If he wants a folk-song for a particular purpose he will write one; as he did, for instance, in the *Suite in D* (1948), written for Prince Charles's birthday.

Tippett's most brilliant and colourful student-contemporary was Constant Lambert, and the view expressed in Lambert's *Music Ho*! that 'folk-songs in England are not a vigorous living tradition' was, and is, generally accepted. Folk-song had served a particular purpose at a particular period of British music; that period was past. There is, moreover, a basic dichotomy between a folk-song style and the requirements of symphonic form; and it is the latter that Tippett has wrestled with.

The years following his period as a student at the Royal College of Music were precarious ones for Tippett. He taught French for a while at a preparatory school, while evolving his technique and idiom as a composer in a comparatively humble capacity. While Constant Lambert pursued, with characteristic zest, the cosmopolitan world of the Russian Ballet, Tippett was drawn instinctively to the less glittering, more humdrum, yet more relevant and peculiarly English world of amateur music-making. If his work is to have a lasting life, a composer needs to have roots, secure and deep; and Tippett, like Vaughan Williams, has always recognized the importance of amateur music-making to the growth of the nation's musicality. His concern with this has covered his whole career and ranges from early operatic ventures, such as *Love in a Village* (1929), which he wrote for the local choral society at Oxted in Surrey, and *Robin Hood*, a one-act ballad opera, which he wrote for the miners of Cleveland in Yorkshire at a time (1931) of industrial depression; it includes his work at Morley College in London, where he remained as Music Director until 1951; it extends finally to his work with the

Leicestershire County Youth Orchestra, whom he took on a tour of Belgium in 1966, and conducted in programmes of music by English composers of this century. His *Shires Suite* (1970) was written for them.

By his fortieth year, the basic pattern of his work had begun to take shape in a way that was remarkably parallel to that of Vaughan Williams thirty years previously. The three most characteristic works by which Vaughan Williams was known by 1914 were the *Tallis Fantasia*, the *Sea Symphony*, and the settings of Housman poems for tenor, piano and string quartet, *On Wenlock Edge*; the three most characteristic works by which Tippett was known by 1945 were the *Concerto for Double String Orchestra*, the oratorio *A Child of our Time*, and the cantata for tenor and piano, on a prose-text by W. H. Hudson, *Boyhood's End*. A large number of compositions before 1935 were later withdrawn.

Tippett's style up to 1946, and his gradual evolution of an instrumental technique, is typified in the three string quartets. His fondness for quick harmonic change, and the interval of the fourth, and wide leaps within the space of a few beats, is already apparent in the *First String Quartet*, which was originally written in 1935, and revised in 1943.[1] The opening Sonata *Allegro* is full in texture throughout, except the cadenzas for the cello which mark the end of the exposition as well as the end of the movement. The tonality (D/A) is both clear and distinctive, with numerous clashes of the major and minor third, cross accents, and rapidly-moving harmonies. The second movement, in the remote key of D flat, develops a soaring melodic line, and grows out of the first 2-bar phrase, with a reprise at [24]. Again, the four instruments play throughout, and the texture is full. The final rondo introduces that added rhythm that so beguiled Tippett at this time. A metrical unit, in this case the ⅛th note (quaver), is treated with unequal bar divisions. But all the instruments move together. This distinguishes this technique from polyrhythm, which is the imposition of one rhythm upon another.

The *Second String Quartet* in F sharp develops further the style of the first. Its timing is important. It was written in 1942, after the *Concerto for Double String Orchestra* (1939) and *A Child of Our Time* (1941), but before *Boyhood's End* (1943) and the *First Symphony* (1945), to which it leads on directly. The opening *Allegro* is a continuous melody, with full four-part texture throughout; a polyphony of long, interweaving lines. The style of the movement is that of a sixteenth-century English madrigal, in which each part may have its own rhythm, and the music is propelled by the forward thrust of differing accents. Bar lines thus form a purely arbitrary division, which was also the case in the quartets of Van Dieren.

1. Dates throughout refer to the year of completion of a work.

The second movement is a fugue, whose minor tonality, and unitary structure, gives the music an intensity which is entirely in contrast with the ensuing *presto*. This once again uses the additive rhythm technique of the finale of the first quartet, and Tippett has aimed at a linear freedom suited for gay, fast music. The beats are alternately short and long, of two and three units, whether quavers or crotchets. It is a ternary movement, in three sections: three varied presentations of a single statement. The finale reverts to a classic sonata-form, whose image is dramatic, Beethoven-inspired. The cantabile second subject effects a marked tonal change into a flat key (E flat/A flat). The various sources of influence in this remarkable work show the chief preoccupations of Tippett at this time.

The *Third String Quartet* (1946) followed the *First Symphony*, and immediately the composer enjoyed the comparative rhythmic freedom of the smaller group. The opening *Grave* develops a recitative-like figure in $\frac{1}{32}$ notes (demi-semiquavers) for all the instruments over a slow pulse. This principle is further expanded in the fourth movement, as well as in certain other works; for instance in the third, slow song ('Compassion') of *The Heart's Assurance*, and in the slow movement of the *Second Symphony*. Thus Tippett sheds a glow of nervous excitement over a prevailingly slow-moving passage. Ripples of rapid sound catch the ear, yet without breaking the stillness. The rest of the first movement is a fugue, with a very long, melodic subject. If the flavour of the second movement, (*Andante*), is medieval, with a $\frac{2}{3}$ metre combined with $\frac{3}{4}$, and material which strongly suggests plainchant, the dance-like character of the third movement (*Allegro molto*) provides an entire contrast with its combination of $\frac{3}{8}$ with $\frac{4}{4}$, unison scales and rhythmic counterpoint. The freedom of such writing is only possible within the medium of a string quartet, since each line is a rhythmic entity of its own.

After the energy of the dance is spent, Tippett introduces a more contemplative mood. Against a held A in the second violin, the three other parts weave independent rhythms, each with different note values; an upward recitative-like phrase for solo cello leads to an *appassionato* phrase, followed by a calm moment, before the process is repeated. The shape of the melody is constructed in seconds, and the sentence is repeated three times, with the role of the instruments altered; the third time leads to a proliferation of the material in each part, and an ecstatic outburst, which forms the end of the movement. After this complexity, the comparative simplicity of the finale (*Allegro comodo*) affords just the right amount of contrast.

Before considering those mainstream works which form the core of his output, there remain some of the smaller vocal and keyboard pieces.

Neither of the two piano sonatas shows Tippett as naturally inclined to this instrument. The first, written in 1937, and revised in 1942, shares some of the same features as the *First String Quartet*, added rhythms, *presto* unisons, and so on, but without the contrapuntal drive. The *Second Sonata*, in one movement, followed *King Priam*, and is altogether tougher in idiom; but despite its formidable appearance on paper, it is predominantly a lyrical work. The little *Organ Prelude* (1945) was written to precede a performance of Monteverdi's *Vespers of 1610*, and quotes extensively from it. It is not really characteristic of Tippett.

On the other hand the two song cycles, *Boyhood's End* (1943) and *The Heart's Assurance* (1951), are fine examples of declamatory recitative and melodic word-setting. Tippett's characteristic added rhythms are shown to be verbally, as well as musically, adaptable, while the exuberant piano part of *The Heart's Assurance*, and its highly contrasted movements, make it, along with the *Third String Quartet*, a lasting contribution to the repertory.

The mainstream of his output has been marked by one or two climactic works, whose gestation and creation have cost great labour over a long period, and which have proved to be the source from which subsequent works have flowed. Thus the *Second Symphony* flows directly from *The Midsummer Marriage*, the *Concerto for Orchestra* directly from the opera *King Priam*. The fact that the seminal compositions tend to be in the form of opera or oratorio, and are not so much settings of words as settings of thoughts, ideas, dreams, is due partly to the fact that he is English, partly to his bent of mind. These mainstream works are the *Concerto for Double String Orchestra* (1939), the oratorio *A Child of Our Time* (1941), the operas *The Midsummer Marriage* (1952), *King Priam* (1962), *The Vision of Saint Augustine* (1965) and *The Knot Garden* (1970).

The first of these, the *Concerto*, has obvious affinities with Vaughan Williams's *Tallis Fantasia*; both composers were inspired by the medium of the string orchestra, which, in this century at least, is chiefly confined to England;[1] both compositions derived from a common source, the old English *Fancy*.

Another source-work for Tippett was Elgar's *Introduction and Allegro* for string quartet and string orchestra. But though Tippett looked on the two orchestras of his *Concerto* as vehicles for *concertante* effects, such as are sometimes found between the *Concertino* and *Ripieno* of the eighteenth century *Concerto Grosso*, the structure was Beethoven-inspired; a dramatic Sonata *Allegro*, a slow movement like a quartet, a Sonata *Rondo*.

1. There are a few notable works for string orchestra by American composers, for instance Barber's *Adagio*, Copland's *Nonet*.

A preoccupation with classical structure also marks the *First Symphony*. Again, the work opens with a dramatic Sonata *Allegro*, on a big scale. The second movement (*Adagio*), however, reaches back beyond Beethoven, to Purcell, with a set of mirror variations on a long ground bass. The *scherzo* reaches back further still, and combines the characteristics of a Beethoven *scherzo* with those of mediaeval hocket, such as shown in the work of Pérotin. The finale is an enormous double fugue.

Like Stravinsky before him, Tippett showed the inclination of many neoclassical composers to reach back to the techniques and inspiration of earlier periods of music, and apply them in his own work. Milner was to do the same. It was logical therefore that, also like Stravinsky, Tippett should re-think the structure of the orchestra itself, and the use of the instruments. The fruits of this line of thought were shown in the *Concerto for Orchestra* (1963).

Following *The Midsummer Marriage*, which was completed in 1952, and produced at Covent Garden in 1955, Tippett wrote several instrumental and orchestral works, such as the Corelli *Fantasia* (1953), the *Piano Concerto* (1955). This phase of his work culminated in the *Second Symphony* (1957). Tippett's idiom evolves markedly in this work. Not only is there a strong influence of Stravinsky, but the music is bolder, fresher than hitherto, with a foretaste of that vigour which Tippett has called a 'toughness' in the fibre of the music, that was to be fully discovered in the next mainstream work, *King Priam*. Once having found this, Tippett did not lose sight of it in the ensuing works. *King Priam* marks a turning-point in his style; the *Second Symphony* already shows this change beginning (see plate 9).

The composer himself has described the process underlying his work on this symphony:

About the time I was finishing *The Midsummer Marriage*, I was sitting one day in a small studio of Radio Lugano, looking out over the sunlit lake, listening to tapes of Vivaldi. Some pounding cello and bass Cs, as I remember them, suddenly threw me from Vivaldi's world into my own, and marked the exact moment of conception of the *Second Symphony*. Vivaldi's pounding Cs took on a kind of archetypal quality, as though to say: 'Here is where we must begin.' The *Second Symphony* does begin in that archetypal way, though the pounding Cs are no longer Vivaldi's. At once horns in open fifths, with F sharps, force the ear away from the C ground. I don't think we ever hear the Cs as classically stating the key of C. We only hear them as a base, or ground, upon which we can build, or from which we can take off in flight. When the Cs return at the end of the symphony, we feel satisfied, and the work completed, though the final chord, which is directed to 'let vibrate in the air', builds up from the base C thus:

$$C^{16} \; C^8 \; G \; C^4 \; D^2 \; A \; C \; E$$

T

It was some years after the incident in Lugano before I was ready to begin composition. While other works were being written, I pondered and prepared the symphony's structure: a dramatic Sonata Allegro: a song-form slow movement; a mirror-form scherzo in additive rhythm; a fantasia for a finale. Apart from the rather hazy memory of the Vivaldi Cs, I wrote down no themes or motives during this period. I prefer to invent the work's form in as great a detail as I can before I invent any sound whatever. But as the formal invention proceeds, textures, speeds, dynamics, become part of the formal process. So that one comes closer and closer to the sound itself until the moment when the dam breaks and the music of the opening bars spills out over the paper. As I reached this moment in the symphony, the B.B.C. commissioned the piece for the tenth anniversary of the Third Programme, but, in the event, I was a year late. It was performed first in the Royal Festival Hall, London, in February 1958, and conducted by Sir Adrian Boult.[1]

One of the vital matters to be decided in the period of gestation before composition, is the overall length; and then the kind of proportions that best fit this length. The symphony takes about thirty-five minutes to play, and its four movements are tolerably equal, though the slow movement is somewhat longer than the others. So it is not a long, spun-out, rhapsodic work, but a short, concentrated dramatic work. And this concentration, compression even, is made clear from the word go. The opening Sonata Allegro makes big dramatic gestures above the pounding opening Cs, and is driven along and never loiters. It divides itself into fairly equal quarters: statement, first argument, re-statement, second argument and coda. The lyrical quality of the slow movement is emphasised by presenting the 'song' of the song-form (after a short introduction) at first on divided cellos and later on divided violins. In between lies a lengthy and equally lyrical passage for all the string body. The wood and brass wind accompany the 'songs' with cluster-like chords, decorated by harp and piano. The movement ends with a tiny coda for the four horns, a sound I remembered from the *Sonata for Four Horns* which I had already written.

The scherzo is entirely in additive rhythm. Additive rhythm means simply that short beats of two quavers and long beats of three quavers are added together indefinitely in a continuous flow of unequal beats. The movement has been called an 'additive structure', which I think very well describes it. At the central point heavy long beats are contrasted against light short beats, in a kind of *tour de force* of inequality, issuing in a climax of sound with *brillante* trumpet to the fore. The movement then unwinds, via a cadenza-like passage for piano and harp alone, to its end.

The finale is a fantasia in that its four sections do not relate to each other, like the four sections of the first movement Sonata Allegro, but go their own way. Section 1 is short, and entirely introductory; Section 2 is the longest and is a close-knit set of variations on a ground; Section 3 is a very gay melody, which begins high up on violins and goes over at half-way to cellos, who take the line

---

1. There was a breakdown during this performance, owing to the work's complexity and shortage of rehearsal time.

down to their bottom note, the C of the original pounding Cs; Section 4 is a coda of five gestures of farewell.

Tippett's imagination is acute, his thought revolutionary, his musical personality complex. An artist who can, in the way he does[1], concern himself with the evanescent and incorporeal world of ideas beyond the confines of time or the senses, to the extent of setting the products of the spiritual imagination on equal terms with those of the world of technics, is both, in the worldly sense, unrealistic and, in the true sense, revolutionary—completing the cycle, and circle, of human life that today is so divided. He seeks with his art to heal that rift between material and technical progress on the one hand, and the things of the spirit on the other. Material abundance, he says, should encourage, not exclude, artistic growth. What better way is there of demonstrating this coming together, this oneness, of different people, or of people who have been driven apart by wars, racial tensions, or other human failings, than by means of an opera or oratorio which, if anything, is the artist's vision of a collective experience?

Tippett is a keen student of Greek literature and ideas; and indeed what better source of material is there than the legends, the mythology of old, which draw on the universal experience of mankind over an untold period of time, and which we know, by Jung's definition, as the 'collective unconscious'? Music's power to unify is one of its underlying characteristics; Tippett's interpretation of this in the contemporary situation is his unique contribution to contemporary music; and just as Stravinsky's aesthetic finds some expression in the words of Picasso, so that of Tippett is found to be paralleled in T. S. Eliot and W. B. Yeats.

The influence of T. S. Eliot is mainly seen in Tippett's attitude towards the problem of music in the theatre.[2] To be able to achieve stage effects is an essential part of an opera composer's technique; nothing can be left to chance; otherwise there is the greatest risk of slipping into the sort of operatic *cliché* which is very commonly found among less experienced composers. The composer needs to treat his libretto as the poet would, if it were to become a poem or a play. If the poet asserts his poetry too strongly, the composer's work is, to some extent, superfluous. A libretto, therefore, needs short lines, simple sentences, which the composer—not the poet—then completes. In order that the experience of an opera should be an immediate one, the material and the language need to be everyday, even ordinary. Eliot's play *The Cocktail Party* is an excellent example of this, and Tippett's own libretti are invariably of this nature.

1. As he described in *Moving into Aquarius.*
2. See *Moving into Aquarius.*

The *Concerto for Orchestra* not only followed *King Priam*; it arose out of it very directly, and used the material, the sonorities and the effects of the opera in a symphonic context. The instruments are grouped into various small *concertini*, and the work explores the combination and interaction of these vividly differentiated groups. The analogy with characters in a play is quite patent: they converse, interlock, juxtapose their contrasting arguments, and eventually revert to silence. In the first movement there are nine *concertini*. The first three (flute and harp; tuba and piano; three horns) are primarily melodic; the second three (timpani and piano; oboe, cor anglais, bassoon, double bassoon; two trombones and percussion) are primarily rhythmic; the third three (xylophone and piano, clarinet and bass clarinet, two trumpets and side-drum) are used for brilliance and speed.

A third of the movement is taken up with the statement of this material; this is followed by three working-out passages, in which the implications of the material are made explicit by instrumental juxtaposition. After the climax (a stroke on the gong) the music returns to the calm of the opening.

The strings are not used until the slow movement, and then only as a small group; eight violins (not divided into 'first' and 'seconds') four violas, five cellos, four basses. Moreover the light tone of the violins, playing in a small group, and capable of great virtuosity, is contrasted with the dark tone of violas, cellos and basses.

The finale uses mixed ensembles, strings and wind. The work as a whole is not so much one in which themes develop into a dramatic climax, which was the Beethoven principle, as a study in the sectional interaction of orchestral colour.

Whereas Eliot interpreted Christianity, Yeats 'wrestled with mythology'. For him, as for Goethe, mythology was reality; the contemporary and the mythological were one. Tippett was most influenced by Yeats at the time of *King Priam*. Helen's song in Act III is pure Yeats; particularly the words: 'For I am Zeus's daughter, conceived when the great wings beat above Leda.' At about the same time as *King Priam*, other settings of Yeats also appear, such as the *Lullaby for six voices*, and *Music for words, perhaps*.

The influence of Jung belongs to an earlier stage of Tippett's work. Apart from Jungian concepts, which he found congruent with his own at a particular period of his life, the metaphysical language seemed to him a way to express religious truths. 'I would know my shadow and my light, so shall I at last be whole,' is the Jungian philosophy which provides the closing moment in *A Child of Our Time*; and the motto which heads this work, taken from T. S. Eliot's *Murder in the Cathedral*, sums up the underlying theme of division and wholeness.

If generalisations about most composers are unsatisfactory, they are even more unsatisfactory in the case of Tippett. He has avoided self-repetition; each work is re-thought *de novo*; and the works written since *King Priam*, for instance the *Concerto for Orchestra* and *The Vision of Saint Augustine*, are in a starker, bolder idiom than those written before; they are still centred round a tonality, but it is a tonality built in fourths rather than thirds which give the work a certain acerbity.

The Operas

Opera, as we have seen, has developed steadily in England since 1945. The year 1955 was a particularly important one, with no fewer than four new productions by prominent composers. These were Lennox Berkeley's *Nelson*, Benjamin Britten's *The Turn of the Screw*, William Walton's *Troilus and Cressida*, and Michael Tippett's *The Midsummer Marriage*. It was the last work which held out the most promise for the future, not just of Tippett's creative career, but of English music in a wider context. Not that the opera was flawless by any means; indeed, if one merely wishes to point out its shortcomings, one will be disconcerted to find that the composer himself has already done so. Certainly it lacks the sense of theatre that Walton's work has in abundance; certainly Britten shows greater fluency and sheer technical adroitness; all this may be conceded: yet to weigh against these shortcomings, if they are shortcomings, Tippett brought nothing less than a totally fresh sense of purpose into opera—namely, dramatic unity through the fusion of opposing principles, the confrontation and the relationship of opposites, the welding of past traditions into the contemporary theatre. He thus sought to make common, age-old, timeless experiences relevant to us today. His music is magical.

Such a creative vision is of a basically different order from that of the composer who sees opera either as a play with music, or as a structure of related songs and choral ensembles. Any competent hack composer—to say nothing of the not-so-competent ones—can add musical icing to a ready-made dramatic cake. But Tippett's art is on an altogether different plane; he approaches the problem of opera from the other end. His concern is to express the eternal in terms of the temporal.[1] The universal, archetypal experience of humanity, which may be found symbolically expressed in mythological legends and folklore, is sought out and discovered by the receptive imagination of the artist, and re-interpreted for his contemporaries. In this respect Tippett is the successor of Berg, though very little influenced by him, if at all.

1. 'A timeless music played in time', as Hermes says at the end of *Priam*.

When *The Midsummer Marriage* was first produced in 1955 it caused bewilderment and confusion. The general impression was that, while the music itself was the equal of any of Tippett's other work (indeed, the *Ritual Dances* are frequently performed as an orchestral suite), the success of the opera as a whole was gravely impaired by an unnecessarily involved and dramatically motionless libretto. If only the composer had not written it himself! If only the dramatic interest equalled the musical!

Thirteen years later the opera was produced again, under Colin Davis. In the intervening years the serialist and *avant-garde* movements of the late 50's and 60's had gathered momentum, with the result that audiences were becoming somewhat less conservative, and more aware of new developments; and so, when *The Midsummer Marriage* was repeated, the public had grown more ready to accept the work on its own terms, and this time it was hailed as an unqualified success. A recording was arranged[1]; the former difficulties seemed, in retrospect, to be more apparent than real.

And yet the opera interprets past dramatic and operatic traditions in a highly personal way; it possesses what Tippett calls 'singularities', which its successor, *King Priam*, does not. *King Priam* is a more readily understood, heroic, tragic opera.

If in *The Midsummer Marriage*, whose theme is love, he did not quite succeed in projecting the somewhat static situation and nature of his characters with the dynamic of structural unity and dramatic urgency, no such qualification applies to *King Priam*, whose theme is war. In *The Midsummer Marriage* he sought to compose a sort of twentieth-century *Magic Flute*; but the symbolism and imagery are difficult to comprehend to anyone not acquainted with Hindu mythology or Fraser's *Golden Bough*. Moreover, the opera consists in a sequence of symbolic ideas rather than a succession of inevitable events; as a result, the conclusion towards which we are drawn, the union of the lovers, does not provide the work with that psychological centre of gravity that it needs if it is to be presented convincingly on the stage. The action may be symbolically meaningful, but that does not necessarily make it relevant to us. But for anyone who can overcome this initial challenge, the spark of true inspiration is there, and Tippett reveals a totally fresh world of artistic experience. When he pursued this in another opera, whose theme and events were of very direct concern to Europeans in the 1960's, the result could hardly fail to be an explosive challenge of the greatest importance to the history of opera and of contemporary music generally.

In *King Priam* Tippett took the traditional story of the sack of Troy

1. Sponsored by the British Council.

by the Greeks, and told it from the Trojan (i.e. the defeated enemy) point of view. Here was a theme that all understood: war, with its pity and its terror. Priam is made a tragic hero. Love is certainly a timeless theme, if ever there was one; but the main advantage of his choosing the Trojan war as the subject for his second opera was that he found not only a great theme, with other subsidiary themes, love included, deriving from it, but also a traditional and well-known story, which would act as a framework for the theme. Imagery there certainly is in *King Priam*, but it is immediately recognizable, relevant and dramatic because we relate it without doubt or difficulty to the events. Moreover, the second opera has a realism not found in the first. If we need points of reference, they are to be found in Wagner, Stravinsky, Brecht, T. S. Eliot.

In *King Priam* Tippett does not confine the action to a single time or place: the duration of the opera is the life span of Priam's son Paris. Scenes also shift. As with his first opera, and *A Child of Our Time*, Tippett wrote his own libretto. A starting-point from which to study the construction and the composition of the work is provided by the four principles which he himself laid down[1], and which form a sort of aesthetic philosophy of his work as an opera composer:

1) Opera is ultimately dependent on the contemporary theatre.
2) The more collective an artistic imaginative experience is going to be, the more the discovery of suitable material is involuntary.
3) While the collective, mythological material is always traditional, the specific twentieth-century quality is the power to transmute such material into an immediate experience of our day.
4) In opera the musical schemes are always dictated by the situations.

Tippett has drawn up a corresponding musical scheme, in accordance with these principles.

ACT I

Scene 1 A chorus of lament is heard off-stage; a baby cries, and a point of light falls on a cradle. The child's mother, Hecuba, wife of Priam, King of Troy, is disturbed by a dream which she cannot understand. This is interpreted by an old man to mean that the child, Paris, will be the cause of his father's death. Priam, therefore, decides that the child must be killed, and orders a guard to do this.

Interlude 1: The old man, a nurse, and the guard reflect on this dilemma; child-murder is a crime, but what if it is your duty?

Scene 2 Some years later Priam's eldest son, Hector, while out hunting, meets his brother Paris, who has been brought up secretly all this time by a shepherd[2]. Paris chooses to go to Troy, and when asked outright, gives his name. Priam

1. In *The Birth of an Opera* (from *Moving into Aquarius*).
2. A common feature of legends; cf. the story of Oedipus.

reflects on this trick of fate. Will the old prophecy come true? He nevertheless accepts his son's choice.

Interlude 2: The old man, nurse, and guard see life as a 'bitter charade'. Hector meanwhile has found a perfect wife in Andromache, while Paris leaves Troy in disgust, and sails to Greece, where the King of Sparta, Menelaus, and his wife, Helen, 'keep open house'.

Scene 3 Paris is enamoured of and captivated by Helen. He persuades her to leave Menelaus and go to Troy with him as his wife. Hermes, the messenger of the gods, comes to him in a dream, and tells him to choose between the three goddesses, Athene, Hera and Aphrodite. Athene appears to him as Hecuba, representing prudence; Hera as Andromache, representing faithfulness; and Aphrodite as Helen, representing the 'eternal feminine' principle[1]. In spite of warnings of the inevitable vengeance that will follow, he chooses Aphrodite.

ACT II

Scene 1 The ten-year Trojan war is now approaching its terrible climax. Hector the soldier chides Paris the adulterer, and expresses more respect for the Greek Menelaus than for his own brother. Priam tries to mediate, and urges them to fight the enemy, not each other.

Interlude 1: Hermes takes the old man (thereby also the audience) over to the Greek camp, to Achilles' tent.

Scene 2 Achilles and his friend Patroclus look back nostalgically to their childhood in Greece. Now, however, Achilles has quarrelled with Agamemnon, the Greek Commander-in-Chief, over the ownership of a captive girl, Briseis, and has refused to fight. But a plan is worked out, whereby Patroclus, wearing Achilles' armour, shall pretend to be Achilles, and go into battle against the Trojans.

Interlude 2: A threat to Troy is foreseen.

Scene 3 Back in Troy, we hear that Patroclus, in Achilles' armour, led the Greeks up to the walls, only to be killed by Hector in single combat. Priam, Hector and Paris sing a hymn of thanks to Zeus. At that moment, from the Greek side, Achilles utters his war-cry of vengeance for Patroclus.

ACT III

Scene 1 Hecuba, Andromache and Helen express their different loves and loyalties; to the city, to the home, to love itself. Hecuba tries to mediate when the other two quarrel. Andromache has an intuitive premonition of Hector's death.

Interlude 1: News of Hector's death spreads: All but King Priam have heard. Who will tell him?

Scene 2 It falls to Paris to tell his father the news of Hector's death and mutilation at the hands of Achilles. He vows to kill Achilles in return; whereupon Priam contemplates the unbreakable cycle of vengeance. Hector killed Patroclus, and Achilles in revenge killed Hector; Paris will in turn seek revenge by killing Achilles; who will then kill Paris? Why was he not killed as a baby?

1. The 3-fold nature of woman is a Freudian conception.

It was the fatal flaw of pity. Yet why should one son (Hector) be allowed to live only if it meant the death of the other (Paris)? Life is a trick, without meaning.

Interlude 2: Instrumental music, to suggest the passage of time; the past leading to the present, and both making up the future.

Scene 3 Hermes brings Priam, unarmed, to Achilles' tent to ransom his son Hector's body. Achilles is moved by pity for the old man—(that 'fatal flaw' again?)—and grants his request. They drink, and their deaths are foretold, Achilles at the hands of Paris, Priam at the hands of Achilles' son, Neoptolemus.

Interlude 3: Hermes prepares the audience for Priam's death and transformation: 'He already breathes an air as from another planet.'[1]

Scene 4 Paris kills Achilles, but too late, since Troy is being sacked by the Greeks and is already burning. Once more the three women come, this time to care for Priam; once more Hecuba and Andromache give place to Helen, who is tenderly addressed by Priam, after he has sent out Paris to a hero's death in the flames of Troy. Priam kisses Helen, who he knows will now return to Greece. He himself then sinks before the altar, where Achilles's son Neoptolemus, as had been foretold, runs him through with a sword.

In telling the story from the Trojan point of view, thus making the old king the central character of his opera, Tippett deliberately challenges us to look at the theme of war through the eyes of compassion and understanding. Priam loved his son Hector just as much as Achilles loved his friend Patroclus; more, if anything, as he was older; therefore he suffered just as much when he was killed. Yet, if we try to find the answer to this human riddle we will not succeed, since human conduct has no satisfactory rational explanation. Priam may curse, he may invoke all the gods he knows, he may turn this way or that, but it is not given to him to understand. War has no meaning. Yet, paradoxically, he does not need to understand in order to provide the solution. He goes to Achilles himself, using only the weapon of pity for an old man. This not only achieves its purpose, but it is a course of action which brings no retribution in its train. On the contrary: the two drink together.

Another thing Priam does. He first of all dismisses Paris; and by doing this he shows that wars are fought by the young, not by the old, and that his function is not on the field of battle. Then he forgives Helen. This is entirely in keeping with the end of Homer's *Iliad*, and lends a truly noble air to the end of the opera. Helen had been the ostensible cause of the whole war, as a result of which Priam's city was destroyed; yet he forgives her. He might well have asked her 'Why?'; but such a question, as we know, can have no answer. The opera ends with the chords depicting the theme of war, sounding, very quietly this

1. For this idea of transformation, compare the myth of the journey of the soul in Plato's *Phaedrus* (247 foll.).

time, for Priam himself. His death at the close of the opera is simply the
final stage of that transformation, which had already begun.

The fusion of opposing principles is everywhere apparent in *King
Priam*: life and death, friend and foe, heaven and hell, choice and
destiny. Tippett's artistry is a receptiveness to the inner as well as the
outer meaning of events. He is concerned with the mysterious nature of
human choice; and the character whose choice is most central to the
whole story is Paris. Paris is much more than a sort of epic Casanova; he
represents that archetypal principle of search, inspiration, passion. But
because his search is directed towards a fantasy, an unreal phantom[1], it
can never be fulfilled. His cry 'Is there a choice at all?' might well be the
motto of the whole opera.

In Act I Priam chooses to have his son killed; later Paris chooses to go
to Troy, and Priam chooses to accept this decision. Most important of all,
Helen chooses Paris, Paris chooses Helen. It seems they are driven by a
force stronger than themselves; yet the choice is theirs. In Act II Achilles
chooses not to fight, Patroclus chooses to take his place; whereupon
Achilles chooses to avenge Patroclus' death. In Act III each of the
three women chooses her loyalty; Paris chooses to avenge Hector, his
brother; finally, Priam makes the two culminating choices of the opera,
to confront Achilles and to forgive Helen. In every case, the choice was
freely taken, freely followed by the deed; in no case could the result of
the deed be foreseen.

The opera moves forward to its appointed end with an irresistible
sweep of inevitability. In Act I the events and the premonitions surrounding Paris, all the more ominous for being vague and unspecified, pile up
and accumulate a dramatic tension that erupts, starkly and violently, in
Act II, the 'war act'. The resolution occurs in Act III, in which the
implications of what has gone before are seen in their true light. This
dramatic inevitability is matched by a remarkable structural cohesion
and balance. The number three is used as a unifying factor. There are
three acts, two of them with three scenes. Three male characters (Priam,
Hector, Paris) balance three female characters (Hecuba, Andromache,
Helen), and they each have trios. The Chorus consists of three people
(old man, nurse, guard). At the opening, the introductory chorus occurs
three times; at the close of the opera, the 'war' chord is sounded three
times; at the centre of the most violent part of the opera, Achilles' war
cry rings out three times.

There are also several points of cross-reference and symbolism in the
opera, which serve to unite the parts into a single compelling whole. For

---

1. For the idea of Helen as a phantom, cf. Plato's *Republic* (IX, 585); also Euripides'
Helena.

instance, Priam's attempt to mediate between his sons' quarrel is balanced by Hecuba's attempt to keep Andromache and Helen apart. Again, on the psychological level, the flames that consume Troy symbolize the burning flame of love that consume Helen and Paris, that ecstasy that brings tragedy in its wake.

But far the greatest unifying factor is the music itself. That fusion of opposites in the personalities of the story is matched by the fusion of words and music, consonance and dissonance, present and past time, that make up Tippett's score. The characters are contrasted by means of motif and instrumentation. The theme of war and killing is given to the brass, woodwind, and timpani. This feature of the orchestration reaches its climax in Act II, the war act, when Tippett leaves out the strings altogether, except the piano and guitar. The latter is used for Achilles' sentimental and nostalgic song. The idea of the home, on the other hand, and the domestic love of women, is expressed by the strings. Hecuba's motif is given out by the violins, in agitated sextuplets, while that of Andromache is a more intensely lyrical melody for cellos alone. The love of Helen and Paris is expressed by flutes, the instrument with traditional erotic associations. The harp is used to suggest the imagery of dreams, and the world of the unconscious. Flute and harp together are used, in Interlude 3 of Act III, for the music of the transformation of Priam.

Tippett's instinct for instrumental *timbre* is nowhere more apparent than in the score of *King Priam* generally, and in his use of the piano in particular. The opera almost amounts to a compendium of writing for the piano, which curiously chameleon-like tends to vary its nature according to its surroundings. The use of piano and xylophone is especially remarkable, and reminds us of Yeats's 'drum, flute and zither'[1]—or rhythm, melody and accompaniment; the rhythm in this case being provided by the somewhat hard and percussive sound of the xylophone.

The underlying motif of the entire opera is made up of two fourths, a perfect fourth with an augmented fourth superimposed

Ex.47   Tippett
                                              King Priam

War motif

This is used either melodically or chordally to express the theme of war, violence, killing. If its appearance is gradual in Act I, in Act II, as we

1. See *Moving into Aquarius.*

would expect, it is the main formative element. It opens the act, played
ff on the timpani

and it brings the act to a blood-curdling close, when it is used to form
Achilles' war-cry

But in addition to this, the augmented fourth is also used to express the
love between Helen and Paris (which takes place off-stage, as this is not
a Romantic opera). The love-scene at the end of Act I begins with it:

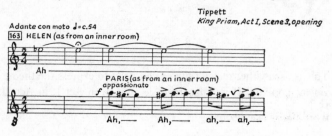

Paris's lyrical outburst later in the same scene is built round it:

Ex.51   Tippett
                                                              King Priam, Act I, Scene 3

The implication of this is quite clear, namely that the addition of the augmented fourth to the perfect fourth produced the motif of war in just as direct a way as the love of Helen and Paris led to war.

In Act I, as we have already said, the motif is introduced subtly; only later do we recall its use, and realize its full implication. It is present in Scene 1 in the violin music which accompanies Hecuba's outburst. In Scene 3, it appears when the identical passage is played on the timpani to introduce each of the three goddesses: and again when Helen is on the point of committing herself to Paris. This reminds us of the opening of the opera, when a solo oboe had played over the crib where the infant Paris lay. Now an oboe again plays, at the words 'how can I choose?', but this time a more menacing phrase

Ex.52   Tippett
                                                              King Priam, Act I, Scene 3

Once the fateful choice has been made, the motif appears more blatantly, boldly stated by the violins.

The motif insistently dominates Act II. It forms a biting, chordal accompaniment to Paris's defence of himself against Hector in Scene 1;

Ex.53
Tippett
King Priam, Act II, Scene I

it gives lyrical shape to Achilles' song in Scene 2; it is used with overwhelming effect, both horizontally in the melody and vertically in the harmony, to build up the three-part texture of the hymn to Zeus, which consists of 36 bars of imitative counterpoint, to a brilliant accompaniment of brass and woodwind.

In Act III Tippett uses the motif retrospectively, to remind us of the theme of war, which is the cause from which the remaining events in the opera stem. In Scene 1, when Helen says to Hecuba (referring to Andromache) 'Let her rave', the motif, played very quietly, just once, as a chord, is enough to remind us that Andromache at least has cause to rave, as her husband Hector is about to be killed. A little later, when Helen sings 'Women like you cannot know what men may feel with me', again the motif sounds out, to remind us what the consequences were of her adultery. The trio of the three women, like that of the men in the previous act, is also built horizontally and vertically round the motif. This trio, however, has a delicate, filigree accompaniment of strings and harp. The notes of the motif are such as to lead to an effect of bitonality—E flat major and D major—and Tippett makes magical use of this tendency.

Ex.54
Tippett
King Priam, Act III, Scene I

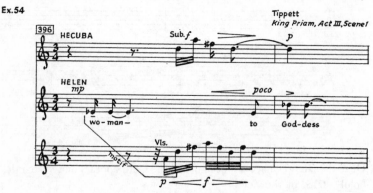

The juxtaposition of two keys a semitone apart also explains the prevalent use of the interval of the second, which is apparent throughout the opera; for instance, at the very opening of the work, in the trumpet fanfare.

At the close of Scene 3, in which Achilles and Priam look ahead to their own deaths, the motif appears again on the timpani, but with an important alteration, a diminuendo. Thus is the final transformation foreshadowed. This occurs during the third interlude, in which the motif is played on the harp as an accompaniment.

When it appears as a sudden brief outburst by the brass, at the beginning of Scene 4, it comes as a shock. The chords introduce Paris the soldier, who has killed Achilles. Thereafter, the motif appears metamorphosed. The three women appear one by one, and each one is introduced, as she had been in Act I, by an identical statement of the motif, made up of three parts each in diminution

Ex. 55

Tippett
King Priam, Act III, Scene 4

From then on the motif is sustained more or less continuously, either by the strings, or by the off-stage chorus. The timpani sound it as a final *ostinato* figure, ff. *marcatissimo*, as Priam is killed; then a moment of stillness; then, as if from eternity itself, it sounds three times, very quietly on the celesta, xylophone, piano, solo cello and double basses. It is as if a bell has tolled, not just for Priam, but for the whole of warring mankind.

After the comparatively direct impact of *King Priam*, Tippett reverted to a more individual and personal interpretation of contemporary opera for his third work, *The Knot Garden*[1]. His libretto for this opera is in direct descent from *The Midsummer Marriage*, and invites participation as well as rapport of understanding from the audience. The 'singularities' return, and Tippett's third opera is a synthesis of several past traditions into a contemporary setting.

1. Première at Covent Garden in December, 1970, conducted by Colin Davis, produced by Peter Hall (formerly Director of the Royal Shakespeare Company).

The title refers to the square gardens of Elizabethan days, with their patterns of flowers or shrub-beds. The ground-plans of these gardens look exactly like Eastern mandalas. The Elizabethan gardens were either lovers' meeting-places or mazes where people became lost. So in this opera the archetypal division is drawn between the rose-garden and the labyrinth. As the personal relations between the characters become warm, the scene appears to turn towards the rose garden; as they become cold, the scene appears more like the cage of a labyrinth.

Of the two main dramatic traditions which underlie Tippett's libretto, the first is the Shakespeare of the late ironic tragi-comedies, like *Measure for Measure*, *All's Well that Ends Well*, and *The Tempest*. These may be described as comedies of forgiveness. Everything is awry, even wicked, cruel and immoral, and can only be restored at the end of the play through an act of contrition, and consequent forgiveness. There is a long, late mediaeval, pre-Shakespearean, Christian tradition of tragi-comedy, which is largely Spanish; Shakespeare introduces a more humanist approach, though his characters often appear arbitrary. Thus, for instance, Isabella in *Measure for Measure* is a too-moral heroine, who has to forgive and marry, by order of the Duke, a man who has committed every sort of crime. In *The Tempest*, forgiveness is suggested to the all-powerful Prospero by Ariel, who recalls his master to a sense of humanity. And even Caliban is to have a measure of pardon.

The other tradition behind *The Knot Garden* is the Shaw of *Heartbreak House*. This play, which Shaw wrote after seeing Chekhov's *The Cherry Orchard*, is a pattern of cross-relationships within a comedy of social manners. *The Knot Garden* could well be an operatic *Heartbreak House* in the sort of permissive young society which Shaw foresaw in *Too True to be Good*.

The operatic tradition is that of *Cosi fan tutte*, which has the same almost arbitrary patterns of relationship, and in which everything is awry until the very end, when the women are contrite and the men forgive. In this theatrical *genre* the story-line is generally of less importance than the patterns of relationship. The opening can often be arbitrary, such as Don Alfonso's wager in *Cosi fan tutte*; and the end occurs simply when all the 'games' have been played—as in Edward Albee's *Who's Afraid of Virginia Woolf?*, which is a recent example of this tradition.

These 'games' imply a fixed set of characters, like pieces in chess. There is also some implied relationship between the characters at the start, which permutates as the work proceeds. In Act I of *The Knot Garden* these initial relationships are set out under the sub-title 'confrontation'. The underlying emotional insecurities, and even cruelties, first reach a climax when the too-moral Denise (a character taken from the examples of women in the French Resistance) denounces the rest, in a big aria. The only alleviation to this is a Blues, a big ensemble.

In Act II, the 'Labyrinth' of the sub-title is in full effect, and the emotional violence breaks surface, as if in a nightmare. This act consists of a series of dialogues and duets. Only at the end of the act is there a hint of alleviation; this is a love-song, which first recalls the nostalgia of Schubert, then the nostalgia of the present day. The archetypal rose-garden forms and fades.

In Act III, subtitled 'Charade', the 'games' as such begin, in the form of charades from *The Tempest*. Five of the seven characters take on parts from *The Tempest* in play scenes alluded to by Prospero. These are not real scenes from Shakespeare's play; of the four 'games', two are hinted at in Shakespeare, one has an exactly opposite outcome, one is not mentioned at all. But these charades are, as in Albee's play, a kind of therapy. The final ensemble, matching the Blues of Act I, deals with the very brief moment of mutual love and acceptance ('Come unto these yellow sands') before separation and departure.

The epilogue for the man and wife is, in spirit not style, Blake. When we are 'all imagination' and not imprisoned by memory, we create the world around us, even to the stars. And the final scene, of man and wife about to join, is taken, in form not words, from the real Virginia Woolf. It comes at the end of her last novel *Between the Acts*—which would have made an alternative title for *The Knot Garden*.

Though the opera has no chorus, and only seven characters, the musical gestures are often large, commensurate with a big theatre. The music itself is multifarious and rich, and all the roles are important. The social problems implied, such as black and white relationships, and homosexuality, are not the essence of the text; yet the statements the characters make about these matters, out of their direct experience of them, are real.

The techniques of film-cutting have suggested the 'jumps' from situation to situation, and scene to scene. But film can cut instantaneously, while opera, for musical reasons, cannot. The 'cut' or 'dissolve' has therefore been provided with a tiny measure of strictly impersonal and unchanging music, which becomes then part of the score. The stage scene at any moment—what the spectators see—is never described in the text, and there are no stage directions beyond some cocktail glasses and a chessboard. The Garden, by implication, is huge, and the night-sky immense; but the cruel dialogues of Act II are hemmed in by their intensity so that the stage space has become temporarily a point.

In his third opera, which again presents contemporary opera with the challenge of a fresh dimension, as *The Midsummer Marriage* did,

U

Tippett achieves a remarkable synthesis between past tradition and present culture. He adheres absolutely to his belief that contemporary opera is ultimately dependent on the contemporary theatre—and indeed contemporary literature, and life in the widest sense. If we accept Dent's classification of opera into mythical, heroic and comic, Tippett's *The Knot Garden* belongs to the first and third. It is certainly not heroic, as *King Priam* is. Indeed, Miranda's 'brave new world' is shown to be an illusion; after the four 'games' are played, the only solution that is possible lies through forgiveness.

VI The contemporary scene

20 Electronic music and the *Avant-garde*

Electronic Music

Electronic music was both inevitable and necessary in the evolution of the Western contemporary tradition; and just as important as its technological basis is its underlying philosophy. It is important to differentiate between creative energy and creative originality; both have their place in different situations. The energy which drives a composer to discover existing sounds, or to invent new ones, is not necessarily synonymous with the originality which invests a sound with musical meaning. To take a simple example, when writing his *Violin Concerto*, Beethoven took the scale of D major—a sound which had been musical common property for centuries. But to raise this from the level of a mere sound to the status of a musical theme called not for energy so much as originality. In thus focusing his creativity onto the 'meaning' more than onto the 'sound', Beethoven was closely reflecting the Romantic philosophy of his age, which we may read, in its literary expression, in the work of E.T.A Hoffmann or Goethe.

In 1920, when Schoenberg first formulated the 12-note technique, it was not possible to foresee the goal of total serialism to which, thirty years later, that path would lead, and towards which his new style of composition represented the first, tentative step. All that was possible was to identify the philosophical basis on which Schoenberg built, which was linguistic, mathematical; the musical extension of Wittgenstein's logical philosophy, and the 'Vienna Circle'.

So today electronic music is at a correspondingly early stage of development. It is impossible to foretell what lies at the end of the path; it is only possible to identify its philosophical *raison d'être*, which, as in the case of Schoenberg's style, is linguistic, mathematical.

Coming at the end of the Romantic period, Schoenberg also realized and took advantage of the climate of *avant-garde* thought in his day, which was broadly speaking, in many branches of philosophic activity, the avoidance of linguistic abuse, and the search for the logical expression of meaning. In evolving the note-row, he was similarly seeking to avoid the 'abuse' of pre-conceived tonal and melodic associations in his music, and to discover the 'new logic'. The numbers of a series, in later serial composition, are precisely analogous to the variables of logical philosophy. The Beethoven-process is thus reversed, and the composer's creative energy is focused onto the 'sound' more than onto the 'meaning'. In fact, the 'meaning' *becomes* the 'sound', and the composer's originality consists in his logical invention of sounds, and the manipulation of the series.

Coming at the end of the serial period, the electronic composer finds that the climate of *avant-garde* thought is still concerned with linguistic and scientific logic, but, in an age of computer-technology, this now takes on an unprecedented scientific precision in the exact analysis of sounds.

Just as the creative energy of the philosophical leaders in Schoenberg's day was directed not to the invention of new philosophical propositions, but to the avoidance of linguistic abuse in the presentation of existing ones, so this principle still holds today, when the climate of thought now favours an even closer inspection and analysis of life as it is, with all the advantages of a scientific age to assist towards this end. It is the main characteristic of an Alexandrian period, such as ours, that its energies are spent in questioning, analysing, discovering what already exists, not in originating new concepts and insights. The mere act of discovery, it is believed today, will bring its own insight.

The electronic composer reflects this philosophy. He explores and explains the nature of sounds, which he breaks down into parameters, then reconstructs. As the technological means of achieving this is so complex, it has taken a much longer time to arrive at a system than Schoenberg took in first evolving his 12-note style. But the principle is similar: the composer is expected to use his energy in logically analysing and synthesizing sounds, not his originality in giving them meaning— such a romantic concept, it is held, belongs to a past age, and to an out-of-date philosophy.

Electronic music is not just a new sort of sound; it is a new way of communicating sound, with a precision hitherto unknown to the musician. Conventional notation allows the performer wide scope for his personal artistic judgement; with each performance, the performer becomes to some extent the composer's colleague in bringing the work to life. Giving rhythmic and dynamic life to a phrase has always been an integral part of the performer's art, and the exact interpretation of a marking, such as mf, or *accel.*, and the exact degree of die-away at the end of a phrase, has always been a matter for the performer's individual judgement. But with the arrival of the computer and the tape recorder the composer of electronic music has become his own performer, to a degree of exactness hitherto undreamt of. On the principle of the parameters, composition has become organized sound; and since it is done by computer, this organization is exact down to the smallest detail.

The story of the beginning of electronic music in Paris and Cologne is well-known. The *musique concrète* of Pierre Schaeffer, and his *Concert des Bruits*, dates from 1948, and studios were built in the early 50's in Cologne (1953), under Stockhausen and Eimert, and Milan (1954) under Maderna and Berio. These developments all took place, significantly, in association with radio stations; and indeed the first piece of electronic music, *Musica su due dimensione* for flute and tape (1951), was composed by Maderna and Dr. Werner Meyer-Eppler, who was a lecturer in communications technique at Bonn University. Parallel developments took place in America, mainly centred on universities; particularly notable, and first, were Ussachevsky and Luening at Columbia. Thereafter composers developed their various concepts of serialism in the new medium; Eimert, Stockhausen, Xenakis, Berio, Barband, and many others.

Electronic music may be said to have begun in England on 15th January 1968, when the first concert of works by British composers took place in London.[1] It was the work of two musicians, Tristram Cary and Peter Zinovieff, and represented the stage then reached in this country. The programme was:

1.	Potpourri	Delia Derbyshire
2.	Diversed mind	Ernest Berk
3.	3 4 5	Tristram Cary
4.	Birth is life is power is death is God is . . .	Tristram Cary
5.	December Quartet	Peter Zinovieff
6.	Contrasts Essconic (for piano and tape)	Daphne Oram and
	Interval	Ivor Walsworth
7.	Partita for unattended computer	Peter Zinovieff
8.	Silent Spring	George Newson
9.	Syntheses 8, 9 and 12	Jacob Meyerowitz
10.	Agnus Dei	Peter Zinovieff
11.	March probabilistic	Peter Zinovieff and Alan Sutcliffe.

The first piece was made in the B.B.C. radiophonic workshop; all the others were made in private studios. This first concert excited considerable interest, but it did show up the handicaps under which most

1. Given by the Redcliffe Concerts at the Queen Elizabeth Hall.

British composers work in this medium without a properly equipped studio. Some of the tapes were merely sound effects, at a primitive stage of development. Electronic composition presupposes sophisticated techniques. Soon, therefore, various somewhat tentative studios began to be assembled—at Manchester and York Universities, at King's College, Cambridge, at Goldsmith's College, and at the Royal College of Music in London, where Tristram Cary began a class.

Cary and Zinovieff jointly gave another concert the following year (February 1969), and this was followed by the setting up of the British Society for Electronic Music, whose chief purpose was to raise money to build a properly equipped national studio.

If this project is still (in 1970) an unfulfilled dream, certain important technical developments have meanwhile been pursued by Peter Zinovieff, whose computerized studio at Putney is far the most advanced in the country. Starting in 1962, he developed an electronic music system, *Musys*, in collaboration with David Cockerell and Peter Grogono. His studio is unique, both in the design of the audio devices, which are controlled directly by digital computers, and in the programmes, which implement a comprehensive and sophisticated language for musicians (see plate 13). This could be adapted by any studio with a simple computer, and a few simple hardware devices and converters.

The musical idea, once compiled, is fed into the faster of the two computers in the form of a programme, which must be exact in every detail. The studio is a hybrid of two types of machine, digital and analogue. The digital part consists of two general purpose computers and devices for feeding information into them. The analogue parts are mostly special purpose machines which convert the essentially numerical signals from the computers into the electronic equivalents of sound pressure waves. The function of the computers could thus be compared with that of an orchestral conductor, and that of the analogue devices with that of the players—except that, in this case, only the conductor has the score.

The digital hardware consists of two D.E.C. PDP8 computers, a disc file and fast paper tape reader/punch, to which a magnetic tape drive is added. The PDP8 computer is cheap and reliable and has a simple interrupt and input/output system, which makes it very suitable for real-time applications. One of the devices connected to the interrupt line is a crystal clock, which delivers synchronizing pulses at 400Hz or a sub-multiple of this frequency: the resulting resolution of 2.5ms has been found adequate for music realized in the studio. For complex pieces, multi-tracking is used, and synchronization between tracks is achieved by recording the 400Hz pulse train on a guide track. There are also 10KHz digital-analogue and analogue-digital converters connected to the faster computer (PDP8/L) but apart from simple experiments in waveform synthesis and simulated reverberation these have been used in visual display systems rather than music.

The computers control the pitch, tuning, amplitude, waveform and envelope of three banks of oscillators, each covering seven octaves; the 'Q', gain and response mode of 64 narrow passband filters, placed at semitone intervals over $5\frac{1}{2}$ octaves for spectrum analysis and synthesis; nine other oscillators and function generators; six amplifiers; two variable response filters; and a number of other devices such as percussion simulators, noise generators (for both white and coloured noise) and reverberation units. Most of the connections between devices are made manually on a patch-panel, but up to twenty of them may be changed during realization by computer-controlled audio switches.

Signals from these devices are mixed and may be monitored both on the oscilloscope and through amplifiers and loudspeakers. A four track recorder and four two track recorders may be used for recording compositions on magnetic tape, but it is one of the great advantages of the studio that it is not necessary to use tape at all until the piece is known to be correct in every detail.

There are two important programmes in *Musys*: the Compiler translates the composer's programme into a data set stored on the disc, and the Performance Programme sends items from this data set to the audio devices at appropriate times controlled by the crystal clock. Eight independent lists of data may be stored by the Compiler, each with its own time scale, so the composer is spared the intricacies of temporal relationships between parts. The language has a *macro facility*, which permits the user to give a name to a sound or structural element, leaving 'gaps' which will be filled by *parameters* when the macro is called. It also allows sections to be repeated or compiled conditionally: these facilities are meant to reflect musical requirements, rather than mathematical requirements.

Either before or during performance, the composer can use a peripheral known as the Button Panel, from which he can monitor, alter and control data going to any of the *Musys* devices; he can also stop, start and adjust the rate of delivery during a performance, and can 'single-shot' the delivery routines by turning a knob which the computer recognizes as a substitute for the clock. An editing programme run in conjunction with the Button Panel enables the data stored on the disc to be altered, providing a way of making fine adjustments which are hard to programme.

In many ways, Zinovieff's studio and programme language are unique in the world. He brought it to the attention of an international audience at a UNESCO conference in Stockholm[1], in June 1970.

If Zinovieff may be considered primarily as a technician who has brought an electronic language within the reach of the composer, Tristram Cary is a composer who has extended his range of expression towards electronic music. Ideas for the manipulation of sound came to him already while he served in the Navy during the war, working in radar. He worked quite independently of Schaeffer's *musique concrète*, and by 1953 he had built up a working studio. But he found little interest or encouragement for electronic experiments at this time, and devoted much time to film work and incidental music for B.B.C. plays. A few conventional compositions were played.

Cary does not consider electronic music as a thing apart from other music; nor does he consider that its function is simply to reproduce the sounds made by existing instruments—if you want a violin tone, you use a violin. He does not see electronic music as a substitute for orchestral music, so much as an extension of it. But its uniqueness consists in the building of sounds, and all Cary's electronic compositions have a very clear scheme and purpose.

3 4 5 deliberately restricts the material, and the only frequencies used are 3, 4 or 5 cycles per second, and their multiples by 10, 10^2, 10^3 and 10^4. This results in three subsonic, nine sonic and three supersonic tones. The subsonic tones, inaudible by themselves, become audible in combination with others, mostly by modulation. The basic combinations are all concordant, but discords arise when harmonics are mixed in certain ways.

Birth is life is power, etc., is based on the music used for Don Levy's multi-screen film shown in the British Pavilion at EXPO '67. This was concerned with a cycle of energy, creative and destructive, and the music is therefore a nine-minute loop.

Cary has combined instrumental with electronic music. *Peccata Mundi* is for choir, orchestra and tape; *Narcissus* for solo flute and tape. The latter, as its name implies, feeds on its own reflection. As the piece proceeds, playbacks at different speeds and directions join the live flute, and these too are recorded, so that the single instrument builds a polyphony round itself. Every nuance, even every mistake, of the performer thus becomes part of the total fabric, as it is played back to him. No modulation or other transformations are employed, which would destroy essential flute quality. Speed changes, however, quadruple, or quarter, the original pitch, and up to thirty-two notes occur together in later passages.

1. *Music and Technology; the Composer in the Technological Era.*

If the basis of *Narcissus* is tonal, that of *Continuum* is temporal. This piece, which was first heard at a Cheltenham Festival concert in 1969, suggests the infinity of time stretching endlessly in both directions from where (or when) we stand. This endlessness is disturbed by temporary events, which bend it but do not essentially change it. This *continuum* in the music is a sound both changing and changeless, within which there are three episodes, each a little longer than the last, and containing at least one element derived from the continuum itself.

This main sound is a texture, a large pile of notes all continuously modulating in pitch, but by different amounts and at different speeds. The overall structure of *Continuum* has affinities, in the broadest sense, with symphonic procedures, as the composer's description shows:

The 'mesh' of sound is presented in a number of different forms, because it is disturbed by events. During the opening passage, we hear some other sounds faint and strangled in the background, as if struggling to get through the mesh. Later in the piece these sounds become definite and forward. The mesh gradually thins, losing its upper frequencies and slowly reducing energy, so that it eventually becomes weak enough to be penetrated by the first event proper. This consists of a 'freezing' by modulation of two blocks of the mesh sound, thrown like a thrombosis across the flow of the continuum. The result is a short passage of dynamic terracing and positional displacements, followed by a new, almost melodic idea in the bass which rises up with the modulated continuum to a climax. At this point groups of supersonic transformations of four notes at a time of the continuum (the audible sound consists of beat notes) make a series of clang-like sounds, while the melodic idea disintegrates and slips away. The continuum reasserts itself, but filtered to a lower sound than before (the event has left its mark).

The second episode (each one rises to a climax and falls back into continuum) also begins by throwing in an interruption which layers and terraces the mesh. The new sound is a development of the undulation idea—notes are slowly moved up and down as much as a fourth or fifth and then 'chopped' at a frequency not necessarily related to that of the frequency modulation. This results in little figures which, like the continuum itself, are similar but never quite the same. These figures build by becoming more numerous (there are twelve at the climax) and two other elements also build; these are (1) the two main elements of episode 1 modulated together (each event 'learns' from the previous one), and (2) the continuum now twisted and tortured by filtering. After the climax the episode 1 element goes, and the 'chop' falls away by gradually thinning out (like ending a round in a way). Finally, all that remains is an exhausted continuum, filtered till only a low rumble remains. This too goes and there is a short silence (it hasn't stopped, but we have lost sight of it).

Out of this silence arises the third episode, which is the most complex of the three. Another almost melodic idea (this was also heard in a choked version at the opening) is built from a rearrangement of the original 'mesh' notes; the filtering of this material is being constantly altered, which means that timbre changes occur within most notes. Added to this is yet another continuum transformation and a development of the 'clang' motive from the first episode. In addition, you hear a choked version of the 'chop' from the second episode, which goes away well before the climax after wandering about like a lost soul in the space between the speakers. Most of this material, as well as moving about, is slightly reverberated, which takes it back in space. The 'clang' sounds are doubled and thrown across from one speaker to the other. Near the climax, some unreverberated (and therefore close) blocks of notes (in eights) appear in rhythmic units and gradually build to the climax (of the piece as well as the episode). The chords here turn into a thick wall of notes, not undulating, whose very density stops the original continuum in its tracks. The melodic strand, by now high in pitch, can be heard wailing and crying behind the heavy curtain of the chord. But both gradually collapse, and again there is a short silence.

In the closing passage the continuum picks up its own pieces in a palindrome of the way we first heard it, and reasserts its power over strangled versions of the 'chop' and the 'clang'. Finally, the 'mesh' rises suddenly and forcefully to its original virility, and we as suddenly turn away, leaving whatever future events there may be to happen unobserved.

The period of the sixties might be called the 'first phase' of the development of electronic music in this country. Composers were made aware of its existence, but they lacked the technical apparatus of a properly equipped studio. Apart from Cary and Zinovieff, several other composers have made individual attempts at electronic effects, notably Ernest Berk, Robert Gerhard and Daphne Oram. Younger composers, including Birtwistle, Connolly and Smalley, have also attempted to embody a simple use of electronics into their compositions. But the electronic composer is just as much technician as composer; either without the other is incomplete.

The avant-garde

The term *avant-garde*, like the terms *romantic* or *contemporary*, is capable of many shades of meaning. It describes an attitude rather than any one style, with the result that it is evident in many different categories of contemporary music-making, and in all countries of the world. Manifestations of the *avant-garde* may be seen today in Los Angeles, New York, London, Paris, Cologne, Vienna, Stockholm or Tokyo. It is polarized between wide and mutually contradictory extremes; between the artless primitivism of pop musicians on the one hand, whose talent is rudimentary and whose compositional technique non-existent; and post-Webern serialists on the other, whose experimental techniques are everything, and can only be described by the term *avant-garde*, since they work consciously on the frontiers of musical knowledge. Or again, between the total abandonment of creative responsibility, the total non-involvement, of the aleatoric school, on the one hand, and the highly sophisticated machine-involvement of the electronic composer on the other. What is the underlying attitude, which we call *avant-garde*, that can possibly be stretched to apply to these widely differing and often contradictory trends?

One of its main characteristics is the element of protest and questioning; and of the mocking of generally accepted standards of concert-music. That *avant-garde* composers are for the most part young is largely due to the protest-core of the aesthetic. The time for protest is when you are young; it sounds more convincing if you are twenty-five; if you leave it until you are forty-five you merely sound disillusioned, tired. When you approach middle-age, you yourself become the object of the withering contempt of a younger generation of protesters. So, one by one, the aesthetic canons on which musical traditions are built are disposed of, until the ultimate goal is revealed: of nihilism, in a figure like John Cage; or of total abstraction and complexity, in the case of the later serialists.

Why, says the *avant-garde*, should music be serious? We will make it frivolous. Why should it involve hard work and laborious technique? We will make it easy, improvised, random. Why should music be dignified? We will distort, mock and parody. Why should a composition necessarily be a work of art, for all time? We will make it ephemeral, here and now. Why should the audience sit in rows? We will have them in informal groups. Why should musicians wear lugubrious, respectable dress? We will do the opposite.

There is thus a considerable affinity between this aspect of the *avant-garde* attitude and the frivolous mood of the 1920's; and it is significant that there has been a recent revival of interest in the work of Satie and Lord Berners by certain groups, such as the Pierrot Players.

It is illogical to assess an ephemeral work by the standards of permanent artistic value, and to approach a satirical or trivial work with the solemnity we reserve for a serious composition. In the case of *avant-garde* music, whose purpose is by definition to make, in some direction, an 'advance', the first question to decide is whether it succeeds in making such an advance, and, if so, what it is. In order to arrive at such an aesthetic conclusion, it is necessary to identify the point at which protest ceases and artistic alignment begins; the point where the composer's intention ceases to be on the periphery of experience, and begins to involve the listener's; for at some point he has to cease his aleatoricism, and invite the performers' collaboration; at some point he has to cease cocking a snook at his audience, and invite their artistic response, if his work is to have even an ephemeral identity. A great number of *avant-garde* works have no identity, or are derivative from one of the dominant trends of Europe or America.

Both pop and jazz are American-derived; most of the absurdities of British attempts in these fields are due to their derivation from American models. But several different and basic influences converged to produce these phenomena. First, a lack of stimulus, particularly among the young, from the complex developments in contemporary music, which meant little or nothing to them; second, just as jazz itself was a negro folk-art born out of protest, so pop followed suit. Elvis Presley had been the well-groomed hero-figure of a generation of post-war adolescents, and it was only a logical step for succeeding groups, the Beatles, the Rolling Stones, to become also the focus for those countless points of difference between teenagers and their elders—which might be expressed politically, in student revolution, in the Black Power movement, in civil rights, in nuclear disarmament; or socially, in the assertion of a carefully publicized 'drop-out' status, by means of unkempt dress and dishevelled appearance, or by means of drug-taking or sexual permissiveness—or by making records.

British jazz also lacks a valid traditional basis; its nature is derivative, with the result that even the most successful British bands compete on unequal terms with their American originals. Jazz is a branch of music in in which the negro has always retained the artistic initiative. In recent years, however, the jazz style has been subjected to treatment and modification by composers of varying shades of allegiance; it has been embodied in a light style by Joseph Horovitz and Ernest Tomlinson; it has been grafted onto other styles (the so-called 'third stream') by Banks and Richard Bennett; it has been given the sort of *avant-garde* treatment usually reserved for other more complex styles of composition, by Howard Riley, Tony Oxley and others.

The *avant-garde* musician is always asking 'Where do we go from here?' Music is for him, therefore, essentially a continuous development, a 'one-upmanship'. He is concerned not with what is 'valid' today; still less with what was 'valid' yesterday; but what is going to be 'valid' tomorrow. If we may say very broadly that pop and jazz developments are, generally speaking, American-derived, those *avant-garde* musicians whose experiments are with more sophisticated forms of music start from the post-Webern situation of European serialism, which they either respond to, or react from.

Two composers who have responded, though differently, are Roger Smalley and John Tavener.

Ten years Davies's junior, Roger Smalley's artistic starting-point is more dogmatically and narrowly confined to the *avant-garde*, whose standard he bears with considerable conviction, and for whom he acts as spokesman. 'Tradition' for him practically amounts to an indecent word. His aesthetic attitude is aptly summarized in a review[1] of six *avant-garde* records:

> I sometimes wonder if I am being wilfully perverse when I condemn so categorically the 'traditional' music of our time—since so many people seem to enjoy it. . . . One only has to try and imagine listening to six records of so-called 'traditional' music (my imagination won't stretch quite that far) and compare the boring, cliché-ridden irrelevancies that *could not fail* to be on offer for 90% of the time, with the vital, imaginative, and stimulating music on these records. Here there is hope even for the composers of those works which are not very interesting because they have at least chosen the path which has the possibility of leading to something original, while the 'traditionalists' will never succeed in becoming relevant whatever they do. I assume that everyone already interested in contemporary music will have bought these records. I am more anxious that those who are not particularly convinced or concerned by contemporary music take advantage of this bargain set and devote several hours of unprejudiced listening to its contents. They will, I am sure, be astonished by the vistas opened up.

The overwhelming naïveté of such an approach to the musical art does not necessarily invalidate Smalley's work as a composer; and it is this that concerns us more than his theories. For anyone except the composer himself, however, there are two basic and logical flaws to be noted: the first is that such an aesthetic reduces the range of artistic choice open to the composer, that 'creative volition' of which Stravinsky speaks, to a contrived one between two irreconcilable opposites—the *avant-garde* on the one hand, the 'traditional' on the other. Thus the whole range of the compositional process is reduced melodramatically to a stark contrast—black or white. Neither art, nor life, is quite so simple as that.

The second flaw is that by its failure to define, it begs more questions than it answers. What is meant by 'traditional'; what is meant by '*avant-*

---

1. *Musical Times*, February 1969.

The pieces which earned this accolade were as follows:

Mayuzumi	*Prelude for String Quartet*	Kagel	*Fantasia*
Lutoslawski	*String Quartet*	Penderecki	*String Quartet*
Juan Allende-Blin	*Sonorities*	David Bedford	*Two Poems*
Stockhausen	*Gruppen*	Berio	*Sequenza V for*
	Carré		*trombone*
	Solo	Carlos Roque	
Ligeti	*Etude I*		*Alsina-Consecuenza*
	Lux Aeterna	Globokar	*Discours II for*
Manricro Kagel	*Match for two cellos & percussion*		*five trombones*
	Music for Renaissance instruments		

garde'? Smalley suggests that the *avant-garde* is what is 'contemporary'—with the implied corollary that the traditional is what is out of date. Thus, if you do not align yourself with the *avant-garde* you are not truly 'contemporary'. To offer the definition that the *avant-garde* is what is new and 'advanced', while the traditional is what is old and un-advanced, does not so much define a style as describe the effect of that style on one particular already-committed recipient. It is also to confuse style with content, what you say with the way you say it—which is a central feature, as will become apparent, of *avant-garde* thinking.

Unfortunately, as we all know, it is not only possible, but most commonly the case, that composers of standing achieve new artistic ends with existing means at their disposal. In other words they have considered the ends (what they say) more important than the means (how they say it). As Smalley is still only twenty-six, it is hardly possible yet to do more than show the general direction in which he is facing. Most of his output so far has been of a formative, exploratory nature. Ironically enough, he is, in one sense, one of the most 'traditional' composers in England today, if by 'traditional' is meant that he accepts what is 'handed down' from someone else. He has accepted in the fullest sense of the word the ideas and techniques handed down by Stockhausen, and he has acted as the advocate and protagonist in this country for Stockhausen's work, in much the same way as Robert Sherlaw Johnson has assimilated and passed on the 'tradition' of Messiaen.

He was born in Swinton in 1944, and at Lee Grammar School (where Peter Maxwell Davies had also been a pupil) he combined science with music. He went to the Royal College of Music in London in 1961, where his composition teacher was Peter Racine Fricker. After the latter left for America[1], there was no one to teach serial techniques. Smalley had studied Stravinsky's *Movements*, and his first serial piece dated from that year. Thereafter his study became more diffuse—with John White, whose compositions at first comprised mainly piano sonatas with a strongly French flavour, until later they became much more experimental; with Alexander Goehr at Morley College, who analysed in detail several works of Mozart, Beethoven, Schoenberg. He also attended the B.B.C. Invitation Concerts, newly instituted by William Glock, at which works by Stockhausen, Berio, and others of the *avant-garde* were introduced to London. In 1965 he was given an award[2], which enabled him to go to Cologne with Brian Dennis and attend Stockhausen's class. The summer of that year saw him at Darmstadt. Since 1967 he has worked from Cambridge, where he was elected a Fellow of King's College.

1. See p. 245.
2. A Countess of Munster award.

So Smalley's formative years occurred in the mid-60's, some ten years after the tide of post-Webern serialism was first felt in London. In his work, therefore, the results of this powerful movement can be seen. The pattern of serialism was by this time clearly recognizable, and thus formed the background to his creative attitude as a composer. What is his attitude? He never felt the slightest dichotomy, or break in continuity, between classicism and serialism. It had been Schoenberg's vision to see that after Mahler's death keys were dead; thus Brahms and Wagner were embodied in Schoenberg and Berg; but serialism did provide one answer to the problem of avoiding tonal chords and regular beats. Smalley has never used a 12-note series, but prefers sets of fewer notes, like a *cantus firmus* or ground bass; nor is he attracted to motivic development, but instead derives the parts from the motif by canon. Up to 1967 he did not use non-pitched percussion instruments, since they add nothing (so he felt) to what has already been said. What is 'advanced' is interesting; what is most 'advanced' is most interesting; what is not 'advanced' is not interesting. It is not possible to do interesting things in the old style; new things require new language and new methods.

His student years were very busy and productive. His compositions between 1962 and 1967 form a 'first period'. Apart from Stockhausen, he was also strongly aware of the work of Maxwell Davies, and in many respects was directly influenced by him; for instance in the use of mediaeval or renaissance pieces as sources of musical ideas; in the idea of parody; in textures and layout generally. Following Davies, he had recourse to the *Mulliner Book*, and the sixteenth-century composer William Blitheman gave him the starting-point, first for two settings of *Gloria Tibi Trinitas*, one for orchestra, the other for orchestra with soloists and choir; next for a *Missa Brevis*, a taxing, virtuoso setting for sixteen solo voices[1], which includes vocal effects such as whispering, shouting, humming and *parlando*. The two *Missa Parodia* (No. 1 for piano, No. 2 for piano nonet) also originated in this way; the Blitheman themes are quoted, only to be deliberately distorted. Another early work (1964/5), *Elegies*, is a strongly dramatic setting of Rilke, for soprano and tenor soloists, and accompaniment of three groups of instruments, strings, brass and bells. Instrumental interludes, and in the middle a Sonatina, separate the four vocal sections, and a characteristic instrumental chord gives rise to the melodic material of the voice parts. In this piece, as in all his other early works, there are implications of tonality; also, as in the *Gloria Tibi Trinitas*, multiple division of the strings. Other pieces of this formative period include a *Septet* (1963), a *String Sextet* (1964), *Variations*

1. First performed by the John Alldis Choir, on 2 May 1967.

v

for Strings (1964), and a *Capriccio* for violin and piano (1966), as well as two song-cycles with instrumental accompaniment, and some short, experimental piano pieces. Then after 1967 his style underwent a change.

Stockhausen's influence has always been all-powerful over Smalley. Not only does the young Englishman perform and propagate the works of his German mentor, and make them the starting point for his own composition, but he has also been persuaded by the older composer's views on the social function of music, and about such mundane matters as the arrangements of concerts, and the relationship of composer, player and audience. Why should an old score be extended into a complex contemporary work? Why should the listener be expected to possess a fund of musical and historical knowledge? Too much intellectual superstructure can well cut him off from the composer.[1] A conversation with John Cage in 1967 also had a decisive influence on Smalley in forming his opinion that the traditional conception of concert-giving is unattractive.

And so from now on he became concerned not so much with the musical material as with the very minutiae of the process of composition; with the continuity not of the motif or harmony, but of all those control-ling factors that hitherto had been subsidiary, or taken for granted. Scales of each controlling factor were graded and systematized (loudness, speed, degree of eventuation and density, rate of change, intelligibility of words and so on), and composition became a rational search for a balance between these factors. The finished piece would thus consist of different combinations of these scales of elements. Spontaneity was impossible, though a limited amount of freedom might be allowed to the performers, who could be invited to listen and take part. Generally speaking, Smalley's music since 1967 is not so technically demanding as that of Maxwell Davies, who looks for a virtuoso standard from the Pierrot Players.

The first work in this new style was *Song of the Highest Tower*, for soprano and baritone soli, chorus, string and brass ensembles and orchestra, which was first heard, with disturbing effect, in the otherwise somewhat decorous atmosphere of a City of London Festival, 1968. The score, which calls for two conductors, consists not so much of notation as such, but of instructions on the manner of performance of the ideas. What matter for the players are durations, dynamics, bowing, mode of tone-production; these are the factors that are 'composed', more than any thematic or motivic invention, which is very simple. The vocal parts consist variously of whispering, murmuring, speaking, shouting.

This piece was followed by *Transformation I* for piano (1968/9), in which Smalley first used electronic modulation, live not pre-recorded.

1. C.f. Busoni's *Die Brautwahl* in Dent's *Ferruccio Busoni*, pp. 183-185.

The work, which was commissioned by the City Music Society, was a preparatory study for *Transformation II*, or *Pulses 5 × 4*.[1] In this piece five groups of four players are placed at random in the hall, and each group is amplified and/or modulated electronically, by combination of the instrumental sounds with sine-tones in a ring modulator.

The instruments consist of: 3 trumpets, 1 percussion (1 group); 3 horns, 1 percussion (2 groups); 3 trombones, 1 percussion (2 groups); The work lasts fifty minutes and is made up of thirty 'Moments'.

The conception is one of a composition in layers of continually fluctuating densities, according to how many of the five groups are playing during each Moment.

The 'pulses' of the title are rhythmic variants, or 'categories of pulsation', of which there are three, each with five sub-divisions. What matters therefore in this case are the rhythmic characteristics of each Moment. Again, the notes played are of secondary importance, and indeed could hardly be simpler, since in each Moment each instrument only plays one note, which is varied constantly by internal vibrations, microtonal inflections, muting and so on. During each Moment only one group plays from notated music; the other 'layers' are provided by groups continuing to develop the last Moment they have played.

This process and principle of composition, which Smalley derived from Stockhausen, rests on the assumption that the composer's art consists not so much of musical ideas or themes as on the constantly fluctuating and variable presentation of the elements of the material. Thus the analogy with logical philosophy is seen to be extremely close;[2] the same intellectual principle governs both—chiefly, that what is important is not what you say but how you say it. Such a principle of composition is not so much an extension of the range of music's experiences as a confining of it within certain selected, concentrated limits, which are thoroughly exploited to the exclusion of other fundamental factors.

Such a trend is directly the reverse of that adopted more than fifty years ago by composers such as Busoni, Schoenberg, Stravinsky—and Webern. Then it was a question of breaking out of the confines of a comparatively narrow tradition into the wider fields of mediaeval, polyphonic and renaissance music, as well as reaching into the unknown paths of the future. Their intellectual curiosity and creative urge was directed towards the constant enlargement of both the extent and the depth of their musical experience. Conversely, however, the *avant-garde*

1. First played by the London Sinfonietta conducted by David Atherton on June 20, 1969.
2. See my *Contemporary Music*, pp. 231–3.

of 1970, of which Smalley is an articulate representative in this country, reverse this process, and seek instead to reduce the range of their musical vision by eliminating whole periods and facets of artistic experience from their thoughts, pronouncing them to be 'irrelevant', and focusing their creative energy with correspondingly greater concentration onto the comparatively limited areas of their own choosing. This process illustrates not only the profound changes that have come about in music, particularly since 1945, but also the illusory nature of 'freedom' where art is concerned. The composer needs constantly to ask: Freedom—from what? Whereas composers of the earlier generation sought freedom from their immediate tradition, and from academic formalism, by the exercise of their creative curiosity, the present generation has inherited the fruits of this freedom; it therefore scarcely needs to invoke the cry of 'freedom' in quite the same way as its forebears did. Yet already, paradoxically, the result of this freedom is showing signs of leading to a narrowing, a rigidity of the art, that is far more restricting, far more rigorous in its demands, than that nineteenth century aesthetic from which earlier composers strove to break free. If this proves to be the case, then it will only be a matter of time before the next generation of composers, in their turn, seek to win their freedom from it. Dogmatism, from whichever quarter, whether 'traditional' or 'avant-garde' is an unsatisfactory basis for the creative artist.

Like Smalley, John Tavener was also born in 1944. Again, therefore, it is premature to suggest more than the general direction in which he is facing—which is unquestionably that of the avant-garde. And though his technique is less complex, and not so mathematically theoretical, as Smalley's—nor is it derived from Stockhausen—nevertheless, the same generating principle inspires both composers: that of concern with, and sophistication in, the manner of presentation of material which by itself may be rudimentary. For instance, the closing section of In alium, whose texture is similar to part of Smalley's Elegies, consists of an improvised glissando within the framework of certain given pitches for sixteen divisi violins, and a pre-recorded solo voice in sixteen canonic parts, gradually dying away to nothing. The notes by themselves mean nothing; there is no thematic material in the accepted sense of that term. The composer's attention is directed towards originality and unexpectedness of effect, not towards the invention of original material.

He studied under Lennox Berkeley at the Royal Academy of Music, and later with the Australian David Lumsdaine; his early pieces include settings of T. S. Eliot's Four Quartets, and of Three Holy Sonnets of John Donne (1963/64), as well as a short religious drama, The Cappemakers

(1964), and a dramatic cantata *Cain and Abel* (1965). The last two are similar in style and both betray a certain awkwardness of word-setting; but in *Cain and Abel*, which is clearly derived from late Stravinsky, Tavener first begins to use that free, improvisatory technique that was soon to become dominant. The work was awarded first prize in the Monaco competition, 1965.

A light work, *Grandma's Footsteps*, and a traditional work, a *Chamber Concerto*, are the prelude to his total adoption of an *avant-garde* style which became apparent in *The Whale* (1966). This is the piece on which his reputation now chiefly rests. It was not performed, however, until 24th January, 1968[1], when it was received with rapturous acclamation. Hardened London critics, whose enthusiasm is not always their most prominent characteristic, even admitted to a sense of exuberant enjoyment and infectious high spirits. The composer's comment gives the clue to his intention: 'the extravagance of the score is something which I feel I may not be capable of when I grow older.' After all, if you are going to throw traditional discipline to the winds, half-measures will not do. And so the work, a dramatic cantata, which lasts forty-five minutes, is an abandoned display of ingenuity, theatrical amusement; it is certainly never dull. It is a word-fantasy, and is constructed, again like Smalley's *Elegies*, with instrumental interludes. It opens with a solemn, documentary reading from the *Encyclopaedia Britannica* on the biological properties of whales; only gradually does the music encroach on the words, until the voice has to struggle to be heard. The composer's ingenuity is directed towards the treatment of noise-effects, some of which are deliberately banal and monotonous; interruptions from a loud-hailer, whispers, snores, grunts, buzzes, hisses; electronic effects; the baritone soloist shouts into an undamped piano, representing the whale's belly; and so on.

Such a work could not be repeated; but the immediate success of *The Whale* opened the door to the young composer. *In alium* was commissioned by the B.B.C. for a 1968 Promenade Concert[2], and the *Introit for March 27*, the Feast of St. John Damascene, was commissioned by the London Bach Society. These were followed by *A Celtic Requiem* (1968/69) which, like *The Whale*, is described as a 'dramatic cantata', and

---

1. By the London Sinfonietta under David Atherton. This was also the first appearance under a new twenty-four-year old conductor of this chamber orchestra, formed specifically to perform *avant-garde* works.

2. At this concert (12th August 1968) three new works were played; Tavener's *In Alium*, Banks's *Violin Concerto*, Musgrave's *Concerto for Orchestra*. In the interval of the concert a 'popularity poll' was conducted to find out which of the three works the chiefly youthful audience would like to hear repeated. Tavener's work was the clear favourite.

in which, also like *The Whale*, and the other works, though its origin may
have been sacred, any traditional religious association is entirely con-
tradicted by the individual presentation of the idea. Though the movements are recognizably traditional (Requiem aeternam, Kyrie, Dies irae,
etc.) in no other sense is the work a 'requiem'. The adult rendering of the
words is parodied by the nonsense interruptions of children as they play
hopscotch; their games have ritualistic overtones for the composer, as
well as suggestions of parody.

For instance, the concluding section *Requiescat in pace* is set against
the words of the nursery rhyme 'Mary had a little lamb,' which ends:

> Mary had a little lamb
>   Her father shot it dead.
> Now it goes to school with her
>   Between two chunks of bread.

This is enacted to an accompaniment of organ and popguns, to say
nothing of Cardinal Newman's hymn, 'Lead, Kindly Light'. The purely
musical material is extremely limited; indeed, the whole work is reduced
to different presentations of the chord of E flat. It is, in this case, no
longer a question of a composition consisting of the treatment and
development of contrasting ideas or thematic material; it is the varied
treatment itself which is the composition.

Tim Souster is Smalley's contemporary, and shares his aesthetic. He
also succeeded him at King's College, Cambridge, as 'composer in
residence'. After studying at Oxford, and with Richard Rodney Bennett,
he attended in 1963 the courses of Stockhausen, Berio and Kontarsky at
Darmstadt, the Mecca of the European *avant-garde*. Most of his recent
works include electronic effects, such as *Tsuwamono-domo* and *Titus
Groan Music*. The first of these is about war on three levels: the personal,
the epic and the political; the second, named after the first of Mervyn
Peake's trilogy of novels, is also political, dedicated to the Greek
composer and freedom-fighter, Theodorakis. Other *avant-garde* composers
of this generation are Brian Ferneyhough and the slightly younger
Michael Finnissy.

Of the former generation, the best known are David Bedford (b. 1938)
and Harrison Birtwistle (b. 1934). Bedford's style is the slenderer of the
two, the more lyrical. Birtwistle's is the more uncompromising and
abrasive, and though he has been closely associated with Peter Maxwell
Davies, both as fellow-student at Manchester, and as co-director of the
Pierrot Players, his music lacks the dimension of parody that Davies
shows; nor does it derive inspiration from the extra dimension of visual
or dance effects, or to any great extent from mediaeval music. His

characteristic *avant-garde* works, such as *Medusa*, or *Interludes from a tragedy*, are built on very simple patterns, and use violent dynamic extremes. He is very interested in electronics, and *Medusa* also required a computer on stage. His only opera so far, *Punch and Judy*, which was first heard at the 1968 Aldeburgh Festival, was a miscalculation in several important respects: the ugliness of orchestral sound palls quickly on the ear, while the scoring and instrumentation combine to make the singers inaudible. Stephen Pruslin's text is equally savage and aggressive. But a sense of drama underlies some of Birtwistle's other orchestral and instrumental works, such as *Verses for Ensembles*, *Tragoedia* and *Chorales*. *Tragoedia* (1965) derived a dramatic form from Messiaen's *Chronocromie*, and was a preliminary study for *Punch and Judy*, while the earlier *Chorales* is an individual interpretation of 'The Martyrdom of St. Catherine' by Pieter Brueghel. Its four sections juxtapose, alternate and repeat similar material in many dimensions and in various perspectives, some blurred, some in focus, like foreground and background.

In many ways Birtwistle is the most uncompromising and determined post-Webern composer in England today. Another who follows a similar path is Justin Connolly, who also went to America on a Harkness Fellowship, and who follows the established *avant-garde* pattern in his concern for method rather than style. He has worked with electronics at Zinovieff's studio.

Several groups have been started in the 60's for the presentation of *avant-garde* works: 'The mouth of Hermes', 'Sonor', 'The Electric Candle', to mention only three. 'The Gentle Fire' is associated with Richard Orton; 'Intermodulation' is the name under which Smalley and Souster present their work to the public. The group known as 'The Soft Machine' played at the first 'Pop Prom', on 13th August 1970; but the ultimate so far in this direction (though who can say what the future holds in store?) is Cornelius Cardew's 'Scratch Orchestra', which he founded in 1969.

Cardew, who was born in 1936, is the John Cage of British music. Indeed, after studying electronic music in Cologne (1957/8), Cardew was associated with Cage and David Tudor, and also made his acquaintance with the music of Christian Wolff and Morton Feldman. His compositions bear deceptively traditional titles, but there any resemblance to traditional procedures ends; more often than not the scores contain lengthy instructions on how to decipher the otherwise unintelligible symbols. Every work is for him a fresh experiment, and every performance too. The only thing, for instance, that is determinate about *Treatise* is that no performance will bear audible relationship to any other performance (see plate 12). The score consists of 193 pages of free graphics, without a single symbol whose meaning has been agreed in advance. You can sing it, play it on any instrument, in any order, backwards or forwards, in part or in whole; you can contemplate it in silence, or act it; but for the final result Cardew disclaims all responsibility. 'My intention' he says, 'is that the player should respond to the situation.'

But what of the audience? An artistic response on the part of the listener has always been the *sine qua non* of any music which lays claim to the status of art. If the nihilistic *avant-garde* composer dissociates himself from the performer, does he also disclaim any concern for the audience? Suppose that a listener were to trespass on a meeting of the Scratch Orchestra in the fond and innocent expectation that he was going to hear a concert:

Place: St. Pancras Assembly Rooms
Date: 2nd April 1970. Thursday evening, 7.50 p.m.
Enter concertgoer.

Heavily Victorian hall. About one hundred seats occupy one half of the floor; the other half is taken up by seven or eight young people seated on the floor, with assorted items of musical and other apparatus.

Audience, ten minutes before the concert, consists of eleven people, and one somewhat bewildered janitor.

Concertgoer refers to his programme—a postcard informing him that this is the 12th presentation of the Scratch Orchestra, and that the date is 2nd April 1970. The reverse side is entirely blank. Perhaps his nearest neighbours might know what was to be played? They say that the participants in the orchestra are not musicians at all; they just enjoy playing. Their instruments appear to consist of a frying pan, blocks of wood, assorted tins. Is that a military drum over there? Someone is busily unpacking a shopping-bag, which evidently contains more utensils, needed no doubt for the performance; a paint tin, what looks like a bag of nails, some iron bars.

Another possible audience-member ventures round the door, only to retreat in haste at the sight that meets his eyes. Those sitting on the floor now number twenty; the audience, so far, twelve.

Various tappings, squeaks, noises. Can this be the concert? Surely not; but it is almost 8 o'clock. The audience is now eighteen. Everyone waits expectantly. More uncoordinated tapping and isolated sounds. Is this all that is meant by *avant-garde*?

Someone with a mallet intently and very deliberately strikes a piece of wood: whereupon four children come in (five–eight age group), who make the loudest noise so far heard, with their golliwog father. The audience is now twenty-three.

A saxophone somewhat surprisingly emits a note; someone claps; someone else utters a vocal sound. Perhaps this is some secret means of communication, like morse code? Or a meditation? Or more likely a leg-pull. Yes, a practical joke. But the date is 2nd April, not 1st April. Several teenagers come in, dishevelled, bored and disconsolate. Evidently *avant-garde* people are unhappy?

More very quiet sounds. Surely this is very tentative for an improvisation? Some of the participants seem to be reading something; a score, maybe?

A rustling of paper; a squeak of a whistle, all unconnected. Someone arrives late with a cornet. Someone else sits with his arm embracing a cello, apparently incapable of playing it. Ah, no! After much deliberation he manages to produce one pizzicato note. Another noise, like the whistle in a Christmas cracker. Over there is a horn player; but he, too, is transfixed, quite unable to play.

The time is now 8.15 p.m. Another violinist comes in, be-jeaned, shoeless. He solemnly selects a chair, sits down, and lays his violin on the floor. Evidently dissatisfied, he then moves to the other side of the room, sits this time on the floor, and meditates. About what, one wonders.

Twenty-four human beings are now reduced to silence; only the occasional *peep* or *plonk* disturbs the placid scene.

Concertgoer is now in a questioning mood. For want of anything resembling music, his thoughts take a dissatisfied turn. Is this all the *avant-garde* has to say about the Western musical tradition? Is this all that is left of the musical art?

(Suddenly a tune is heard—on a musical box.)

Is it meant to be a joke? If so, each concertgoer must supply his own punch-line; nobody else will.

(Two more elderly people arrive—surely not *The Times* critic?)

The participants are obviously indulging their private rite of this particular spring; a private meeting of meditation for their own edification. An audience is an affront in such a gathering—an unwarrantable intrusion; neither valued nor necessary.

Concertgoer reflects that there is a saloon just opposite, where his custom would be, on the contrary, highly valued.

Exit concertgoer.

21   Serialism and Romanticism

Categorization is an inadequate way of considering a composer's work; if he is a composer of any marked individuality, whose music bears the imprint of his personality, he will create his own category. Nevertheless, it is equally true that the great increase in musical activity in this country since 1945, and the vastly greater general interest in music-making at all levels has led directly to a correspondingly increased response by composers. Demand has, to some extent, created supply; moreover, the highly variegated demand by different groups and different trends has created a highly variegated supply; largely occasional and ephemeral perhaps, but all an essential part in a vital and growing tradition.

Serialism
One of the strongest trends, and one which made the most exacting demands to any who succumbed to its siren voice, was the serialist/ *avant garde* movement that began to be noticeably felt in the 50's. It largely focused on a small group of composers centred round the B.B.C., where William Glock was Head of Music from 1959.

The most senior of those composers who today reflect the trend of serialism is Benjamin Frankel. He was born in 1906, and in his case it was a gradual assimilation of Schoenberg's ideas, not a sudden conversion; he was not born into an environment which accepted the 12-note principle as a *fait accompli*. On the contrary, his musical growth has been a slow and cumulative process, which is reflected in his compositions. Frankel developed his own 12-note style, because Schoenberg alone appeared to him to offer a technical discipline which he, Frankel, needed. He came to serialism practically unwittingly, instinctively; then he worked consciously and quite alone, in an attempt to arrive at his own technique, which was not comparable with anybody else's, but which arose absolutely from the 'classic example' of Schoenberg. Frankel's large output culminates in seven symphonies, the first of which was not written until 1960. All the symphonies are, to a greater or lesser extent, serial.

Prominent among those who have worked within the Schoenberg tradition is Elizabeth Lutyens. With Humphrey Searle, she was the pioneer of the 12-note technique at a time (in the forties) when it was hardly heard of in this country. Moreover, as the wife of Edward Clark, and one of the founders of the Macnaghten concerts in 1931, she has been actively concerned with matters to do with contemporary music concerts in this country, and the musical politics that appear to be inseparable from them, for very many years. Needless to say, she has not infrequently been at the centre of controversy. Her close acquaintance with William Glock has secured for her works a hearing at his Dartington Summer School, and since 1960 in radio concerts. Indeed, the trend towards serialism, which reached a peak in the 60's, was in no small measure the result of her influential and crusading voice.

She was born in 1906, the daughter of the architect, Sir Edwin Lutyens. She studied first in Paris, then at the Royal College of Music under Harold Darke, the organist of St. Michael's, Cornhill. Her first public performance consisted of a ballet *The Birthday of the Infanta*, conducted by Constant Lambert. Gradually during the thirties her works reached audiences, through the L.C.M.C., or her own Macnaghten Concerts, or Adolph Hallis. Later she regularly featured in I.S.C.M. programmes, starting in 1939, when her *Second String Quartet* was played at the Warsaw Festival[1]. This is a conventional work; dissonant, though hardly revolutionary. It was gradually, after about 1940, that she embarked on the path of 12-note composition, starting with the first of the *Six Chamber Concertos*, Op. 8. It was a path which, particularly at that time in England, called for qualities of musical vision and personal determination. She had to be prepared for her voice to be, for many years, a lone one crying in a particularly lonely wilderness. In retrospect we are now able to detect, and identify, that goal of total serialism towards which Schoenberg's 12-note style represented the first step. It was an all-demanding technique of composition, through which only the strongest musical personality could assert itself. Such a success in the personal adoption of the serial world is seen in the later works of Gerhard[2], in which his individual characteristics of style remain stronger and more important than the technical procedures he adopted. But his achievement is exceptional, and, in this country at least, unique.

But for the pioneer Elizabeth Lutyens in 1940 this path lay in the unseen future. Her works since then, of which there are over seventy, as distinct from her incidental film scores, represent her gradual movement

---

1. When Rawsthorne's *Symphonic Studies* were also played (see p. 43).
2. See p. 183/5.

along that path. In a number of them, her idiom and style is indistinguishable from that of countless other European composers at this time. Schoenbergian dodecaphony was the common technique of the *avant-garde* in the 40's and 50's; the more refined Webernian serialism followed after.

The adoption of dodecaphony, and a totally chromatic tonality, presents the greatest problems of balance and texture in orchestral works; not so much in chamber works, which use fewer instruments. Moreover, Lutyens's style is best suited to small-scale works. A highly expressive score, and an early one, is the soprano cantata *O Saisons, O Châteaux* (1946); it has a clarity and a brevity which is lacking in some of the orchestral works, such as the densely concentrated *Three Symphonic Preludes* (1942) or *Music for Orchestra I* (1954). Indeed, writing for voices tends to bring out the lyricism in Lutyens—such works as the *Wittgenstein Motet* (1953) and *Quincunx* (1957), for instance, have a focal point. Wittgenstein's philosophy is germane and highly relevant to Schoenberg's[1], and in translating into music such apparent imponderables as 'The world is everything that is the case', or 'The existence and non-existence of atomic facts is the reality', Lutyens was retracing the path that Schoenberg had trod thirty years earlier. She simply, if unconsciously, substituted one series of symbols (a note-row) for another (the *variables* of logical philosophy). The musical characteristics of the resulting composition are precisely analogous to the linguistic characteristics inherent in Wittgenstein's text in the first place. It is one of the most apt pieces ever composed, since the 12-note technique was linguistic in origin. Lutyens's motet is not a setting of words so much as a realization of ideas.

She has written a large number of scores since 1960 for B.B.C. performance, many directly commissioned—starting with the *Wind Quintet*, Op. 45, (1960). These include orchestral works—*Music for Orchestra II* (1962) 'for Edward Clark,' who had died that year, and *Music for Orchestra III*, (1964); also *Symphonies* for piano, wind, harp and percussion (1961), and several works for voice and instrumental ensembles. In these later works Lutyens found herself confronted with the severest test of all—a ready audience. The path of the 12-note technique can only lead the composer through progressive refinement of idiom, until all inessentials are pared away. Webern is the prototype in this respect. Lutyens' style is slender and lyrical; but all too easily, as in *Quincunx*, the melodic line can be lost among the notes. Her idiom is the *lingua franca* of European serialism; but her musical personality does not shine through it with the strength and brilliance of Gerhard.

1. This point is dealt with in greater detail in my *Contemporary Music*, pp. 231/3.

Many composers have since followed along the Schoenberg—Webern path; among them the Scottish composer Iain Hamilton, who was born in Glasgow in 1922. Like his contemporary Fricker, he emigrated to America in 1961, where he was Professor at Duke University, North Carolina; also like Fricker, he was awarded a Clements memorial prize, for a String Quartet, and a Koussevitzky Prize, for his *Second Symphony* (1950). Unlike Fricker, however, he is more doctrinaire in his approach to the post-Webern situation; and the strict serialism of his *Sinfonia for Two Orchestras* (1959), which was a direct reflection of the then Continental *avant-garde*, caused an uproar when it was first heard at an Edinburgh Festival concert that year. He has, however, written several works in lighter vein, such as a *1912 Overture* (1958), and a *Concerto for jazz trumpet and orchestra*.

A similar versatility, and a certain artistic ambiguity, marks the work of the younger composer, Richard Rodney Bennett. His major works are unquestioningly 12-note, yet he combines this with a remarkable fluency; already his work so far includes as many as five operas, two symphonies, a major choral work, *Epithalamion*, a *Piano Concerto*, and numerous other pieces, including scores for films, radio, television and theatre, which call for a less intellectual style. He is also an accomplished pianist, and his penchant for jazz led to a jazz ballet, and several pieces for jazz ensemble.

More directly in line from Schoenberg (not so much from Webern) is Alexander Goehr, the son of the conductor, Walter Goehr. At Manchester, his name was bracketed with Davies and Birtwistle in the 'Manchester Group', though his work has since followed a more recognizably conventional path than that of his two student contemporaries. After Manchester he studied under Messiaen in Paris, and his piano *Capriccio* (1958) is dedicated to Messiaen's wife, the pianist Yvonne Loriod. Goehr is widely-travelled, spending much time in Europe and America, and active as a teacher, lecturer and writer. He taught analysis and composition at Morley College, and two of his pupils were Roger Smalley and Anthony Gilbert. He later taught at Yale (1968/9).

The idiom of his work is that of the orthodox European post-Schoenberg tradition; concentrated, dense, proliferating in detail, and instrumental rather than vocal—indeed, his vocal and choral works (*The Deluge* and *Sutter's Gold*) are the least satisfactory among his output. Concertos include the *Violin Concerto* (1962), *Romanza for cello* (1968) and *Konzertstuck for piano* (1969); symphonic works include *Little Symphony* (1963) and *Symphony in one movement* (1970). The final movement of the *Little Symphony* is particularly indicative of Goehr's style. In it, the composer seeks to combine the features of both slow movement and finale. 'I particularly like this type of movement,' he says, 'which combines different tempi and musical inventions, although it always raises the biggest problems of clarity and continuity, and imposes a particular stress on the performers.' In this movement, the various styles of recitative, finale material, and chorale, alternate in a mosaic of rich texture, leading to a coda (*Adagio*) based on the symphony's opening. Rather than thematic invention, Goehr prefers the invention, and development, of texture. This is particularly apparent in his chamber music.

Apart from instrumental composition, Goehr has also had considerable operatic experience. His first opera *Ardern must die* was written, in German, for the Hamburg State Opera (1967), while his theatre work ranges from an early ballet to Greek plays, as well as feature and television films. He is associated with the Brighton Festival, where, in 1969, he directed the Music Theatre Ensemble in Birtwistle's *Down by the Greenwood Side* and Walton's *Facade*, as well as his own *Naboth's Vineyard*—a morality in the style of a chamber opera, combining music and mime. It has been described by the composer as a 'dramatic madrigal'. It was the first of a trilogy, the other two pieces being *Shadowplay-2* and *Sonata about Jerusalem*. Goehr's 'Music Theatre' is comparable with Davies's works for the Pierrot Players, and Britten's Church Parables.

The works of his pupil Anthony Gilbert, though still comparatively few in number, are also very much the products of their period, the 60's. The trend of serialism decisively influenced Gilbert at a formative stage of his development. Though only two years Goehr's junior (he was born in 1934), his work so far shows him to be a more outright *avant-garde* composer, and less innately romantic, than his teacher. His first pieces, such as the *Missa Brevis*, Op. 4, and the *Sinfonia*, Op. 5, are serial miniatures; later pieces, such as *Nine or Ten Osannas*, Op. 10, and *Mother*, Op. 15, written for the Pierrot Players, are *avant-garde* miniatures, using a certain amount of aleatoricism. One of his largest scores is *Music in Twelve Regions* (Op. 6), written in 1965 'in memoriam Edgard Varèse'. This is scored for two orchestral units, and derived, like Hamilton's *Sinfonia*, from Stockhausen's *Gruppen*, rather than from anything of Varèse. It employs a formidable, but not unusual, array of instruments, including a Hammond organ and amplified bass guitar, and calls on most tricks of the *avant-garde* trade, in a highly organized welter of orchestral effects.

Also contemporary with Gilbert, and three years his junior, is Gordon Crosse, who, after studying at Oxford under Wellesz, sought the stimulation of a continental environment by going to Rome, in 1962, and working under Petrassi. His contacts with the academic world, first at Oxford, and later at Birmingham, where he was appointed Composition

Fellow in 1966, have given his use of serialism a different dimension—a modalism, which somewhat recalls Maxwell Davies's style. His output is varied and variable, and includes several operas (*Purgatory* is the best known) as well as other theatrical works, and school and choral pieces.

Another composer whose comparatively small output reveals a painstaking study of Schoenberg's 12-note technique is Hugh Wood. Like Goehr, his works contain a romantic core; as indeed do those of a large number of composers of widely differing style. Romanticism is still a strong force in British music today.

Romanticism

Though an adequate and universally acceptable definition of *Romanticism* is impossible, there is probably a broad measure of agreement about what is implied by the term *Romantic* when it refers to music. We might call it that residue, in a score, of sound-for-its-own sake, which is still left over when the analyst has done his work. Historically speaking it is music based on a harmonic style of composition, as that of the nineteenth century was; its appeal is to the heart more than to the head; it tells a story (*roman*); it fills a need in the human spirit, of quest, of imagination, of picture-painting, of pleasure in sound, which nothing else equally can. In a sense, therefore, romanticism is a pre-requisite of any music that aspires to anything more than ephemeral interest. And indeed, is not a man who sits down to write a symphony, instead of following the more lucrative and rational occupations of commerce or industry, a living embodiment of that mixture of imaginative idealism and unrealistic foolishness that we describe by the single, all-inclusive word *romanticism*?

Romanticism is only possible in a period of active confidence. Indeed, historically speaking, it was the rock-firm confidence of composers after about 1770 in the newly-established principles of diatonic harmony, the nuts and bolts of the harmonic style of composition, that gave birth to the period of music that saw by far the greatest manifestation of the human spirit of romanticism, namely the nineteenth century. The nineteenth century was certainly a period of overwhelming confidence. And by this reckoning of romanticism, if you maintain your confidence when the grounds on which it rests are no longer firm, your art runs the risk of becoming decadent.

It is a commonplace that many twentieth-century composers, starting with Busoni and Debussy, ceased to have confidence in this aesthetic of romanticism and attempted to modify the harmonic foundation on which it rested. The long line of those contemporary composers who have since questioned the harmonic structure of music and, as it were, divided up the spoils of the nineteenth century, is also common knowledge. But it is all too easy to exaggerate the effects of an experiment. Many critics have mistakenly interpreted the experiments of a particular composer as representing the one true direction in which contemporary music is really facing. They mistake an individual composer's personal developments for those of the tradition within which he works; in their bid to avoid at all costs appearing Beckmesserish, they mistake appearance for reality, in a way that no composer ever would. It is a particularly prevalent form of intellectual snobbery which causes a critic to simplify contemporary music, and to present it as a straight choice between the work of whatever composer he sees as 'advanced' on the one hand, and all the rest, whom he labels 'reactionary', on the other. You do not see the view if you are facing the wrong way; and the fact that many composers have questioned the concept of *romanticism* does not cause the whole corpus of romantic music to become thereby instantly redundant and irrelevant. Music history is made, not by trends, but by traditions. Moreover, one should wait to see the results of an experiment before announcing, and assuming, its success.

The late flowering of romanticism in British music, which has already been referred to[1], was, at least in part, the expression of confidence by a newly emerging school of composers. Centred round Vaughan Williams, Holst and Arnold Bax, it was a movement which formed the background for many composers, before and after 1945, who wrote symphonies, or large orchestral works: William Wordsworth, for instance, whose five symphonies and three concertos form the core of a large output. His particular pleasure is in nature—mountains, storms, spacious views, ever-changing colours—which he translates into symphonic sounds. Moreover, he admits to the force of emotion; and what could be more incurably romantic a view than that? Concord, discord, tonality—the data of romantic music—are for him reality, and he has never pursued originality for its own sake. His music is a quiet, restrained contemplation of the world's tribulations and triumphs.

> *Enough if something from our hands have power*
> *To live, and act, and serve the future hour.*

A composer whose personality reflects many sides of the romanticism between the wars is Arthur Bliss, who was born in 1891. In 1953 he succeeded Bax as Master of the Queen's Musick, and his career has included a number of administrative posts, including the B.B.C. His early compositions culminated in the *Mêlée Fantasque* (1921) and *A Colour Symphony* (1922); but it is the more intimate, less outwardly original works written since his return from California in 1925 which

1. See p. 11.

have proved longer lasting, such as the *Clarinet Quintet* (1931) and the *Pastoral: Lie Strewn the White Flocks* (1928). His symphonic works include two concertos, *Meditations on a Theme of John Blow* (1955), and *Discourse for Orchestra* (1957); his large output (over one hundred works) comprises opera, ballet and innumerable smaller pieces.

Representing an Establishment of a very different order stands Alan Bush, whose adherence to the Communist Party acts as a positive stimulus to his composition. After the conventionally English musical training of the Royal Academy of Music, and a period under John Ireland, he went to Berlin (1929–31) to study philosophy and musicology at the Humboldt University. The rise of Nazism, as well as his contact with Brecht and Hans Eisler, influenced him in adopting Marxism in 1934, though he had for a long time been associated with music in the working-class movement.

So his early instrumental compositions, which tended towards a sophisticated chromaticism, now gave place to vocal and choral compositions of a direct simplicity. Instead of piano pieces he wrote workers' choruses; instead of string quartets he wrote marching songs; and he adopted a simple style. Like Vaughan Williams, he wanted an idiom which all could understand; unlike Vaughan Williams, however, his message was political. His search for a national style has been a search for a topic, and a musical modalism, which would unite the working class. His ballad-operas *Wat Tyler* and *Men of Blackmoor* are each concerned with the unjust exploitation of the working-class, the one in the middle ages, the other in the nineteenth century. And when writing *Men of Blackmoor* Alan Bush and his wife visited a Northumbrian mine, and acquainted themselves with the folk-songs and speech idioms of that part of the country. His operas have so far only been produced in Germany; *Wat Tyler* in Leipzig, 1953; *Men of Blackmoor* in Weimar, 1956; *The Sugar Reapers* in Leipzig, 1966; *Joe Hill* in Berlin, 1970.

Such direct tone-painting from his choral and vocal works spills over into his orchestral composition. His *Third Symphony*, the *Byron Symphony*, in which each movement depicts an episode, or aspect, of Byron's life, culminates in the hero's death for the cause of Greece. In this work romanticism and politics combine; and they make uneasy partners. Just as Bush's thematic material appeals to the musically unsophisticated, so his plots, and musical schemes, reveal a naïveté which cannot but exclude a large number of his compatriots. While he may seek to unite one section of the population, this is against the other half. His *Byron Symphony* finishes with a choral finale; but there any resemblance to Beethoven ends. Beethoven's vision was for all men, and it was one of love.

Another composer of substantial symphonic works, who combines

w

academic learning with a nationalistic colour, is the Welshman Daniel Jones. Twelve years Bush's junior, he is both interested in philosophy and familiar with many languages. After graduating in English at the University of Wales, he wrote his M.A. thesis on 'The relations between Literature and Music in the Elizabethan period'; he has since written a number of essays and articles on a variety of highly original topics, including Music-Aesthetics, in which he is a contemporary pioneer. He was a friend of Dylan Thomas, and on the poet's death became literary trustee of the estate. He constructed *Under Milk Wood* from the unfinished manuscripts, and edited *A Prospect of the Sea*. He wrote his *Fourth Symphony* (1954) in memory of Dylan Thomas, and has recently edited the poems.[1] He appears as Dan Davies in Dylan Thomas's *Portrait of the Artist as a Young Dog*.

Jones's compositions consist of several symphonic poems and other orchestral pieces, six symphonies, piano works and chamber music; an oratorio, *St. Peter*, an opera, *The Knife*, and several other choral works. His romanticms is tempered by metaphysical ideas, which give his music a distinctive flavour. In 1935 he devised a scheme of Complex Metre, from which the German composer Boris Blacher later derived his 'Variable Metre' system. Jones's Complex Metres, however, have an expressive and formal purpose, and are usually confined to small appreciable units, whereas Blacher's system is mathematically based, and the unit becomes so extended that it is barely detectable to the listener.

Complex time signatures (9.2.3/8) give Jones's melody a distinctive and subtle quality, as well as a new basis for formal construction. Working from that basis, he evolved complex metrical patterns. The music gains from the unifying element of a fixed pattern, but the pattern itself is asymmetrical. In the *Sonata for Three Kettledrums*[2], for instance, (1947) the metrical patterns of the different movements are:

$$
\begin{array}{ll}
\text{i Moderato} & \dfrac{4.3.2.3.3}{4} \\[2ex]
\text{ii Allegro assai} & \dfrac{3.2.3.2.2.3.2.2.2.3.2.2.3.2.3.3.2.3.3.3.2.3.3.2}{4} \\[2ex]
\text{iii Lento e solemne} & \dfrac{9.8.6.4.3.2.3.4.6.8.}{8} \\[2ex]
\text{iv Agitato} & \dfrac{3}{4}\ \dfrac{9}{8}\ \dfrac{2}{4}\ \dfrac{6}{8}\ \dfrac{4}{4}\ \dfrac{3}{8}
\end{array}
$$

An example of the use of 'Complex Metres' occurs in three of the six movements that make up the *Sixth Symphony* (1964). The six movements

1. *The Poems of Dylan Thomas*, (Dent).
2. *The Score*, June 1950.

are arranged into three pairs as follows:

I (a) *Maestoso*   The prelude, containing the symphony's basic theme, played in unison.

(b) *Agitato*   The metrical pattern $\frac{5}{8} + \frac{2}{4}$ is maintained in the main section; in the subsidiary section $\frac{4.5}{4}$; in the development section $\frac{5}{4} + \frac{5}{8}$

II (a) *Sostenuto*   A slow movement

(b) *Con brio*   A scherzo, without middle section

III (a) *Capriccioso*   Variations, played continuously, with the metrical pattern $\frac{6.4.3.2}{4}$

(b) *Vivace*   Resembles I (b) in structure, but with the metrical pattern $\frac{4}{4} + \frac{3}{8}$

[This symphony, which, like the fourth, was commissioned by the Royal National Eisteddford, is free in its tonality, but highly organised in its structure. The whole work derives from a single theme, and the tonal centres of the six movements are regular, and balanced—D, G sharp, B, F, G sharp, D.

If Jones's 'Complex Metres' recall the rhythmic development of Stravinsky, and in particular the additive rhythm technique which Tippett embodied into his style, he also invented a system of extended modes, which are somewhat reminiscent of Messiaen's music before 1950. Jones conceives of a mode that arrives not necessarily at the octave above the starting-note, but at some other one. A musical *continuum* is formed by continuing the mode upwards. Thus, for example:

Ex. 56   Daniel Jones

In this example the mode extends over a minor ninth; the starting-note is a semitone higher each time. Intervening notes are not considered; for instance, the note C can only occur at the point, and pitch, shown at *. The use of these modes has been confined to chamber music for a small number of instruments.

Several composers of the next generation as well have continued this symphonic growth, with works on a large scale: Wilfred Josephs,

Nicholas Maw, Jeremy Dale Roberts, Patric Standford, Arthur Butterworth and several others. All derive recognisably from the English
romanticism of the 30's; all use a familiar form of tonality; yet within
these broad limits their individual styles differ.

Wilfred Josephs, who was born in 1927, achieved what is practically
unknown for a British composer, a sudden, and spectacular, international
notoriety. This came in December, 1963, when his *Requiem*, Op. 39, won
the 'First International Competition for Symphonic Composition of the
City of Milan and La Scala'. His subsequent success as a composer—
performances, commissions and so on—stemmed from that point, though
it was by no means his first work, nor his first prize.

The *Requiem* caught the public fancy, particularly in America[1], in a
way that few works do; certainly those of unknown composers. It was
played in 1967 in Cincinnati and New York.

It is an act of remembrance for the untold millions of Jews who were
murdered in Europe under Hitler. It was originally conceived in 1961,
during the time of the Eichmann trial. Perhaps the artistic representation
of this chief crime of our age required, for its full effect to be realized, a
Jewish composer. Only he would feel the consanguineous horror at
the sufferings of his fellow Jews; only he could express, on behalf of the
world-wide Jewish community, what it is appropriate should be expressed—and no more. We recall Schoenberg's *A Survivor from Warsaw*.
We also recall another work, which, strangely, was also awarded an
international prize in 1963, but without creating such a sensational, and
very obvious, *succès d'estime*—more strangely still, it was the work of a
composer who was himself, in his own person, a survivor from Warsaw—
Andrzej Panufnik's *Sinfonia Sacra*. The very title, *Requiem*, appealed to
the public mood at this time, as Britten had shown the previous year. But
Josephs' work is more personal, and contains none of the immediate
juxtaposition of opposites that Britten's *War Requiem* has. The spirit of
protest is entirely absent; it is replaced by a dignified sorrow, a quiet
hope.

Josephs first wrote a *String Quintet*, Op. 32, in memory of those Jews
who had died: three slow movements, called *Requiescant pro defunctis
Iudaeis*. Later, he incorporated this quintet into a choral work, a setting of
the traditional Hebrew prayer of mourning, the Kaddish. Just as the
mood of this *Requiem* is prevailingly quiet, so is its tempo prevailingly
slow; yet nowhere does the Kaddish text mention death or the dead.
Though it is a funeral meditation, it is concerned only with life and with
the glorification of God. The three String Quintet movements (*Requiescant*,

1. It was first played in this country by the Hallé Orchestra in Sheffield, 29 October 1966.

Lacrimosa, Monumentum) carry the burden of grief, and become progressively slower, simpler, less rhetorical. Interspersed as they are, as interludes to the text, they correspond in this respect to the Wilfred Owen poems of Britten's work. The six vocal movements express the acceptance of God's will, and the traditional Messianic hope of the Psalms and the Prophets, in a mood of fervent and profound submission. There is one purely orchestral movement, *De profundis*. The scheme of the work as a whole is thus:

(Adagio 3/4)	1	*Requiescant*	string quintet	1st section
(Adagio 3/4)	2	*Yitgadal*	chorus and orchestra	
(Allegro ritmico 4/4)	3	*Yehey Sh'mey Raba*	chorus and orchestra	2nd section
(Poco Andante 3/4)	4	*Yitbarach*	baritone solo and orchestra	
(Adagio 4/4)	5	*Lacrimosa*	string quintet	3rd section
(Adagio 4/4)	6	*Yehee Shem*	baritone solo, chorus and orchestra	
(Grave 6/4)	7	*De Profundis*	orchestra	
(Pesante 3/4)	8	*Ezri Meyim*	baritone solo, chorus and orchestra	4th section
(Piú Adagio 4/4)	9	*Monumentum*	string quintet	
(Adagio 4/4)	10	*Ohseh Shalom*	baritone solo, chorus and orchestra	

However, the Hebrew text was not used to restrict the work to Jewish dead. On the contrary, though it was a Jewish tragedy that first triggered off the composition, Josephs wished to underline the universality of his artistic aims by avoiding the many established associations, both musical and liturgical, of the Roman Mass for the Dead. It was his hope that the listener would be able to submerge himself in the feeling inspired through the music by the text, without being distracted by any such specific associations; and the profoundly moving impact made by the La Scala première amply fulfilled this hope.

The very original emotional character of the work results partly from the layout of the forces employed. When Josephs first started planning the extension of the *Quintet* into a ten-movement choral and orchestral work, begun and interspersed by quintet movements, he entertained the idea of rescoring the quintet music for orchestra. But by deciding against this, and instead keeping the original quintet of two violins, viola, and two cellos, he produced a work of strongly individual dynamic design. The music rises out of, and finally sinks again into, near-silence, and the use of a quintet of solo strings adds an extra dimension to the dynamic possibilities of normal orchestral scoring. By contrast with the biggest fortissimo the quintet can produce, even the quieter passages for chorus and orchestra assume a character of massive strength. The few loud outbursts are in turn able to make a striking impact, since the contrast with the quintet enables the composer to keep to a soft dynamic through a large proportion of the choral and orchestral music.

The impact of Josephs' *Requiem*, which is sung in Hebrew, in phonetic transliteration, derives partly from the direct expressiveness and warmth of the vocal line, partly from the harmonic idiom. This is both highly individual, yet flexible, and consistent as need be both with the quasi-modal style of a plainsong-like section, and with the semitonal brilliance of a climax-point; the third movement illustrates both these aspects. This harmonic and melodic consistency derives from a simple 4-note chord which is capable of almost limitless variation of colour, by the constant permutation of its constituent notes:

Ex. 57   Wilfred Josephs
                                Requiem

Motivic chord

By the inflection of each note either way, either singly or in combination, a wide range of progressions and chords is possible. For instance, if the E is changed to E♯ (F♮) and the B to B♭, harmony in fourths is suggested; the work opens in this way. Many types of triads can be arrived at; one example, for instance, results from the two lower notes (C, E) being moved up a tone (to D, F♯). No. 6 ends with this chord (transposed down a semitone). Moving triads occur in several places (for instance in No. 8); the major seventh chord moves in its entirety, in No. 3, and No. 4. The four notes may be spelt out melodically, in modified form, as at the opening of No. 10; the inversion of the chord leads to the minor 2nd, or minor 9th, with which the work closes.

Indeed, a most interesting parallel may be drawn between the even-chord movement of the unaccompanied choral *Amen* with which Britten ends the *Dies Irae* of his *War Requiem*, which again occurs at the end of the work, and the even-chord movement of *Ohseh Shalom* at the end of Josephs' *Requiem*. Both move step-wise; in both the movement arises from the nature of the thematic material. But the harmonic change in the

Josephs is subtler; the final die-away leaves the implications of the parent chord unresolved. Britten, however, instead of dying away on the tritone, round which his entire work has been built, allows the chorus to subside onto a comfortable and reassuring F major triad.

Wilfred Josephs wrote a large number of early works while still a schoolboy, which he later destroyed. A certain parental mistrust of the musical profession led him to qualify as a dentist in 1951; and his study at the Guildhall School under Alfred Nieman (1954-6) was carried on simultaneously with the practice of dentistry. A year in Paris under Max Deutsch, 1958/9, enlarged his musical range decisively; this was the period when Boulez was presenting the *avant-garde* in his *Domaine Musicale* concerts. But Josephs was not easily swayed. 'The 12-note style,' he said in 1964, 'has come and gone for me, and I have found my own style in works that have appeared abroad—seldom in England'; which is the fate of many a British composer.

Yet Josephs was not entirely unknown before the *Requiem*; the *Viola Concertante*, Op. 30, was commissioned in 1961 for a chamber orchestra in Birmingham. He was particularly in demand as a composer of light-weight works, and of radio and television incidental music; his flair for light music had been shown in the *Comedy-Overture 'The Ants'*, Op. 7, which depicts the ant-like movement of Londoners in the Underground during the rush-hour; and *Twelve Letters*, Op. 16, a setting of Hilaire Belloc's 'A Moral Alphabet'. Light music, indeed, forms a strong element in his musical personality. He has since written a very large amount of incidental and background music for feature films, documentaries, television and theatre shows, which calls for little beyond fluency, and whose *raison d'être* is economic. Light works form a fair proportion of his large output.

But for his development of a personal idiom the turning point came with the *Concerto da Camera*, Op. 25, the first work that he wrote after his study with Max Deutsch. Thereafter, his works with opus numbers are divided between symphonies, concertos and several large-scale chamber works; important works for piano—*14 Studies*, Op. 53, *29 Preludes*, Op. 70—and various dramatic, or semi-dramatic entertainment pieces, which are more direct in idiom, such as *Adam and Eve*, Op. 61.

The *Second Symphony* was the first major work to be heard and 'officially' commented on in this country. When it was known that Josephs had won the Milan prize, his symphony was included in the 1965 Cheltenham Festival, and played there on 5th July. It is a striking work in structure and idiom, and breaks new ground in both respects. The first movement, which lasts almost half the total twenty-five minutes, is an exposition of the material, which is treated in the ensuing shorter

movements. The second movement is an intermezzo, while the third combines slow movement and scherzo; the fourth, *Grave*, is the symphony's
heart, which Josephs originally conceived as a synthesis to the opening
movement's thesis, while the finale *Prestissimo leggiero*, never rising above
p, is a fleeting, ghostlike re-working of the first movement at twelve
times the speed. The harmonic idiom is freely tonal, with a dimension of
expression that comes from an acquaintance with serial techniques.

Two important commissions from America resulted from the *Requiem*;
the *Third Symphony* ('Philadelphia') was commissioned by the Chamber
Symphony of that city; and a large-scale choral work, for adult and
children's choruses, *Mortales*, was commissioned for the Cincinnati May
Festival, in May 1970.

The *Third Symphony* is tailored to an orchestra of thirty-six players. It
was written in the very short space of two months (June/August 1967),
and adheres to a classical four-movement structure. *Mortales* followed a
period of reassessment, and introduces new techniques, such as aleatoricism.

Maw, like Josephs, also studied under Max Deutsch in Paris. His
most characteristic works, in a so far fairly small output, are *Scenes and
Arias* (1962) for soprano, mezzo-soprano, contralto and orchestra (a
setting of two anonymous mediaeval poems), a *String Quartet* (1965),
Sinfonia (1966) and *Sonata for 2 Horns and Strings* (1967). He achieves a
certain opulence and fullness by the gradual and deliberate spelling out of
a harmonic situation, by thematic cross-reference, and build up of a
complex texture, often from lightweight material. The music finds its
fullest expression when the pulse is slow moving, and the rate of harmonic
change correspondingly leisurely. In purely vocal works his characteristic
romanticism is less noticeable. The vocal line, for instance, in the songs
The Voice of Love (1966) is serially derived, and various devices are
directly influenced by Britten. Moreover, Maw's first opera, *One-Man
Show*, was spoilt by a libretto of shattering triviality, against which the
music was powerless; but for his second opera, *The Rising of the Moon*
(1970), which was the first ever to be commissioned by Glyndebourne,
the librettist Beverley Cross, in spite of some unnecessary complications
of plot, provided a comedy of considerable scope for the composer's
gradually evolving harmonic style.

Several composers of this generation modify the romantic tradition in
the light of their own style, and in accordance with evolving contemporary
styles. Jeremy Dale Roberts, who was born in 1934, strove first to emulate
Debussy and Tippett, whose imaginative power he most respected; this
is reflected in his earliest works, such as the *Suite for Flute and Strings*

(1958) and *Florilegium* (1961). Later, he developed an increasing interest in *timbre*, a keener-edged melodic line, in such pieces as *Capriccio for Violin and Piano* (1967), and *Sinfonia da Caccia* (1966). He is a composer, like Tippett, who seeks to translate the imaginative experiences of life—a year in the Cameroons, the Egyptian desert, nature, French epic poetry—into aurally perceptible sound.

Patric Standford's romanticism, on the other hand, has been tempered by a study of various contemporary techniques, new and not so new, under Malipiero, Lutoslawski and Messiaen. Like Bennett, he includes light music and film music in his output; but his most characteristic orchestral works are the fruits of a personal imagination. After the *Second String Quartet* and *Stabat Mater* (1966) he developed a greater freedom of style, and later works such as *Chiaroscuro* (1967) and *Notte* (1968) are an attempt to combine atmospheric and aleatoric techniques into the traditional disciplines of thematic composition. His student contemporary at the Guildhall School of Music was the conductor, James Stobart, who has since performed many of Standford's works with the New Cantata Orchestra, which he founded.

In spite of the adulatory fervour which surrounded the name of Sibelius in the thirties, the two Scandinavian masters of the Romantic symphonic tradition, Sibelius and Carl Nielsen, have had curiously few English disciples. Two composers, however, whose symphonies are directly descended from them are Robert Simpson and Arthur Butterworth. Both have so far written three symphonies. Simpson is the author of detailed studies of Nielsen and Bruckner, where his allegiance clearly lies. Butterworth is a Mancunian, and his music has strong connections with the North of England; his *Third Symphony*, for chorus and orchestra, is called *Moorland*. He was an orchestral trumpeter in the Scottish National and Hallé Orchestras until 1961, and his main works are symphonic. His *First Symphony* (1957) was directly influenced by Sibelius, while his *Second Symphony* (1965) was in memory of the Sibelius and Nielsen centenary (1865–1965). He considers tonality, in the form of the 'basic symbols' in sound (the octave, fifth, third and so on), to contain the basis of meaning common to all human beings. His music also contains a ruggedness, a certain greyness, which is Butterworth's impression of the architecture of the North of England, and the character of his fellow Northerners—to say nothing of the English weather.

It is perhaps understandable that any British composer of this tradition should be bracketed with either Sibelius or Nielsen. However, in the case of William Bardwell such a comparison is not justified. His *First Symphony* (1966), though duly ascribed to the Nielsen influence[1], is more of a

1. In *The Times* of 25 March 1966.

personal essay in orchestral timbre and symphonic structure by a composer whose work up to then had concentrated chiefly on chamber and vocal works. His idiom is simple and expressive, though not naïve, and he has a preference for instruments of an intimate and quiet character, such as the mandolin, for which he has written a concerto. Three years at the Royal College of Music, under those twin champions of orthodoxy, R. O. Morris and Gordon Jacob, were followed by three years under Nadia Boulanger in Paris. His output is small, the result of painstaking deliberation, fastidious revision and, occasionally, withdrawal. Performances of his works have been very intermittent, and none of them is published.

His orchestral works are focused onto two symphonies. The first is in three movements, of which the second (Andante) was written separately and before the other two, which were later added. Not surprisingly perhaps the *Second Symphony* is more integrated as a symphony, and more refined orchestrally. Written four years after the first (1970–71), its four movements gradually enlarge in structure, and increase in tension as the music proceeds.

Two ideas dominate the first movement; a slow, legato melody for the strings, woodwind and light percussion, which opens the symphony; and a more rhythmic, percussive figure, associated with the brass, with a background of agitated *tremolando*, which forms the core of the development, and against which the opening melody is later set at a moment of rich climax.

The second movement (*Allegro non troppo*) uses *pizzicato* strings like a harp. As the composer says, he takes up at the point reached by Tchaikowsky in the scherzo of his *Fourth Symphony*. In the middle section of the movement, Bardwell gives the cellos and basses the *pizzicato* material, but *arco*, at a low register, and in close position. This forms a background for free, improvisatory material, largely in the percussion. The movement closes with the harp taking over the *pizzicato* material, inverted (bar 49), while the melody is given this time to the flute and piccolo (pp, *dolcissimo*).

The third, slow, movement is a fugue, whose sharply defined, rather dramatic subject mounts to a solemn climax in the brass before dying away to nothing. The finale (*Allegro spiritoso*) has as its framework an ostinato trumpet theme, whose entry is always marked by the same chord. The intervening episodes call for a high degree of orchestral virtuosity, and include a timpani figure, canon for the strings, characteristic use of the brass, and so on. The melody of the opening movement is briefly recalled before the end, when the orchestral chord that has persisted throughout the finale is increased to include the full orchestra, transposed, and spread out over the last thirteen bars, until it closes the symphony on a note of brilliance, yet remains unresolved.

Many of his vocal and choral compositions have Eastern and Spanish affiliations; and, indeed, since 1967 he has chosen to live in Spain, in a remote corner of Alicante province. The *Chinese Cantatas* (1952) (on poems from Ezra Pound's *Cathay*) evoke an Eastern spirit, without slipping into pastiche. The *Serranillas* (1961), six poems by the Marqués de Santillana, and *La Lechuza* (1968), three poems of Antonio Machado, are set for voice and piano; *Dardi d'Amore* (1967), three sonnets by Guido Cavalcanti, is set for *a capella* choir, and is freely expressive in a traditional idiom.

The Romantic tradition was not only symphonic, though a number of symphonists have worked within it; choral and vocal music has provided just as important an outlet.

The senior representative of this aspect of the tradition is Charles Orr, who was born in 1893, the year before Peter Warlock. He shared with Warlock the friendship of Delius, and interpreted the romanticism of the inter-war years solely in terms of song-writing. Many song-composers shared this influence—George Butterworth, Ivor Gurney, Gerald Finzi, Armstrong Gibbs—all of whom came within the dominating influence of Vaughan Williams. Unfortunately, Charles Orr was subject since birth to most severe attacks of eczema, and this gravely handicapped his work. He was at the Guildhall School of Music, and also studied privately with Edward Dent. His first, and strongest, formative influence was the expressive strength of German Lieder; he heard Elena Gerhardt in 1912, and decided to concentrate his creative energy onto song-writing, much as Hugo Wolf did. He made translations for performance in English of Hugo Wolf's songs—though these remain unpublished.

While Finzi concentrated as a song-writer on words by Thomas Hardy, Orr focussed his attention primarily on the poems of A. E. Housman; and there lies his strength. In his poetry Housman represented the mood of nostalgic romanticism that was peculiarly characteristic of this period. Most of Orr's thirty-five published songs were written before 1939, though six appeared in the 50's, including settings of Helen Waddell's *Mediaeval Latin Lyrics*. Twenty-four are Housman settings: Housman was to Orr what Mörike was to Wolf.

The expressive, Purcell-derived *parlando* style that was to mark the style of later song-writers, such as Tippett and Britten, is quite foreign to Orr. Instead, the melodic line is square, but invariably appropriate for the mood and rhythm of the words; and the colour is primarily harmonic and dramatic, as in the case of Wolf. There is no trace of a pseudo-folk style, which is the bane of many a British composer who wrote beneath the shadow of Vaughan Williams. Moreover, the piano writing is conceived in terms of the instrument, a part in its own right. Chromatic subtlety marks the harmonic movement, based naturally on the acceptance of key-based tonality, which goes without saying among composers of this tradition. Warlock greatly admired Orr's work, and it is fitting that Orr in return should have dedicated to his fellow song-writer one of his most effective, and largest, Housman settings, *The Carpenter's Son*.

Younger than Orr, though working within the same tradition, is Bernard Naylor; but his considerable output is predominantly choral, and predominantly sacred. He is one of the very few composers who have effectively carried the tradition of English Romanticism into the church. Born in 1907, he was a pupil of Vaughan Williams, Holst and Ireland at the Royal College of Music, and his first compositions, which included a symphonic poem, an opera, and a *scena* for tenor and orchestra, were derivative from these sources. He has divided his time between this country and Canada, where he has been active as a teacher and conductor, as well as composer. Between 1935 and 1947 he wrote nothing of any consequence. After 1947, however, he began to compose again, and his mature works date from this year: fifty-three songs and choral works, six chamber music compositions, and a 'modern mystery' for three characters and string quartet—*The Cloak*, by Clifford Bax.

Though both derive from a common musical source, Naylor uses more metrical licence than Orr. Whereas Orr uses a harmonic chromaticism, Naylor develops a greater tonal freedom. His point of departure was the ecclesiastical choral style of singing of King's College, Cambridge; and so, in one sense, his work represents the first fruits of the new style of choral music introduced by Boris Ord.[1] Resonance and homogeneity are the key to the character, quality and effect of his, at first sight, somewhat disjointed vocal textures. He composes to a scheme, rather than a theme; he works with a melodic or rhythmic idea, which is simple, unadventurous accessible to amateurs, yet distinctive. The music is governed by tonal centres rather than keys, and achieves its effect more by the expressiveness of each phrase, and each word within the phrase, than by any strong, or particularly memorable vocal line. Naylor's most characteristic works are *King Solomon's Prayer*, a cantata for voices and orchestra, *Stabat Mater*, for women's voices and orchestra, and the *Nine Motets*. These works, and his numerous other cantatas and motets, stand out the more so in a period when church music is at a low ebb. But, curiously, the *Nine Motets*, which depict the chief landmarks of the Christian year—Advent, Christmas, Epiphany, Ash Wednesday, Good Friday, Easter Day,

1. See p. 14.

Ascension Day, Whitsunday and Trinity Sunday—are all settings of Old
Testament texts, largely Isaiah; and this casts a certain mood of nostalgia
over the work, which is reinforced by recollections of the choral texture of
Bax (particularly such a work as *Mater Ora Filium*, which is the prototype
for Naylor's choral style), and occasionally a suggestion of the dramatic
excitement of Walton.

Another graduate of Oxford University, and thirteen years Naylor's
junior, Geoffrey Bush also follows the established tradition; like Naylor
he did not fully achieve a sense of musical direction until comparatively
late, with his *Dialogue* for oboe and piano (1960). But he had begun to
write down notes at the age of ten, when he was a chorister at Salisbury
Cathedral; this, and the teaching of John Ireland, formed his background.
Bush is a scholar as well as a composer and, like Vaughan Williams, is
concerned to find out for himself something of the past legacy of British
music. His historical assessment of the past leads him to the conclusion
that influences from France and Italy have generally been beneficial to
British music, as can be seen in the Madrigalists and Purcell; while those
from Germany (Handel, Brahms, Mendelssohn, Wagner, Schoenberg)
have been almost entirely destructive of the endemic tradition.

His music is light and direct. His orchestral scores, which are easily
approachable, and usually within the scope of amateurs, include two
symphonies, several concertos for cello, oboe, piano and trumpet, and
three overtures. His *Concerto for Light Orchestra* was written for a B.B.C.
Light Music Festival, while his *Music for Orchestra* (1967) was written
for the Shropshire County Youth Orchestra.

Directness of approach also characterizes his operas, which are all
short, and of one act. *The Blind Beggar's Daughter* is a ballad opera, very
much in the Vaughan Williams tradition, 'for young people of all ages'.
If the Cap Fits, with a libretto by the composer from Molière's 'Les
Précieuses Ridicules', is a satirical comedy; his next libretto, *The Equation*,
from John Drinkwater's 'X=O', is a tragedy.

But if Bush remains on the fringe as far as opera is concerned, his most
characteristic work is undoubtedly in the smaller chamber music forms,
such as the two piano *Sonatinas*, and particularly the songs. These
range from the simply diatonic, *Five Spring Songs* (1944), to the more
freely declamatory and chromatic, *Greek Love Songs* (1964), and include
three settings with various orchestral groupings. Bush's style is aptly
suited to the comparatively short form of a song, and in them he combines
freedom with a simplicity of effect. The piano is integrated into the voice
part, and is not an independent entity.

Born in 1921, the year after Bush, Adrian Cruft also derived his earliest
musical experience as a chorister in an English cathedral—in his case,

Westminster Abbey. English polyphony is part of his fibre. He is one of a distinguished musical family, who have been orchestral musicians for five generations;[1] and after learning the double bass from his father, Eugene Cruft, he played this instrument in several orchestras. Though his orchestral output includes three overtures, and a *Divertimento* for strings (1963), most of Cruft's work is choral, and predominantly religious. His use of the diatonic vocabulary has become progressively more refined, and he is particularly inclined towards the use of triads with conflicting tonality. His church compositions are largely intended for liturgical use; particularly characteristic are the two settings of the *Te Deum*, the *Magnificat*, and the *Mass for St. Michael*, which was written in 1962 for Coventry Cathedral. But a work which derives extra expressive power from the additional dimension of drama, as well as from the use of mediaeval words, is the chamber cantata, *Alma Redemptoris Mater* (1967). In this, the choral writing is simpler, and the harmony more static, than in earlier works, and the effect is of a stark grandeur, at a slow-moving pace. The scoring (contralto and baritone solo and choir, accompanied by flute, oboe, violin, cello and organ) is similar to that of the cantata *Crucifixus pro nobis* by Cruft's teacher, Edmund Rubbra.

Representative composers of this tradition, belonging to the next generation, are Bryan Kelly, who was born in 1934, and Christopher Brown, who is nine years his junior. Kelly was a choirboy at Worcester College, Oxford, before proceeding to the Royal College of Music. His technique is that of a *Kapellmester*, whose function is to oblige with whatever is requested: a church service, a light overture, something for a choir to sing at a festival, a children's opera. One of his most performed works is the Evening Service, based on Cuban rhythms.

Christopher Brown attended Westminster Abbey Choir School, and later was at King's College, Cambridge, and the Royal Academy of Music. His work so far has been predominantly choral, in direct line from Naylor and Cruft.

The adoption, and the adaptation, of a traditional idiom, based on tonality, has tended in the case of several composers already mentioned towards some of their most effective scores being written in a lighter vein, with none of the more portentous and weighty implications of different, less readily-accessible idioms. It is a most natural tendency; and there is also a considerable number of composers whose work is quite unashamedly intended as entertainment.

Among the best known is Malcolm Arnold, who after a period of study at the Royal College of Music, and service in the army during the war,

1. His elder brother John is now Music Director of the Arts Council of Great Britain.

was principal trumpeter in the London Philharmonic for eight years. He has been notably successful in his film scores, of which he has written over eighty; and in addition to the immediate, and by no means irrelevant, financial reward for his labours, he was awarded a Hollywood Oscar for *The Bridge on the River Kwai*, and an Ivor Novello award for *The Inn of the Sixth Happiness.*

The style of his symphonic and chamber music is unassailably diatonic, and if not always subtle or profound, it has a direct simplicity, coupled with a humorous touch. This finds its niche in such a work as *A Grand Grand Overture*, Op. 57, which started the Hoffnung Musical Festival on 13th November 1956[1]. This was the occasion when long-suffering London musicians released some of the pent-up tension of the previous fraught and agonized decade, and let down their musical hair in an orgy of musical jokes—some, it must be admitted, funnier than others, and some whose point could only be detected by the connoisseur. Arnold's piece, for three vacuum cleaners, one floor polisher, and full orchestra, enshrines the Song of the Hoover into an orchestral texture; no mean feat, and one unsurpassed before or since. Moreover, his *Concerto for two pianos* (1969) delighted the Prom audience for whom it was written. He is a polished popular entertainer.

Arnold lives in Cornwall, and detects in the Cornish a highly-developed sense of humour. It is, he says, 'the land of male-voice choirs, brass bands, Methodism, May Days, and Moody and Sankey hymns'; also of the deserted engine-houses of the tin and copper mines, which 'radiate a strange and sad beauty'. All this is reflected in his *Four Cornish Dances*, light and brilliant pieces which show the essence of Arnold's music; as do his earlier *Scottish Dances*, and the two sets of *English Dances*, which are his best-known works among a huge output.

John Addison is a contemporary of Arnold, born one year earlier in 1920, and one who is also primarily concerned with film work. His light film-style has been used in several concert scores, such as the ballet suite *Carte Blanche*, and a *Serenade* for wind quintet and harp.

Another contemporary, Denis Blood, is an Irish composer, born in Dublin, who describes himself, with appropriate Irish sophistry, as a 'serious light composer'. His overture *Bravade*, and his *Capriccio* for piano and orchestra, are just that. After studying at Oxford, where he was an organ student, then at the University of South Carolina, Blood was associated with Muir Mathieson and the Rank Film Organisation, before setting out on a nomadic career.

If his output is slender, and unpublished, the same cannot be said of Ernest Tomlinson, who was first a Manchester Cathedral choirboy, and

1. See p. 139.

studied the organ, piano, clarinet and composition at Manchester before, and immediately after, the war. His light orchestral pieces aim to be 'unpretentious and tuneful', and he has written a large number of orchestral works in this vein—suites, dances, overtures, and light opera. His best-known tune is *Little Serenade*, which has often been used as a signature-tune for radio and television programmes; the sort of tune few can identify, but most can hum. Tomlinson has also written several works which integrate jazz groups with the symphony orchestra— *Sinfonia '62*, *Symphony 65*; and *Concerto for 5* (concerto for five saxophones and orchestra). His most recent concern is with electronic music, and he is now building up a studio at his home near Preston in Lancashire. His underlying purpose is 'to communicate with ordinary people by any means available'. With this end in view he founded in 1969 a Northern Concert Orchestra, which is intended to be a popular orchestra for the concert hall, to fill the gap between the majority of people to whom 'serious' music signifies little, and the minority who can derive pleasure from the standard symphonic repertoire, and the even smaller minority who are sympathetic to the *avant-garde*.

If the term 'light music' can be taken by different musicians to have several shades of meaning, each of them somewhat pejorative, the style of Joseph Horovitz is perhaps better described as witty and ingenious, rather than light. Like Tomlinson, he uses jazz idioms where it suits him; like Arnold he found a niche in the Hoffnung concerts.

Though born in Vienna, Horovitz has lived in this country since 1938. After studying at Oxford, he went to the Royal College of Music, and thereafter for a year to Nadia Boulanger. His name first became known in the 50's with his light ballets, such as *Les Femmes d'Alger* and *Alice in Wonderland*. Other notable successes in this unusual *genre*, which he has made peculiarly his own, are *Concerto for dancers* and *Let's make a ballet*. Horovitz himself conducted performances, such as those of the Ballets Russes and the Intimate Opera Company, for whom he wrote the comic operas *The Dumb Wife* and *Gentlemen's Island*.

Musical wit is notoriously elusive; one man's joke is another man's poison. Horovitz brings to bear not only great technical accomplishment, which raises his work above the level of incidental music, but, even more important, the appropriate limitation of musical material, so that the listener's attention is not diverted and aroused by too weighty and complex possibilities of development. Too much thematic contrast would imply symphonic development, which is not appropriate in such a style; too little variety, however, can very quickly induce boredom. Humour and timing go together, and a score such as the *Four Dances for Orchestra* (from *Femmes d'Alger*), with its dramatic sparkle, or the *Jazz harpsichord concerto*, with its absurd juxtaposition of two entirely opposed traditions, derive from these extra dimensions a vitality which is lacking from the other more conventional pieces, such as the various concertos, and chamber works.

For the Hoffnung concerts, where you had to be funny at all costs if you were to survive, Horovitz collaborated with Alistair Sampson in a series of parodies; first, *Metamorphoses on a Bedtime Theme*, which presented a television commercial ('Sleep sweeter—Bournvita') in the style of Bach, Mozart, Verdi, Schoenberg and Stravinsky; second, *Horroratorio*, which ridiculed the old oratorio style in a work which celebrated the wedding of two delightful characters, Master Frankenstein and Miss Dracula. Like a true comic, Horovitz builds his musical jokes on a serious foundation; the audience will laugh more if they can laugh away something that they recognize as being inherently real, yet stupid.

If Horovitz is a frequent performer of his own works, this applies to a number of other musicians. However incapable some of the most eminent composers may be of directing an orchestra, or playing what they themselves have written, there are also those whose music is first conceived from the point of view of the executive artist. The theatre has produced several. Marc Wilkinson is one, whose eighty plays include *The Royal Hunt of the Sun*. Christopher Whelen is another, whose starting-point was his work as Musical Director of the Old Vic; he was also assistant conductor with the Bournemouth and Birmingham orchestras. He is almost exclusively a theatre composer, with 150 productions to his credit in theatre, ballet, television and radio. Two other highly practical musicians of the theatre are Thomas Eastwood, and the Australian Malcolm Williamson. Eastwood, who was a pupil of Boris Blacher, and then of Erwin Stein, is best known for his opera *Christopher Sly* (1960); he has also set sail on the comparatively uncharted waters of television opera, with his contemporary interpretation of the Good Friday story, set in East Berlin, *The Rebel* (1969). His idiom fits Rudolph Reti's definition of 'pantonality'[1]. On the other hand, Williamson, another Stein pupil, fills a need mainly in the field of more conventional opera. The style of his compositions, which include numerous orchestral and chamber works as well as opera, varies according to the audience; he is also much in demand as an organist and pianist, as well as a composer.

Another most prolific pianist/composer is Ronald Stevenson, whose best-known composition so far is his *Passacaglia* on D.S.C.H. (D-E flat-C-B). His links with the grand, romantic age of piano-playing of Liszt or Busoni are both explicit and implicit in this monumental work,

1. See Reti, *Tonality, Atonality, Pantonality*.

as indeed in Stevenson's work as a whole. He is of Scottish and Welsh ancestry, born in 1928, and strongly aware of the Celtic side to his nature, as well as of his working-class origin. This, and an acute social conscience, have given his music a thrust, an edge, which is highly distinctive. Stevenson sets out both to win an immediate rapport with the ordinary listener, wherever he may be found (which his first performance of the *Passacaglia*, in Cape Town in December 1963, certainly achieved), and also, somewhat more remotely, to seek an ideal of a 'world music', a universal language of understanding. If the world-weary Westerner may smile ruefully at such a hopelessly unattainable goal, many artists and composers have attempted to take at least the first steps towards it, however faltering; notably Busoni, who has been the chief model for Stevenson, whether as pianist, as man, or as artist in the widest sense.

Stevenson's output includes numerous choral works and songs, many of which are settings of Blake, with whose visionary qualities he finds himself in close affinity. But pride of place must be given to the piano works. The Busoni influence is all-pervasive on Stevenson. He researched for many years into Busoni's life and work, and after 1955 he continued this, while also studying orchestration in Rome with a Busoni pupil, Guido Guerini. This research and study culminated in a massive study of Busoni[1]; and the *Passacaglia*, written 1960/62, which is the most important of his hundred compositions so far, represents the consummation of these Busoni-orientated years. The parallels with the latter's *Fantasia Contrappuntistica* are quite overt.

The work forms in contemporary music what biologists would call a 'sport'. It runs contrary to evolutionary trends; it is, logically and rationally speaking, impossible. Whereas the commonest trend today is towards a fragmentation of both style and content, Stevenson builds his eighty-minute structure on the proven capacity of the piano for architectural growth, and on a wide-ranging technical basis which extends from Bach's contrapuntal style to the extravagant gestures of the high Romantic period, and including certain more experimental devices of today. Other composers, such as Kenneth Leighton, have been directly influenced by Busoni's famous *Fantasia*; or, such as Robert Sherlaw Johnson, have explored pianistic experiment. Those who have derived inspiration from Bach are legion. But Stevenson has sought to combine all these traditions, with a few others for good measure, into one enormous structure.

Moreover, he has successfully avoided the ever-present tendency of performer-composers, to slip into derivative gesture; as he does in certain other works, such as the later harpsichord sonata, for instance.

1. So far unpublished.

The *Passacaglia* is based on the musical letters of the name of D. Shostakovitch (D.S.C.H.) Stevenson was greatly impressed by the Russian composer's works[1], particularly the Eighth String Quartet, the tenth Symphony and the First Violin Concerto.

His work is in three parts, of which the first is built round the classical concepts of sonata and suite; the second is concerned with the primeval ideal of 'world music' (Tippett would call it archetypal), and introduces a picture of 'emergent Africa'; the third forms the dramatic climax of the whole work, with a 'tribute to Bach' and a triple fugue.

Stevenson's views as a composer are perhaps best summed up in his own words:

My main interest in music is in the epic. This is an epic age, it seems to me, and only epic forms can fully express its aspirations. I absorb in my music elements from the East and from Africa, as well as from Western culture. In my future work, I hope to find points of coalescence in world music; there are musical forms which are common to all nations (for instance variation, and the relationship between Hindu and European music of such forms as *Kirtanam* and *Khyal*, comparable with sonata and rondo structures respectively); and although there are many nations, there is only one human race. I'll use any technique which will enable me to achieve these objectives. My aim is to base my music in reality, and to allow it to tend towards abstraction, but *never* to take abstraction as a premise and so lose all connection with life, which is so much larger than the musical world.

1. He presented an incomplete copy of the *Passacaglia* to Shostakovitch during the 1962 Edinburgh Festival. It was first played in this country by John Ogdon in 1966, at the Aldeburgh and Cheltenham Festivals.

22 Lennox Berkeley and Priaulx Rainier

A traditional idiom has been used in highly contrasted ways by two senior composers, both pupils of Nadia Boulanger: Lennox Berkeley and Priaulx Rainier.

Lennox Berkeley, who was born in 1903, developed a distinctive style within the traditional idiom, and has maintained it consistently. His most characteristic features are a textural lightness and lucidity, a harmonic piquancy, an eighteenth-century *galanterie*, and a thematic brevity; and these intrinsic qualities are more effectively realized in the more intimate forms than in the large structures; in works of limited and precise emotional range, rather than in those of broader sweep or more profound import; in such orchestral works as the *Serenade* or *Divertimento*, rather than in the symphonies; in chamber operas, such as *A Dinner Engagement*, or *Ruth*, rather than in the more heroic, grand opera *Nelson*; and particularly in songs and chamber music.

Berkeley spent five years in France (1928-1933) under Nadia Boulanger, when he also met some of the French composers of this period—Poulenc, Milhaud, Honegger, Sauguet. The influence of Fauré, Ravel, Stravinsky was very strong on him; his style was firmly orientated at this time towards a French logic, precision and clarity, rather than towards an English romanticism or modalism.

Many parallels can be seen in Berkeley's music with the styles of other composers and other periods. The closest is with Mozart; the *Divertimento*, the *Horn Trio*, *A Dinner Engagement*, to mention just three examples, are entirely Mozartian in conception. Among French composers, he has close affinities with Fauré and Poulenc; with Fauré particularly in the songs, though Berkeley's harmonic style is piquant and without Fauré's subtlety; with Poulenc in his melodic and harmonic style. The second set of *Ronsard Sonnets* was dedicated to Poulenc's memory. Among British composers, he and Britten share many qualities. A similar receptivity to literature and the poetic image, which finds its chief outlet in song-writing; a similar interest in opera, and particularly chamber opera—Lennox Berkeley's works were performed by the English Opera Group, one of them at Aldeburgh; a similar concern for church music. Points of contrast, however, between the two composers are equally instructive. Berkeley's style has not evolved as much as Britten's has; he has written little if any *Gebrauchsmusik* for the less talented or amateur performer—indeed, though his work does not call for virtuoso performance, polish and refinement are essential ingredients in his musical personality; finally, unlike Britten, he is one of the oldest-established teachers in this country, and his numerous pupils at the Royal Academy have included Richard Bennett and Nicholas Maw.

His works cover every *genre*. Among the first of his orchestral works to win distinctive recognition were the *Serenade* for string orchestra, and the *Divertimento* for chamber orchestra; among chamber works, the *Sonatine* for violin and piano. His characteristically short-winded melodic style, aptly suited to such a piece as the *Sinfonietta*, which Berkeley wrote for Anthony Bernard's London Chamber Orchestra, is not so amenable to the more sustained development and growth of the symphonies. He has also written concertos for piano and violin, and some early piano pieces; he himself is a pianist.

Berkeley's songs include poetry from many sources, and the words, depending on their content, add a correspondingly extra dimension to his pliant style. His response to a text resembles Britten's in this respect. Berkeley's most intense and powerful expression is reserved for those texts with a religious significance: the Donne settings, or the *Four Poems of St. Teresa of Avila*. His strong religious sense finds expression in several sacred works, some of them liturgical. His early *Stabat Mater* (1946), dedicated to Britten, was for six solo voices and instruments; his later *Magnificat* (1968) was more in the grand manner of the older choral tradition, and was written for performance in St. Paul's Cathedral during a City of London Festival.

His first opera, as in the case of Britten, was his most successful. The librettist for *A Dinner Engagement* was Paul Dehn, who also co-operated in the later work, *The Castaway*. In the brilliant writing of Dehn's libretto, Berkeley found the perfect foil. The short-winded, ridiculous plot, and its total lack of innuendo or intricacy, ideally suited Berkeley's style; the result was a highly successful comic opera. The story of the next opera, *Ruth*, was biblical, with a libretto by Eric Crozier, while *The Castaway* was an adaptation by Paul Dehn of the Homeric story of the ship-wrecked Odysseus and the princess Nausicaa.

It appears that, just as English composers during the inter-war years responded in a mood of romantic nostalgia to the movements that occurred

on the continent of Europe some twenty years previously, so the wistful-
ness and the elegance that characterised the music of certain French
composers in the twenties, of whom we may chiefly mention Poulenc,
was reflected—again some twenty years later—in the work of Berkeley.

Priaulx Rainier was born in 1903 in South Africa, and spent her childhood in a remote region of Natal. Her first indelible musical impressions
were the indigenous sounds of African life—children, birds, animals;
primal sounds, heard as if from a great distance. She came to London to
study at the Royal Academy, and has stayed ever since. She began to
compose comparatively late, and was under Nadia Boulanger just before
the outbreak of war in 1939; it is from this year that her first important
work, though not her first work, dates—the *First String Quartet*. Over the
next period of about twenty years her output consisted mainly of chamber
music and songs, in which she pursued her characteristic idiom: simple
melodic and rhythmic patterns used repetitively and cumulatively, with
frequent use of unison and octaves; an absence of counterpoint, and a
harmony built on an individual use of triadic tonality, not simply diatonic.
The rhythmic style of the *String Quartet* is extended in the *Sinfonia da
Camera*, which Walter Goehr performed in 1947, and which belongs
within the same 'Morley College' genre as Tippett's works for string
orchestra, or Seiber's *Besardo Suite*.

Her songs are short, and directly effective; two of them, *Ubunzima* and
Dance of the Rain, are for voice and guitar. *Ubunzima*, written in 1948,
is a setting of a Bantu poem; *Dance of the Rain* (1947), adapted by the
Afrikaans poet Uyo Krige, evokes memories of the Zulus and the
rhythm of Africa. The material is largely pentatonic, with sharply defined
verbal rhythm. The later *Cycle for Declamation* (1953) is also a study in
verbal rhythm, for solo voice.

The *Barbaric Dance Suite* (1949) for piano similarly uses percussive
piano texture; its basis was the sound of African marimbas—discs
played with hammers, with dried gourds underneath acting as resonators.
The *Five keyboard pieces* (1951) are more abstract.

Rainier has been closely associated with the singer Peter Pears. He
commissioned *Cycle for Declamation* (1953) as well as *The Bee Oracles*
(1970); he also gave the first performance of the *Requiem* (1956) at the
Aldeburgh Festival that year. This remarkable twenty-minute piece (see
plate 14), is a setting, for tenor and unaccompanied choir, of a text by
David Gascoyne, whose qualities of intense vision, coupled with a chilling,
declamatory rhetoric, are matched in every nuance by the composer. The
work is prefaced by two quotations, which give its clue. One, from Pierre
Jean Jouve, reads: 'Grant that we may first taste thee on the day of our

death, which is a great day of peace for souls at one; the world full of joy, the sons of men reconciled.'

The *Requiem* falls into four sections, and these are shared between soloists, semi-chorus and full chorus. The text was specially designed for a choral setting, with alternate sections for choir and soloist. The choral writing is homophonic, not polyphonic, and stark in its rhythmic strength. The solo part is partly integrated, in concertante style, partly providing structural links with passages of dramatic recitative. The work has a strange grandeur, and stands among the distinctive pieces of unaccompanied choral music of the contemporary period, and without any of the traditional English influences.

In the unfolding of Rainier's style, it represents the end of a period; in it she uses the triad for the last time to any great extent. From this point onwards her work changes, and by the late 50's a development of style took place. In response to the trend of the time, her works became much more abstract, though their idiom is still tonal, not serial; and also in the 60's she wrote several large orchestral works. The change can be detected in two chamber works for the oboe, written for Janet Craxton; the *Pastoral Triptych* (1960) for solo oboe, and the oboe quartet *Quanta* (1962).

An absence of thematic material was nothing new to Rainier; her music had from the start been athematic. Now the rhythmic patterns became more sophisticated, the tonality more chromatic, based on semitones more than on triads, and the texture more varied. The title *Quanta*, which was given to the piece only after it was finished, and the composer realized that it could have no conclusion, derives from quantum theory in physics, and indicates the structure of the work—and indeed of other works from now on. Energy exists in space, independent of matter; particles bunch together, and fly off; so the work has no orthodox form, and it springs from one initial impulse. Interchanging textures alternate, and build up to a long slow section; a final 'spinning' texture leaves the work quite unresolved.

The first of the large orchestral works was first heard the previous year, 1961. *Phalaphala* is built on interlocking orchestral rhythms and textures, much as *Cycle for Declamation* had been a study in verbal rhythm. The material of both works has a certain primitive quality.

The occasion of *Phalaphala* was Boult's tenth anniversary with the London Philharmonic Orchestra (1960), and the programme of the work, therefore, is one of celebration. It is based on the ceremonial horn used when the African chief summons the tribe.

Two major orchestral works followed: the *Cello Concerto* (1964) and the orchestral suite *Aequora Lunae* (1967). The *Cello Concerto* was written for a 1964 Promenade Concert, and fulfilled a long-standing wish to write for the instrument. Rainier had a sister cellist, and also a cousin who played in public at the age of eight; she was thus very acquainted in early life with the sound of the instrument.

Her scheme for solving the problem of enabling the so lo instrument's expressive but not penetrating quality to be heard against a background of orchestral tone was to avoid the conjunction of soloist and orchestra, except when the textures, instrumentation, colour and disposition were such that the cello could penetrate or interplay with the orchestral groups in juxtaposition without strain, and without reducing the proper volume of the orchestral dynamics.

Nevertheless, the concerto contains certain contradictions. In many ways, the traditional conception of a solo concerto is irreconcilable with an abstract idiom. Though, at least visually, the score contains a prominent solo line, it is not a virtuoso concerto in the traditional sense. The solo part is difficult, but the unsuspecting soloist who expects the satisfyin g rewards of a showpiece concerto, like the Dvorak or the Elgar, will be disappointed.

Rainier's concerto is in two movements, *Dialogue* and *Canto*; and though the cello writing is more *cantabile* and *legato* than in other works of this period, the overall mood is sombre, elegiac and slow-moving. In the first movement, as the title implies, unfinished cello phrases are taken over by the orchestra, and vice versa. The middle section of the movement is slower. In the *Canto* movement, the scoring is much lighter and the material quite different; it is more in the nature of a free rhapsodic solo with orchestral interjections and comments. The work ends with a *Cadence* and *Epilogue*, where the pace quickens. The *Cadence* takes the place of a formal *Cadenza*. Here the instruments interplay, solo wind or strings and solo cello, in lighter, gayer, florid passages, all on an equal footing. This brief section resolves into the Epilogue, which is reminiscent of the *Canto*, but here the orchestral voices are reduced to the slightest sounds between the long-drawn phrases of the solo instrument, which bring the movement to a pianissimo close.

The solo cello, with its power of rhetoric, dominates the concerto as a whole. Though the orchestra is never merely accompanying the solo instrument, after the introduction there are no long *tuttis*; but it plays its important part in the work in comment, in opposition, and finally in acquiescence to the final statement of the solo part. Groups of instruments are characteristic of the work, but the percussion is used primarily to sharpen sounds at moments of tension, and as a means of extending resonances, not as a body in itself.

But her largest work of this period is the orchestral suite *Aequora Lunae*. Rainier worked at St. Ives in Cornwall, and she not only knew Barbara Hepworth, to whom *Aequora Lunae* is dedicated, but shared something of her abstract aesthetic. It is by no means far-fetched to compare what Rainier expresses in terms of abstract musical sounds with what Hepworth expresses in abstract sculpture.

Rainier finds St. Ives an excellent environment for work; and she first made the acquaintance of Barbara Hepworth and Ben Nicholson when she stayed one summer, using a fisherman's loft as a studio. She was the only musician in this community of artists, though Tippett was also associated with her, and Barbara Hepworth, in the arrangements for the St. Ives Festival in Coronation year (1953). The years leading up to this were taken up in preparatory work for it, and so Rainier composed little during this period (1951–53).

But the spirit of the place infected her; how could it do otherwise? The form of land and sea; space; the identity of the human with the natural; the purity of life, unfiltered by city-living. The basis of her work was profoundly affected through this contact with Hepworth and Nicholson. She concentrated on essentials of technique, and eliminated all unnecessary parts of a work; she attempted in a composition not to capture the whole of an experience, but to state just enough to 'open the doors of experience' for the listener; she sought a purity of aim, and the avoidance of everything banal and obvious. 'The music and rhythm of lines created by light and shadow, and by the boundaries where form and space meet'[1] were interpreted in sculpture by Barbara Hepworth— and in music by Rainier.

The musical content in Ben Nicholson's work is even more explicit than in Hepworth's; Hodin compares his still lifes with the construction of fugues—subject, counter-subject, episodes and so on. To quote Nicholson's own words: 'the kind of painting which I find exciting is . . . both musical and architectural, where the architectural construction is used to express the musical relationship between form, tone and colour.' This was the background for Rainier's later abstract works.

Aequora Lunae is a continous piece in seven sections, each one descriptive of one of the moon's seas. The abstract patterns of this uninhabited world give rise to small particles of sound, which in turn generate further patterns, or molecules. Rhythm is the pulsating energy which surrounds all matter, only waiting to be released; different particles move at different speeds, and set up varying degrees of rhythmic patterns. In a sense, as is

---

1. Quoted from Hodin, *The Dilemma of Being Modern*, pp. 128–134: 'Barbara Hepworth —The meaning of abstract art'.

the case with a serial style, such abstraction can only produce static music; each particle is a thing in itself, as it reacts on its surrounding matter, before giving way to the next. So it inevitably follows that this score lacks the overall drive of a dynamic continuity which comes from contrapuntal writing, or from thematic development. In place of themes, Rainier substitutes textures; in place of the melody that thematic composition implies, she gives correspondingly greater importance to rhythm.

The seas chosen as titles for the seven parts form a metaphysical Cycle of Fertility, which could be described in a figurative way as follows:

Mare Imbrium:	Rain—the contribution, the beginning.
Mare Fecunditatis:	Fertility—the potential in all existence.
Mare Serenitatis:	Tranquillity—the calm before movement.
Mare Crisium:	Crises—releasing of activity.
Mare Nubium:	Clouds—the vapours transcending and forming.
Oceanus Procellarum:	Tempest—chaotic disturbances.
Lacus Somnorum:	Dreams—the sea sleeps in lakes and moves in sleep.

The orchestra is often divided into two parts: one half of the string body attached to the brass and hard-sounding percussion, the other to the woodwind and dulcet percussion. This division creates acoustical opportunities. Dense chord clusters move as composite sounds with frequent changes of colour through their transfer from one instrumental group to another. The opposition of dark and light-coloured instrumental tone plays a large part in the structures of the work.

A special feature is the number of solos for wind instruments. These form linear movements between chord clusters, and sometimes are the link between parts, either as conclusions or introductions. The percussion is enlarged with three steel plates, high, low and medium, and a set of antique cymbals, tuned to specific pitches. Each of the parts has its distinctive orchestration.

After these large-scale instrumental works, Rainier returned to vocal composition, for the first time since the *Requiem*, with *The Bee Oracles* (1969). This setting of Edith Sitwell's poem 'The Bee-Keeper', commissioned by Peter Pears, was first sung publicly at the Aldeburgh Festival in 1970. The scoring is for tenor soloist, with flute, oboe, violin, cello and harpsichord. The choice of text is usually the first and strongest guide to a vocal composition; this, like that of the *Requiem*, is a powerful structure, rich in mystical imagery.

The poem is a recognition and an affirmation of the mystery and hope of all creation. In the music are embodied two rhythms, one represented by the instrumental writing, forming *particular* rhythms linking and unlinking, always moving towards and in support of the second and *fundamental* rhythm, represented by the vocal line. The syllabic repetitions upon which the vocal line is based create a pulsation, flooding in and out of the instrumental textures. This continuous interplay, such as is found in Rainier's earlier works, produces a structure perpetually forming and re-forming; a kind of 'honeycomb' in sound.

The introduction to the 'Hymn of Being' is used as an incantation in the form of a chant, which recurs in shortened versions between the verses, each of which is a paean to the elements, Earth, Water, Fire, Air, Sun and Thunder.

> *This was the song that came from the small span*
> *Of thin gold bodies shaped by the holy Dark . . .*

23 Teacher/Composers

The greatly increased interest in music in this country since 1945, concomitant with a growing tradition, is actively reflected at the educational level in schools, universities and colleges. Several new universities have opened their doors to music students since 1960, and they have brought fresh thinking to bear, each in their own way, on the basic principles governing that perennially controversial issue, musical training and education. Some of the more idealistic and experimental ideas bear little or no resemblance to the traditional practices carried on in the older-established institutions. Among the new universities, Sussex and York have already established an identity, while the younger Surrey still remains to be proven.[1]

It is a long-established practice in this country to separate the performer from the non-performer. If you are a performer, you attend one of the conservatory institutions in London or elsewhere; if you are a non-performer you attend a university. It is an unfortunate dichotomy, with its roots firmly in the past, and one which is in sharp distinction to the American practice, which includes performance as a perfectly respectable and, indeed, most important academic discipline. In this country the dichotomy has an important and unfortunate corollary, which dictates that what a composer is called on to teach in an academic institution is, generally speaking, limited to academic subjects. Moreover, it is the traditionally established practice in this country that teaching appointments are made primarily on academic qualifications, not on executive or creative ability. The two do not necessarily go together, though they often may. But a composer who is also a noteworthy musicologist, such as Wellesz, is a great rarity.

Whereas in America, learning about music, and learning the performance of music, go hand in hand as part of the same essential discipline, in this country, generally speaking, they do not. There are, however, certain indications that this long-established impediment to the free

1. See p. 375, App. 11.

evolution of the contemporary musical tradition is at least being called in question. A very considerable number of composers are occupied, directly or indirectly, with the business of teaching; and though many would perhaps consider teaching as primarily a convenient economic haven, there is no question that a great deal is being achieved within a (broadly defined) teaching environment.

York University, for instance, under the direction of Wilfrid Mellers, is an active performing centre, which boasts no fewer than six composers on its staff, who cover a wide range of sympathy. David Blake's work has been so far largely choral, culminating in *Lumina*, written for the Leeds Festival, 1970; while the more experimental, *avant-garde* side of the spectrum is represented by Richard Orton and Bernard Rands. Rands, like Mellers before him, acquainted himself with American procedures during a two-year Harkness Fellowship in that country, which he spent at Princeton and Illinois, and his compositions, such as *Actions for Six*, are in the main Western *avant-garde* tradition; some are intended for the classroom, such as *Sound Patterns, I and II, for Young Players*.

His colleagues John Paynter and Peter Aston have also concerned themselves with musical education at classroom level; Aston's compositions represent the more conservative side of the spectrum, and he has done musicological research into the manuscripts in the library of York Minster. Robert Sherlaw Johnson, on the other hand, is one of the most enlightened, if single-minded, advocates of Messiaen's music, which he frequently plays. As a composer, he developed a form of serial technique with his *First Piano Sonata* (1963); but his was a French rather than a Viennese serialism; it was derived from Boulez more than from Webern. At this time (1963), the fashion of serialism was reaching a sophisticated stage. He pursued Boulez still further (particularly the latter's *Third Piano Sonata*) in the *First String Quartet* (1966) and *Improvisation* I, II and III for violin and piano (1966/7). Indeterminacy and improvisation, which together constitute aleatoricism, were pursued in *Improvisation* V (1968), though Johnson sees in the admittance of a Cage-derived 'chance' element an unacceptable challenge to both composer and performer. Instead, he pursues the Messiaen-Boulez path of sound organisation: highly complex but strictly logical, with the elements of music (pitch, rhythm, duration and so on) graded into various relationships. The *Second Piano Sonata* is not only a development of this type of serialism; it also introduces a new type of 'graphic' notation, and various new playing techniques (such as the use of the fingers directly on the strings). In addition to these *avant-garde* instrumental works, Johnson's output also includes some shorter sacred vocal pieces.

At the other end of the country, Southampton University includes among its staff the highly active and prolific composer Jonathan Harvey, whose formative works so far reflect a wide range of diverse influences, from Britten to Stockhausen, from Messiaen to Maxwell Davies. Tonality is for him the background against which he composes, and his aesthetic is a blend of technical enquiry and religious idealism. As a result of this, his commissions have come from widely differing groups; from Maxwell Davies's Pierrot Players, for whom he wrote *Cantata III* for soprano and six instrumentalists (1968), which exploits the relationship between pitch and tempo, as expounded by Stockhausen; and from the more venerable Three Choirs Festival, for whom he wrote *Cantata IV*, *Ludus Amoris*, for speaker, soloists, choir and orchestra; a mystical work, with seventeenth-century Spanish text, moving gradually from the absence to the presence of God.

Another centre of active music-making is at Cardiff University, under the energetic direction of Alun Hoddinott. His colleagues in other Welsh colleges include William Mathias, who is on the staff at Bangor, and Ian Parrott, the Professor of Music at Aberystwyth; both belong in the traditionalist camp.

Hoddinott's compositions are predominantly orchestral and instrumental. Extreme practicality marks all his work, whether as a composer, or as an arranger of concerts for Cardiff University, or for the Cardiff or Dynevor Festivals. His output numbers over fifty works: early pieces such as the *Clarinet Concerto*, Op. 3, are diatonic, but later, starting with the *Nocturne*, Op. 5, he developed a total chromaticism. He has also attempted to use serial methods in a melodic way, to unify a piece. His extrovert style is best represented in all its varied aspects in his orchestral output: the *Second Symphony*, for instance, contains dramatic, romantic gestures, and is pronouncedly more conservative than *Variants*; moreover, he is by no means averse from writing in a lighter vein. He played the violin from an early age, and this is reflected in his strong leaning towards chamber music.

Birmingham is served by two much contrasted musicians. John Joubert is a South African, whose music, like Hoddinott's, is approachable and practical, but differs from Hoddinott's in that it is more sturdily traditional, and predominantly for voices. His cantatas include three unaccompanied motets *Pro Pace*, and his operas range from *Silas Marner* to *Under Western Eyes*.

Peter Dickinson is a versatile musician of wide interests and sympathies; he is as much a writer as a composer, as much concerned with introducing British composers to a public at Birmingham[1] as with lecturing and

1. At the Birmingham and Midland Institute, through the University of Birmingham Department of Extramural Studies.

performing. Three seasons in the U.S.A. served to widen his musical horizon, when he met Varèse, Cowell and Cage, and his fifty-odd works, which have been played as much in America as in this country, reflect his diverse enthusiasms.

Technical craftsmanship marks the work of three traditionally-orientated composers centred on Oxford University. Though in no sense of the word breaking new ground, and entirely devoid of any social, satirical or intellectual overtones, Kenneth Leighton's work is sure and meticulous in its deliberate effect. His career has been marked by the award of several international prizes: a Busoni prize at Bolzano for the *Fantasia Contrappuntistica*; at Trieste for the *Symphony*, Op. 42; at Hanover for the *Piano Trio*, Op. 46. Tonality for him has been enriched by serialism, rather than superseded by it, as the *Piano Variations*, Op. 30, and the *Second Piano* Concerto, Op. 37, bear witness. A tendency towards contrapuntal complexity is matched elsewhere by a strong sense of a *scherzando* style. But his idiom throughout has remained remarkably constant.

Malcolm Lipkin, born in Liverpool in 1932, is tutor for the extra-mural department of Oxford University. His more conventional works, such as the *Violin Sonata* (1957) and the *Second Violin Concerto* (1962), both written for Yfrah Neaman, are harmonically conceived; therefore the listener's point of reference is the standard repertoire of other works in the same categories. In more recent works, particularly *Sinfonia di Roma* (1958–1965), and *Mosaics for Chamber Orchestra* (1966), he uses a more linear technique, serially derived. A short motif is submitted to varied treatment throughout the work. Unity and variety are thus obtained, while the single source-material ensures consistency. This method is particularly well shown in the *Sinfonia di Roma*, which is a twenty-minute piece, conceived in the form of an arch; a central scherzo, unrestrained and fierce, introduced and followed by a slow section.

This conception was used by Panufnik in his *Sinfonia Elegiaca*, and indeed Lipkin's score bears a certain surface resemblance to Panufnik's, though his (Lipkin's) sonority is more diffuse, his material less economically used.

The twenty-five works that make up Christopher Headington's output, though they include a *Violin Concerto*, are primarily for small chamber music combinations or voices. Though he attempted to escape from a diatonic style, according to the trends of the time, by experimenting with serialism in one work, *Three Poems of Rainer Maria Rilke* (1960), he uses a traditional idiom simply to communicate and to give pleasure. He is

1. Dr Leighton was appointed Reid Professor of Music at Edinburgh in 1970.

Staff Tutor in music of Oxford University Department of Extra-mural Studies, and has written several educational articles and books.

The Professor at Cambridge University, predominantly the birthplace and home of the new choral tradition, is the Scottish composer Robin Orr.[1] After a conventional training at the Royal College of Music, and later at Cambridge under Dent, he went to Siena to study under Casella, and thereafter to Nadia Boulanger. His output is slender, and apart from functional pieces for organ and choir (he was the organist at St. John's College), some chamber music and songs, centres chiefly on two works, the *Symphony in One Movement*, and the one-act opera, *Full Circle*. Both had Scottish premières; moreover, Orr is also chairman of the Scottish Opera. Teaching and administration take away his time from composition.

Music in the North of England is focused on Newcastle, the home of the Northern Sinfonia, where the first Arts Festival took place in 1969. David Barlow, who has held a lectureship there since 1951, is a composer whose output is small but distinctive. His basic romanticism, derived from Ireland, Bax and Vaughan Williams, was most apparent in his two early symphonies, written in 1950 and 1959 respectively. A period of re-thinking in 1962, at the time when the serial trend was at its height, led to his adoption of a modified form of serialism, first in two chamber music works, the *Concertante Variations* for oboe and string trio, and the *Introduction, Theme and Variations* for string trio; then in two orchestral works, *Microcosms* for string orchestra (1964), and *Five Preludes After The Tempest* (1965) for chamber orchestra. *Microcosms* uses an alternation between lyrical and *secco* playing, while the *Five Preludes* are serially based on a 3-note cell (E-C-F).

Barlow's comparatively few works over the following years include some pieces for chamber orchestra, *Homage to John Clare* (1966), *November 1951* (1968), and a *String Quartet* (1968), which is in the form of variations for cello and strings; but his culminating work so far is his opera *David and Bathsheba*, which was first seen at the Newcastle Festival in 1969. This work, with a libretto by Ursula Vaughan Williams, is simpler and less cerebral than Barlow's work of the previous years. It is directed at a wider public. Uriah the Hittite is even allowed a popular tune, but against the accompaniment of a 12-note chord.

The text is taken from Samuel II (11, v.2, and 12, v.24), and tells the story of David's adultery with Bathsheba, and the sending of her soldier-husband, Uriah, to the hottest part of the fighting, thus ensuring his death. Nathan, the prophet, enters at a dramatic moment, and angrily upbraids David, telling him the parable of the rich man taking away the

1. He was appointed in 1965, in succession to Thurston Dart.

one possession of the poor man; David gives judgement, and is self-condemned. As a 'punishment' Bathsheba's child was to die, and David repents in sackcloth and ashes, and by fasting. But when the child eventually dies, he calls for fresh robes, saying that while the child lived there was hope, but that after his death there was none. The opera ends, as it began, with a kind of catharsis; the ever-returning spring after a cold winter is symbolic of new birth.

The opera is in one act, with a Prelude which is a thematic storehouse. The biblical story is concerned with David's guilt, and the 'conscience-motif', first heard in the Prelude, is a sequence of three notes (C-D-B), pursued upwards or downwards. Muted strings at the close signify the acceptance of their child's death by David and Bathsheba.

The composers who devote a proportion of their time to teaching at the many London institutions represent, as might well be expected, a wide range of musical sympathy. Of those already mentioned, Humphrey Searle has taught at the Royal College since 1965, and Lennox Berkeley at the Royal Academy since 1946. The doyen of traditionalists is Gordon Jacob, whose long list of compositions is predominantly instrumental, and entirely diatonic and straightforward. The younger Richard Stoker, on the other hand, is an enquiring musician, who assimilates ideas from many directions.

His elder colleague John Gardner, who has taught at the Royal Academy since 1956, is a highly active and versatile musician. Like Alwyn, Chagrin, and many other composers, he commutes, as it were, between the ivory tower and the market-place. He studied at Oxford before the war, and after serving in the R.A.F., he was a repetiteur at Covent Garden, 1946–1952. He was at Morley College after 1952, and in 1965 became Director of Music. Since 1962 he has taught at St. Paul's Girls School; he has also taken more than his share of committee-work.

He attracted attention with an early work, the *Symphony No. 1*, Op. 2 (1947); a direct work, straightforward in tonality and structure, and owing a good deal to the Sibelius movement of the romantic thirties—as, indeed, was expected of British symphonists at this time. This work was played under Barbirolli at a Cheltenham Festival concert in 1951, and repeated in London the following year. It was followed the next year by another work for Cheltenham, *Variations on a Waltz by Carl Nielsen*, Op. 13, and a choral work, *Cantiones Sacrae*, Op. 12, for the Three Choirs Festival. Here Gardner's characteristically extrovert style, and direct, confident choralism, are unimpeded, right from the D major opening chorale '*Ein feste Burg*'. The final *Magnificat* is taken from an earlier *Nativity Opera*, Op. 3, that he wrote with Tyrone Guthrie.

1952 was a busy year for Gardner, and he also wrote a ballet, *Reflection*, Op. 14, for the Sadlers Wells Theatre Ballet, from which he later took an orchestral suite. This was followed five years later by his opera *The Moon and Sixpence*, which was a remarkable first venture into the just-unfolding world of repertory English opera. Gardner's ability to write for voices, coupled with his considerable operatic experience, ensured for his work a practical success.

But his career reflects the swing of the pendulum of taste at this time. He rejected dodecaphony, preferring instead a directly exciting music, which can more easily be memorable and become known. He was thus compelled to seek outlets other than those of the prevailing trends.

He has a considerable penchant for jazz piano-playing, which he once put to effective use in the tavern scene from *Wozzeck*. This lighter side of his work is shown in the *Suite of Five Rhythms* (Rumba, Waltz, Pizzi-cato Blues, Sentimental Song, Five-beat Boogie) written for a B.B.C. light music concert in 1960; also in the *Five Hymns in Popular Style*, which were written for school choirs at the Farnham Festival in 1963. This is perhaps the most performed of all his compositions; it is his *Pomp and Circumstance*, the work by which he is most widely known. Because it also represents a movement towards experimentation in church music at this time, Gardner's comments on it are relevant:

Lowering the brow of the Church is all the rage these days, and it is probable that many of the attempts to bring the atmosphere of the Espresso bar to the chancel are as hypocritical as they are misguided. The fact remains, however, that until the nineteenth century, the styles of secular and sacred music tended to go hand in hand. Thus we find composers using the same turns of phrase to express both erotic love and pious adoration, a practice condemned by some, but one which undoubtedly arose from an attitude towards life which saw it whole, and which allowed God to be praised for having endowed us with the pleasures of the senses as well as with the delights of the spirit.

In these five hymns I have been inspired particularly by the example of Malcolm Williamson, to whom they are dedicated, and by the wonderful poetry of Bishop Heber, Henry Lyte and Mrs. Adams, so full of simple pro-found thoughts, expressed in language which is both noble, evocative and memorable. Popular art in the best sense, in fact!

The tunes are my own except in the case of the second hymn, which is based upon E. J. Hopkins' famous melody 'Ellers', associated by me always with the last Evensong of the school term. I can still feel, as I play or sing this lovely tune, my boyish pleasure in being swept this way and that, in a state of mingled ecstasy and anguish, upon the contrary currents of expectation and nostalgia that flow so strongly from both words and music.

Gardner sees in a jazz or popular style the possibility of achieving some-thing of that common touch which is so conspicuously lacking from the more cerebral contemporary techniques, and which reached such heights in the American Musical in the hands of George Gershwin, Irving Berlin, Cole Porter, and others of that tradition.

Most of Gardner's main works since the late 50's have been for voices. He returned to the Farnham Festival in 1967 with *Proverbs of Hell*, Op. 85, a setting for unaccompanied chorus of Blake's writings, assembled by John Ormerod Greenwood, who had earlier arranged an anthology of Shakespeare texts for *The Noble Heart*, Op. 59, which was Gardner's contribution to the 1964 Shakespeare anniversary festival. The *Herrick Cantata*, Op. 49 (1961), is a suite of independent poems, like the early *Cantiones Sacrae*, and the *Seven Songs*, Op. 36 (1957) by various poets. Only once has he set a long narrative—*The Ballad of the White Horse*, Op. 49 (1959), and in that case he has divided up Chesterton's vast poem into eight short, interlinked sections, like a suite.

Later choral pieces include the *Four Wanton Ballads*, Op. 81 (1965), light-hearted and pseudo-modal; and the *Cantata for Christmas*, Op. 82 (1966), traditional yet individual; also simply felt, unquestioning, yet rhythmically fresh, after the new choral tradition.

Three traditionalist composers, who are on the staff of the Royal College, use a tonal idiom in highly contrasted ways. Bernard Stevens has very clear views on the place and function of music, and has deliberately kept his style in conformity with his Marxist aesthetic.[1] He has no wish to write for a small coterie. He sees 'the crisis in contemporary art-music'[2] as threefold:

1. The limited performance of art-music;
2. The isolation of contemporary art-music from contemporary popular music;
3. The simultaneous existence of contradictory idioms in contemporary art-music.

There can hardly be a composer anywhere who would not agree at least with the first of these points, certainly as far as his own work is concerned. In Stevens's case it is undeservedly all too true, and at least three of his most important works, the *Piano Concerto* (1955), the *Second Symphony* (1964) and the *Variations for Orchestra* (1964) have not been performed at all. One of his earliest works is also one of his most characteristic, the *Violin Concerto* (1943), written for Max Rostal. Wedge-like harmonic movement over a pedal G immediately sets the mood of serious intensity, which is a marked feature of his style, with a certain Elgarian luxuriance

1. See his article *The Soviet Union* in *European Music in the Twentieth Century*.
2. The title of a paper (1948).

of melody. His harmony is often subtle, though a fondness for pedal-points occasionally gives the music a somewhat static quality. He has certain musical affinities with the Tudor madrigalists (a legacy from R.O. Morris), with Shostakovitch, and, among British composers, with Rubbra.

An absence of theory is a source of strength in Stephen Dodgson's music, coupled with an unfailing desire to write gratefully for a performer the sort of phrase that will reveal the true characteristics of his instrument. Such an idea may be said to be common to many composers; but Dodgson's art is also refined, gentle, aristocratic. The underlying elements of tonal music—rhythm, harmony, melody—are in his case uncomplicated in essence, though capable of considerable complexity in detail. His themes are simple, not naïve, and are recognizable as much from their rhythmic as their melodic contours. He is not concerned to explore technical innovations which may lead to an aesthetic *cul de sac*; his is no life-task to map out uncharted musical territory. In his desire to write music that gives spontaneous pleasure, his temperament is more Mediter-ranean than Germanic. His melodic line is continuous, not fragmented. He is no pursuer of musical systems, and has no desire to explore the attenuated rhythms or the cluttered and complex technique that he sees as the characteristics of so much German-influenced music. The simplicity of the diatonic scale he sees in historical perspective, as a basic source of strength, while chromaticism is a basic source of decadence or weakness, whether it is used by Dowland, Gesualdo or Wagner.

Dodgson is not influenced by systems, though he is conversant with that of Hindemith. His cantata *The Soul's Progress* is scored like Hinde-mith's *Apparebit repentina dies*. But those composers with whom he has a particular affinity are Debussy, Shostakovitch, Janacek, in whose work he admires power, subtlety, and economy. He is particularly fond of quoting Verdi's dictum, when he said he was not a learned composer, only an experienced one.

He was written extensively for the orchestra. His early work received scant attention, and only occasional performance, and it was not until the *Serenade* for viola and orchestra that he began to achieve success. This work was hastily revised in the space of about one week, just prior to a broadcast in May 1956. This year also saw the masterly *Guitar Concerto*, which was not performed until March 1969. This work has not only chiefly established his reputation, but it is also a fine example of his mature style. He has written of it:

I have been writing for the guitar on and off for fifteen years. Like Rodrigo, I don't play the instrument. In fact, a direct confrontation with its formidable technique would be far more likely to inhibit than assist my developing sense of its resources. My tutelage began with Julian Bream, and has continued under

John Williams—as fortunate a combination of teachers as any composer could wish for.

I had written this concerto (in 1956) during an August spent in a deserted farmhouse in a steep Wiltshire valley of startling beauty. The farmhouse's reversion from manor to nature extended at the time to a top storey full of birds (I was alarmed to meet an owl on the staircase the day I arrived), and the house is now declined into irreparable ruin. During intervals of writing the concerto, I rode the shepherd's Welsh pony, followed the straw-baler, collected giant mushrooms and hacked the nettles. I've never written a work, the circumstances of whose composition stand out more vividly in my mind. I've since learned that Hippenscombe, as this intensely romantic spot is called, had previously inspired another English composer to an orchestral tone poem.

Looking back at the atmospheric environment, I am surprised at the classicism of the concerto. I've always believed that the exact placing and timing of the orchestral *tutti* is the paramount consideration in any concerto's design. With the guitar, it is, of course, vital to avoid confusion in anyone's mind about when the soloist should be heard and, conversely, where the orchestra may be given its head. I have tried to make a virtue of this necessity. The slow movement, for example, depends for its architecture on the span and precise point of arrival of its single passage for the whole orchestra.

The orchestra contains no oboes, but *three* clarinets instead; chosen for their complete tonal contrast with the guitar (whose *ponticello* effects do have some affinity with the double-reed sound). The pair of horns also have their moments, very simple ones, when they prove their suitability as a tonal foil.

The first movement (*Allegro comodo*) has a central episode in place of the standard development section, but the principal ideas of the movement, with their tendency to irregular accentuation, gradually invade this episode and so graft it onto this overall design. The slow movement (*Lento*) is a free variation on the opening wind music-tune in the flute. The finale (*Molto vivace*) is a rondo with two very clearly defined episodes, and although the argument is closely knit as between soloist and orchestra, the latter is allotted definite architectural points where it may speak up boldly. This movement makes considerable use of *pizzicato* strings as a propulsive partnership for the soloist.

The musical idiom—which is not consciously of any adherence—is largely based on the age-old triads (which, unlike Hippenscombe, will never crumble) and the concerto does not quibble about being in D major.

Dodgson's fondness for the Czech composer Janacek is revealed in certain of his later orchestral works. The *Nocturne* for strings (1960), which is a short movement lasting some six minutes, is an act of direct homage, based on *Goodnight* from Janacek's Piano Pieces (first set), *By overgrown tracks*. The *Sinfonietta* (1964) is an indirect homage; it is scored for the largest orchestra that Dodgson has ever used, and its sinfonietta character, as with Janacek's work of the same title, comes from the shortness of the movements, of which there are six, some with reduced.

orchestration. Like Janacek's, Dodgson's *Sinfonietta* begins with open fifths in the wind. As with so many of Dodgson's works, this had to wait several years before being performed.[1]

The chamber music style is inherent in Dodgson's intimate and precise musical personality. All his chamber works are written for specific performers. His acquaintance with Philip Jones at the R.C.M. led to two works for brass instruments for the Philip Jones Brass Ensemble; the same principle applied to other works. The bassoon concerto was for Martin Gatt, the guitar works for John Williams, the cello sonata for Anna Shuttleworth. The proportion and the overall sonority are finely judged in all the ensemble works, to allow each individual instrument to be heard to fullest advantage.

He has written comparatively few vocal works, mainly because there has been no occasion for them. A recent work, *Cadilly*, is a 'narrative entertainment', written for the Grosvenor Ensemble: a miniature concert opera, with text by David Reynolds, which could well form the basis of a television puppet show. Dodgson's ability to enter into a lighter métier was well illustrated when he wrote a new overture for *The Mikado*[2], when it was produced at Sadler's Wells, following the expiry of the Gilbert and Sullivan copyright. In the words of an unwitting tribute which appeared in *The Times*: 'the woodwind especially were on their best form, and the overture emerged with a lightness and charm which it too rarely possesses.'

Philip Cannon, born in 1929 of mixed English and French parentage (his mother Burgundian, his father English), is five years Dodgson's junior, and like Dodgson has bent his traditional idiom to a personal style, independently of any system. His starting point is unimpeachably respectable: the *Symphony Study: Spring* (1949) dates from his period of study at the Royal College of Music. Similarly, the early *Concertino* (1951) is light, readily approachable in its largely pentatonic material, and undemanding on the listener. It is in direct line with Walter Leigh's famous harpsichord *Concertino* of 1934. Like Leigh, Cannon has written extensively for voices, and his output includes an opera *Morvoren* (1963) and a choral work *Son of Science* (1961). This 'cantata for the machine age' calls for various choral effects—shouting, hissing, muttering. Moreover, Cannon explores a more experimental idiom in his *String Quartet* (1964); but his true style is a simple, somewhat slender lyrical modalism. One of his most characteristic works is *Cinq Chansons de Femme* (1952) for soprano and harp, settings of old French ballads, which unpreten-

1. It was first played on 18 June 1970, by the Bournemouth Orchestra.
2. This is recorded on HMV CLP 1592.

tiously, and effectively, exploit the dramatic potential of different folk-song styles.

Not only in universities and colleges has there been a marked increase of musical activity in recent years. In schools also there has been a much greater level of music-making by schoolchildren—the performers and music-lovers of the future. In many cases composers are also involved, and benefit in a most direct way. One of the most striking examples is the boys' choir of Wandsworth School, which their Director of Music, Russell Burgess, has built into a highly effective musical ensemble, and which has excited the interest of at least one familiar composer—Benjamin Britten.

Another marked feature of recent years is the spread of County Youth Orchestras, who frequently surprise and impress audiences by their high standard. There can be few more direct ways of interesting school-children in music than by assembling those who wish to play in an orchestra, drawn from the schools in a county. Many counties have achieved excellent results, taking their example from the National Youth Orchestra. Those counties whose achievements are particularly interesting, and who have also commissioned works from British composers, are Essex, Shropshire and Leicestershire. The last named, which formed its Youth Orchestra in 1948 through the infectious enthusiasm of the County Music Adviser, Eric Pinkett, is perhaps particularly deserving of mention because of its association with Michael Tippett. Every member of the orchestra has been taught in a Leicestershire school, by a peripatetic staff. Since 1965 Tippett has frequently conducted the orchestra in this country and abroad, and composed for them the *Shires Suite*. In 1969, for a German tour, he conducted a characteristic repertoire, including music by Bryan Kelly, Butterworth, Delius, Copland and Charles Ives. For Gershwin's *Rhapsody in Blue* the orchestra was joined by Richard Bennett as piano soloist. Tippett also arranged for the orchestra to appear at the Bath Festival. Other composers who have directly benefited from the Leicestershire Schools Symphony Orchestra are Alan Ridout, William Mathias and Malcolm Arnold.

The combination of pupils from different schools in a district can often lead to most worthwhile results; the combined talents of several schools is more than any one school can achieve alone. An instance of this was shown in February 1970, when sixteen schools in the Richmond area were brought together through the Richmond-upon-Thames Schools' Music Association for the performance of a specially commissioned work—Panufnik's *Thames Pageant*—a work with strong local connections, as the composer lives nearby.

Contemporary Music Societies formed since 1945

Outside the teaching environment, the great increase in activity since the war has been matched, to some extent, by the formation of several small societies and ensembles, mainly in London, whose concern is the performance of new music.

The senior of these is the *Society* (originally *Committee*) *for the Promotion of New Music* (S.P.N.M.). This was the brain-child of a remarkable musician, who describes himself as 'Roumanian by birth, British by nationality and cosmopolitan by inclination'—Francis Chagrin. As well as a composer of orchestral and chamber works, music for films, radio and television, and some pieces in a lighter vein, Chagrin in 1951 was also the founder and conductor of his own ensemble, which became known for performing the lesser known repertory, and works of the serenade or divertimento category.

The necessity of a society which would adopt as its policy the encouragement and professional performance of music by young, untried composers came to Chagrin in December 1942, at the darkest moment of the war. Such a society would be a service provided by more senior composers to help their younger colleagues, whose work was unknown or unperformed. Professional performers of repute would be invited to give their services. Chagrin thus nailed his colours firmly to the mast of idealism.

But the anomaly inherent in the public performance of unknown works had been already brought into focus by the Patron's Fund concerts at the Royal College of Music in 1919[1], when Hugh Allen, in order to counter public indifference, changed their status from public *concerts* to public *rehearsals*. This distinction between a workshop, or studio, recital, and an unqualified public concert has always been recognized by the S.P.N.M., whose primary purpose was from the start to give a hearing to new works. By definition, programmes would consist almost entirely of first performances: the performance would be followed by discussion, led by a 'first speaker', who was usually a composer or musician of some note, drawn from the ranks of the Committee, whose comments would, theoretically at least, be respected by the hopeful young tyro. At the first such studio recital, on 2nd April 1943, the discussion was led by Michael Tippett.

In this respect Chagrin's S.P.N.M. differed markedly from the L.C.M.C., which Dent had founded some twenty years earlier, and whose concerts were inclined more to European than to British composers. Whereas the older society presented balanced, public concerts of contemporary works from all countries, including some British ones, the

1. See p. 18.

S.P.N.M. gave in effect public rehearsals, followed by discussion, of untried works. In many cases, inevitably the first performance was also the last.

It is hardly surprising that this somewhat cumbersome procedure came under heavy criticism in the course of the following years. The chief anomaly lay in the relegation of the audience to the role of unnecessary, even superfluous, and occasionally embarrassed spectators. If the unknown works, and unknown composers, were not alone enough to daunt all but the hardiest and most curious of the very limited public, it was hardly to be expected that they would pay to hear works played, only to be informed afterwards, perhaps, that the music was of questionable value. Inevitably, audiences were frequently very small, and funds very low. Moreover, if the L.C.M.C. was afflicted by committee problems, these were as nothing compared with the S.P.N.M., whose enormous committee read like a musical *Who's Who*, and over the years contained most of the warring factions of musical London. A serious financial problem in 1965 produced the disturbing suggestion from one committee rebel that, as the composer's situation had improved, the S.P.N.M. should cease to exist. This, however, was not agreed. Then, quite unexpectedly in 1967, the Society was left a legacy from one of their audience[1] of over £100,000.

From this stemmed problems of a different sort for the hard-pressed committee. How was this money to be used? Recital-discussions, workshop performances and public orchestral rehearsals of new works had always been their pattern; but now, particularly with the advent of other societies, it did not see its purpose primarily as a concert-giving organization. The 'service to the young composer' which Chagrin originally visualized, could be given in other ways, such as weekend seminars.

It is only to be expected that the policy-direction followed by any committee should be the common denominator of the views of its more articulate and vociferous members; and the S.P.N.M. has always attracted the *avant-garde* into its ranks, who have naturally tended to promote works of an experimental nature, particularly electronic or jazz-derived. This trend has been particularly noticeable since about 1968, and indeed is shared by other societies such as the Macnaghten Concerts and the Park Lane Group. This appeared to be where the popular mood lay. This mood also led to the formation of two instrumental ensembles: the Pierrot Players, formed by Davies and Birtwistle, mainly for the performance of their own works; and the London Sinfonietta, formed for the performance of *avant-garde* music of all countries.

1. Arthur Paul, a keen amateur, once a pupil of Matyas Seiber.

The Park Lane Group, named after Park Lane House where the first meetings took place, is a society begun in 1956 by three students of the Guildhall School of Music, chiefly to provide a platform for young performers. The intention thus differs from the S.P.N.M., though their chamber music recitals frequently include British works. The recitals fall under two main headings, 'Young Artists and Twentieth Century Music', and 'Music Today', which consists mainly of *avant-garde* works.

The principle of a performer/composer partnership was followed by another highly gifted musician, the pianist Ian Lake. Finding himself in 1959 at that awkward point at the beginning of his artistic career when his student days were over but his engagement diary disarmingly empty, he decided to make his London début and introduce the works of new composers at one and the same time. The critics would be sure to pay attention if contemporary music were played; there might be other young instrumentalists who would join with him, who were also faced with the same barriers in the London concert world; perhaps even composers might welcome the idea. So was born Music in our Time; small recitals beginning in November 1960 in out-of-the-way halls. Composers from the start were found to be not only interested, but eager to co-operate; their problems were similar to Lake's, if not more pressing. For his first series Lake obtained the co-operation of John White, Ronald Lumsden, Donald Street, Edwin Roxburgh and Duncan Druce. Other players and composers joined the enterprise in the years that followed—and benefitted mutually.

The Redcliffe Concerts of British Music were formed, officially, in 1964, though the formation of the society followed some concerts which were given over a number of years before then. These first took place in a church in Redcliffe Square, London, from which the name of the society is taken. Later they were given in the Arts Council Drawing-Room at 4, St. James's Square. Most societies already mentioned gave recitals in this room up until the mid-60's; they could be described collectively as the 'St. James's Square Concerts'. The Redcliffe Concerts gradually evolved into an annual season, which since 1967, and the opening of the Queen Elizabeth Hall and Purcell Room, has taken place on the South Bank. The policy governing this Society is that the problem of performing the work of the contemporary British composer is best solved by matching it, in a programme, with other works, mainly British, but not necessarily exclusively so, which will serve to bring it into focus. Orchestral and chamber concerts blend first performances with more established works; and no one trend is followed. As Ian Lake found with his Music in our Time Festival, the clearest and most reliable advocate of a score is often the composer himself, and the Redcliffe Concerts have invited several composers to co-operate directly, either by contributing works, or by performing, or, in the case of better established composers, by directing programmes of their own works. Peter Maxwell Davies, Rubbra and Fricker have contributed to these 'composer's choice' concerts. Among other composers who have directly contributed are Geoffrey Bush, Anthony Milner, Peter Zinovieff, Tristram Cary and Andrzej Panufnik.

There can be no conclusion to an account of a tradition which is so varied, and growing so fast. This is a story that has a beginning and a middle, but no end. The evolution that Vaughan Williams foresaw has gathered pace in recent years to an extent unparalleled in the musical history of this country. That London is now the musical capital of the West is due to a combination of many factors, social, historical and geographical. Out of the enormous range of music-making, there has emerged what is perhaps the most important, certainly the most lasting, thing of all: an environment in which the British composer can work; an active tradition, for which these pages are an attempt to present some of the evidence.

VII

Appendices

Cause for concern

There can be no one today connected with music, or music-making, in this country, either directly or indirectly, who is not aware of the ever-growing undercurrent of criticism concerning the B.B.C. The steady trickle of complaint has grown into a considerable torrect in recent years, and the publication in 1969 of the B.B.C.'s manifesto, *Broadcasting in the Seventies*, merely served as a focal point round which the various dissident voices could concentrate. Even when due allowance has been made for the extravagant and vociferous claims of the professional complainers, and the outraged vanity of frustrated artists, there remains an irreducible hard-core of dissatisfaction, which is both widespread and genuine, and which sooner or later will require radical solution.

The B.B.C. has, since its inception over forty years ago, held the monopoly in this country of sound broadcasting. This has been both its strength and its weakness. It has built up in that period a very consider-able bureaucratic power, which has concentrated the administrative decision-making into the hands of a small group.

But now, the quantity and range of music in this country, particularly of contemporary music, has increased immeasurably since 1945; the Composers' Guild alone now numbers some 450 names; and the total number of concerts, whether contemporary or not, in London alone, is quite incalculable. In range and diversity, music-making today is vastly greater than it was even twenty years ago.

Yet there still remains only one B.B.C. Moreover, the growth of television has, on the whole, not provided an outlet so far for contem-porary music; generally speaking this, and serious music generally, remains the preserve of radio, rather than television. This has meant that a very much greater concentration of administrative power, and artistic responsibility, rests in the hands of the small group who direct the affairs of the B.B.C. Music Department. The Head of Music, and his immediate associates, can decide, from the immense amount of available material, what shall be heard on the radio up and down the country; and, perhaps more importantly, what shall not. Against their wish there can be no alternative.

This power is beyond reason. It places more responsibility into few hands than is possible for them to discharge fully. In sheer quantity of music hours, the B.B.C. is far the largest patron in the country; that this patronage should be in the hands of an oligarchy, however well-intentioned, gives them an influence and prominence out of all proportion to any man's capacity. Moreover, the B.B.C.'s control has extended over far more than just radio programmes; the Promenade Concerts, for instance, are directly controlled; other festivals and organizations are indirectly controlled. A nationwide accumulation of influence has concentrated a great deal of power into few hands, and the danger consists in the use of such power to influence artistic ends. To their credit, the B.B.C. have over the years broadcast a great number of contemporary works, generally of a reasonably high standard, which would not otherwise have been heard. Their service in this respect is impossible to calculate. But there is a debit side to the ledger, which consists, in the main, of the development of a rigid hierarchy of power, that has set its own pace and made its own rules. Generally speaking, it has been intended to operate fairly, within its own terms of reference; but it puts a premium on the less desirable features of bureaucracy, such as inefficiency and secrecy; and occasionally it condones corrupt practices.

The B.B.C. Music Department has not kept pace with the enormously increased range of contemporary music, with the result that only part of the mosaic-like pattern of today's tradition of British music is represented in radio programmes. An extreme instance of this limitation occurred in the early 60's, when the newly-appointed Head of Music, William Glock, exercised the power vested in his position to promote particular composers of the serialist and *avant-garde* school. Those who were not of this persuasion were disregarded, and their works were not broadcast. In this way the serial fashion found an influential advocate, and the newly-founded 'Invitation Concerts' promoted partly the continental *avant-garde*, partly those composers in this country who followed suit, such as Lutyens, Goehr, Birtwistle and Smalley. A trend was thus set, which was undesirable because it was lopsided and unrepresentative.

The vitality of a musical tradition consists primarily of the active collaboration between composer and performer at the point where it matters, which is the concert platform. To attempt to subordinate such a profitable, free, variable and creative partnership to the rigid, inhuman dictates of a bureaucracy will almost certainly stifle its growth. In the case of the B.B.C. it has meant that a large number of the developments in contemporary music in this country have not featured in radio programmes.

As for the manifesto *Broadcasting in the Seventies*, it caused widespread dissatisfaction, both within the B.B.C. and in the country as a whole, when it was published. The grounds of complaint were twofold. First, within the B.B.C., and among those most closely concerned, it caused a dispute about power. This found its expression in various letters to the *Times*.[1] Second, there was widespread alarm up and down the country that, because the Third Programme and Radio Three appealed only to a minority, and was patently uneconomic, certain reductions might be made in order to save money. The cost of the Third Programme is the highest—£665 per hour—yet its audience is the lowest—50,000. And so proposals were made in the manifesto to disband certain orchestras, chiefly the Scottish Symphony Orchestra, and to relegate the Music Programme to V.H.F. These proposals were defeated, largely due to the militant strength of the Musicians' Union.

But the controversy about money, and the audience/finance ratio, was a side-issue in comparison with the central one, which is the administrative organization of the B.B.C. If you permit an authoritarian monopoly to exist, you cannot reasonably complain if it behaves in an authoritarian way. The only lasting solution is to change the basis of its function, and to re-define the purpose it serves.

Unfortunately, public debate naturally tends to focus on economic arguments. These are the easiest understood by the majority of people; moreover, *Broadcasting in the Seventies* appeared to lay great stress on programme-costing; and any suggestion of cutting programmes to save cost caused the loudest protest from B.B.C. producers and staff. And so public attention became focused onto the apparent, immediate problem of lack of money, while the more basic, underlying problem became correspondingly obscured.

Monopoly-power is highly undesirable, even dangerous. Not only is there an absence of competition, but artistic questions are made the subject of bureaucratic protocol, with a strongly built-in tendency towards secrecy, intrigue and corruption. It is, perhaps, only too natural that the same handful of composers, and the same limited number of executive artists, should reappear regularly in radio programmes, to the comparative exclusion of their colleagues, whose livelihood is quite unreasonably jeopardised. It is quite essential in a public service such as the B.B.C. that

1. Starting on 19 January 1970.

z

justice should not only be done, but invariably be seen to be done; otherwise secrecy breeds greater suspicion. Unfortunately, certain composers have been manifestly excluded from receiving what is their due; and in the case of performers also, the moral correctness of a policy of exclusion has occasionally been shown to be, to say the least, open to question.

The conclusion is inescapable that the monopoly should be broken, and that smaller, independent and autonomous units should take its place. The days of Reithian paternalism are now past. In the 30's, when the musical developments of this country—its orchestras, its institutions, its public—were at a formative stage, as was the B.B.C. itself, the enlightened guidance of one dominant figure was probably both inevitable and desirable; but now the situation is vastly more complex, and calls for a correspondingly different administrative machine. The growth and spread of music, to say nothing of the growth and spread of the B.B.C. itself, and its multifarious departments in both radio and television, calls for a much more flexible approach, if anomalies are not to result.

An academic proposal:
Degree Course in music for the
University of Surrey

In 1965, after it was decided that the Battersea College of Technology was to become the new University of Surrey at Guildford, and that the University was to include a Faculty of Music, preparations were made for drawing up a new degree course. The scheme was put forward by Dr. Hans Heimler and Francis Routh.

The most characteristic features of the new university were its strong technological and scientific bias, which was due to its origin, and its proximity to London. First, therefore, a study was made of the general nature of academic music in this country, and also in twelve selected American universities. From this study certain underlying principles became clear, and certain basic differences between the British and the American systems, which helped to decide the nature of the Surrey proposal. These may be briefly summarized:

1 A general lack in this country of specialized training in the various branches of music. Just as other disciplines and sciences have certain basic divisions, (for instance between physics and chemistry, or between medicine and surgery), this also applies in music. Yet although there are certain exceptions, such as Cambridge, Manchester and Edinburgh Universities, these divisions have not been, on the whole, academically recognized. The student simply studies 'music'.

2 A traditional dichotomy in this country between 'practical' and 'academic'; between music making on the one hand, and the academic study of it on the other. This dichotomy was seen to be contrary to the generally-accepted American practice; it also seemed to contribute to the view that the university is something of an ivory tower, remote and exclusive, and that the study of music as an academic discipline is to some extent irrelevant to the practising musician. This was clearly undesirable.

3 Arising from this, it has not been the general practice in this country (again with certain exceptions) to include composers and executive musicians on the staff of universities, except in an 'academic' capacity. This again is contrary to the American practice; moreover it appeared to

have had the result of failing to encourage officially an interest in contemporary music, and its rapidly growing developments—and this deficiency led in some cases to the students themselves seeking a remedy.

4 The summer school, which is such a pronounced feature of American musical life, does not generally speaking feature in the British academic year, which is divided into three terms, not two.

The general principles which were followed in the Surrey proposal had the following broad intentions in mind:

1 The Degree course should aim to strike an adequate balance between theoretical and practical musicianship. It should provide the future professional musician both with a relevant and adequate training in his specialized branch of music, and with a background of more general musical knowledge.

The main branches of music were taken to be Composition, Conducting, Performing, Musicology, and Technology.

Musicology includes those more traditional disciplines associated with the study of historical styles, as well as the more sophisticated ramifications of this, such as aesthetics, palaeography, notation and ethnomusicology, which are at present hardly taught at all.

Technology includes the numerous advances made since 1945 in the science of acoustics, in recording and broadcasting, and in the use of electronic equipment. The very fact of recording has introduced a fresh dimension into our musical experience. Clearly a technological university, such as Guildford, would offer a unique opportunity in this respect, and the Degree course would be devised in conjunction with the Physics department.

2 Apart from the more formal aspects of the undergraduate programme, equal stress should be laid on attendance at concerts and recitals, and on participation in university performances, which might be seen as an important service provided by the music department for the university community. This would also partly help the student to see music in a wider, social context.

3 Future growth should be allowed for in postgraduate research, particularly in the field of computer-technology, which is in its infancy still in this country. The experience of other countries shows that studios involving expensive electronic equipment have been established either by radio stations or by universities. A university with a strong technological bias seems therefore a reasonable environment for such a studio, where musicians of the future can become acquainted with contemporary techniques, which are the tools of their trade.

The proposal therefore was made for a four-year course, leading to an

Honours Degree. The first year would be common to all students; a general background introduction to those fundamentals of musical technique, theoretical, practical and historical, without which no musician, whatever his ultimate specialization, is properly equipped. During this first year the student would decide which more specialized option he would choose to follow for the remaining three years.

The second year would begin this process of specialization. The first option would include one of the branches of practical or theoretical music: Composition, Conducting, Performing, Musicology. The second option would include recording techniques, acoustics and electronics. This option would be known as the *Tonmeister* option, named after the similar course at the Nordwestdeutsche Musikakademie in Detmold— one of the few in Europe to introduce such a study.

After the second year the student would pursue his particular specialization in a wider environment. Those who specialized in one of the subjects of the first option, in addition to an overall, general development of musicianship in history, orchestration, acoustics, and other common, fundamental techniques, should concentrate more specifically on that particular subject, in readiness for the final examination. In composition, preparing a work of some substance, which would show a technical and an imaginative ability; in conducting, the study and rehearsal of a wide range of scores; in performing, the study and practice of a comprehensive repertoire; in musicology, the preparation of an original thesis. During the third year a student in the first option might well work extramurally, and return for his final examination at the end of the fourth year; while for the student who specializes in the second *Tonmeister* option, such extramural, or industrial, experience during the third year would be essential; he might well work in a broadcasting or recording studio.

In this way not only would the student relate theoretical and practical musicianship, but the work of the university would be seen as an important contribution to the wider musical community, which it serves.

Orchestral Concert Analysis
For One Season

Season: September 1968–September 1969

TABLE SHOWING THE PROPORTION OF CONTEMPORARY BRITISH WORKS
PERFORMED BY THE MAIN ORCHESTRAS IN THE BRITISH ISLES

Orchestra or Society	Conductor or Artistic Director	No. of concerts	No. of items played	No. of works by British composers	No. of works by living British composers	No. of first performances, commissions
1. B.B.C. Symphony Orchestra	Head of Music: William Glock	14	33	1	1	—
2. Bournemouth Symphony Orchestra	Constantin Silvestri	101	196	20	19	1
3. Brighton Philharmonic Society	Herbert Menges	20	70 (app.)	9	5	—
4. City of Birmingham Symphony Orchestra	Assistant Conductor: Harold Gray	38	128	9	2	1
5. English Chamber Orchestra	Raymond Leppard	14	47	3	3	2
6. Hallé Orchestra and Concert Society	Sir John Barbirolli	55	214	16	9	1
7. London Mozart Players	Harry Blech	15	60	7	7	3
8. London Philharmonic Orchestra	Bernard Haitink	72	215 (app.)	27	6	1
9. London Symphony Orchestra	Andrè Previn	34	109	5	4	1
10. Northern Sinfonia	Rudolf Schwarz	35	51	2	2	—
11. New Philharmonia Orchestra	Artistic Adviser: The Earl of Harewood, Hon. President: Otto Klemperer	37	96 (app.)	10	9	1
12. Royal Liverpool Philharmonic Society	Charles Groves	59	154	24	9	2
13. Royal Philharmonic Orchestra	Rudolf Kempe	55	190 (app.)	16	10	2
14. Royal Philharmonic Society	Chairman: Sir Thomas Armstrong	8	28	8	4	3
15. Scottish National Orchestra	Alexander Gibson	64	80	12	10	—
16. Ulster Orchestra	Sergiu Comissiona	22	71	3	1	—
	TOTALS	643	1,742	172	101	18

Notes and comments on this table

1. Public concerts only. Studio broadcasts not included. Orchestra also appeared under 14.

2. 75th anniversary season. Concerts presented in southern and western districts of England; also three London concerts.

3. 44th season of orchestral and choral concerts, presented by various orchestras and artists, including the Brighton Philharmonic Orchestra.

4. Including two London concerts. 49th season. Hugo Rignold withdrew as principal conductor in 1968 after 8 years.

5. London season only. Orchestra, formed in 1961, specializes in eighteenth-century music, and is particularly associated with the Aldeburgh Festival.

6. 111th season, including celebrations of the Berlioz centenary. Three London concerts, and concerts in Manchester only (including industrial concerts).

7. 24th season. London concerts only. Orchestra specializes in concerts of the Haydn/Beethoven period.

8. 36th season. Does not include all out of town and school concerts.

9. London concerts only, 'International series'. 65th anniversary season.

10. 10th anniversary season. Ten programmes repeated.

11. 5th season. Orchestra re-constituted in 1964.

12. 130th season. Nine programmes repeated, including industrial concerts.

13. London season only.

14. 157th season. Various orchestras presented, six English, two foreign.

15. 19th season. Concerts given in Edinburgh (22), Glasgow (26), Aberdeen (8) and Dundee (8), with programmes repeated. Works are shown only once, with the number of performances in brackets Scottish composers were prominently featured.

16. 3rd season. Concerts presented in Ulster Hall.

General Comments

Most orchestras aim to attract 'internationally renowned artists', particularly the main London orchestras, whose principal conductors are thus all non-British. The best known star-conductor of the season was Pierre Boulez, who usually conducted his own works. He was later appointed as conductor to the B.B.C. Symphony Orchestra, which he was to share with the New York Philharmonic. He also presented four concerts with the L.S.O. of Schoenberg/Berg/Webern. The Birmingham orchestra followed suit, with the appointment of another French conductor, Louis Frémaux, who also simultaneously directs another orchestra in Lyons.

Both the N.P.O. and L.S.O. presented almost identical Walton concerts, conducted by the composer, at opposite ends of the season (L.S.O. on 25th September 1968; N.P.O. on 6th July 1969).

Only the L.P.O. presented a concert to commemorate the tenth anniversary of the death of Vaughan Williams, though André Previn was later to record the Vaughan Williams symphonies with the L.S.O.

A marked leaning can be seen towards the British music of the pre-1939 generation: Elgar, Delius, Vaughan Williams, Holst and Bax.

The tables exclude Christmas carols and Handel's *Messiah*.

WORKS BY LIVING BRITISH COMPOSERS
(as listed above)

(* denotes first performance)

Total number of works by living British composers

1. B.B.C. SYMPHONY ORCHESTRA

Birtwistle	*Nomos*	1

2. BOURNEMOUTH SYMPHONY ORCHESTRA

Alwyn/Hassall	*Prologue*	
Bliss	*Discourse for orchestra*	
	Piano Concerto	
Britten	*Cello Symphony*	
	Diversions for piano left hand	
	Four sea interludes (Peter Grimes)	
	Sinfonia da Requiem	
	Young Person's Guide to the Orchestra	
Panufnik	*Sinfonia Sacra*	
Rawsthorne	*Divertimento*	19
Steel	**Overture 'The Island'*	
Tippett	*Corelli Fantasia*	
	Concerto for double string Orchestra	
	Little music for strings	
	Prelude, brass, bells and percussion	
	Ritual Dances from 'The Midsummer Marriage'	
	Symphony No. 2	
Walton	*Symphony No. 1*	
Williamson	*Symphony No. 2*	

3. BRIGHTON PHILHARMONIC SOCIETY

Britten	*Passacaglia ('Peter Grimes')*	
	Variations on a theme of Frank Bridge	
Rawsthorne	*Overture, 'Street Corner'*	
Salzedo	*Song in the Night* (harp solo)	5
Walton	*Overture 'Scapino'*	

WORKS BY LIVING BRITISH COMPOSERS

*Total number
of works by
living
British composers*

4. CITY OF BIRMINGHAM SYMPHONY ORCHESTRA
   | Rawsthorne | Overture, 'Street Corner' | |
   | Wellesz | *Symphony No. 7 | 2 |

5. ENGLISH CHAMBER ORCHESTRA
Goehr	*Konzertstuck for piano and orchestra	
Maw	Nocturne	3
Reizenstein	*Concerto for Strings	

6. HALLE ORCHESTRA, HALLE CONCERTS SOCIETY
Arnold	Scottish Dances	
Britten	Cello Symphony	
	Young Person's Guide to the Orchestra	
Dankworth	Tom Sawyer's Saturday	
Hoddinott	Symphony No. 3	9
Josephs	*Symphony No. 2	
McCabe	Variations on a theme of Hartmann	
Musgrave	Concerto for Orchestra	
Walton	March 'Crown Imperial'	

7. LONDON MOZART PLAYERS
Arnold	Oboe Concerto	
Berkeley	Four Poems of St. Teresa of Avila	
Britten	Simple Symphony	
Maw	*Sinfonia	7
Routh	*Dialogue for violin and Orchestra	
Tavener	*Introit for the Feast of St. John Damascene	
Tippett	Little Music for Strings	

8. LONDON PHILHARMONIC ORCHESTRA
Britten	Violin Concerto (2 perfs.)	
Goehr	*Suite, 'Arden Must Die' (2 perfs.)	
Rubbra	Symphony No. 7	
Walton	Belshazzar's Feast	
	Façade	
	Partita	

9. LONDON SYMPHONY ORCHESTRA
Bennett	*Symphony No. 2	
Walton	Belshazzar's Feast	
	Cello Concerto	4
	Johannesburg Festival Overture	

WORKS BY LIVING BRITISH COMPOSERS

*Total number
of works by
living
British composers*

10. NORTHERN SINFONIA

| Britten | *Sinfonietta* | } 2 |
| Milner (Arthur) | *Diptych* | |

11. NEW PHILHARMONIA ORCHESTRA

Britten   *Les Illuminations*
            Serenade
            Violin Concerto
            War Requiem
            Young Person's Guide to the Orchestra
Goehr   **Romanza for cello and Orchestra*
Walton   *Belshazzar's Feast*
            Johannesburg Festival Overture
            Violin Concerto

       } 9

12. ROYAL LIVERPOOL PHILHARMONIC SOCIETY

Arnold   *Symphony No. 6*
Britten   *Cantata 'St. Nicolas'*
            Young Person's Guide to the Orchestra
Crosse   **For the Unfallen*
McCabe   **Harpsichord Concerto*
Walton   *Overture, 'Portsmouth Point'*
            Suite from 'Henry V'
Williams   *Penillion*
Williamson   *Sonata for two pianos*

       } 9

13. ROYAL PHILHARMONIC ORCHESTRA

Josephs   **Symphony No. 3*
Mathias   **Symphony No. 1*
Rawsthorne   *Overture 'Cortèges'*
Tippett   *Concerto for Double String Orchestra*
Walton   *Symphony No. 1*
            Variations on a theme of Hindemith
            Viola Concerto
            Violin Concerto
Williamson   *Overture, 'Santiago d'Espado'*
            Suite from 'Our Man in Havana'

       } 10

WORKS BY LIVING BRITISH COMPOSERS

Total number
of works by
living
British composers

14. ROYAL PHILHARMONIC SOCIETY

Britten	*Violin Concerto*	
Gerhard	**Symphony No. 4*	4
Musgrave	**Clarinet Concerto*	
Walton	**Capriccio Burlesco*	

15. SCOTTISH NATIONAL ORCHESTRA

Arnold	*Overture 'Tam o'Shanter'*	
Berkeley	*Divertimento* (2 perfs.)	
Britten	*National Anthem*	
	The Building of the House	
Davie	*Diversions on a theme of Thomas Arne*	
Dorward	*Concerto for wind and percussion* (4 perfs.)	10
Musgrave	*Clarinet Concerto* (4 perfs.)	
Orr	*Overture, 'The Prospect of Whitby'* (2 perfs.)	
Rawsthorne	*Elegiac Rhapsody for Strings* (4 perfs.)	
Wilson	*Concerto for Orchestra* (2 perfs.)	

16. ULSTER ORCHESTRA

Britten	*The Building of the House*	1

SUMMARY OF CONTEMPORARY COMPOSERS REPRESENTED
IN ORCHESTRAL CONCERTS 1968/9

Composer	No. of works	No. of Perform- ances	Composer	No. of works	No. of Perform- ances
Alwyn	1	1	Milner, Arthur	1	1
Arnold	4	4	Musgrave	2	6
Bennett	1	1	Orr	1	2
Berkeley	2	3	Panufnik	1	1
Birtwistle	1	1	Rawsthorne	4	8
Bliss	2	2	Reizenstein	1	1
Britten	16	24	Routh	1	1
Crosse	1	1	Rubbra	1	1
Dankworth	1	1	Salzedo	1	1
Davie	1	1	Steel	1	1
Dorward	1	4	Tavener	1	1
Gerhard	1	1	Tippett	6	8
Goehr	3	4	Walton	14	19
Hoddinott	1	1	Wellesz	1	1
Josephs	2	2	Williams	1	1
Mathias	1	1	Williamson	4	4
Maw	2	2	Wilson	1	2
McCabe	2	2			
	(43)	(56)		(42)	(59)

Total works :   85

Total performances :   115

16 repeats of works by different orchestras.

14 repeats of works by the same orchestra (L.P.O. and S.N.O.).

Societies and Organizations:
Concert Analysis For One Season

Season: September 1968–September 1969

TABLE SHOWING THE PROPORTION OF CONTEMPORARY BRITISH WORKS PERFORMED

	Society or Organization	Musical or artistic director	No. of concerts	No. of items played	No. of works by British composers	No. of works by living British composers	No. of first performances
1.	B.B.C. Premenade Concerts (1969)	William Glock	52	184 (app.)	41	24	8
2.	Macnaghten Concerts	Committee Chairman: Colin Mason	7	26	13	12	10
3.	Music in Our Time	Ian Lake	9	53 (app.)	32	29	20
4.	Park Lane Group	Committee Chairman: John Woolf	17	83 (app.)	24	24	4
5.	Pierrot Players	Peter Maxwell Davies / Harrison Birtwistle	5	17	15	14	8
6.	Redcliffe Concerts of British Music	Francis Routh	7	36	34	25	15
7.	Robert Mayer Children's Concerts	Sir Robert Mayer	7	32	7	6	1
8.	Society for the Promotion of New Music	Committee Chairman: Susan Bradshaw	4	22	22	22	19
9.	South Bank Summer Music (1969)	Daniel Barenboim	14	50 (app.)	0	0	0
	TOTALS		122	503	188	156	85

Notes and comments on this table

1. 75th season of Henry Wood Proms, 18th July/13th September 1969. 18 orchestras and 18 choirs contributed to the season. Centenary of death of Berlioz, and birth of Henry Wood, marked by the Berlioz *Requiem* in the first concert.

2. Founded 1931. Concerts were presented in the Victoria and Albert Museum, Wigmore Hall, St. Pancras Assembly Rooms, and elsewhere.

3. 9th Festival, 15th/18th October 1968. Recitals presented in Holborn Central Library, Conway Hall, St. Pancras Church.

4. 13th season. Recitals mainly at Wigmore Hall; season also included French electronic music, and joint promotion of Berlioz's *Beatrice and Benedict* with the Camden Festival. (*see App. V*).

5. 2nd season. Concerts on South Bank, and in Universities. Works repeated, particularly Schoenberg's *Pierrot Lunaire*, Davies's *Antechrist*.

6. 5th season. Concerts presented on the South Bank.

7. Founded 1923. Various orchestras presented in the Royal Festival Hall on Saturday mornings; programmes mainly light and varied.

8. 25th anniversary year. As well as public concerts, this Society also promoted two 'Workshops', a composers' weekend seminar with the American composer Milton Babbitt (June 1969), and sponsored certain other events.

9. The 2nd season of a series of 'international celebrity' concerts, 17th/31st August, set up in rivalry to the Proms. This series enjoys the dubious distinction of being the only one in the country to show no interest whatever in the British composer, whether living or not. The concerts in 1970 featured Schoenberg's Chamber Music. One concert was repeated.

WORKS BY LIVING BRITISH COMPOSERS

(as listed above)

(* denotes first performance)

*Total number
of works by
living
British composers*

1. B.B.C. PROMENADE CONCERTS

Arnold	*Concerto for two pianos and orchestra*	
Bedford	*Two poems for chorus on words of Kenneth Petchen*	
Bennett	*Piano concerto*	
Berkeley	*Magnificat*	
Bliss	*Concerto for two pianos*	
	Royal Fanfare (Prince Albert's 150th anniversary)	
Britten	*Children's Crusade*	
	Sinfonia da Requiem	
	The Golden Vanity	
Bush (Alan)	*Scherzo for wind with percussion*	
Cooke	*Variations on a theme of Dufay*	24
	Young Person's Guide to the Orchestra	
Davies	*Worldes Blis*	
Gerhard	*Alegrias: divertissement flamenco*	
	Symphony No. 4	
Goehr	*Three pieces from 'Arden must die'*	
Mellers	*Yeibichai*	
Tavener	*The Whale*	
Tippett	*Sonata for four horns*	
Walton	*Battle of Britain March*	
	Belzhazzar's Feast	
	Partita	
	Suite: Façade	
Wood (Hugh)	*Cello Concerto*	

2. MACNAGHTEN CONCERTS

Bedford	*Fun for all the family*	
Cardew	*The great digest*	
Connolly	*Cinquepaces for brass quintet*	
Davies	*The Shepherd's Calender*	
Dennis (Brian)	*Z'noc*	12
Downie	*Tantra I*	
Howarth	*Variations for brass quintet*	
Rowland	*Degrees for chorus and brass quintet*	

WORKS BY LIVING BRITISH COMPOSERS (continued)

*Total number
of works by
living
British composers*

Self	*Nukada*	⎫
Smalley	*String Sextet*	⎬ (12)
Tippett	String Quartet No. 2	⎪
Williamson	*The Growing Castle*	⎭

3. MUSIC IN OUR TIME

Austin	*Three Poems of Brian Jones*	⎫
Bardwell	*Sonata for tuba and piano*	
Birtwistle	*Four Interludes for clarinet, piano and drum*	
Britten	Suite Op. 6	
Bush, G.	Four Songs from Herrick's 'Hesperides'	
Cardew	Third winter potato	
Dalby	*Pindar is dead*	
Davies	Alma Redemptoris Mater	
Dodgson	*Four moods of the wind for piano*	
Druce	*Jugalbundi*	
Finnissy	*Song 9*	
Forbes	*Four Psalms, for soprano and organ*	
Freeborn	*Two variants for piano*	
Goehr	Three pieces	
	Fantasias	
Harvey	*Transformations of 'Love bade me welcome'*	29
Maguire, E.	*Chamber Music for three clarinets, piano & harp*	
Mason, D.	*Three songs of Christopher Dandy*	
Moore	*Violin Sonata*	
Moss	*Three piano pieces*	
Patterson	*Trio for wind*	
Smalley	Capriccio I, for violin and piano	
Standford	*Ave Maria, for soprano and organ*	
	Wayward Thoughts (song cycle)	
Warren	Two songs by W. B. Yeats	
White	*Piano Sonata No. 35*	
Wilson, C.	*Trio for trombone, tuba and piano*	
	Theme and variations	
Wordsworth	Four sacred sonnets of John Donne	⎭

4. PARK LANE GROUP

Berkeley	Four Ronsard Sonnets	⎫
Britten	Cello Sonata	⎬
	The Poet's Echo	⎭

WORKS BY LIVING BRITISH COMPOSERS (continued)

		Total number of works by living British composers
Dalby	Piano Trio	
Davies	Trumpet Sonata	
Ferneyhough	Sonata for two pianos	
Forbes	Partita	
Frankel	Pezzi pianissimi	
Gardner	*Partita for solo cello	
Gerhard	Cello Sonata	
	Fantasia for guitar ·	
	Hai-Kai songs	
	Libra	
	Nonet	24
Hoddinott	Piano Sonata No. 4	
	*Piano Sonata No. 5	
Lord	*The Wife of Winter (song cycle)	
Lutyens	Piano e Forte	
	Stevie Smith poems	
Maw	Chamber music for wind quartet and piano	
Musgrave	A song for Christmas	
Rainier	A cycle for declamation	
Stevenson	*Harpsichord Sonata	
Wood	Piano pieces	

5. PIERROT PLAYERS

Birtwistle	*Cantata	
	*Linoi	
	Medusa	
	*Melodica	
Davies	Antechrist (4 perfs.)	
	*Eight songs for a Mad King	
	Fantasia and two poems (Purcell realisation)	14
	L'homme armè	
	Piano pieces	
	Stedman Caters	
Druce	*Jugalbundi	
Gilbert	*Mother	
Harvey	*Cantata 3	
Various	*A Garland for Dr. K.	

6. REDCLIFFE CONCERTS OF BRITISH MUSIC

Banks	*Equation (part I)	
Berk	*Sychrome	

WORKS BY LIVING BRITISH COMPOSERS (continued)

*Total number
of works by
living
British composers*

Berkeley	*Four poems of St. Teresa*	
Birtwistle	*Four interludes from a tragedy for Basset Clarinet with tape*	
Bliss	*Clarinet Quintet*	
Cary	*Narcissus for flute and tape*	
Casserley	*The Final Desolation of Solitude*	
Collier	*The Barley Mow*	
	Workpoints	
Davies Hugh,	*Shozyg I*	
Gerhard	*String Quartet No. 1*	
Henshilwood	*Sonata 6*	
Jenkins (Karl)	*Down the Road*	
Maw	*Sinfonia for Chamber Orchestra*	25
Routh	*Dance Suite for String Quartet*	
	Dialogue for Violin and Orchestra	
Rubbra	*Cantata di Camera*	
	Discourse for Harp and Cello	
	Lauda Sion	
	Pezzo ostinato	
	String Quartet No. 3	
	The Jade Mountain	
Sutcliffe	*Spasmo*	
Tippett	*Little Music for Strings*	
Zinovieff/		
Connolly	*M-piriform*	

7. ROBERT MAYER CONCERTS FOR CHILDREN

Arnold	*Overture, 'Tam O'Shanter'*	
Britten	*Young Person's guide to the Orchestra*	
Dankworth	*Tom Sawyer's Saturday*	6
Jacob	*Trombone concerto*	
Mathias	*Sinfonietta*	
Walton	*Prelude and Fugue, 'The Spitfire'*	

8. SOCIETY FOR THE PROMOTION OF NEW MUSIC

Allen	*String Trio*	
Anderson	*Sound Frames*	
Birtwistle	*Interludes for a tragedy*	
Chapple	*Concert piece for piano quartet and tape*	
Connolly	*Music for Voice II, Prose*	
Dennis (Brian)	*Abstract II*	

WORKS BY LIVING BRITISH COMPOSERS (continued)

		Total number of works by living British composers
Gilbert	*Missa Brevis*	
Johnson	*Improvisation V*	
	Piano Sonata No. 2	
Jones (David)	*Spirals*	
Le Fanu	*Soliloquy for solo oboe*	
Negro	*Sonata Breve*	
	Wind Quintet	
Newson	*This Gap of Time*	
Orton	*Wind Quintet*	22
Rees	*And then she dropped her overcoat on the chair*	
Riley	*Alliance/Structures*	
	Three fragments for clarinet and piano	
Rowland	*Immensitie*	
Self	*Material*	
Shrapnel	*Memories of childhood*	
Steinitz		
(Richard)	*Taku*	

APPENDIX V

Festivals in the British Isles:
Analysis 1969

TABLE SHOWING THE PROPORTION OF CONTEMPORARY BRITISH WORKS PERFORMED

Name of Festival	Date	No. of concerts	No. of works played	No. of works by British composers	No. of works by living British composers	First performances or commissions	Artistic director or chairman of committee	Remarks
1. ABERYSTWYTH	Nov. 12–19	3	not specified	—	—	—		Concerts by Pierrot Players/ Birtwistle, Davies.
2. ALDEBURGH	June 7–29	51	120 (app.)	40 (app.)	25 (app.)	5	Benjamin Britten Peter Pears Imogen Holst	22nd Festival. Also included exhibitions, lectures, films, outdoor events, ballet, and Festival Club.
3. BATH	June 13–29	34	125 (app.)	39 (app.)	22	4	Colin Davis Michael Tippett Jack Phipps	Also included poetry reading, lectures, exhibitions, antiques fair, wine tasting, tours, and a Costume Ball.
4. BATH BACH FESTIVAL	Oct. 18–25	16	30 (app.)	—	—	—	Cuthbert Bates	All Bach, with City of Bath Bach Choir.
5. BATTLE	July 18–27	5	30 (app.)	2	—	—	H. C. Alexander	
6. BERLIOZ CENTENARY	—	41	24	—	—	—	The Earl of Drogheda	Included travelling exhibition, photographs, manuscripts, etc.
7. BISHOP'S STORTFORD	April 12–20	6	35	25	1	—	Lt.-Col. R. J. Venn	
8. BOXHILL	June 13–21	4	42	17	—	—	Susi Jeans	Early and Baroque music only.

Name of Festival	Date	No. of concerts	No. of works played	No. of works by British composers	No. of works by living British composers	First performances or commissions	Artistic director or chairman of committee	Remarks
9. BRIGHTON	May 7–18	16	45 (app.)	7	5	2	Ian Hunter	3rd Festival. Featured Czech music, with the Czech Philharmonic, also jazz, with films and a master class, cabaret, exhibitions and a conference.
10. BROMSGROVE	Apr. 19–May 10	11	45	19	9	2	Harold Taylor	10th Festival. Also included films, theatre, exhibitions. Concerts held in schools, colleges and churches.
11. CAMDEN	May 3–June 1	38	130 (app.)	14	14	6	Jack Henderson	Featured 20th century Swedish music and art, as well as unusual operas by Rossini, Berlioz and Scarlatti. Also poetry, exhibitions, drama and other amusements.
12. CAERPHILLY	Oct. 26–29	4	not specified	—	—	—	—	2nd Festival. including drama and exhibition, folk music.
13. CALDER VALLEY	Mar. 29–Apr. 5	3	14 (app.)	2	2	1	E. Fletcher	Commission to Yorkshire composer.

	Dates						Director	Notes
14. CARDIFF	Mar. 2–8	8	30 (app.)	18 (app.)	14 (app.)	7	Alan Hoddinott	Festival of 20th century music.
15. CHELTENHAM	July 4–13	24	101 (app.)	25	25	16	Frank Howes John Manduell G.A.M.Wilkinson	25th Festival. Featured Roussel and Schubert.
16. CHIDDINGSTONE	Aug. 23–31	13	25 (app.)	—	—	—	not specified	Seminars, art exhibition.
17. DARTINGTON (Summer School)	Aug. 2–30	28	106	18	13	2	William Glock	16th Summer School at Dartington, included teaching, masterclasses, daily concerts.
18. DARTINGTON (Course of British Music)	Jan. 17–19	3	7	7	4	1	Francis Routh	Weekend course, included lectures and open forum.
19. DAWLISH	June 2–July 5	4	not specified	—	—	—	W. J. Holman	16th Festival, included art exhibition, drama, films
20. DUBLIN	Jan. 5–10	11	44 (app.)	18 (app.)	18	4	Gerard Schürmann	Festival featured Irish composers.
21. EDINBURGH	Aug. 24–Sep. 13	62	158 (app.)	12	6	2	Peter Diamand	23rd Festival, featured Italian music and art. Also theatre and film festival, exhibition and military tattoo.
22. ENGLISH BACH	June 16–July 13	43	164	14	8	1	Lina Lalandi Sir Jack Westrup	7th Festival. Concerts in Oxford and London, featuring Bach and the *avant-garde*, particularly the Greeks Skalkottas and Xenakis; also Berlioz and Roussel.

Name of Festival	Date	No. of concerts	No. of works played	No. of works by British composers	No. of works by living British composers	First performances or commissions	Artistic director or chairman of committee	Remarks
23. GLYNDE-BOURNE	May 25–Aug. 3	60	4	—	—	—	John Pritchard	Festival opera, founded in 1934. An opera commissioned for this season from Nicholas Maw, 'The Rising of the Moon', was postponed until 1970.
24. GUILDFORD	Mar. 7–16	8	32	4	4	1	Richard Welton	First festival, presented by the Students' Union of the new University of Surrey. Included jazz, drama, films, poetry-reading and cabaret.
25. HARLOW	July 12–16	16	35 (app.)	5	3		Harlow Arts Council	Numerous fringe events, and lunch-time recitals by local artistes.
26. HARROGATE	Aug. 5–16	19	66 (app.)	15	7	2	Clive Wilson	4th festival. Many events apart from music, such as 'International literary conference'.
27. HASLEMERE	July 18–26	13	60 (app.)	13	—		Carl Dolmetsch	45th festival. Exclusively early music.
28. HINTLESHAM	July 11–27	2	5	—	—		Mrs. D. Macrae Moir	19th festival. Opera by Gluck, and 18th century music.

	Dates						Director	Notes
29. KING'S LYNN	July 25–Aug. 2	13	56 (app.)	16 (app.)	3	—	Ruth, Lady Fermoy	19th festival. Strong leaning towards choral singing, madrigals, etc., through connection with Cambridge University.
30. LEICESTERSHIRE SCHOOLS	Apr. 28–May 2	2	27	15	7	1	Eric Pinkett	21st anniversary of Leicestershire County School of Music. Several concerts also given in various other schools.
31. LITTLE MISSENDEN	Sep. 27–Oct. 5	5	20 (app.)	6 (app.)	4	3	Patricia Harrison	10th Festival.
32. LLANDAFF	June 1–12	10	32	3	2	—	—	—
33. LOWER MACHEN	July 6–12	4	17 (app.)	2	2	—	—	—
34. LUDLOW	June 21–July 6	4	27 (app.)	6	1	—	Joan Knight	10th Festival, mainly Shakespeare in Ludlow Castle.
35. MACCLESFIELD	May 5–25	15	60 (app.)	32	9	2	Neil Chaffey Walter Isaac	2nd Festival. Theme: British music, arts, drama and international films. Numerous exhibitions and attractions, including Adlington Hall, Gawsworth Hall, Jodrell Bank.
36. MINEHEAD and EXMOOR	July 13–27	11	35 (app.)	5	2	—	Timothy Reynish	7th Festival.
37. MONTROSE	Aug. 30–Sep. 6	4	30 (app.)	10	3	—	James Morrison	7th Festival, including opera, variety, art exhibitions.

Name of Festival	Date	No. of concerts	No. of works played	No. of works by British composers	No. of works by living British composers	First performances or commissions	Artistic director or chairman of committee	Remarks
38. NEWCASTLE	Oct. 3–18	31 (app.)	131 (app.)	42 (app.)	30	2	Michael Emmerson	1st Festival. Also included films, drama, art exhibitions, lectures. Special feature of David Barlow, 'composer of the year', ten of whose works were played, including a new opera, and a commissioned work.
39. PERSHORE	June 20–29	4	25 (app.)	3	1	1	Rev. J. D. Crichton	9th Festival. Local plays and exhibitions.
40. ROYAL NATIONAL EISTEDDFORD OF WALES	Aug. 3–10	8	—	—	—	—	John Roberts	Music is only one part of the festival of literature, drama, arts and crafts. Only specified performances were Mozart's C Minor Mass, Brahm's Requiem.
41. ST. ALBANS	June 23–28	9	84	33	3	—	Peter Hurford	5th international organ festival, featuring competitions for organists, lectures and master-classes. 7 pieces by British composers also formed the subject of a lecture-recital.

42. St. ENDELLION	July 9–Aug. 7	7	24	5	1	—	—	11th Festival. Purcell and Schumann chiefly represented.
43. SOUTHERN CATHEDRALS FESTIVAL	July 24–27	4	25	16	6	1	President: The Archbishop of Canterbury	Joint Festival of Chichester, Salisbury and Winchester Cathedrals. Strong liturgical leaning, including centenary tribute to Walford Davies (1869–1941).
44. STRATFORD ON AVON	April–Sept.	7	15 (app.)	5	—	—	Dr. Levi Fox John Strickson	200th anniversary of the Garrick Jubilee gave the music an 18th century emphasis.
45. STOUR	June 24–29	9	3 (recitals unspecified)	3	1	1	Alfred Deller	Largely early music, with one contemporary work.
46. STROUD	Oct. 12–26	5	1	1	1	1	Rev. Peter Minall	Drama-in-church, poetry, exhibitions included. One new opera was given five performances.
47. SWANSEA	Oct. 6–19	8	not specified	—	—	—	—	—
48. THREE CHOIRS FESTIVAL	Aug. 24–29	13	40 (app.)	8 (app.)	4	3	Christopher Robinson	An almost entirely sacred choral festival, held in Worcester Cathedral.

Name of Festival	Date	No. of concerts	No. of works played	No. of works by British composers	No. of works by living British composers	First performances or commissions	Artistic director or chairman of committee	Remarks
49. UNIVERSITY COLLEGE OF SWANSEA	Feb. 2–9	6	20 (app.)	—	—	—	—	Details not specified.
50. UNIVERSITY OF YORK	Mar. 1–9	12	32 (app.)	7	7	4	Wilfrid Mellers	A music week to mark the opening of the new Lyons Concert Hall. Most of the concerts featured the work of the University staff.
51. VALE OF GLAMORGAN	Sep. 7–13	4	not specified	—	—	—	Christopher Cory	—
52. WINDSOR	Sep. 17–27	20	49 (app.)	10	2	1	Yehudi Menuhin, Ian Hunter	1st Festival, by the team who, until 1968, directed the Bath Festival. Numerous extra events connected with Windsor.
53. YORK MYSTERY PLAYS, FESTIVAL OF THE ARTS	June 20–July 13	44	181 (app.)	29	17	6	Councillor J. M. Wood	Numerous exhibitions and local events, as well as the Mystery Plays; also Festival Club and Costume Ball.

APPENDIX V (Continued)

FIRST PERFORMANCES/COMMISSIONS LISTED AS ABOVE

2. **ALDEBURGH FESTIVAL**

Britten	*Children's Crusade, Op. 82*
	Suite for harp, Op. 83
Crosse	*Purgatory* (one-act opera)
	The grace of Todd (one-act opera)
Knussen	*Fire*

3. **BATH FESTIVAL**

Daves	*Cauda Pavonis, for piano* (based on Schubert's Op. 90, No. 1)
McCabe	*Sostenuto (Piano Study No. 2)*
Ridout	*Variants and Alleluias for organ and orchestra*
Tippett	*Shires Suite*

9. **BRIGHTON FESTIVAL**

| Birtwistle | *Down by the Greenwood Side* |
| Goehr | *Konzertstuck for piano and orchestra* |

10. **BROMSGROVE FESTIVAL**

| Banks | *Equation I and II* |
| North | *Ludes for harp and string trio* |

11. **CAMDEN FESTIVAL**

Collier	*London Street Cryes*
Josephs	*Oboe Concerto*
	Trio for Flute, Violin and Cello
Joubert	*Under Western Eyes* (Opera)
Newson	*June is a month in the summer*
Patten	*What its like to be alive*

13. **CALDER VALLEY FESTIVAL**

| Butterworth | *The Night Wind* |

14. **CARDIFF FESTIVAL**

Gardner	*Partita*
Hoddinott	*Violin Sonata*
Hughes (Arwel)	*In Memoriam, John Hughes*
Ogdon	*String Quartet*
Rees	*The cat's paw among the silence of midnight goldfish*
Smith-Brindle	*Piano Quintet*
Wynne	*Mosaic*

15. **CHELTENHAM FESTIVAL**

Berkeley	*Symphony in one movement*
	Triptych for organ
Brockless	*Fantasia Adagio and Fugue for organ*
Bush (Alan)	*Time Remembered, Op. 67*

FIRST PERFORMANCES/COMMISSIONS *(cont'd)*

15. CHELTENHAM FESTIVAL *(cont'd)*
    Cary   *Continuum*
    Davies (Hugh)   *Quintet*
    Davies (P. M.)   *St. Thomas Wake*
    Hearne   *Piano Piece II*
    Hoddinott   *Sinfonietta No. 2*
    Jacob   *Bassoon Quintet*
    Jones (Daniel)   *Tenor Songs*
    Lockwood   *Glass Water*
    Metcalf   *Chorales and Variants*
    Orton   *Cycle for 2 or 4 players*
    Phillips   *Ornamentik*
    Steel   *O Praise the Lord of Heaven*

17. DARTINGTON (SUMMER SCHOOL)
    Bush (Alan)   *The Freight of Heaven*
    Lord   *The History of the Flood*

18. DARTINGTON (WEEKEND COURSE)
    Young   *String Trio*

20. DUBLIN FESTIVAL OF 20th CENTURY MUSIC
    Bodley   *String Quartet*
    McCabe   *Capriccio (Piano Study No. I)*
    Schürmann   *Seven studies of Francis Bacon*
    Victory   *Three legends*

21. EDINBURGH FESTIVAL
    Goehr   *Nazredin*
    Damilton   *Pharsalia*

22. ENGLISH BACH FESTIVAL
    Davies   *Ecce Manus tradentis*

24. GUILDFORD FESTIVAL
    Wordsworth   *The Festival Overture*

25. HARLOW FESTIVAL
    Stevens   *Choriamb*

26. HARROGATE FESTIVAL
    Mellers   *The Word Unborn*
    Orton   *Kiss*

30. LEICESTERSHIRE SCHOOLS FESTIVAL OF MUSIC
    Kelly   *Overture 'Sancho Panza'*

31. LITTLE MISSENDEN FESTIVAL
    Benger   *Robert Frost Songs*
    Osborne   *Fantasia for cello and piano*
    Saunders   *Diversions*

35. MACCLESFIELD FESTIVAL
    Goehr   *Nowomiya* Op. 27
    McCabe   *Sonata for Clarinet, Cello and Piano*

38. NEWCASTLE
    Barlow   *Concertante Music for horn, cor anglais and orchestra*
                       David & Bathsheba (Opera)

39. PERSHORE FESTIVAL
    Parrott   *Mosaics, for organ*

43. SOUTHERN CATHEDRALS FESTIVAL
    Mathias   *An Admonition to Rulers*, Op. 43

45. STOUR MUSIC
    Tranchell   *Murder at the Towers*

46. STROUD FESTIVAL
    Hopkins (Anthony) *Rich Man, Poor Man, Beggar Man, Saint*

48. THREE CHOIRS FESTIVAL
    Harvey   *Ludus Amoris*
    Maconchy   *And Death Shall Have No Dominion* (Dylan Thomas)
    Mathias   *Psalm 150*

50. UNIVERSITY OF YORK MUSIC WEEK
    Davies (Hugh)   *Cuysac*
    Johnson   *Trika*
    Mellers   *Life Cycle*
    Orton   *Piano ring*

52. WINDSOR FESTIVAL
    Berkeley   *Windsor Variations*

53. YORK MYSTERY PLAYS FESTIVAL OF THE ARTS
    Birtwistle   *Melodica*
    Davies   *Solita for solo flute*
    Gilbert   *Mother*
    Orton   *Divisions III*
    Rands   *Wildtrack I*
    Tate   *Illustrations for Brass Bands*

This list does not include biennial or triennial festivals, which did not take place in 1969; nor festivals which were not specifically of musical interest. Those not mentioned, therefore, include: Ashington, Billingham, Bristol, Buxton, City of London, Hackney, Hemel Hempstead, Leeds, Rolleston, Tees-side, Wallasey, and over fifty Folk Festivals.

Classified Select Bibliography

I—COMPOSERS a) Books and articles about a composer. Authors listed alphabetically.
          b) Books and articles by a composer, titles listed alphabetically.

II—GENERAL Books and articles referred to in the text, or of general relevance to the music of the contemporary period. General histories and works of reference are not included.

Abbreviations

C	*The Chesterian*	Pub. by J. & W. Chester Ltd.
CM	*Church Music*	Pub. by the Church Music Association
Co	*Composer*	The journal of the Composers' Guild of Great Britain
E	*Encounter*	
FMN	*Faber Music News*	Pub. by Faber Music Ltd.
IT	*Ideas of Today*	
L	*The Listener*	Pub. by the British Broadcasting Corporation
LCMM	*London College of Music Magazine*	
LM	*London Magazine*	
LLT	*Life and Letters today*	
MaMu	*Making Music*	Pub. by the Rural Music Schools Association
ML	*Music and Letters*	Pub. by the Oxford University Press
MM	*Music and Musicians*	
MMR	*Monthly Musical Record*	
MO	*Musical Opinion*	
MQ	*Musical Quarterly*	Pub. by G Schirmer Inc., New York

407

MR	*Music Review*	
MS	*Music Survey*	
MT	*Musical Times*	Pub. by Novello & Co. Ltd.
NS	*New Statesman*	
OIQ	*Organ Institute Quarterly*	
OP	*Opera*	
PR	*Performing Right*	Pub. by the Performing Rights Society
PRMA	*Proceedings of the Royal Musical Association*	
RAMM	*Royal Academy of Music Magazine*	
S	*The Score*	
SO	*Soundings*	
T	*Tempo*	Pub. by Boosey & Hawkes Ltd.
TT	*Time and Tide*	

I—Composers (a) = about
(b) = by

ALWYN, W.
  (b)   *Ariel to Miranda*   (Adam, Inter-
                                                      national Review
                                                      316-17-18, 1957)
                         The technique of film music (Focal Press 1957)
                         *Twentieth Century French   (Chatto & Windus
                            Poetry*   1969)

APIVOR, D.
  (b)   *Bernard Van Dieren*   (MS vol. 3, no. 4,
                                                      1951)
                         Contemporary music and the (The Critic 1946)
                            British scene

ARNOLD, M.
  (a) Goddard, S.   *Malcolm Arnold*   (L vol.51, 1954)
      Mitchell, D.   *Malcolm Arnold*   (MT Aug. 1955)
  (b)   *I think of music in terms of* (MM July 1965)
                            sound

BANKS, D.
  (a) Mann, W.   *The music of Don Banks*   (MT Aug. 1968)
  (b)   *Converging streams*   (MT June 1970)
                         Third stream music   (MM June 1970)

BARDWELL, W.
  (a) Spero, C.   *William Bardwell*   (Co 39, 1971)

BEDFORD, D.
  (a) Nyman, M.   *Stockhausen and David   (L vol. 83, 1970)
                            Bedford*

BENNETT, R. R.
  (a) Blyth, A.   *Penny for an opera*   (MM Nov. 1967)
       Bradshaw, S.   *Richard Rodney Bennett*   (L vol. 81, 1969)
                       The music of Richard   (L vol. 69, 1963)
                       Rodney Bennett
       Dawney, M.   *The contemporary string* (Ma Mu 67,
                       quartet   Summer 1968)
       Downes, E.   *A man of principle*   (MM May 1970)
                       (on the opera *Victory*)
       Jacobson, B.   *Friday's child*   (MM Nov. 1964)
       Maw, N.   *Richard Rodney Bennett*   (MT Feb. 1962)

BERKELEY, L.
  (a) Barker, F. G.   *At last the admiral sings* (MM Oct. 1954)
                      (on 'Nelson')
       Berkeley, M.   *Lennox Berkeley's Third*
                       Symphony   (L. vol. 82, 1969)
       Cooper, M.   *Lennox Berkeley*   (L vol. 69, 1963)
                       Lennox Berkeley and his (L vol. 61, 1969)
                       new (2nd) *symphony*
       Dean, W.   *Lennox Berkeley and*   (L vol. 52, 1954)
                       'Nelson'
       Dickinson, P.   *The music of Lennox*   (MT May 1963)
                       Berkeley
                       Berkeley on the keyboard (MM April 1963)
                       Berkeley's Music today (MT Nov. 1968)
                       Lennox Berkeley   (MM Aug. 1965)
       Headington, C.   *The instrumental music of* (C XXXII, 193,
                       Lennox Berkeley   1958)
       Holst, I.   *Lennox Berkeley's 'Stabat* (C XXVIII, 178,
                       Mater'   1954)
       Hull, R.   *The music of Lennox*   (C XXII, 153,
                       Berkeley   1948)
                       The style of Lennox Berkeley (C XXIV, 162,
                                          1950)
       Klein, J. W.   *Some reflections on*   (C XXIX, 181,
                       Berkeley's 'Nelson'   1955)
       Le Fleming, C.   *The shorter works of Lennox* (C XXVII, 174,
                       Berkeley   1953)
       Lockspeiser, E.   *The music of Lennox*   (L vol. 38, 1947)
                       Berkeley
       Mason,   *The progress of Lennox*   (L vol. 56, 1956)
                       Berkeley
       Redlich, H.   *Lennox Berkeley*   (MS vol.3, no. 4,
                                            1951)

BERKELEY, L. *(cont'd.)*

Vogel, A.	*Lennox Berkeley*	(C XXXIII, 198, 1959)
(b)	*Counting the beats*	(Co 12, 1963)
	The Magnificat	(L vol. 80, 1968)
	The sound of words	(Times, 28.6.62)
	Truth in music	(Times Lit. Supp. 3.3.66)

BIRTWISTLE, H.

(a) Henderson, R.	*Harrison Birtwistle*	(MT March 1964)
Nyman, M.	*Harrison Birtwistle's 'Punch and Judy'*	(L vol. 80, 1968)
	Harrison Birtwistle	(MM Sep. 1969)
	With reference to Birtwistle's 'Medusa'	(L vol. 82, 1969)

BLAKE, D.

(a) Larner, G.	*David Blake*	(MT April 1968)
(b)	*Lumina*	(MT April 1970)
	Lumina	(L vol. 83, 1970)

BLISS, A.

(a) Crisp, C.	*The ballets of Arthur Bliss*	(MT Aug. 1966)
Foss, H.	*Arthur Bliss & J. B. Priestley*	(L vol. 42, 1949)
Goddard, S.	*Bliss and the English tradition*	(L vol. 35, 1946)
Jefferson, A.	*Bliss, composer royal*	(MM Oct. 1965)
Mahony, P.	*Sir Arthur Bliss: 75th birthday*	(Co 20, 1966)
Thompson, K. L.	*Catalogue of Bliss's works*	(MT Aug. 1966)
(b)	*As I remember (autobiography)*	(Faber 1970)
	Four aspects of music	(Co 22, 1966/7)
	Violin Concerto	(MT June 1955)

BRIAN, H.

(a) Foreman, R. L. E.	*The symphonies of Havergal Brian*	(Co 33, 1969)
Orga, A.	*The largest symphony in existence* (Brian's 'Gothic')	(L vol. 76, 1966)
Simpson, R.	*The later works of Havergal Brian*	(MT Nov. 1959)
	The unknown English composer	(MM Jan. 1961)

BRITTEN, B.

(a)　　　　　　　　　　　*i-books*

| Boys, H. (with Crozier, Duncan & Piper) | *The Rape of Lucretia* | (John Lane The Bodley Head 1948) |

| Brook, D. | *Composers' gallery* | (Rockliff 1946) |

| Forster, E. M. (with Sackville-West, Slater) | *Peter Grimes* | (John Lane, The Bodley Head 1945) |

| Gishford, A. (ed) | *Tribute to Benjamin Britten on his fiftieth birthday* | (Faber 1963) |

| Holst, I. | *Britten* | (Faber 1966) |

| Howard, P. | *The operas of Benjamin Britten* | (Barrie & Rockliff 1969) |

| Keller, H. | *Benjamin Britten: a commentary on his works from a group of specialists* | (Rockliff 1962) |

| Lindler, H. | *Benjamin Britten: das Opernwerk* | (Musik der Zeit Boosey & Hawkes 1955) |

White, E. W.	*Benjamin Britten. A sketch of his life and works*	(Boosey & Hawkes 1954 2nd ed.)
	The rise of English opera	(John Lehmann 1951)
	Benjamin Britten. His life and operas	(Faber 1970)

ii—magazines & periodicals

| Berkeley, L. | *Britten's 'Spring Symphony'* | (ML vol. 31, 1950) |

| Blom, E. | *Britten's 'Roman' opera* | (L vol. 36, 1946) |

| Boys, H. | *Benjamin Britten* | (MMR Oct. 1938) |
| | *Benjamin Britten and The Rape of Lucretia* | (Con Brio, Autumn 1946) |

| Boys, M. | *Britten, Verdi and the Requiem* | (T Autumn 1968) |

| Bradshaw, S. | *Britten's 'Cantata Academica'* | (T Spring 1960) |

| Brown, D. | *Britten's three canticles* | (MR vol. 21, 1960) |

| Carpenter, R. | *Baines and Britten: some affinities* | (MT April 1956) |

| Coleman, B. | *Britten's 'Billy Budd'* | (T Autumn 1951) |
| | *Britten's 'Gloriana'* | (T Summer 1953) |

| Crozier, E. | *Britten's 'Billy Budd'* | (T Autumn 1951) |
| | *Britten's second opera* | (T March 1946) |

BRITTEN, B. (*cont'd.*)

	Forward to 'Albert Herring'	(T Summer 1947)
Dawney, M.	*Britten's church music*	(T Autumn 1967)
Dent, E. J.	*The Beggar's Opera*	(L vol. 40, 1948)
Evans, P.	*A Midsummer Night's Dream*	(T Spring 1960)
	Britten in merrie England ('Gloriana')	(L vol. 76, 1966)
	Britten's Cello Sonata	(T Summer 1961)
	Britten since the 'War Requiem'	(L vol. 71, 1964)
	Britten's new church opera ('The burning fiery furnace')	(L vol. 75, 1966)
	Britten's Pushkin songs	(FMN Summer 1968)
	Britten's 'War Requiem'	(T Spring 1962)
	'Curlew River'	(FMN Summer 1965)
	Interpreter and idiom	(FMN Autumn 1966)
	Sonata structures in early Britten	(T Autumn 1967)
	Owen Wingrave	(MT May 1971)
Fiftieth birthday issues (various contributors)		T Winter 1963
Foss, H.	*Britten and 'Peter Grimes'*	(L vol. 34, 1945)
Goddard, S.	*Britten as an instrumental composer*	(L vol. 42, 1949)
Halsey, L.	*Britten's Church Music*	(MT Oct. 1962)
Hamburger, P.	*Mainly about Britten*	(MS, vol. 3 no. 2, 1950).
Headington, C.	*Britten's music and its significance today*	(C Spring 1960)
Holst, I.	*Britten's 'Let's make an opera'*	(T Winter 1950)
	Britten's 'Nocturne'	(T Winter 1958)
	Britten's 'Saint Nicholas'	(T Winter 1948)
Howard, C.	*Britten's first new opera for six years* ('A Midsummer Night's Dream')	(MM June 1960)
Jacobs, R. L.	*The significance of Peter Grimes*	(L vol. 35, 1946)
Keller, H.	*Britten and Mozart*	(ML vol. 29, 1948)
	Britten's 'Beggar's Opera'	(T Winter 1948)

BRITTEN, B. (*cont'd.*)

	Benjamin Britten and the young	(L vol. 42, 1949)
	Benjamin Britten's Second Quartet	(T March 1947) (cf. Times 26.x.62)
	Britten's 'Sinfonia da Requiem'	(L vol. 59, 1958)
	Two interpretations of 'Gloriana'	(T Winter 1966)
Klein, J. W.	*Britten's 'Gloriana'*	(T Summer 1953)
	'Billy Budd'	(L vol. 64, 1960)
McDonald, O. H.	*The semantics of music* ('Serenade', 'On this island')	(MS vol. 1, no. 4, 1948)
Malcolm, G.	*The new opera by Benjamin Britten* ('A Midsummer Night's Dream')	(L. vol. 63, 1960)
Mason, C.	*Benjamin Britten*	(MT March, April 1948)
	Britten's new Requiem	(L vol.67, 1962)
Mason, R.	*Britten's 'Billy Budd'*	(T Autumn 1951)
Mellers, W.	*Benjamin Britten and English opera*	(L vol. 63, 1960)
Mitchell, D.	*A neglected masterpiece: Britten's 'Gloriana'*	(L vol. 70, 1963)
	Britten's 'Let's make an opera'	(MS vol. 2, no. 2 1949)
	Owen Wingrave	(L vol. 25, 1971)
	More off than on 'Billy Budd'	(MS vol. 4, no. 2, 1952)
	The later development of Benjamin Britten	(C XXVII, 171 & 172, 1952)
Noble, J.	*Britten's 'Songs from the Chinese'*	(T Autumn 1959)
	'Greater than Grimes' ('Billy Budd')	(MM Feb. 1964)
Piper, J.	*Britten's 'Billy Budd'*	(T Autumn 1951)
Plomer, W.	*Britten's 'Gloriana'*	(T Summer 1953)
Porter, A.	*Britten's 'Billy Budd'*	(ML vol. 33, 1952)
	Britten's 'Gloriana'	(ML vol. 34, 1953)
	Britten's 'Prodigal Son'	(L vol. 79, 1967)
Robertson, A.	*Britten's 'War Requiem'*	(MT May 1962)
Roseberry, E.	*Britten's Purcell realisations and folk-song arrangements*	(T Spring 1961)
	Britten's 'Missa Brevis'	(T Spring 1960)

BRITTEN, B. (cont'd,)

		The music of 'Noye's Fludde'	(T Autumn 1958)
	Shawe-Taylor, D.	*Britten's comic opera*	(L vol. 37, 1947)
	Squire, W. H.	*The aesthetic hypothesis of 'The Rape of Lucretia'*	(T Sep. 1946)
	Stein, E.	*Analysis of String Quartet No. 2*	(Boosey & Hawkes 1946)
		Britten's 'Noye's Fludde'	(T Summer 1958)
		Britten's 'Spring Symphony'	(T Spring 1950)
		Britten's 'The Turn of the Screw'	(T Winter 1954)
		Form in opera: Albert Herring	(T Autumn 1947)
		Gloriana	(L vol. 49, 1953)
	Stevenson, R.	*War Requiem*	(L vol. 78, 1967)
	Tippett, M.	*A birthday tribute*	(Co 12, 1963)
	Tranchell, P.	*Britten and Brittenites*	(ML vol. 34, 1953)
	Walsh, S.	*Two interpretations of 'Gloriana'*	(T Winter 1966)
	Warrack, J.	*Britten's 'Cello Symphony'*	(MT June 1964)
	White, E. W.	*A musician of the people*	(LLT April 1939)
		Billy Budd	(L vol. 46, 1951)
	Whittall, A. M.	*Benjamin Britten*	(MR vol. 23, 1962)
		Tonal instability in Britten's 'War Requiem'	(MR vol. 24, 1963)
	Wright, A.	*Britten at home*	(MM Aug 1955)
(b)		*Conversation with Benjamin Britten*	(T Feb. 1944)
		Early influences: a tribute to Frank Bridge	(Co 19, 1966)
		Frank Bridge, 1879–1941	(FMN Autumn 1966)
		How to become a composer	(L vol. 36, 1946)
		On receiving the first Aspen award	(Faber 1964)
		The composer and the listener	(L vol. 36, 1946)
		The wonderful world of music (with Imogen Holst)	(Macdonald 1968)

BUSH A.

(a)	Chapman, E.	*Wat Tyler*	(L vol. 56, 1956)
	Goddard, S.	*Alan Bush: propagandist and artist*	(L vol. 71, 1964)

BUSH, A. (*cont'd.*)

	Mason, C.	*Alan Bush in high middle age*	(L vol. 63, 1960)
	Orga, A.	*Alan Bush, musician and Marxist*	(MM Aug. 1969)
	Ottaway, H.	*Alan Bush's 'Wat Tyler'*	(MT Dec. 1956)
	Payne, A.	*Alan Bush*	(MT April 1964)
	Stevenson, R.	*Alan Bush—committed composer*	(MR vol. 25, 1964)
(b)		*In my seventh decade*	(Kahn & Averill 1970)
		Music and the people	(MM Oct. 1956)
		Strict counterpoint in Palestrina style	(Joseph Williams 1948)
		The mind in chains	(Muller 1937)
		The second international congress of composers and music critics	(MT Sep. 1948)
		The study and teaching of musical composition	(MT Dec. 1952)
		What does music express?	(Marxism Today July 1963, April 1964)

BUSH, G.

(a)	Rooper, J.	*Geoffrey Bush*	(MT Dec. 1967)
(b)		*Musical creation and the listener*	(Muller 1954)
		Prophet in his own country (Sterndale Bennett)	(Co 21, 1966)

BUTTERWORTH, A.

(b)		*Music in the North*	(Co 12, 1963)

BUTTERWORTH, G.

(a)	Rippin, J.	*George Butterworth, 1885–1916*	(MT Aug/Sep. 1966)
	Thompson, K. L.	*A Butterworth catalogue*	(MT Sep. 1966)

CANNON, P.

(a)	Myers, R.	*Philip Canon*	(MT Nov. 1965)

CARDEW, C.

(a)	Parsons, M.	*Cornelius Cardew*	(L vol. 78, 1967)
(b)		*A Scratch Orchestra: draft constitution*	(MT June 1969)
		Cage and Cunningham	(MT Sep. 1964)
		Notation—Interpretation etc.	(T Summer 1961)

CARY, T.
  (b)   *Electronic Music*   (Faber 1972)
                                                                 Electronic Music : call for   (MT April 1966)
                                                                action
                                                                 Electronic Music today   (MT Jan. 1968)
                                                                 Electronic Music, its creation, (PR 53, May 1970)
                                                                protection and exploitation
                                                                 Florentine Eggheads   (Co 29, 1968)
                                                                 Moving pictures at an   (Co 25, 1967)
                                                                 Exhibition (Expo 67)
                                                                 Sproggletaggle   (Co 18, 1966)

CHAGRIN, F.
  (b)   *A Quarter-century of*   (Co 26, 1967/8)
                                                                  new music
                                                    (Society for the promotion of new music)

COOKE, A.
  (a) Clapham, J.   *Arnold Cooke's Symphony*   (MR vol. 7, 1946)
                                               Arnold Cooke : the   (MS vol. 3 no. 4,
                                               achievement of twenty years 1951)
      Mason, C.   *Arnold Cooke*   (MT March 1967)
  (b)   *A birthday conversation*   (Co 24, 1967)
                                               Paul Hindemith I   (MS vol. 2, no. 1,
                                                                    1949)
                                             Paul Hindemith II   (MS vol. 2, no. 2,
                                                                    1949)

CROSSE, G.
  (a) Waterhouse, J.   *The music of Gordon Crosse*   (MT May 1965)
  (b)   *My Second Violin Concerto*   (L vol. 83, 1970)

CRUFT, A.
  (a) Rubbra, E.   *The music of Adrian Cruft*   (MT Aug. 1969)
      Stevens, B.   *Adrian Cruft*   (Co 19, 1966)

DAVIES, P. M.
  (a) Chanan, M.   *Latent bombast*   (L vol. 82, 1969)
      Henderson, R.   *Peter Maxwell Davies*   (MT Oct. 1961)
      Murphy, M.   *Maxwell Davies—who*   (CM April 1969)
                                             were you?
      Northcott, B.   *Peter Maxwell Davies*   (MM April 1969)
      Payne, A.   *Maxwell Davies's five*   (T Spring 1965)
                                             motets
      Pruslin, S.   *Maxwell Davies's Second*   (T Summer 1965)
                                             Taverner Fantasia
      Smalley, R.   *Recent works by Peter*   (T Spring 1968)
                                             Maxwell Davies

DAVIES, P. M. (*cont'd.*)

Waterhouse, J.	*Peter Maxwell Davies and his public image*	(L vol. 71, 1964)
	Maxwell Davies: towards an opera	(T Summer 1964)
	Meeting point	(MM Oct. 1964)
(b)	*A letter*	(Co 15, 1965)
	Set or series	(L vol. 79, 1968)
	Recent works	(L Vol. 81, 1969)
	The origins of 'Vesalius'	(MM Dec. 1969)
	The young British composer	(S 15, March 1956)
	The young composer in America	(T Spring 1965)

DELIUS, F.

(a) Beecham, T.	*Frederick Delius*	(Hutchinson 1959)
Special issue, with other contributors		(T Winter 1952)
(Foss, Holland, Hutchings, Mitchell, Squire)		
Fenby, E.	*Delius as I knew him*	(Quality Press 1936)
Hutchings, A.	*Delius*	(Macmillan 1949)
Klein, J. W.	*Delius*	(T Winter 1961)
Payne, A.	*Delius*	(T Winter 1961)
	Delius' Requiem	(T Spring 1966)
Warlock, P.	*Delius*	(Bodley Head 1923)

DICKINSON, P.

(a) Dommett, K.	*Peter Dickinson*	(MM May 1969)
Lovett, L. (with Blackburn)	*Judas in our time*	(MM April 1967)
Norrington, R.	*Peter Dickinson*	(MT Feb. 1965)
(b)	*A note on 'The Judas Tree'*	(MT April 1967)

EASTWOOD, T.

(b)	*Writing an opera for television*	(Co 25, 1967)

FRANKEL, B.

(a) Gill, R.	*The music of Benjamin Frankel*	(L. vol. 41, 1949)
Keller, H.	*Frankel and the symphony*	(MT Feb. 1970)
Mason, C.	*The music of Benjamin Frankel*	(L vol. 48, 1952)
Vaughan, D.	*Benjamin Frankel's Sixth Symphony*	(L vol. 81, 1969)
Wood, R. W.	*Benjamin Frankel*	(MS vol. 3 no. 4, 1051)

FRANKEL, B. (*cont'd.*)

(b)   *His music caught the*   (MM Dec. 1956
                                 meaning of words
                                 (on Gerald Finzi)
                                 On reaching a seventh   (L vol 83, 1970)
                                 symphony
                                 Sonata form?   (L vol. 73, 1965)
                                 The bold step forward in   (L vol. 75, 1966)
                                 music

FRICKER, P. R.

(a) Bradbury, E.   *Fricker's developing art*   (L vol 56, 1956)
     Cox, D.   *Fricker and an American*   (L vol. 67, 1967)
                         story
     Evans, P.   *Fricker and the English*   (L vol. 64, 1960)
                         symphony
     Larner, G.   *The choral music of Peter*   (MT Oct. 1958)
                         Racine Fricker
     Mason, C.   *Fricker and his generation*   (L vol. 51, 1954)
                         Peter Racine Fricker   (L vol. 43, 1950)
                         The recent music of   (L vol. 60, 1958)
                         Racine Fricker
     Peart, D.   *Fricker's Fourth Symphony*   (L vol. 77, 1967)
     see also under Hines, R. S.
(b)   *The vanishing composers*   (Co 13, 1964)

GARDNER, J.

(a) Goodwin, Noel   *John Gardner's opera*   (MT May 1967)
                        'The moon and sixpence'.
     Halsey, L.   *John Gardner's choral music*   (MT Jan. 1967)
(b)   *A Russian contrapuntist*   (Co 17, 1965)
                        (Taneiev)
                        Not about 'The moon and   (MM May 1957)
                        sixpence'
                        Testing genius by analysis   (Co 24 1967)
                        The slopes of Parnassus   (Co 21 1966)
                        (Fux)

GERHARD, R.

(a) A tribute to Roberto Gerhard on his 60th
     birthday by various contributors   (S 17, September
                                                 1956)
     Bradshaw, S.   *Roberto Gerhard and his*   (L vol. 62, 1959)
                        new symphony
     Drew, D.   *Gerhard as symphonist*   (L vol. 57, 1957)
                        Roberto Gerhard   (L vol. 83, 1970)
     Kay, N.   *Late harvest*   (MM March 1970)

GERHARD, R. (*cont'd.*)

Keller, H.	*Roberto Gerhard's two ears* (Fourth Symphony)	(L vol. 82, 1969)
Mason, C.	*A Modern Spanish composer in England*	(L vol. 53, 1955)
	A Spanish composer in exile	(L vol. 60, 1958)
	Roberto Gerhard	(L vol. 73, 1965)
	Roberto Gerhard and 'The Duenna'	(L vol. 45, 1951)
	Roberto Gerhard's First Symphony	(MT Feb. 1962)
Orga, A.	*Roberto Gerhard 1896–1970*	(MM Oct. 1970)
(ed.)	*Roberto Gerhard: Selected Essays*	(Kahn and Averill 1971)
(b)	*Composition with twelve notes*	(see under Rufer, J.)
	Is new music growing old?	(Pb. Ann Arbor, Michigan, Vol. 62, no. 18, Aug., 1960)
	Some lectures by Webern	(S 28 Jan. 1961)
	Tonality in twelve-tone music	(S 6 May 1952)
	Twelve-note technique in Stravinsky	(S 20 June 1957)
	The Plague	(L vol. 71, 1964)

GILBERT, A.

(a) Hopkins, G. W.	*The music of Anthony Gilbert*	(MT Oct. 1968)
(b)	*On not writing for serpents*	(L vol. 83, 1970)

GOEHR, A.

(a) Goodwin, N.	*Ardern must die*	(MM May 1967)
Northcott, B.	*Goehr the progressive*	(MM Oct. 1969)
Wood, H.	*Alexander Goehr*	(L vol. 67, 1962)
	The music of Alexander Goehr	(MT May 1962)
(b)	*Ascents and descents* (Symphony in one movement)	(L vol. 83, 1970)
	For my performers (Romanza for Cello & Orchestra)	(L vol. 79, 1968)
	Naboth's Vineyard	(MT July 1968)
	The importance of being Schoenberg	(MM July 1965)
	Towards the Twelve-Note System (with Walter Goehr)	(in 'European Music in the Twentieth Century' Routledge 1957)

HAMILTON, I.
  (a) Mason, C.   *The recent music of Iain*   (L vol. 58, 1957)
                      Hamilton

          Milner, A.   *Some observations on the* (MT July 1956)
                      music of Iain Hamilton

  (b)   *Serial composition today*   (T Autumn/
                      (see under Still, R.)   Winter 1960)

HARVEY, J.
  (a) Brown, D.   *Jonathan Harvey*   (MT Sep. 1968)
  (b)   *Stockhausen: theory and* (MR vol. 29, 1968)
                      music

HODDINOTT, A.
  (a) Thomas, A. F.   *Alun Hoddinott*   (MT Oct. 1955)

HOROVITZ, J.
  (a) Bradbury, E.   *Joseph Horovitz, a survey* (MT April 1970)
  (b)   *The importance of*   (Co 34, 1969/70)
                      Pleasants—I
                      The importance of   (Co 35, 1970)
                      Pleasants—II
                      (see under Pleasants, H.)

IRELAND, J.
  (a) Arnell, R.   *John Ireland 1879–1962* (T Spring/Summer
                                     1962)

          Brooke, J.   *The music of John Ireland* (MT Nov. 1958)
          Foss, H.   *John Ireland*   (MT Aug. 1962)
          Holland, A. K.   *John Ireland at 75—an* (T Summer 1954)
                      appreciation

          Ottaway, H.   *Ireland's shorter piano* (T Autumn 1959)
                      pieces

                      Complete catalogue of (Boosey & Hawkes
                      Ireland's works, compiled 1968)
                      by Ernest Chapman

JOHNSON, R. S.
  (a) Aston, P.   *The music of Robert*   (MT March 1968)
                      Sherlaw Johnson

JONES, D.
  (a) Keeffe, B.   *Daniel Jones: his*   (L vol. 61, 1959)
                      achievements & views

          Loveland, K.   *A new symphony from Wales* (MM Feb. 1959)
                      Jones's 'The Knife'   (MM Dec. 1963)
          Stewart, A.   *Daniel Jones's opera*   (MT Nov. 1963)
  (b)   *An attempt to formulate* (S 11 March 1955)
                      general aesthetic principles
                      through music-aesthetics

JONES, D. (*cont'd.*)

	Some metrical experiments	(S 3 June 1950)
	The problem of clear presentation	(S 5 Aug. 1951)

JOSEPHS, W.

(a) Jacobson, B.

	My friend the composer	(Chicago Daily News, 16.3.68)
	Prize Requiem	(MM Feb. 1964)

JOUBERT, J.

(a) Chisholm, E.   *John Joubert's 'Silas   (MT Sep. 1961)
                        Marner'*

Dickinson, P.   *A composer interviewed   (Co 31, 32, 1969)*
(b)   *Under Western Eyes   (MT May 1969)*
                    see under Glendenning, F.

LAMBERT, C.

(a) Foss, H.   *The music of Constant   (L vol. 47, 1952)
                    Lambert*
                    *Constant Lambert   (MT Dec. 1951)
                    (1905–1951)*

Searle, H.   *Constant Lambert   (MS vol. 3 no. 2,
                                              1952)*

(b)   *Music Ho!   (Faber 1934)*

LEIGHTON, K.

(a) Cockshott, J. *The music of Kenneth   (MT April 1957)
                    Leighton*

LIPKIN, M.

(a) Good, H.   *The music of Malcolm   (MT Dec. 1969)
                    Lipkin*

LUTYENS, E.

(a) Henderson, R. *Elisabeth Lutyens   (MT Aug. 1963)*
    Larner, G.   *Frozen music : Elisabeth (L vol. 76, 1966)
                    Lutyens at sixty*

    Mason, C.   *The art of Elisabeth   (L vol. 66, 1961)
                    Lutyens*

    Payne, A.   *Elisabeth Lutyens,   (L vol. 81, 1969)
                    Nicholas Maw*
                    *Lutyens's solution to serial (L vol. 70, 1963)
                    problems*

    Weissmann, J. *The music of Elisabeth (L vol. 44, 1950)
                    Lutyens*

MATHIAS, W.

(a) Walsh, S.   *The music of William   (MT Jan. 1969)
                    Mathias*

MAW, N.

(a)   *Nicholas Maw's new opera*   (MT July 1970
                                 ('The rising of the moon') & T Spring 1970)
        Bradshaw, S.   *Nicholas Maw*   (MT Sep. 1962)
        Dawney, M.   *The contemporary string*   (Ma Mu 67,
                                 quartet   Summer 1968)
        Northcott, B.   *Nicholas Maw*   (MM March 1970)
        Payne, A.   *Composer in search of a*   (MM Aug. 1964)
                                 language
                                 Nicholas Maw's 'One man   (T Winter 1964)
                                 show'
                                 Nicholas Maw's String   (T Autumn 1965)
                                 Quartet

        see also under Lutyens E. and Musgrave, T.

(b)   *Boulez and tradition*   (MT March 1962)

MILNER, A.

(a) Bradbury, E.   *The music of Anthony*   (L vol. 72, 1964)
                                 Milner
                                 Milner's The 'Water and   (MT Feb. 1963)
                                 the Fire'
        Dawney, M.   *Liturgical music by three* (CM vol. 2 no. 17
                                 composers   Feb. 1967)
        Jacobs, A.   *The music of Anthony*   (MT Sep. 1958)
                                 Milner
        Stevens, D.   *Anthony Milner's*   (MT July 1959)
                                 'Variations for Orchestra'
(b)   *English contemporary*   (in 'European Music in
                                 music   the Twentieth Century'
                                                              Routledge 1957)
                                 Music and Liturgy   (*The Month*, London
                                                              1966)
                                 Music in a vernacular   (PRMA 91, 1964/5)
                                 Catholic liturgy
                                 The Instruction on   (*Worship* Vol. 41, no. 6
                                 Sacred Music   June/July 1967
                                                              Collegeville, Minnesota)
                                 The Lunatic Fringe combed (MT Oct. 1956)
                                 The vocal element in melody (MT March 1956)
                                 Roman Spring   (MT Oct. 1969)

        see also under Hines, R. S.

MUSGRAVE, T.
  (a) Bradshaw, S.   *Newcomers: Musgrave*   (C XXXV, 203,
                         and Maw   1960)
                         Thea Musgrave   (MT Dec. 1963)
      Kay, N.   *Thea Musgrave*   (MM Dec., 1969)
  (b)   *Starting-points*   (L vol. 81, 1969)
                         (Clarinet Concerto)
                         The Decision   (MT Nov. 1967)

NAYLOR, B.
  (a) Halsey, L.   *Bernard Naylor's Nine*   (MT July 1961)
                         Motets

ORAM, D.
  (a) Parfitt, I.   *Oramics*   (LCMM Spring
                                            1969)

ORR, C. W.
  (a) Barford, P.   *C. W. Orr*   (MR Aug. 1960)
      Copley, I. A.   *An English song-writer* (Co 29 198)
      le Fleming, C.   *The music of C. W. Orr* (C XXIX, 182,
                                            1955)
      Northcote, S.   *The songs of C. W. Orr* (ML vol. 18, 1937)

PANUFNIK, A.
  (a) French, P.   *The music of Andrzej*   (T Spring 1968)
                         Panufnik
      Hall, B.   *Andrzej Panufnik and his* (T Winter 1964)
                         'Sinfonia Sacra'
      Truscott, H.   *Andrzej Panufnik*   (T Autumn/Winter
                                            1960)

PARROTT, I.
  (a) Thomas, A. F.   *Ian Parrott at 50*   (MT March 1966)
  (b)   *A guide to musical thought* (Dobson 1955)
                         Encouragement for new (MT Feb. 1946)
                         composers
                  (on the Society for the promotion of new music)
                       Method in orchestration (Dobson 1957)
                       Pathways to modern music (Unwin 1947)
                       The music of an adventure (Regency Press 1966)

RAINIER, P.
  (a) Amis, J.   *Priaulx Rainier*   (MT July 1955)
      Glock, W.   *The music of Priaulx*   (L. vol. 38, 1947)
                         Rainier
  (b)   *The new world of*   (IT vol. 15, no. 3)
                       modern music   (April-May-June
                                            1967)

RANDS, B.

  (a) Small, C.   *Bernard Rands*   (MT Oct. 1967)
  (b)   *Sibelius and his critics* (MR vol. 19, 1958)
                        The use of canon in Bartok's (MR vol. 18, 1957)
                        Quartets

RAWSTHORNE, A.

(a)	Blom, E.	*Alan Rawsthorne*	(L vol. 33, 1945)
	Cox, D.	*Rawsthorne: style and idea*	(L vol. 69, 1963)
	Crankshaw, G.	*The art of Alan Rawsthorne*	(C XXX 186, 1956)
	Foss, H.	*Rawsthorne's new concerto*	(L vol. 39, 1948)
	Goddard, S.	*Alan Rawsthorne and the orchestra*	(L vol. 66, 1961)
	Hoddinott, A.	*Rawsthorne at sixty*	(MT May 1965)
		Rawsthorne's concertos	(L vol. 75, 1966)
		The achievement of Alan Rawsthorne	(L vol. 73, 1965)
	Howells, H.	*A note on Alan Rawsthorne*	(ML vol. 32, 1951)
	Keller, H.	*Film music: Rawsthorne's 'Leonardo'*	(MT Jan. 1956)
	Mason, C.	*Alan Rawsthorne*	(MT March 1950)
	Mellers, W.	*Rawsthorne and the English tradition*	(L vol. 70, 1963)
		Alan Rawsthorne and the Baroque	(T March 1946)
		Rawsthorne's recent development	(L vol. 44, 1950)
	Myers, R.	*Composer of delicacy*	(MM May 1965)
(b)		*The Ballades of Chopin*	(Co 16, 1965)

REIZENSTEIN, F.

(a)	Bush, A. (and Wilde, D.)	*Franz Reizenstein, 1911–1968*	(RAMM 196 Summer 1969)
	Carner, M.	*Franz Reizenstein*	(TT 13.x.51)
		In memory of Franz Reizenstein	(AJR Inf. Dec. 1968)
		Voices of Night	(TT 5. vii. 52)
	Henderson, R.	*English by adoption*	(L vol. 65 1961)
	Jacobs, A.	*Reizenstein's 'Voices of Night'*	(MT Aug. 1952)
	Keller, H.	*Reizenstein en Face; an unique achievement*	(MR vol. 13, 1952)
	Mason, C.	*An opera for broadcasting*	(L vol. 49, 1953)
	Ottaway, H.	*Reizenstein and the English Oratorio*	(L vol. 63, 1960)
	Parfrey, R.	*Night school composer*	(Co 31, 1969)

REIZENSTEIN, F. (*cont'd.*)

Redlich, H.	*Modern profiles III— Franz Reizenstein*	(MR vol. 12, 1951)
Routh, F.	*The creative output of Franz Reizenstein*	(Co 31, 1969)
Sackville-West, E.	*An opera for broadcasting*	(NS 2. viii. 52)
Times, the	*articles on Franz Reizenstein*	(28. vii. 52; 17. xii. 59: 17.x.68)
Weissmann, J.	*Reizenstein's 'Genesis' and its antecedents*	(L vol. 60, 1958)
	Reizenstein's recent music	(L vol. 57, 1957)
	The music of Franz Reizenstein	(L vol. 47, 1952)
(b)	*Composer and string player*	(L vol. 77, 1967)
	Hindemith's 'Marienleben'	(L vol. 72, 1964)
	Hindemith : some aspersions answered	(Co 15, 1965)
	(in answer to H. Redlich in MR, Aug. 1964)	
	Paul Hindemith	(L vol. 71, 1964)

RUBBRA, E.

(a)	Crankshaw, G.	*Rubbra and the symphony*	(C XXIX 181, 1955)
	Dawney, M.	*Liturgical Music by three contemporary composers*	(CM vol. 2 no. 16, Dec. 1966)
	Evans, E.	*Edmund Rubbra*	(MT Feb & March 1945)
	Goddard, S.	*Rubbra's new symphony* (Sixth Symphony)	(L vol. 52, 1954)
	Hutchings, A.	*Edmund Rubbra and the liturgy*	(L vol. 43, 1950)
		Rubbra and the symphony	(L vol. 40, 1948)
	Mellers, W.	*Rubbra and the dominant seventh*	(MR vol. 1943)
		Rubbra and the symphony	(L vol. 41, 1949)
		Rubbra's Anglican Mass	(L vol. 62, 1959)
		Rubbra's recent chamber music	(L vol. 47, 1952)
	Ottaway, H.	*Edmund Rubbra and his recent works*	(MT Sep. 1966)
		Rubbra's Sixth Symphony	(MT Oct. 1955)
		Rubbra and the symphony	(L vol. 58, 1957)
	Payne, E.	*Edmund Rubbra*	(ML vol. 36, 1955)
		Some aspects of Rubbra's style	(MR vol. 16, 1955)
	Truscott, H.	*The music of Edmund Rubbra*	(L vol. 72, 1964)

RUBBRA, E. (*cont'd.*)

Westrup, J. A.   *Rubbra and the symphony*   (L vol. 28, 1942
                                                        also: L vol. 54, 1955)

see also under Hines, R.S.

(b)   *Choral music*   (L vol. 79, 1968)
                        Counterpoint   (Hutchinson 1960)
                        R. O. Morris, an   (ML vol. 30, 1949)
                        appreciation
                        Second String Quartet   (MR vol. 14, 1953)
                        Rubbra looks at his eight
                        symphonies   (L vol. 85, 1971)

SCOTT, C.

(a) Demuth, N.   *Cyril Scott*   (L vol. 75, 1966)
(b)   *Bone of contention*   (The Aquarian
                        (autobiography)   Press 1969)

SEARLE, H.

(a) *An interim report on Humphrey Searle's music*   (MS vol. 1 no. 5,
                                                        1948)

Gorer, R.   *Humphrey Searle and the*   (L vol. 58, 1957)
                        serial symphony
                        The opera of the absurd   (L vol. 71, 1964)
                        ('The photo of the Colonel')

Lockspeiser, E.   *Humphrey Searle*   (MT Sep. 1955)
                        Humphrey Searle and   (L vol. 54, 1955)
                        James Joyce

Rayment, M.   *Searle ; avant-garde or*   (MT June 1964)
                        romantic?

Seaman, G.   *The music of Humphrey*   (L vol. 64, 1960)
                        Searle

Walsh, S.   *Humphrey Searle's*   (L vol. 81, 1969)
                        'Hamlet'

(b)   *'A note on Gold Coast*   (MS vol. 3 no. 1,
                        Customs'   1950)
                        Composition with twelve   (see Rufer, J.)
                        notes
                        Four works   (L vol. 79, 1968)
                        (Piano Sonata, Song of the Sun, The Canticle of
                        the Rose, Progressions)
                        Hamlet   (MT April 1969)
                        Opera of the absurd   (MM March 1964)
                        ('The photo of the Colonel')
                        What is the truth about   (MM June 1956)
                        12-note music?
                        Searle is also the author of books and articles on
                        Liszt, Schoenberg and Webern (e.g. *Grove's
                        Dictionary*)

SEIBER, M.

(a)	Fricker, P. R.	*Matyas Seiber's chamber music*	(L vol. 70, 1963)
	Keller, H.	*A master's piece* ('Ulysses')	(L vol. 80, 1968)
		Matyas Seiber, 1905–1960	(T Autumn/Winter 1960)
		Matyas Seiber	(MT Nov. 1955)
		Matyas Seiber and his twelve notes	(L vol. 51, 1954)
		Seiber and the rebirth of the String Quartet	(L vol. 54, 1955)
	Mason, C.	*The musical personality of Matyas Seiber*	(L vol. 57, 1957)
	Weissmann, J.	*Matyas Seiber : style and technique*	(L vol. 45, 1951)
	Wood, H.	*Matyas Seiber*	(MT Nov. 1960)
(b)		*A note on 'Ulysses'*	(MS vol. 3 no. 4, 1951)
		Composing with twelve notes	(MS vol. 4 no. 3, 1952)
			(see also Rufer, J.)
		The I.S.C.M. plans and Prospects	(C XXII 151 1947)

SMALLEY, R.

(a)	Walsh, S.	*Roger Smalley*	(FMN Summer 1968)
		Roger Smalley	(MT Feb. 1968)
		Roger Smalley	(MM June 1969)
(b)	*Pulses*	*5 × 4*	(MT June 1969)
		Stockhausen and development	(MT April 1970)
		Stockhausen's piano pieces	(MT Jan. 1969)

STEVENS, B.

(a)	Hutchings, A.	*Introduction to Bernard Stevens*	(L vol. 35, 1946)
	Stevenson, R.	*Bernard Stevens*	(MT June 1968)
(b)		*Music in the Soviet Union*	(in 'European Music in the Twentieth Century' Routledge 1957)

STEVENSON, R.

(a)	Bush, A.	*Ronald Stevenson's 'Passacaglia'*	(Co 14, 1964)
	Dawes, F.	*An 80-minute movement*	(MT June 1968)
	Orga, A.	*Ronald Stevenson*	(MM Oct. 1968)

STEVENSON, R. (*cont'd.*)

	The piano music of Ronald Stevenson	(MO March 1969)
Scott-Sutherland, C.	*The Music of Ronald Stevenson*	(MR vol. 26, 1965)
(b)	*Busoni's 'Arlecchino'*	(MT June 1954)
	Passacaglia on D.S.C.H.	(L vol. 82, 1969)
	Reflections after a première (on the 'Passacaglia')	(Vita Musica, Johannesburg, Aug. 1964; reproduced in the handbook of the 19th Aldeburgh Fest. 1966)

STOKER, R.

(a) Townend, R.	*Richard Stoker*	(MT May 1968)

TIPPETT, M.

(a) Amis, J.	*A child of our time*	(L vol. 45, 1951)
	Seven years' hard labour ('The Midsummer Marriage')	(MM Feb. 1955)
Atkinson, M.	*Michael Tippett's debt to the past*	(MR vol. 23, 1962)
Bowen, M.	*Recognition for 'The Midsummer Marriage'*	(MM June 1968)
Crankshaw, G.	*The art of Michael Tippett*	(C XXV 204, 1960)
Dickinson, A.	*Round about 'The Midsummer Marriage'*	(ML vol. 37, 1956)
Glock, W.	*Four new English operas*	(E April 1955)
Goddard, S.	*Michael Tippett and the symphony*	(L vol. 43, 1950)
	Michael Tippett's operas	(L vol. 69, 1963)
	Tippett's 'Ritual Dances'	(L vol. 49, 1953)
	Tippett's Second Symphony	(L vol. 59, 1958)
Goehr, A.	*Tippett at sixty*	(MT Jan. 1965)
Goodwin, N.	*Michael Tippett: a new orchestral perspective* (Concerto for Orchestra)	(L vol. 71, 1964)
Kemp, I. (ed.)	*A symposium on his 60th birthday*	(Faber 1965)
Mason, C.	*Michael Tippett*	(MT May 1946)
	Michael Tippett's opera ('The Midsummer Marriage')	(L vol. 53, 1955)
	Tippet and his oratorio	(L vol. 38, 1947)

TIPPETT, M. (*cont'd.*)

	Michael Tippett's Piano Concerto	(L vol. 56, 1956)
	Michael Tippett's Piano Concerto	(S June 1956)
Mellers, W.	*Michael Tippett in 1957*	(L vol. 57, 1957)
	Michael Tippett and the String Quartet	(L vol. 66, 1961)
	Tippett and the Piano Concerto	(L vol. 61, 1959)
Milner, A.	*An introductory note to Tippett's* '*The Midsummer Marriage*'	(MT Jan. 1955)
	Rhythmic technique in the music of Michael Tippett	(MT Sep. 1954)
	The music of Michael Tippett	(MQ vol. 50, 1964)
	Tippett's Piano Concerto	(S 16 June 1956)
Pirie, P.	*Tippett at sixty*	(L vol. 72, 1964)
Rubbra, E.	*The Vision of St Augustine*	(L vol. 75, 1966)
Souster, T.	*Michael Tippett's 'Vision'*	(MT Jan. 1966)
Wetherell, E.	*Music for Priam*	(MM June 1962)
Woodward, I.	*Tippett looks ahead*	(MM March 1969)
(b)	*A child of our time*	(L vol. 33, 1945)
	At work on 'King Priam'	(S 28 Jan. 1961)
	Moving into Aquarius	(Routledge 1959)
	On 'King Priam'	(OP May 1962)
	Schoenberg's letters	(Co 15, 1965)
	The Festival and Society	(MT June 1969)
	Some categories of judgement in modern music (Bath Festival)	(SO no. 1, Autumn 1970)
	see also under Hines, R. S.	

TOMLINSON, E.

(b)	*Light music in the modern world*	(Co 23, 24, 25, 1967)

WALTON, W.

(a) Aprahamian, F.	*Walton and his new symphony* (Second Symphony)	(L vol. 64, 1960)
Avery, K.	*William Walton*	(ML vol. 28, 1947)
Blom, E.	*The later William Walton*	(L vol. 34, 1945)
Cooper, M.	*The unpredictable Walton*	(L vol. 58, 1957)
Evans, P.	*Sir William Walton's manner and mannerism*	(L vol. 62, 1959)

WALTON, W. (*cont'd.*)

Foss, H.	*Entertainment*	(L vol. 40, 1948)
	The music of William Walton	(L vol. 33, 1945)
Goddard, S.	*William Walton*	(L vol. 36, 1946)
Hassall, C.	*Walton's First opera*	(MM Dec. 1954)
Howes, F.	*The music of William Walton*	(Oxford University Press 1965)
	Walton's opera	(L vol. 69, 1963)
Layton, R.	*Walton and his critics*	(L vol. 67, 1962)
Mellers, W.	*Sir William Walton and Twentieth-Century opera*	(L vol. 52, 1954)
Mitchell, D.	*Some observations on William Walton*	(C XXVI 169 and 170, 1952)
	The modernity of William Walton	(L vol. 57, 1957)
Ottaway, H.	*Walton and his critics*	(L vol. 83, 1970)
Reid, C.	*Sixty years of William Walton*	(MM March 1962)
Reizenstein, F.	*Walton's 'Troilus and Cressida'*	(T Winter 1954)
Rutland, H.	*Walton's new Cello Concerto*	(MT Feb. 1957)
Sitwell, O.	*Laughter in the next room* (Autobiography, vol. 4)	(Macmillan 1949)
Warrack, J.	*Walton's 'Troilus and Cressida'*	(MT Dec. 1954) (MT Feb. 1955)
(b)	*Contemporary music, its problems and its future*	(Co 20, 1966)

WARREN, R.

(a) Acton, C.	*The music of Raymond Warren*	(MT Oct. 1969)
(b)	*A musician in Ulster*	(Co 34, 1969/70)
	Music in Northern Ireland	(Co 12, 1963)
	Music in the plays of W. B. Yeats	(Co 20, 1966)

WELLESZ, E.

(a) Dawney, M.	*Liturgical music by three contemporary composers*	(CM vol. 2 no. 18 April 1967)
Mellers, W.	*Egon Wellesz: an 80th birthday tribute*	(MT Oct. 1965)
	The music of Egon Wellesz	(L vol. 44, 1950)
	Wellesz and Bruckner	(L vol. 57, 1957)
	Wellesz at eighty	(L vol. 73, 1965)

WELLESZ, E. (*cont'd.*)

Nettel, R.	*Later chamber music of Egon Wellesz*	(L vol. 54, 1955)
Redlich, H.	*Egon Wellesz—an Austrian composer in Britain*	(MR vol. 7, 1946)
	Wellesz and the Austrian symphonic tradition	(L vol. 46, 1951)
Reti, R.	*Egon Wellesz, musician and scholar*	(MQ vol. 42, 1956)
Ridley, A.	*The later works of Egon Wellesz*	(Co 18, 1966)
Schollum, R.	*Die neuesten werke von Egon Wellesz*	(Osterr. Musik-zeitschrift 1968, no. 4)
	Egon Wellesz	(Osterreichischer Bundesverlag, Wien, 1965)
Thomas, A. F.	*Background to Wellesz' 'Incognita'*	(C XXVI 169, 1952)

(b) Wellesz' large output of books and articles are listed in Schollum's works. The following are additional:

Bruno Walter, 1876–1962	(ML vol. 43, 1962)
Die Bakchantinnen (a summary)	(L vol. 65, 1961)
E. J. Dent and the International Society for Contemporary Music	(MR vol. 7, 1946)
'Monteverdi's Vespers'	(MT June 1946)
Recollections of Schoenberg	(Co 17, 1965)
Reminiscences of Mahler	(S 28 Jan. 1961)

WHELEN, C.

(b)	*Sir Arnold Bax*	(MM Dec. 1953)
	Thoughts on television opera	

WILLIAMSON, M.

(a)	Mason, C.	*The art of Malcolm Williamson*	(L vol. 69, 1963)
		The music of Malcolm Williamson	(MT Nov. 1962)
	Walsh, S.	*Williamson the many-sided*	(MM July 1965)
(b)		*On being a tonal composer*	(L vol. 73, 1965)

WORDSWORTH, W.

(a)	Bayliss, S.	*William Wordsworth*	(C XXIV 162, 1950)
	Goddard, S.	*William Wordsworth*	(MT Oct. 1964)
		William Wordsworth's Symphonies	(L vol. 65, 1961)
	Hamburger, P.	*A note on William Wordsworth*	(MS vol. 3, 1951)
	Kennedy, M.	*William Wordsworth and his contemporaries*	(L vol. 69, 1963)

II—General

List of books and articles referred to in the text, or of general relevance
to the music of the contemporary period.
(authors listed alphabetically)

ALLDIS, J.	*Modern choral music*	(Co 33, 1969)
AMIS, J.	*O rare Hoffnung*	(MT Dec. 1960)
ARUNDELL, D	*The critic at the opera*	(Benn 1957)
BACHARACH, A. L.	*British music of our time*	(Pelican 1951)
BEECHAM, T.	*A mingled chime*	(Hutchinson 1944)
	80th birthday issue	(MM April 1959)
BLOM, E.	*Music in England*	(Pelican 1942)
BOULT, A.	*Sir Adrian Boult at 80*	(MT April 1969)
BOURKE, G.	*Sir Thomas Beecham*	(MM April 1954)
BRIGGS, A.	*The history of broadcasting in the United Kingdom* (3 vols.)	(Oxford 1961, 1965 and 1970)
BUTCHER, A. V.	*A. E. Housman and the English composer*	(ML vol. 29, 1948)
CAMPBELL, S. S.	*The Royal School of Church Music*	(MT Jan. 1952)
CABELL, R.	*Sir Thomas Beecham*	(MT May 1961)
CAREY, C.	*He pioneered opera in English* (on E. J. Dent)	(MM Oct. 1957)
CARNER, M.	*The Committee for the Promotion of New Music*	(MT Oct. 1945)
	Of men and music	(John Williams 1944)
CASTILLEJO, D.	*A counter report on Art patronage*	(Castillejo 1968)
CHISSELL, J.	*Dartington*	(MT Sep. 1950)
CLARKE, E.	*Institute of Contemporary Arts*	(MT Sep. 1947)
CLARKE, M.	*The Sadler's Wells Ballet*	(Black 1955)

CLUTTON, C.   *Organ building in Britain today*   (MM Oct. 1969)
                   The British organ   (Batsford 1963)
                   (with Niland, A.)
                   The organ, its tonal structure   (Grenville Pub. Co.
                   and registration   1950)
                   (with Dixon, G.)
COLE, H.   *London Music, winter 1965/6*   (Co 19, 1966)

COLLES, H. C.   *The Royal College of Music*   (Macmillan 1933)
                   A Jubilee Record, 1883–1933
                   Voice and verse in England   (Oxford 1928)
COMMONWEALTH   (Co 19, 1966)
MUSIC

COMPOSERS'   *Catalogues of music by British*
GUILD   *Composers*
                   vol. 1 *Chamber Music*
                   vol. 2 *Orchestral Music*   (Composers' Guild
                                                       1970)
CROZIER, E.   *Composer and librettist*   (Co 18 1966)

DARTINGTON   *Music. A report on musical*   (PEP 1949)
                   life in England, sponsored by the
                   Dartington Hall Trustees
                   see under Chissell
DAVIES, H.   *International Electronic Music*   (MIT Press
                   Catalogue   Cambridge, Mass.
                                                       1968)
DAWNEY, M.   *New liturgy : New music*   (Co 33, 1969)
                   The New Wave Composer   (The Tablet 16.
                                                       viii. 69)
DEALE, E. M.   *A catalogue of contemporary*   (Music Association
                   Irish composers   of Ireland 1968)
DENNIS, B.   *Experimental music in schools*   (Oxford 1970)
                   Metamorphosis in modern   (T Autumn 1966)
                   culture
                   (the parallel evolution of
                   music and painting)
DENT, E. J.   *Ferruccio Busoni, 1866–1924*   (Oxford 1933)
                   Opera   (Penguin 1940)
                   Ralph Vaughan Williams   (MT Oct. 1952)
                   The pianoforte and its influence (S 18 Dec. 1956)
                   on modern music
                   The future of music   (Pergamon Press)
                   see under Carey, Lewis, Trend,
                   Wellesz and Westrup

DIEREN, B. Van	*Down among the dead men*	(Oxford 1935)
ELKIN, R.	*Queen's Hall, 1893–1941*	(Rider 1944)
FOX-STRANGWAYS,	*Cecil Sharp*	(Oxford 1955)
A. H.	(with Karples, M.)	
FELLOWES, E. H.	*Memoirs of an amateur musician*	(Methuen 1946)
	see under Warner	
FENBY, E.	*Beecham crowns his service to*	(MM Dec. 1959)
	Delius	
	Delius after twenty years	(MM June 1954)
	see under Delius, Threlfall	
FOSS, H.	*A neglected composer*	
	(Van Dieren)	(L vol. 36, 1947)
	Cecil Gray	(MT Nov. 1951)
GASCOYNE, D.	*Collected Poems*	(Oxford 1965)
GLENDENNING, F.	*The Church and the Arts*	(SCM 1960)
(ed.)	(symposium)	
GODFREY, D.	*Memories and Music*	(Hutchinson 1924)
GOOSSENS, E.	*Don Juan de Mañara*	(Co 26, 1967/8)
	Overture and beginners	(Methuen 1951)
GRAY, C.	*A survey of contemporary music*	(Oxford 1924)
	Contingencies	(Oxford 1947)
	Musical Chairs—life and	(Home and Van
	memoirs	Thal 1948)
	Peter Warlock	(Cape 1934)
	Predicaments	(Oxford 1936)
	Sibelius	(Oxford 1931)
	The History of Music	(Kegan Paul 1928)
GRIGORIEV, S. L.	*The Diaghilev Ballet, 1909–1929*	(Constable 1953)
HALE, A.	*Ruling the musical radio waves*	(MM May 1959)
HAREWOOD, Lord	*Erwin Stein* (obituary)	(T Autumn 1958)
HEDGES, A.	*BBC centralisation—a threat*	(Co 22, 1966/7)
	to provincial music?	
HINES, R. S.	*The composer's point of view*	(Oklahoma 1963)
	(Essays on Choral Music by	
	composers, incl. Fricker,	
	Milner, Rubbra, Tippett)	
	The orchestral composer's	(Oklahoma 1970)
	point of view	
	(essays by composers, incl.	
	Fricker, Tippett)	
HODIN, J. P.	*The dilemma of being modern*	(Routledge 1956)
HOFFNUNG, G.	*A bit of a lark*	(MM Nov. 1958)
	The Hoffnung Music Festival	(MM Jan. 1957)
	see under Stiff, Amis	

HOLST, I.   *Gustav Holst's manuscripts*   (Co 27, 1968)
                     The music of Gustav Holst   (Oxford 1968)
HOUSMAN, A. E.   see under Butcher, Quinlan

HOWES, F.   *The Cheltenham Festival*   (Oxford 1965)
                     The English Musical   (Secker &
                     Renaissance   Warburg 1966)
HUGHES, R.   *'South Place'—A home of*   (MT Feb. 1953)
                     Chamber Music
HUNTER, I.   *Bath revives the 18th century*   (MM May 1955)
                     (on the 1st Bath Festival)
HURD, M.   *Immortal Hour : the life and*   (Routledge 1962)
                     period of Rutland Boughton
JENKINS, G.   *Making musicians.*   (Co 22, 1966/7)
                     The Gulbenkian report 18 months
                     later
JESSEL, C.   *British music on show*   (Co 29, 1968)
                     (Music Information Centre,
                     London)
KUBELIK, R.   *Our plans at Covent Garden*   (MM Nov. 1955)
KENNEDY, M.   *Edward Elgar*   (Oxford 1968)
                     The works of Ralph Vaughan   (Oxford 1964)
                     Williams
LAKE, I.   *A dream of a festival*   (Co 27, 1968)
                     ('Music in our time')
LARNER, G.   *New music and old scores*   (Co 17, 1965)
                     (on broadcasting new music)
LEITH HILL MUSIC FESTIVAL, 1905–1955   (Pullinger (Epsom)
                                                   1955)
LEWIS, A.   *Edward J. Dent, a birthday*   (MT July 1956)
                     tribute
LONG, N.   *Music in English education*   (Faber 1959)
LOVELAND, K.   *Wales is making Festival Music*   (MM June 1958)
MACNAGHTEN, A.   *The story of the Macnaghten*   (MT Sep. 1959)
                     Concerts
MASON, C.   *Music in Britain*   (Longmans 1964)
MIDDLETON, D.   *The Courtauld-Sargent Concerts*   (MR Vol. 27, 1966)
MORLEY COLLEGE   see under Stuart
NEEL, B.   *The story of an orchestra*   (Castle Press 1950)
                     (The Boyd Neel Orchestra)
NETTEL, R.   *The Englishman makes music*   (Dobson 1952)
NEWSON, G.   *Electronic Odyssey*   (Co 26, 1967/8)
ORIANA MADRIGAL SOCIETY see under Peck

PATRICK, P. H.   *Composer, computer and*   (Co 35, 1970)
                       audience

PAYNTER, J.   *Sound and silence*   (Cambridge 1970)
                       (with Aston, P.)

PECK, R.   *The Oriana Madrigal Society,*   (MT Oct. 1954)
                       1904–1954

PHELPS, L.   *A short history of the organ*   (CM 67, no. 1)
                       revival
                       Perspective   (OIQ Winter 1964)
                       Thoughts on the future of the   (International
                       organ   Society of organ
                                                   builders. Inf. no. 1,
                                                   Feb. 1969)

PIKE, A.   *The ordering of the*   MR vol. 23, 1962)
                       all-combinatorial set

PINKETT, E.   *Time to remember*   (Leicestershire EC,
                       (on the Leicestershire Schools   1969)
                       Symphony Orchestra)

PIRIE, P.   *The lost generation*   (MT April 1955)

PLEASANTS, H.   *Death of a music?*   (Gollancz 1961)
                       Serious music—and all that jazz (Gollancz 1969)
                       The agony of modern music   (Simon & Schuster
                                                   N. Y. 1965)

QUINLAN, J.   *A. E. Housman and British*   (MT March 1959)
                       composers

RADCLIFFE, P.   *Bernhard (Boris) Ord,*   (King's College,
                       1897–1961   Cambridge, 1962)

RADMALL, P.   *Max Rostal and the*   (C XXX 184, 1955)
                       contemporary composer

RAYMENT, M.   *The McEwen Memorial*   (Co 28, 1968)
                       Concerts

RAYNOR, H.   *Influence and achievement*   (C XXX 185, 1956)
                       (20th century English song)

REDLICH, H.   *New British operas*   (C XXIX 182,
                                                   1955)

REID, C.   *Thomas Beecham*   (Gollancz 1961)

RILEY, H.   *Aleatoric procedures in*   (MT April 1966)
                       contemporary piano music
                       Webern's Variations, Op. 27   (MR vol. 27, 1966)

ROSENTHAL, H.   *Opera Annual, 1954/5*   (Calder 1954)
                       Opera at Covent Garden, a   (Gollancz 1967)
                       short history
                       Two centuries of opera at   (Putnam 1958)
                       Covent Garden

ROUTH, F.	*Contemporary Music—an introduction*	(English Univ. Press 1968)
	The patronage and presentation of contemporary music (ed.)	(Redcliffe Concerts 1970)
	The Redcliffe Concerts	(Co 26, 1967/8)
ROUTLEY, E.	*Church Music and Theology*	(SCM 1959)
	Is Jazz Music Christian?	(Epworth Press 1964)
	The Church and Music	(Duckworth 1950)
	Twentieth Century Church Music	(Jenkins 1964)
RUFER, J.	*Composition with twelve notes*	(Rockliff 1954)
SADLER'S WELLS	*Twenty five years of Sadler's Wells Opera*	(MM April 1956)
SCHAFER, M.	*British composers in interview*	(Faber 1963)
SHARP, C.	*English folk song: some conclusions*	(Mercury Books 1965)
SHAW, W.	*The Three Choirs Festival*	(Baylis, Worcester, 1954)
SHORE, B.	*Sixteen symphonies*	(Longmans 1949)
SIMPSON, R.	*Bruckner and the symphony*	(MR vol. 7, 1946)
	Carl Nielsen symphonist	(Dent 1952)
	Guide to modern music on records	(Blond 1958)
	Sibelius and Nielsen—a centenary essay	(BBC 1965)
	The essence of Bruckner	(Gollancz 1967)
	The Symphony (ed.)	(Pelican 1967)
STANFORD, C. V.	*Interludes, Records and Reflections*	(John Murray 1922)
	Pages from an unwritten diary	(Arnold 1914)
STEIN, E.	*Form and performance*	(Faber 1962)
	Orpheus in new guises	(Rockliff 1953)
	see under Harewood	
STIFF, W.	*Hoffnung taught us how to laugh with music* (obituary notice)	(MM Nov. 1959)
STILL, R.	*Serial composition today* (in reply to Iain Hamilton)	(T Spring 1961)
ST. JOHN, C.	*Ethel Smyth: a biography*	(Longmans 1959)
STUART, C.	*Morley College Music*	(MT Sep. 1951)
SWINYARD, L.	*The Royal Festival Hall Organ A Symposium*	(MO, 1954)

TAYLOR, M.   *A Festival for 'The City'*   (MM Jan. 1962)

TAYLOR, S.   *Charles Kennedy Scott*   (MT Nov. 1951)

THRELFALL, R.   *Delius in Eric Fenby's MSS*   (Co 31, 1969)

TILLYARD, H. J. W.   see under Velimirović

TREND, J. B.   *Dent*   (S 22 Feb. 1958)

VELIMIVORIC, M.   *H. J. W. Tillyard, patriarch of* (MQ vol. 54, 1968)
                     Byzantine studies
WALTER, B.   *Gustav Mahler* (tr. Galston)   (Kegan Paul 1937)
                     Theme and Variations   (Hamish Hamilton
                                                        1947)
WARNER, S. T.   *Edmund Fellowes as editor*   (MT Feb. 1952)

WESTRUP, J. A.   *Dent as translator*   (MR vol. 7, 1946)

WHITMAN, G.   *Diary of a Quarter-Wit*   (Co 35, 1970)
                     (on microtonal music)
                     Introduction to microtonal   (Brit. & Cont.
                     music   Music Agencies
                                                        1970)
WHITTALL, A.   *Post-twelve-note-analysis*   (PRMA 94, 1967/8)

WILKINSON, M.   *Two months in the 'Studio di*   (S 22 Feb. 1958)
                     fonologia'
WILLIAMS, P.   *The European organ*   (Batsford 1966)

WOOD, H.   *My life of music*   (Gollancz 1938)

YOUNGER
GENERATION   *Short composers' self-portraits* (MT March 1960)
                     Addison, Butterworth, Cannon,
                     Cole, Cruft, Dodgson,
                     Hoddinott, Kelly, Salzedo,
                     Whettam
ZINOVIEFF, P.   *A computerised Electronic*   (Electronic Music
                     Music Studio   Reports I. Utrecht
                                                        1969)
                     Musys   (Brit. Soc. for
                     (with Grogono, P. and   Electronic Music
                     Cockerell, D.)   1970)
                     The special case of inspirational (LM July/Aug.
                     computer music scores   1969)

Acknowledgements

The sheer quantity of material available presents the student of contemporary music with an embarrassment of riches which he cannot hope to comprehend unaided; and it has been my very good fortune to have been helped by those composers whose work forms the substance of this study. To them therefore, collectively, for their unstinting co-operation and forbearance, my first and chief acknowledgement is made.

I am also indebted to the staffs of many libraries for so freely and generously making available to me the works in their possession. Chiefly I am happy to acknowledge the unique value of the Music Information Centre, administered by the Composers' Guild of Great Britain. This incomparable collection of scores, discs and tapes by British composers—the starting-point for a work of this kind—together with facilities for their use, was made freely available to me over a long period of time, through the courtesy of the Composers' Guild; to their staff, Elizabeth Yeoman and Leslie Glaze, I owe a deep debt of gratitude for providing this much-valued service, and so making my task proportionately simpler. Other libraries whose services have proved of great value are the Central Music Library of the Borough of Westminster, and the B.B.C. Music Library, and to their staffs also I record my obligation.

Many publishers have given great assistance; notably Alfred Lengnick & Co., Ludwig Doblinger (Vienna), Schott & Co., Boosey & Hawkes, J. & W. Chestea, Mills Music, Faber Music, Universal Edition, Oxford University Press and the University of Oklahoma Press. In this connection I am particularly indebted to Mr. Charles Avenell, Mr. Michael Vyner, Mr. Jeremy Caulton, Mr. Robin Hogg, Mr. Martin Kingsbury, Mr. Anthony Wright, Mr. John Andrews, Mr. Martin Hall, Mr. Alan Frank, Mr. Malcolm Binney and Mr. James Fox.

Among those who have rendered specific kindnesses are Mr. Barrie Iliffe, Music Director of the British Council, Professor Frederick Rimmer, University of Glasgow, Mr. Julian Hodgson, Dr. H. Zelzer, until recently

DD*

Director of the Austrian Institute, London, who read and commented on the chapter on Egon Wellesz; Mr. Edgar M. Deale, who supplied information about Irish composers; also Dr. Hans Heimler, Mr. David Wilde, Mr. Peter Marr, Miss Elizabeth Holbrook, Sir Adrian Boult, Dame Ninette de Valois, Miss Carol Spero, Mr. David Castillejo, Mr. Michael Dawney, Mr. Richard Townsend, Mr. Ian Lake, Miss Muriel K. Whiteman, Mrs. M. Montagu-Nathan, Mr. Edmund Smith, Mrs. Margaret Reizenstein, Mr. Angus Morrison, Mrs. Camilla Panufnik, Mrs. Gerhard, Mr. Ernest Chapman, Mr. James Murdoch, Mr. John Woolf, and many others, all of whom have assisted in various ways, and whose services I acknowledge with gratitude. The typescript was painstakingly prepared and edited by Mrs. Louise Jenkins and Mrs. Vanessa Cunningham, whose work I greatly appreciate.

Index

441